Imperial Technology and 'Native' Agency

This book explores the impact of railways on colonial Indian society from the commencement of railway operations in the mid-nineteenth to the early decades of the twentieth century.

The book represents a historiographical departure. Using new archival evidence as well as travelogues written by Indian railway travellers in Bengali and Hindi, this book suggests that the impact of railways on colonial Indian society were more heterogeneous and complex than anticipated either by India's colonial railway builders or currently assumed by post-colonial scholars.

At a related level, the book argues that this complex outcome of the impact of railways on colonial Indian society was a product of the interaction between the colonial context of technology transfer and the Indian railway passengers who mediated this process at an everyday level. In other words, this book claims that the colonised 'natives' were not bystanders in this process of imposition of an imperial technology from above. On the contrary, Indians, both as railway passengers and otherwise influenced the nature and the direction of the impact of an oft-celebrated 'tool of Empire'.

The historiographical departures suggested in the book are based on examining railway spaces as social spaces – a methodological index influenced by Henri Lefebvre's idea of social spaces as means of control, domination and power.

Aparajita Mukhopadhyay is a history lecturer at Goldsmiths, University of London.

Imperial Technology and 'Native' Agency
A Social History of Railways in Colonial India, 1850–1920

Aparajita Mukhopadhyay

LONDON AND NEW YORK

First published 2018
by Routledge
2 Park Square, Milton Park, Abingdon, Oxon OX14 4RN

and by Routledge
711 Third Avenue, New York, NY 10017

Routledge is an imprint of the Taylor & Francis Group, an informa business

© 2018 Aparajita Mukhopadhyay

The right of Aparajita Mukhopadhyay to be identified as author of this work has been asserted by her in accordance with sections 77 and 78 of the Copyright, Designs and Patents Act 1988.

All rights reserved. No part of this book may be reprinted or reproduced or utilised in any form or by any electronic, mechanical, or other means, now known or hereafter invented, including photocopying and recording, or in any information storage or retrieval system, without permission in writing from the publishers.

Trademark notice: Product or corporate names may be trademarks or registered trademarks, and are used only for identification and explanation without intent to infringe.

British Library Cataloguing-in-Publication Data
A catalogue record for this book is available from the British Library

Library of Congress Cataloging-in-Publication Data
Names: Mukhopadhyay, Aparajita, author.
Title: Imperial technology and 'native' agency : a social history of railways in Colonial India, 1850–1920 / Aparajita Mukhopadhyay.
Description: Abingdon, Oxon ; NewYork, NY : Routledge, 2018. | Includes bibliographical references and index.
Identifiers: LCCN 2017056528| ISBN 9781138226685 (hardback : alk. paper) | ISBN 9781315397108 (e-book)
Subjects: LCSH: Railroads—Social aspects—India—History. | Railroad travel—Social aspects—India—History. | India—Civilization—1765–1947. | India—History—British occupation, 1765–1947.
Classification: LCC HE3298 .M85 2018 | DDC 385.0954/09034—dc23
LC record available at https://lccn.loc.gov/2017056528

ISBN: 978-1-138-22668-5 (hbk)
ISBN: 978-1-315-39710-8 (ebk)

Typeset in Times New Roman
by Florence Production Ltd, Stoodleigh, Devon, UK

For my parents

Contents

Acknowledgements		ix
Glossary		xi
	Introduction	1
1	On time? Railway time and travel-discipline in colonial India	20
2	A ticket to control? Limits of railway travel-discipline in colonial India	41
3	A shared space? Contestation of station spaces and railway travel-discipline in colonial India	83
4	Chariots of equality? Travelling in railway carriages and social transformation in colonial India	108
5	To eat or not to eat? Railway travel, commensality and social change in colonial India	141
6	A nation on the move? Railway travel and conceptualisations of space in colonial India	164
7	Shared spaces, shifting identities: Railway travel and notions of identity and community in colonial India	187
	Conclusion: All aboard the train? Technology transmission and social transformation in colonial India	213
	Bibliography	227
	Index	240

Acknowledgements

Originally this book was intended be a replica of my PhD dissertation that I submitted to the School of Oriental and African Studies, London in 2013. But in the intervening years I decided to substantially revise, alter and expand the dissertation. As such, with new chapters added and some old ones discarded or published elsewhere, in its current form this book resembles only the broadest contours of my PhD dissertation.

Given the long journey this book has traversed, I have been indebted to individuals and institutions for their support. It will be, however, difficult to even start recounting my debts, intellectual and otherwise without thanking Peter Robb (my PhD supervisor) and Ian Kerr. It will not be an exaggeration to claim that both Peter and Ian have lived with this project in more ways than one and have generously shared their time, knowledge, constructive criticism and gentle humour. Over the years Ian has read most parts of this manuscript in one form or other and has always offered useful critique as well as consistent encouragement. Ian's encyclopaedic knowledge of the history of Indian railways remains a source of inspiration. My intellectual debts to Peter and Ian cannot be sufficiently articulated in the confines of these pages.

I would also like to express thanks, albeit belated, to Joya Chatterji and Tirthankar Roy, examiners of my PhD dissertation. Both Joya and Tirthankar's comments and suggestions have helped me to re-think crucial concepts that have proven significant in writing this manuscript.

Thanks are also due to many fellow scholars and friends who over the years have unhesitatingly shared their knowledge, time and critical insights. Though for reasons of brevity here I do not proffer a list of names of scholar/friends who have shaped my thoughts; I hope my private acknowledgement of intellectual camaraderie will rectify this lacuna. I am also thankful to those scholars and colleagues who generously commented on various parts of this manuscript presented as conference papers in London (SOAS, Birkbeck, UCL), New Delhi, Princeton, Yale, Oxford, Tours, Albuquerque, Helsinki, Philadelphia, New Mexico and Seattle.

This book would not have taken this shape without the help I received from the staff of the Asia and Africa Reading Room in the British Library. They not only endured my never-ending demands for documents and books with efficiency, but also enlivened my days with humour and friendship. The library of the School of Oriental and African Studies too, proved invaluable for this project.

This book was written in a period of transition, both professional and personal. Unsurprisingly therefore, I have drawn upon my husband, parents and sister for emotional support. I would not have been able to write this book without my husband's presence and support. He not only believed in my ability to finish the project, but kept aside his own forthcoming monograph manuscript to share caring responsibilities of our newborn daughter so that I could continue to write. His academic specialisation in the History of Early Modern Europe and the History of Science has also helped me to widen my own research interests. My parents and my sister offered consistent emotional support and have lived with this project since my PhD days. This book is dedicated to my parents for encouraging me to pursue my goals. Last but not least, this book has grown with my daughter. I hope one day she will enjoy reading it.

I also owe a special thanks to Robert Langham, Senior Publisher for History, Routledge for believing in this project. The shortcomings of this book, however, remain solely mine.

Aparajita Mukhopadhyay

Glossary

Anna	A currency unit formerly used in India. One anna was 1/16th of a rupee.
Aryavarta	Literally 'abode of the excellent ones'. In the texts used in this study the word means 'land of the Aryans'.
Bhadralok	Gentleman; a well-mannered person. A word with significant socio-economic connotation in colonial and post-colonial Bengal.
Bhisti	A Muslim water bearer/carrier.
Desh	Country.
Desh Bhraman	Travelling around the country.
Dharamsala	A waiting place for travellers managed by Hindus.
Durga Pujo	Annual autumnal festival of Bengali Hindus celebrating the goddess Durga.
Ghat	A landing place near a river or other water bodies.
Grahak	Customer.
Jati	A group defined by various common economic, political, social and cultural factors.
Paani Panrey	A Hindu water bearer/carrier usually of high caste.
Raj	(Sanskrit: to rule). Used with the definite article (the Raj), the word usually signifies British rule in India.
Serai	A waiting place for travellers managed by Muslims.
Swadesh	One's own country; a conjunction of two Sanskrit words *swa* (self/own) and *desh*.
Swajati	One's own *jati*; a conjunction of two words *swa* (self/own) and *jati*.

Introduction

> The strong barriers of the most rigid and exclusive caste systems in the world have been penetrated on every side by the power of steam. In India for many years past, caste prejudices have been practically extinguished within the fences of a line of railway and the most sacred Brahmin will now contentedly ignore them rather than forgo the luxury and economy of a journey by rail, while everywhere the usually impenetrable and lethargic eastern has been aroused out of sleep, has learned to move with alacrity and even to acquire the virtues of punctuality, under the uncompromising and imperious tuition of the locomotive whistle.[1]

The above words of sanguine belief in the transformative powers of steam comes from G.W. MacGeorge who once served as the officiating consulting engineer for railways for the Government of India. In many ways, MacGeorge was voicing a wider and certainly a long-standing view common among colonial officials about the ability of steam in general and railways in particular to induce social change in colonial India.[2] It will not be an exaggeration to claim that though railways in India were primarily introduced to fulfill the economic and military needs of an expanding colonial administration,[3] their moral and social role in 'improving India' was considered to be equally if not more significant.[4] Indeed, as encapsulated in the aforementioned quote, in colonial India, railways were expected to accomplish specific purposes, including, but not limited to, dissolving social barriers and particularities based on religious, caste and regional identities; and creation of a perception of time and punctuality, qualities that Indians allegedly lacked. Equally important was railways' putative role in forging India into a 'nation' by integrating her far-flung and disparate regions in a spatial whole.[5] In short, railway promoters and colonial administrators of India hoped that railways will succeed in accomplishing hitherto unprecedented social transformations.

This confidence in the instrumentality of railways to transform India, however, is not surprising as the belief in the ability of technology to initiate social change was a popular credo of the nineteenth-century world. Writing in 1846 the Italian statesman Cavour expressed his faith in the railways in the following words:

> The influence of railways will extend on the whole planet. In the most civilised countries, railways will boost industry, their economic outcomes will be magnificent since the beginning, and they [railways] will accelerate the progressive movement of the society.[6]

Certainly, Cavour was not alone in his optimism for railway-propelled changes. Similar expectations, though varying in specifics, were expressed by political grandees as well as intellectuals in both Europe and beyond.[7] Indeed, in Meiji Japan, introduction and expansion of railways was promoted by invoking very similar language used by railway builders and enthusiasts in Europe and USA.[8] Given this, it is hardly surprising that in colonial India railways were expected to perform social miracles. But unlike Europe, USA or for that matter Japan, India was a colony. Consequently, the benefits of introducing railways in India were argued to be more compelling than other 'civilised' parts of the world. For instance, echoing comparable sentiments contained in the above quote by G.W. MacGeorge, an anonymous railway promotional pamphlet demanded introduction of railways in India in the following words:

> Iron and steam has civilised mankind let us give India the benefit of the discovery.[9]

Evidently then, railways in India were to perform a dual function. At one level, the iron horse was to transform Indian economy and society. At another, railways were to usher modernity in India; thus, offering India and Indians the advantages of civilisational progress. Thus, either way, railways, the 'mighty engine of improvement', were to awaken India from its 'slumber, unshackling chains of superstition and prejudice' while infusing her with new ideas that would prove beneficial for the material and moral well-being of her people.[10]

A tool of empire? Railways as an agent of social change

Imperialists such as Hardinge and Dalhousie or railway promoters such as Chapman and Stephenson, however, were not the only ones who believed in the idea of steamborne social progress. Correspondence between R.M. Stephenson, the pioneer promoter of railways in Eastern India and prominent members of nineteenth-century Bengali society such as Debendranath Tagore, Moti Lal Seal, Ram Gopal Ghosh and others suggest that contemporary Indians too shared similar convictions.[11] Though it is beyond the scope of this discussion to elaborate upon the complex nuances and genealogies of these Indian responses to a new technology[12] relevant here will be to note that a belief in socially beneficial and transformative role of steam was not confined to Indian elites. Pamphlets and travelogues published in Bengali and Hindi in the mid-nineteenth century indicate a broader interest and a relatively wider diffusion of notions about railways as instruments of progress.[13]

More importantly perhaps, despite a clear awareness of railway technology being both foreign and colonial, a belief in the idea of railways having benefited Indian society lingered well into the twentieth century and beyond, permeating even post-colonial scholarship.[14] At risk of speculation one may suggest that this continued conviction in socially transformative abilities of railways is perhaps, as Ian Kerr has suggested, a reflection of how for many post-colonial scholars the negative aspects of railways (economic, military) are outweighed by their positive accomplishment, i.e., their role in creating the Indian nation.[15] Whether or not one agrees with Kerr, there is, however, little doubt that there is a broad consensus in current historiography about the positive transformative effects of railways on Indian society.[16] What is more, this positive verdict is rather commonplace in both railway and non-railway scholarship. Thus, for instance, whether it is railway-specific arguments made by Ian Kerr, Laura Bear, or more recently, Ritika Prasad; or indirect though vital treatment of railways by Manu Goswami, Kumkum Chatterjee or Harriet Bury, the social impact of railways is delineated largely in terms of engendering collective, i.e., 'national' sentiments among Indian railway passengers.[17] Similarly, railway travel is also argued to have contributed to the spatial imagining of India as a nation, adding crucial visual dimension to an emergent 'geo-body' of cartographic, photographic and literary representations.[18]

Thus, broadly speaking, current historiographical assumptions invest railway travel experiences of Indians as having spawned a notion of India both as a spatial entity and as a community with underlying similarities. At an apparent level, this image of railway-induced 'imagined community' mirrors the expectations of colonial railway promoters. There is however, a singular difference. Post-colonial scholars argue that Indian passengers did not forge bonds of unity merely as a consequence of sharing communal spaces as a part of their railway travel experiences. Rather, it was the conditions in which the majority of Indian passengers travelled (unsanitary, crowded carriages) as well as the racially informed discriminatory practices of railway employees that engendered a 'national' identity vis-à-vis the colonisers. Though some scholars such as Manu Goswami, Laura Bear and more recently Ritika Prasad have alluded to the presence of fissures in this imagined 'national' identity;[19] nevertheless, the emphasis largely remains on the ways in which railway travel experiences spawned wider, pan-Indian affiliations, transcending religious, caste or linguistic particularities. The endurance of this historiographical assumption can be gauged by the fact that a recent tome on Indian railways waxes eloquent about the contribution of railways, underlining how the network made India into a nation by connecting historically and geographically disparate regions and people.[20]

Historiographically speaking therefore, hitherto, the role of the iron horse in creating a nation and national identity have not been doubted – a somewhat surprising outcome given that it also implies a consensus with colonial claims that is otherwise denied about neutrality of technology, especially in a colonial context.[21] This scholarly consensus alongside a near absence of any systematic enquiry into the impact of railways on colonial Indian society have consequently offered me an entry point to ask a relatively narrow and hitherto neglected question: did railways wrought social transformations along the lines assumed by both the colonial administrators and post-colonial scholars? This book makes an attempt to answer the question. But as is usually the case with projects of historical inquiry, the book too does not intend to provide either final or conclusive answers.

Additionally, for reasons of analytical coherence and a desire to avoid wading in unknown academic waters, the book does not offer a detailed exploration of the pre-railway history of communications in India except for acknowledging pre-existing patterns of mobility and circulation.[22] Similar considerations have also influenced the decision to not attempt to trace historical evolution of perceptions of time; notions of identities (caste and religion amongothers) or conceptualisations of territories in either pre-colonial or colonial India except for underscoring how railway operations either added new layers to existing ideas or modified them.[23]

At a related level, the book makes no claim to assess and compare all the forces for social change in colonial India.[24] In short, this book focuses on railways and the expectations raised about its wider social impact largely by looking at Indian experiences to a radically new system of transport. This has allowed a re-appraisal of the role of the iron horse on colonial Indian society, while simultaneously underlining the presence of Indian agency and the complexities and diversity of Indian responses. Thus, clearly the book has modest aims. This, however, does not diminish its contribution. Quite the contrary, the book represents a historiographical departure inasmuch as it focuses on specific aspects of Indian society, which are assumed to have been transformed under the impact of railways to assess the degree of change. And by demonstrating complexities of Indian responses to an imperial technology, this book also offers a nuanced understanding of technology transfer in a colonial milieu and agency of the colonised, more of which shortly.

This railway-centered approach however, should not be interpreted as ignoring other 'technologies of communications'.[25] If anything, this book builds upon as well as contributes to the wider genres of the social history of technology, history of technology transfer and history of social space in both South Asia and beyond.[26] Broadly speaking, in a relatively recent historiographical shift, scholars have emphasised the significance of contexts in examining technology transfer in colonial South Asia, thus adding richly to our knowledge of the interlinkages between the role of technologies of communication, empire and social change.[27] Additionally, these analyses have shown that there were both practical and ideological limits to Western technological superiority, reminding us of the vital difference between 'technology-in-practice and technology in discourse'.[28] Agreeing with these conclusions and developing them further through a railway specific approach, this book also argues for the need to pay closer attention to the context of technology transfer as much as the process itself, if not more.[29] After all, railways in India operated in a colonial milieu and as such, negotiations and even collaboration with existing conditions, both social and otherwise, were often the norm. Our assessment of railways' transformative impact cannot ignore this vital reality. At the same time however, the book also departs from current historiography by suggesting a more robust and influential presence of 'native'/ Indian agency in shaping the nature and direction of the impact of railway technology transfer in colonial India.

Simply put, this book makes a case for moving beyond what may be described as 'Headrick-Adas model',[30] i.e., thinking through technology transfer, especially in a colonial context merely as an imposition from above, wherein at best the role of the 'natives' is limited to either forced acceptance of a new technology or at worst gawking in wonder. Based upon a diverse range of sources (see next section), this book underlines the ways in which Indians adapted, adopted as well as appropriated the proverbial 'tool of empire' for ideological as well as mundane, practical reasons. This is evidenced, among other things, in the ways in which Indian railway passengers negotiated with colonial/railway authorities – a process, which, as subsequent chapters will demonstrate, had more heterogeneous and even divisive impact on colonial Indian society than we currently imagine. In other words, this book pushes our understanding of the role of railways in engendering social transformations in colonial India towards a more radical direction by suggesting that Indians played a crucial role in shaping the consequences of the former on the latter.

At a related level therefore, the book takes exception to the argument that Indian railway passengers did not exert any influence over railway operations in colonial India and were mere recipients of decisions forced upon them. In the historiography of Indian railways as it now stands, 'native' passengers appear only as a collective, almost a homogenous group that lacks both differentiation and agency. This insignificance of Indian railway passengers, in spite of their numerical strength,[31] has traditionally been explained as symbolic of their unequal status in a railway system operating within a colonial context. This view, though not entirely inaccurate, however, overlooks evidence, which points to the importance of Indian passengers for railway operations in colonial India. This is not an attempt to discount the realities of crowded third-class carriages in which most Indian passengers travelled. But this is to suggest that Indian railway passengers had access to a narrow negotiating window with the railway/colonial authorities largely as a consequence of pecuniary and other socio-political considerations that dictated the everyday workings of railway operations. Moreover, though not all Indian passengers were treated equally and the access to this negotiating window varied both with the social status of Indian railway passengers as well the relative strength of their numerical significance; nevertheless, Indian railway passengers were aware of this possibility of negotiation and consequently often made demands underlining either superior social status or religion, caste, gender and even professional identities.

In short, notwithstanding 'the routine discomforts and indignities' that provided a 'collective and simultaneous'[32] register of railway travel experiences; Indian passengers did not see themselves as a monolithic category. Nor was race the only notion of identity that offered unifying impulses.[33] More importantly perhaps, this demand-response mechanism between Indian passengers and colonial/railway authorities demonstrate how the former influenced railway operations at an everyday level, thereby also shaping its wider impact. Given this, the book argues for a notion of Indian railway passengers as a differentiated and articulate group, a suggestion that also offers a new analytical index to identify and acknowledge diverse outcomes of the interactions between a technology and the society in which it was transposed.

For the record: official and unofficial archive of colonial Indian railways

The historiographical departures proposed in this book are based on an extensive use of both 'official' and 'non-official' sources,[34] including hitherto unused archival records. The former mainly consists of the correspondence between the agents of railway companies based in India with their Board of Directors in London and with the various government agencies of colonial Indian administration.[35] This particular body of records has been crucial to this project as it provides vital information about the earliest decades of railway operations (1853–1870s), a usually neglected period in the context of appraising the impact of steam on Indian society. Additionally, these records also demonstrate the ways in which from the outset of railway operations in colonial India, the policies and facilities evolved through an interaction of pecuniary needs, the local and the regional contexts and passenger demands. To take an example, in Chapter 5, this voluminous body of correspondence has enabled me to show the presence of a complex, dynamic and evolving refreshment arrangement for Indian passengers, an aspect either woefully neglected or altogether ignored in current railway scholarship. This new archival source however, has been used in conjunction with what may be defined as the standard archive of the colonial Indian railways as well as the 'native newspaper reports' series.[36] But crucially, this book also uses a substantial body of unofficial sources primarily in the form of travelogues written by Indian railway travellers mainly in Bengal and Hindi, including some of the earliest railway related writings published in these languages.[37] Use has also been made, though not extensively, of travel guides, guidebooks and tourist pamphlets.

The decision to use two distinct kinds of sources: the official and the unofficial, has been influenced by a desire to analyse both objective and subjective aspects of railway journeys.[38] Railways increased the number of people travelling together. This was also accompanied by the necessity to travel under conditions, which were at once more intimate and impersonal. The rules of railway travel were very different, the necessary physical proximity and communication with other travellers and railway employees were unprecedented. For instance, to buy tickets passengers had to communicate with the ticket booking clerks and had to make their way through the ticket counters – all this was definitely new and a necessary part of railway travel. Yet, travelling became more impersonal, by which I mean the possibility of travelling with strangers and also the inviolable rules of travel (at least in theory) that were administered through railway employees who had no rapport with the passengers. And though passenger experiences varied, depending primarily though not exclusively on which class of carriage one travelled in; nonetheless, all passengers had to adapt to the travel practices introduced by a new mode of transit. In other words, the objective conditions of railway travel produced subjective and often novel experiences.[39] More importantly perhaps, railway passengers interpreted new experiences spawned by railway journeys in ways that had social implications.

A simultaneous perusal of both official and the un-official sources therefore has allowed a window into passenger responses to objective and subjective facets of railway journeys. Additionally, the unofficial sources, especially the travelogues, offer Indian voices, an element that though not entirely missing from the official records, always runs the risk of being mediated or somehow inauthentic.[40] Neither of these advantages however, does not even remotely imply a claim to recover railway journey experiences of all Indian railway passengers. But it does provide an opportunity to reflect upon issues that influenced passenger experiences of railway journeys mainly by cross examining official and unofficial sources and extrapolating on the basis of it. A case in point is the issue of railway employees demanding bribes from passengers. Official records attest to the presence of bribery as an 'ubiquitous menace' thus offering a scale of the problem.[41] Surely one can discount this description as an instance of colonial authorities singling out Indian railway employees and deploying a stereotype of 'corrupt natives'.[42] But interestingly, contemporary travelogues by Indian railway passengers substantiate these official claims, while also adding new details. For instance, authors such Surendranath Ray, Ghosthabihari Dhar or Prabhat Chandra Dube recounted their own experiences of bribes being demanded by all sorts of railway employees, often in collusion with the members of the railway police.[43] Such evidence indicates that regardless of the official sources' silence on the subject, upper-class passengers were not immune from demands for bribe. More significantly, these instances add to our understanding of Indian passengers' (in this case elites) everyday experiences of railway travel, thus underlining the significance of non-official sources complementing the official one. But at the same time, since the bulk of these unofficial sources are also personal narratives, i.e., travelogues; adding a caveat acknowledging the limitations of the former will not be amiss.

First, though written in the vernacular and therefore in principle catering to a wider audience, these texts were written by a specific social group: urban, Western educated and upper-caste/class. As such, as subsequent chapters will show, the notions and sentiments expressed in these texts had a specific socio-economic resonance. Second, most of the travelogues used in this book are in Bengali and therefore represent a regional response. This disproportionate use of Bengali travelogues is mainly a consequence of a relative lack of Hindi travelogues in the late nineteenth century.[44] Nevertheless, the claim to glean an 'Indian response' based primarily, though not exclusively, on Bengali sources can quite rightly be problematic. Finally, the authors of these travelogues constituted a minority of railway travellers.[45] Their railway experiences therefore, do not tell us directly about the majority of Indian passengers. For instance, none of these travelogues contain any first-hand account of travelling in low-class crowded carriages or discomfort experienced from lack of access to toilets. If such issues made it between the covers of these travelogues, then the discussion was based entirely on indirect observations. Despite these limitations however, there is a possibility that the travelogues reached a wider audience, directly or indirectly.[46] Also, it is perhaps not without significance that the authors, who often self-published their travel accounts, kept the prices of these texts low, or in some extreme cases distributed them free, presumably to attract a wider clientele.[47] Additionally, although these travelogues were personal narratives, they were by no means private. On the contrary, the travelogues were written to be read if only because the authors used this fairly new literary medium to convey much wider messages than descriptive accounts of sites and travels. Last but not least, though certainly elitist, as hinted above, it can be argued that the travelogues had a wider influence than merely literary, for example, verbal, visual and so on.

Additionally, the timing of these texts is instructive. Most of these travelogues were written from the late nineteenth to early twentieth century and are of course symbolic of the growth of the book printing industry in colonial India. But they also represent a wider shift that characterised the period, which was the changing relation between different social groups, print language, public sphere and the growth of mass mobilisation largely around issues of identity.[48] The content of these travelogues, it can be argued, was shaping attitudes and framing ideas that were influential. They created a filter for experiencing railways in specific ways and it can be fairly assumed that they established the frame or the context in which railway experience was interpreted. It is not a coincidence that the authors of these texts hinted at the difficulties faced by those who travelled in lower-class carriages, without any direct experience of it and linked the conditions of travel to a wider political narrative about the colonial context of railway operations in India. These authors therefore were clearly using a textual medium to take upon themselves the role of representing those sections of Indian society that arguably lacked such devices. This not only offered these authors opportunities to unambiguously self-fashion a position between the colonial state (claiming paternal beneficience) and the majority of Indians; but at the same time these texts were also producing and re-producing social norms, in this case how to interpret railway experiences, through hegemony.[49]

This however, should not be taken to mean that 'ordinary' travellers had no way of being influenced by railway encounters, especially issues of proximity, confinement and new travel practices, without an elite mediation. In truth, until the end of the nineteenth century railways were relatively limited in their location and impact.[50] Additionally, many Indians were too poor to pay for their own travel by train, or lived a long way from a railway connection, geographically and without good local travel. But nonetheless, railways affected an unprecedentedly large number of people from a wide cross section of society. As Ian Kerr has noted, by the turn of the twentieth century, for an increasing number of people, the railway was a palpable part of everyday life –first-hand experience through railway travel, daily encounters with tracks or passing trains and newspaper stories about aspects of railway experience affected many people.[51] Additionally, as hinted above, the objective conditions of railway travel practices affected all railway travellers, albeit in varying degrees. Similarly, ideas and sentiments about territory, identity and nationhood possibly influenced those whose railway experiences were interpreted through other filters such as an access to a particular kind of education or membership of a specific social group. Thus, even if railways

Introduction 9

did not do much, directly, for many people until a certain period, yet their physical presence and ideas about them from a variety of sources may have had a wide impact.

Railway spaces as social spaces: a note on methodology

This book assesses the impact of railways on colonial Indian society by examining railway spaces as social spaces.[52] The decision to use social space as an analytical tool has been primarily influenced by Henri Lefebvre's idea that roads, railways and other forms of infrastructures are materialisations of social relations in space.[53] This choice has been further bolstered by the sources used in this study, which reveal how different social groups, both Indian and British, wanted to dominate railway spaces by exerting their superior claims based on notions of social status, race, religion or caste.[54] The use of social space as a conceptual category however, is not entirely novel. In the context of South Asia, both Ravi Ahuja's work on colonial Orissa, as well as Ritika Prasad's recent volume on railways and everyday life in colonial India have effectively used the idea of social space. While the focus of Ahuja's work is mainly economic; Prasad has applied the concept in rather limited way.[55] As such, here the use of social space as a methodological fulcrum that underpins this appraisal of the role of railways on Indian society certainly charts new territory. This said, the way Ahuja has approached the 'problem' of social space in a sequence of seven hypotheses, juxtaposing them against common colonial conceptualisations of space, remains relevant for thinking through the relationship between colonialism and production of space. More specifically, the first two hypotheses of Ahuja's conceptual framework, which are production and conflict, are also particularly relevant to this project as will be explored later.

Railway operations created new social spaces and modified the existing ones. New railway spaces included stations, platforms, waiting rooms, refreshment rooms and carriages etc.; while spaces such as *serais* and *dharamsalas* became a part of railway organisation.[56] But this difference between old and new is mainly one of nomenclature.[57] Railway operations did not produce spaces out of a vacuum. Drawing upon Ravi Ahuja's hypothesis of production of space, which underlines the conditions in which social space is historically produced and reproduced, here I suggest that the production of railway spaces took place within earlier produced spaces and responded to the demands and challenges presented by pre-existing spatial practices. For instance, this process is clearly illustrated when the Eastern Indian Railway Company's Board of Directors decided to construct *serais* for Indian railway passengers in the vicinity of larger stations. Deliberating on the question of sanctioning capital for the construction of *serais*, the Board admitted:

> Hitherto the Government of India [the East India Company] and native princes provided serais and dak bungalows at convenient distances on all the principal roads. Since the railway company had succeeded to the rights of

the Government as proprietors of the chief roads, they had inherited the acknowledged obligation and are bound to provide suitable resting places for the travellers.[58]

At one level this declaration reads like a transfer of moral responsibilities of governance from one agency to another. But there is little doubt that such munificence was also prompted by a desire to claim superior rights over social spaces, which hitherto had been (though incompletely) the preserve of others.[59] Similar tendencies can also be noticed in the debates around railway authorities' demands to impose a standardised tariff for passengers staying at *serais* and *dharamsalas*. In this case, the owners of *serais* and *dharamsalas* contested railway administrations' claims on the ground that prevalent norms were more flexible and offered travellers various options. This dispute can certainly be read as suggestive of a wider shift visible under colonial governance from personal or private transactions to a commercial system accessible to anyone. At the same time, it is also plain that here is a classic case of pre-existing spatial practices challenging the emergent one through production of new social spaces.

Such outcomes however, may not appear surprising if one bears in mind that social space 'in addition to being a means of production, it is also a means of control and hence of domination, of power'.[60] Here Ahuja's hypothesis of conflict offers a useful tool to understand how the production and reproduction of railway spaces in colonial India was marked by an uneven process of contestation by different social groups – a process that, as we will see, also mediated the impact of steam on Indian society. Simply put, railway spaces were sites wherein Indian passengers occasionally, as a wider collective and more often as smaller groups (caste, religious or social status based), contested the superior claims of each other as much as that of the railway/colonial authorities' claims over the passengers. As hinted above, this process is clearly visible in all sources. Here however, I desist using any illustrative examples mainly because the subsequent chapters will amply substantiate my claims. But as a way of anticipating later arguments it can be noted that conflict and contestation over railway spaces are most clearly evident in the day-to-day functioning and management of railways, especially in the interactions between the demands made by Indian railway passengers and the responses of the railway authorities.

This process, though dynamic, was nonetheless characterised by uneven access to political power by different contending groups. Hence, the unevenness of these interactions also adds to our understanding of the conflict through which railway spaces and spatial practices were produced and how these spaces were tools of asserting social control and domination. The desire to dominate railway spaces is also demonstrated in the ways in which competing claims were made to appropriate railway spaces by one group over others for a variety of reasons that were often contradictory. For instance, the appropriation of the railway spaces in the twentieth century by the nationalist leaders was primarily ideological, more or less designed to challenge the superior claims of the railway/colonial authorities over a well-acknowledged tool of political control. But railway spaces were also appropriated in more practical ways by railway passengers, including but not limited to a large number of pilgrims; railway employees (as the recent example of bribery indicates) and even criminals, many of whom plied their trade exclusively on railways.[61] This book therefore, uses production and reproduction of railway spaces and the competing claims over them as a clue to understand and explicate the complex and heterogeneous impact of railway operations on colonial Indian society.

Scope, organisation and chapter scheme

This book covers approximately six decades: from 1855 to 1920. The chronological scope has been primarily influenced by a general lack of scholarly interest in the early decades of railway operations in colonial India. Broadly speaking, in most studies on Indian railways, including some of the most recent ones,[62] the density of information usually increases by the late nineteenth century, with the twentieth century enjoying maximum coverage. This leaves us with very little detail to hand on the early decades of railway operations – a significant oversight, especially if one wants to identify elements of continuity and change, an important component in assessing the degree of railway induced changes. By accessing a hitherto unused body of archival sources, this book covers an important period of the expansion of railway operations underlining not only the evolution of railway policies, but more crucially, how Indians responded to a new means of transit. The choice of dates has also been shaped by the fact that in August 1855, the first trains ran from Calcutta to Raniganj thus inaugurating the 'railway age' in Eastern and Northern India; and 1920 is a convenient end point to ascertain the degree of change attributable to railways alone and to contextualise these changes within a wider socio-political framework.

The territorial focus is primarily the Indo-Gangetic plain and Bengal, though comparisons with other areas have occasionally been made, thus justifying the ambitious, if somewhat pretentious use of the word 'India' in the title. This geographical scope has been shaped by two considerations. *One*, though disrupted by the events of 1857–1858, the area between Calcutta to Delhi, being strategically important for the colonial administration, received the earliest unbroken railway communication. This area therefore, potentially offers continued assessment of Indian interactions with railways. And, *two*, the two major languages of the region, Hindi and Bengali, have offered a substantial body of unofficial sources, thus allowing me to incorporate both these sources.[63] Though this geographic focus has limited the analysis to those railway companies that operated in the region;[64] comparisons have been made with other regions wherever relevant. The book is divided into seven chapters, excluding the introduction and the conclusion. The following paragraphs offer a thumbnail sketch of the chapters.

Chapter One: Imposition of railway time-discipline was/is considered to be one of the most important aspects of the introduction of the railway in colonial India. Broadly speaking, railway timetables are assumed to have imposed an unprecedented time discipline on colonial India primarily by introducing a travel-discipline. Arguably railway timetables were also one of the most efficient tools of the colonial state to bring Indians within the ambit of 'colonial time', thereby disciplining them. But were railway timetables as successful in imposing their regime on Indian society as currently claimed? Using new evidence this chapter interrogates the ability of railway timetables to impose time and travel-discipline in colonial India; while also exploring the wider, social implications of the process.

Chapter Two: This chapter continues with the theme of imposition of travel-discipline and its social implications by looking at railway tickets – a hitherto unexplored theme. In fact, this chapter is the first of its kind in Indian railway history to be devoted exclusively to railway tickets. Tickets, alongside timetables were/are noted as the twin tool of the colonial state to transform Indian society by introducing a rigid travel mechanism, presumably to influence their behaviour beyond railway travel. By using a combination of sources this chapter questions our current assumptions about the putative role of railway tickets in imposing travel-discipline in colonial India.

Chapter Three: This chapter focuses on railway spaces, especially station infrastructure: the platforms, waiting sheds and rooms and toilets at the station. Once again, historiographically, the focus of this chapter is unique. Singling out station infrastructure, this chapter illustrates how railway spaces evolved through an interaction between operational exigencies of railway administrations and negotiations by Indian railway passengers played out in the wider context of government interventions. The chapter investigates how far the image of railway spaces influencing social transformations in colonial India is historically sustainable.

Chapter Four: Developing on the theme of railway spaces and the impact of railways on Indian society, this chapter focuses exclusively on railway carriages – a contentious historiographical site. This chapter reappraises our historical understanding of train carriages as a site of the imposition of railway travel-discipline that in turn contributed to the creation of homogenous racial/national experiences with significant social implications both within and beyond the confines of the compartments.

Chapter Five: Continuing with the discussion of railway spaces this chapter focuses on refreshment arrangements for Indian railway passengers. By bringing new evidence the chapter argues that, as opposed to our current historiographical assumptions, refreshment arrangements for Indian passengers did not have socially unifying consequences. Additionally, the chapter widens and complicates our existing assumptions about refreshment provisions in colonial India's railways by underlining the presence of Indian agency and their role in shaping the former.

Chapter Six: One of most significant colonial assertions about the transformative capacity of railways was its ability to create a 'nation' – both in imagination and in reality. The post-colonial scholarship too, though with minor modifications, continues to accept that railways created a 'national' space in India. Arguably, this creation of a 'nation' was achieved by homogenisation and conceptualisation of the territory, depriving regions of their characteristics and imbuing them with wider, trans-local identities. This chapter departs from this dominant scholarship. It contests the claims of the creation and completeness of 'national' space and the role of railways in the process. It also illustrates contestations over the production of spaces by offering multiple, often contradictory conceptualisations of territories, thus hinting at long-term implications for colonial Indian society and beyond.

Chapter Seven: This chapter appraises the impact of railways on notions of identity and community. Hitherto railway travel has been associated with creating a notion of 'Indian' identity – glossing over notions of identity based on religion, caste, gender and social status. By a critical examination of the travelogues and Indian-language newspaper reports, this chapter challenges this historiographical orthodoxy, while arguing for a more differentiated and heterogeneous impact of railways on notions of identity and community.

The themes explored in the chapters are expected to meet the main objective of this project, i.e., whether railways, the celebrated 'tool of empire' succeeded in transforming colonial Indian society in ways imagined by her imperial masters. Any answers to this question are also likely to contribute to our understanding of the nature of colonialism both in India and beyond, especially the issue of the gap between colonial rhetoric of technology-borne social transformations and the realities of colonial governance and colonised societies.

Notes

1 G.W. MacGeorge, *Ways and Works in India: being an account of the public works in that country from the earliest times up to the present day* (London, Archibald Constable and Company, 1894) Part II: 'Railway in India', Chapter 1, p. 221.
2 At the heart of such expectations was the belief that Indian society remained unchanged for centuries, a feature that allegedly made India and Indians non-dynamic and averse to change. See, for instance, MacGeorge, 'Ways and Works', p. 220. Such ideas however, were not confined to one individual. More importantly, this notion of 'unchanging Asiatic', as is now well acknowledged, provided much needed ideological justification for imperial control, especially the claim that colonial control will infuse much needed change in Indian society and in the habits and beliefs of Indians. For a succinct overview of the various ideological underpinnings of colonial rule in India see T. Metcalf, *Ideologies of the Raj* (Cambridge, Cambridge University Press, 1st edition, 1995).
3 For a useful account of the various factors that influenced the introduction of railways in colonial India, see I. Kerr, *Engines of Change: The Railroads That Made India* (Westport, Connecticut, Praeger, 2007), Chapter 2.
4 Contemporary documents, either railway related or otherwise, are replete with such sentiments. See W.P. Andrews, *Indian Railways and their probable results, with maps and an appendix, containing statistics of internal and external commerce of India* (London, T.C. Newby, 3rd edition, 1848); MacGeorge, 'Ways and Works'.
5 MacGeorge, 'Ways and Works'; Andrews, 'Indian Railways'; J. Danvers, *Indian railways: their past history, present condition, and future prospects* (London, Effingham Wilson, Royal Exchange, 1877), IOR.
6 Cavour, C. *Des chemins de fer en Italie* (Paris, Plon Fréres, 1846), p. 8. I thank Francesco G. Sacco for translating the excerpt from French to English.
7 For a comprehensive account of railway development in the nineteenth century world see C. Wolmar, *Blood, Iron and Gold: How the Railroads Transformed the World* (New York, Public Affairs, 2010).

8 T.R. Grunow, 'Trains, Modernity, and State Formation in Meiji Japan' in B. Fraser and S. Spalding (eds) *Trains, Culture and Mobility: Riding the Rails* (UK, Lexington Books, 2012) pp. 235–261; S. Ericsson, 'Importing Locomotives in Meiji Japan: International Business and Technology Transfer in the railroad industry'; *Osiris*, 13, Number 1; 1998; pp. 129–153.
9 Pamphlet addressed to the Secretary of State for India, 1853, in Home Correspondence 'B', copies of letters sent, 1849–1879, L/PWD/2/68, IOR.
10 Andrews, 'Indian Railways'. The quote can be found in the preface to the second edition, page VII.
11 See R.M. Stephenson, 'Report upon the practicability and advantages of the introduction of railways into British India with the official correspondence with the Bengal Government and full statistical data respecting the existing trade upon the line connecting Calcutta with Mirzapore, Benaras, Allahabad and the North-West frontier'; 1844, London, L/PWD/2/43, IOR.
12 D. Chakrabarty, 'The Colonial context of Bengal Renaissance: a note on early railway-thinking in Bengal', *Indian Economic and Social History Review*, II, 1 (March 1974), pp. 92–111.
13 For instance, writing in 1841, i.e., a little over a decade before the first trains ran on Indian soil, Pandit Ratneshwar, a school teacher, expounded on various benefits of railway locomotion on Indian society in the pages of his travelogues *Patramalika*. Similar thoughts were also expressed in Bengali pamphlets published in 1855, the year in which the railway operations commenced in Eastern India. See P. Ratneshwar, *Patramalika* (Agra, Agra School Book Society, 1841); A.K. Dutta, *Bashpiya Upadesh* (Calcutta, Tattwabodhini Press, 1855); K. Moitra, *Bashpiya Kal O Bharatiya Railway* (Srirampur, Srerampore Press, 1855).
14 Here and hereafter in this book I use the word post-colonial in a strictly chronological sense, i.e., post-1947. The idea that railways benefited Indian society most tangibly by forging a 'nation' continues to influence even popular perceptions about colonial Indian railways. Good and accessible evidence can be found in the comments that accompany the YouTube videos of Shyam Benegal's old but still clearly popular television series *Yatra*. The popularity can be gauged by the fact that the series was originally aired on Indian television in 1986 but still enjoys substantial viewership on YouTube. See also the blog: https://thereel.scroll.in/800696/the-dd-files-shyam-benegals-yatra-packed-all-of-india-in-a-train (accessed 14 December 2016).
15 J. Hurd and I. Kerr (eds) *India's Railway History: A Research Handbook* (Leiden; Boston, Brill, 2012), pp. 113–114.
16 Though generalised, the observation is not off the mark and has been noted by Smritikumar Sarkar in his recent volume. See S. Sarkar, *Technology and Rural Change in Eastern India, 1830–1980* (New Delhi, Oxford University Press, 2014), p. 5. This favourable assessment of impact of railways on colonial Indian society contrasts with how the role of railways on colonial Indian economy and more recently on ecology and environment has been assessed. The literature on the impact of the railway on Indian economy is extensive. For a useful overview see Hurd and Kerr, 'India's Railway'; pp. 44–46; and D. Thorner, *Investment in Empire: British railway and steam shipping enterprise in India, 1825–1849* (Philadelphia, University of Pennsylvania Press, 1950). For the impact of railways on the environment, see P. Das, *Colonialism, Development, and the Environment: Railways and Deforestation in British India, 1860–1884* (New York, Palgrave Macmillan, 2015); I. Iqbal, *The Bengal Delta: Ecology, State and Social Change, 1840–1943* (UK, Palgrave Macmillan, 2010), Chapter 6; R. Prasad, *Tracks of Change: Railways and Everyday Life in Colonial India* (New Delhi, Cambridge University Press, 2015), Chapter 3.
17 I. Kerr, *Engines of Change: The Railroads That Made India* (Westport, Connecticut, Praeger, 2007); L. Bear, *Lines of the Nation: Indian Railway Workers, Bureaucracy,*

and the Intimate Historical Self (New York, Columbia University Press, 2007); R. Prasad, *Tracks of Change: Railways and Everyday Life in Colonial India* (New Delhi, Cambridge University Press, 2015); M. Goswami, *Producing India: from colonial economy to national space* (Chicago, University of Chicago Press, 2004); H. Bury, 'Novel spaces, Transitional moments: Negotiating Texts and Territory in 19th century Hindi travel accounts', in I. Kerr (ed.) *27 Down: New Departures in Indian Railway Studies* (Hyderabad, Orient BlackSwan, 2007), pp. 1–38; K. Chatterjee, 'Discovering India: Travel, History and Identity in late 19th century and early 20th century India', in D. Ali (ed.) *Invoking the Past: The Uses of History in South Asia* (Delhi, Oxford University Press, 1999), pp. 192–227.

18 S. Ramaswamy, *The Goddess and the Nation: Mapping Mother India* (Durham: Duke University Press, 2010); C. Pinney, *Photos of the Gods: The Printed Image and Political Struggle in India* (UK, Reaktion Books, 2004); M. Edney, *Mapping an Empire: The Geographical Construction of British India, 1765–1843* (Chicago: London, University of Chicago Press, 1997).

19 Goswami, 'Producing', p. 116; Bear, 'Lines', p. 46; Prasad, 'Tracks', p. 59. Of these, Prasad perhaps comes closest in scrutinising heterogenous impact of role of railways on notions of identities in colonial India.

20 B. Debroy, S. Chadha and V. Krishnamurthi (eds), *Indian Railways: The Weaving of a National Tapestry* (New Delhi, Penguin Random House India, 2017).

21 M. Mann, 'Torchbearers upon the Path of Progress: Britain's Ideology of a 'Moral and Material Progress' in India'; and R. Ahuja, '"The Bridge-Builders": Some Notes on Railways, Pilgrimage and the British "Civilizing Mission" in Colonial India' in H. Fischer-Tine and M. Mann (eds) *Colonialism as Civilizing Mission: Cultural Ideology in British India* (London, Anthem Press, 2004).

22 For a comprehensive discussion on pre-railway mobility in India see C. Markovits, J. Pouchepadass and S. Subrahmanyam (eds) *Society and Circulation: Mobile People and Itinerant Culture in South Asia* (Delhi, Permanent Black, 2002); also R. Ahuja, '"Opening up the Country"? Patterns of Circulation and Politics of Communication in Early Colonial Orissa', *Studies in History*, 20, 1, n.s. (2004), pp. 73–130.

23 There is no denying that these critical concepts and notions or the meanings attached to them have evolved over time, often acquiring new dimensions under colonial rule. But for reasons of analytical coherence and brevity in this study discussions of such themes have been confined to acknowledgement of the presence of longer and more complex processes.

24 Among other things, historians have identified education, legal reforms and land reforms as having transformed Indian society in varying degrees under colonial rule. Here comparison has been eschewed (unless relevant) mainly to underline linkages between railways and social change, a somewhat neglected historiographical theme.

25 I borrow the word 'technologies of communications' from Amelia Bonea's recent title, A. Bonea, *The News of Empire; Telegraphy, Journalism, and the Politics of the Reporting in Colonial India c.1830–1900* (New Delhi, Oxford University Press, 2016), p. 2.

26 In the context of South Asia this book adds to existing studies such as D. Arnold, *Everyday technology: Machines and the Making of India's Modernity* (Chicago: London, The University of Chicago Press, paperback edition, 2015); C. Dewey, *Steamboats on the Indus: The Limits of Western Technological Superiority in South Asia* (New Delhi, Oxford University Press, 2014); D.K. Lahiri Chaudhuri, *Telegraphic Imperialism: Crisis and Panic in the Indian Empire, c.1830–1920* (UK, Palgrave Macmillan, 2010); S. Sarkar, *Technology and Rural Change in Eastern India, 1830–1980* (New Delhi, Oxford University Press, 2014); N. Sinha, *Communication and Colonialism in Eastern India: Bihar, 1760s-1880s* (London, Anthem Books, 2012). In a global historiographical context, the book contributes to the growing body

16 *Introduction*

of literature on the social history of technology. See S. Bradley, *The Railways: Nation, Network and People* (UK, Profile Books, 2015); M. Cooper, *Brazilian Railway Culture* (UK, Cambridge Scholars, 2011); T. Van Hoy, *A Social History of Mexico's Railroads: Peons, Prisoners, and Priests* (USA, Rowman and Littlefield, 2008).

27 In many ways the following titles exemplify this shift: R. Ahuja, *Pathways of Empire: Circulation, 'Public works' and Social Space in colonial Orissa* (Hyderabad, Orient Longman, 2009); N. Sinha, *Communication and Colonialism in Eastern India: Bihar, 1760s–1880s* (London, Anthem Books, 2012); D. Arnold, *Everyday technology: Machines and the Making of India's Modernity* (Chicago and London, University of Chicago Press, paperback edition, 2015); C. Dewey, *Steamboats on the Indus* (New Delhi, Cambridge University Press, 2014).

28 Bonea, 'The News', p. 21.

29 D. Arnold, Science, *Technology and Medicine in Colonial India*, The New Cambridge History of India, III.5, (Cambridge, Cambridge University Press, 2000), Chapter 4; Prasad, 'Tracks of Change'; Chapter 2; and Bonea, 'The News of Empire'; Chapter 2.

30 M. Adas, *Machines as the Measure of Men: Science, Technology and Ideologies of Western Dominance* (Ithaca and London, Cornell University Press, 1989); D. Headrick, *The Tools of Empire: Technology and European imperialism in the nineteenth century* (New York, Oxford University Press, 1981); D. Headrick, *Power over Peoples: Technology, Environments, and Western Imperialism, 1400 to the Present* (Princeton, Oxford, Princeton University Press, 2010).

31 Up until the turn of the twentieth century, revenue from freight traffic grew slowly and without any remarkable increase. The coaching traffic or revenue earned from passengers thus supplied the much-needed profit, with Indian passengers travelling in third and fourth-class carriages constituting 97 per cent of the total passenger traffic. For passenger statistics see Reports to The Secretary of State for India in Council on Railways in India, in Parliamentary Papers, V/4 Series, IOR.

32 Prasad, 'Tracks of Change', p. 57.

33 As the following chapters will show, social status or rank (broadly defined) played a key role in shaping Indian passenger demands, at times even often more than race. Historiographical shifts have already alerted us to the significance of social rank in both colonised societies as well as in the metropole, especially notions of 'white subalternity'. See for instance, D. Cannadine, *Ornamentalism: How the British saw their Empire* (London, The Penguin Press, 2001); H. Fischer-Tiné, *Low and Licentious Europeans: Race, Class and White Subalternity in Colonial India* (Hyderabad, Orient Blackswan, 2009); S. Mizutani, *The Meaning of White: Race, Class, and the 'Domiciled Community' in British India 1858–1930* (New York, Oxford University Press, 2011). In this book, however, I use the category of 'respectable natives' as employed by both the colonial administration and Indian railway passengers themselves to argue for both a wider influence of role of status in colonial encounters and agency of Indians in shaping these interactions. At the same time, I think that both race and status were varyingly influential in shaping colonial relations and therefore one needs a closer scrutiny of specific cases rather than an overall explanation.

34 'Official' archive refers to the voluminous railway data maintained by different administrative agencies associated with the behemoth that was (and is) the Indian railways; while the 'unofficial' archive include railway related sources in a variety of textual and other formats that is not part of colonial railway records.

35 I claim this source as hitherto unused because I have not come across any reference to the use of these correspondences in any secondary literature on the Indian railway. The railway companies whose correspondence has been consulted include the Eastern Indian Railway Company, the Eastern Bengal Railway Company, the Calcutta and the South-Eastern Railway Company, the Oudh and Rohilkhand, the Indian Midland Railway and a series called 'Railway letters miscellaneous', which contained letters

Introduction 17

from several railway companies on diverse issues. For details see Letters to and from Railway Companies: 'A', 'B' and 'C' series, L/PWD/2 series, IOR.

36 For a detailed list of sources see bibliography. By standard archival resources I mean records that are often consulted by railway historians. This includes the records of the Public Works Department (Railway department); proceedings of the railway departments of the Government of India and the local government agencies and selections from Indian languages newspaper reports translated in English.

37 For a comprehensive list of travelogues used see J.F. Blumhardt (ed.) Catalogue of Bengali printed books in the library of the British Museum, 1886; and The catalogues of the Hindi, Punjabi, Sindhi and Pushtu printed books in the library of the British Museum, 1893; IOR. The use of the word earliest is based on the date of the publication in relation to commencement of railway operation. For instance, among Bengali sources I have used Jagomohan Chakrabarty's account of his travels to Rajmahal from Howrah the year in which a direct railway connection became available between the two places. Similarly, I have used Akshay Kumar Dutta and Kalidas Moitra's account of railways published in 1855, the year railway operations commenced in Eastern India. Among Hindi sources, I have included Pandit Ratneshwar's account of watching a working and miniature model of train in Bombay as early as 1841. See bibliography for a detailed list of sources consulted.

38 Here objective aspects imply new travel practices associated with railways such as buying tickets, consulting timetables or using the platforms and waiting rooms; while subjective alludes to the ways in which Indian passengers experienced and interpreted the objective conditions.

39 As Wolfgang Schivelbusch's pioneering work shows, railway journeys produced novel experiences – of space and time, self, fellow-travellers and landscape. W. Schivelbusch, *The Railway Journey: the industrialization of time and space in the 19th century* (Berkeley, Los Angeles, The University of California Press, 1986 edition).

40 See S. Amin, Event, *Metaphor and Memory: Chauri Chaura 1922–1992* (Delhi, Oxford University Press, 1995); R. Guha, *Elementary Aspects of Peasant Insurgency in Colonial India* with a foreword by James Scott (Durham, Duke University Press, 1999, first published in 1983).

41 See Chapter 2 for a discussion of bribes demanded by railway employees (Indian and Eurasians) and its implications for the imposition of railway travel-discipline.

42 In perception of India's colonial administrators 'natives' were dishonest, prone to chicanery, characteristics that also rendered them unfit for self-rule.

43 While Surendranath Ray and Prabhat Chandra Dube complained about luggage booking and ticket booking clerks respectively for demanding bribes; Ghosthabihari Dhar wrote an advisory in his five-volume travelogue warning readers of both corrupt railway employees and railway thieves and criminals. See S. Ray, *Uttar Paschim Bhraman* (Calcutta, Pashupati Press, 1907), p. 7; P. Dube, *Darjeeling* (Mahishadal, 1910), p. 20; G.B. Dhar, *Sachitra Tirtha Yatra Vivaran* (Calcutta, The Bengal Medical Library, 1913), advertisement before the preface. These however, are not the only instances of railway employees being criticised for demanding bribe. Similar complaints were made by authors of other travelogues as well as widely reported in Indian languages' newspapers.

44 V. Dalmia, *Nationalization of Hindu Traditions: Bharatendu Harishchandra and Nineteenth Century Benaras* (Delhi, Oxford University Press, 1996), p. 328.

45 Statistically speaking, passengers in upper-class carriages (first and second) constituted 1 per cent of total coaching traffic. This included both Indians and Europeans, the latter outnumbering the former. Given this, one may safely claim that the authors of these travelogues were a miniscule minority of Indian railway passengers. For passenger statistics see Reports to The Secretary of State for India in Council on Railways in India, in Parliamentary Papers, V/4 Series, IOR.

18   *Introduction*

46 There is evidence to believe that travelogues enjoyed a wide readership. See Chatterjee, 'Discovering India', p. 197. Neither can one rule out the possibility that the ideas and sentiments expressed in the travelogues did not influence those who did not or could read these texts as diffusion of textual ideas among a non-literate audience can take a variety of forms (oral, aural, visual). See C.A. Bayly, *Empire and Information: Intelligence Gathering and Social Communication in India, 1780–1870* (Cambridge, Cambridge University Press, 1996); F. Orsini, *Print and Pleasure: Popular Literature and Entertaining Fictions in Colonial North India* (Ranikhet, Permanent Black, 2009); S. Freitag, 'More than Meets the (Hindu) Eye: The Public Arena as a Space for Alternative Vision', in R.H. Davis (ed.), *Picturing the Nation: Iconographies of Modern India* (Hyderabad, Orient Longman, 2007); A. Mukhopadhyay, 'Colonised Gaze? Guidebooks and Journeying in Colonial India', *South Asia: Journal of South Asian Studies*, 37, 4, 2014, pp. 656–669.

47 Dharanikanta Lahiri Chaudhuri and Ghosthabihari Dhar, authors of two Bengali travelogues, distributed the texts for free as they wanted people to read these accounts and benefit from them.

48 B. Anderson, *Imagined Communities: Reflections on the Origin and Spread of Nationalism* (London, New York, Verso Books, 2006 edition).

49 A. Gramsci, *Prison Notebooks* (ed.) (New York, Columbia University Press, 1992). Besides Gramsci, as Henri Lefebvre once reminded us, hegemony is also useful in examining the actions of the bourgeoisie, especially in relation to space. See H. Lefebvre, *The Production of Space*, trans. D. Nicholson-Smith (Oxford, Basil Blackwell, English translation first published in 1991), pp. 10–11.

50 The current historiography about infrastructure and transport projects in colonial India shows that up until the turn of the twentieth century railways faced serious competition from other means of transport such as boats, carts and caravans. See R. Varady, 'Rail and Road Transport in Nineteenth Century Awadh: Competition in a North Indian province' (unpublished PhD dissertation) University of Arizona, 1981. Also, R. Ahuja, *Pathways of Empire: Circulation, 'Public works' and Social Space in colonial Orissa* (Hyderabad, Orient Longman, 2009); N. Sinha, *Communication and Colonialism in Eastern India: Bihar, 1760s-1880s* (London, Anthem Books, 2012).

51 For a comprehensive discussion of how railways became imbedded in South Asian popular culture, see I. Kerr, 'Cultural Dimensions of India's Railways: Representation, Representations and Sources', in Kerr and Hurd, 'Handbook'; pp. 96–135. See also, Sarkar, 'Technology and Rural Change'; pp. 288–290.

52 In this book, the use of the word railway space denotes a reference to both geographical/natural spaces that were railway authorities' property as well as social space as defined by Henri Lefebvre. Lefebvre, 'The Production'; pp. 26–27; 32.

53 Lefebvre, 'The Production', p. 26.

54 As David Harvey's work shows, there is a close link between control of space and control of the politics of the place. See D. Harvey, *The Condition of Postmodernity: An Enquiry into the Origins of Cultural Change* (Oxford, Blackwell, 1990), Chapter 14. For a discussion of how the 'spatial turn' may offer possibilities to explore aspects of India's railway history and its wider impact see I. Kerr (ed.), *Railways in Modern India* (New Delhi, Oxford University Press, 2001), pp. 14–18.

55 Ahuja, 'Pathways of Empire'; Prasad, 'Tracks of Change'. Ahuja uses social space for his entire analysis, while Prasad uses the concept only in the second chapter of her book. Also see M. Goswami, 'From Swadeshi to Swaraj: Nation, Economy, Territory in Colonial South Asia, 1870–1907', *Comparative Studies in Society and History*, 40:4 (October 1998), pp. 609–636.

56 The cases of *serais* and *dharamsalas* were quite complex as the shift towards railways was both formal and informal. Formal arrangements entailed either *serais* or *dharamsalas* being constructed by railway companies or their proprietors became

sub-contractors of railway companies and as such these sites became part of official provisions for accommodating Indian railway passengers. The informal arrangement on the other hand, was one in which private individuals, owners of *serais* and *dharamsalas* offered similar services to passengers without entering into any negotiations with the railway authorities. See Letters to and from the agent of the Eastern Indian Railway Company to the Board of Directors, dated June 1864 and April 1865 in L/PWD/2/91 and L/PWD/2/93, IOR.

57 Stations, platforms and carriages etc. were indeed new; but not in the sense of being social spaces. Though one can certainly think of them as new sites.
58 'Memorandum on Report of the Sanitary Commissioner' in Letters to and from the agent of the Eastern Indian Railway Company to the Board of Directors dated December 1865, L/PWD/2/81, IOR. The company finally decided to construct serais Letters to and from the agent of the Eastern Indian Railway Company to the Board of Directors, dated June 1864, L/PWD/2/91, IOR.
59 One cannot, however, also rule out the role profit played in this decision, especially at a time when demands for night-long accommodation from passengers were increasing. See 'Translation of an anonymous petition', dated 24 February 1865, in Proceedings of the Railway Department, Government of Bengal, P/163/35, IOR.
60 Lefebvre, 'The Production'; p. 26.
61 The appropriation of railway spaces by 'railway criminals' is a fascinating narrative. Though a discussion of this theme is beyond the scope of this book, I have written about it elsewhere, see A. Mukhopadhyay, 'Lost in Transit? Railway Crimes and the Regime of Control in Colonial India', in S. Ghosh, E. Rashkow and U. Chakrabarti (eds), *Memory, Identity and the Colonial Encounter in India: Essays in Honour of Peter Robb* (New Delhi, Routledge India, 2017).
62 For instance, the sources used and examples proffered in Ritika Prasad's otherwise excellent contribution mostly concerns late-nineteenth to early twentieth century. In fact, the density of sources used by Prasad shows a remarkable gap of the early decades of railway operations in India. Prasad, 'Tracks of Change'.
63 Kumkum Chatterjee and Harriett Bury have looked at Bengali and Hindi travelogues respectively. But hitherto, no attempt has been made to use Bengali and Hindi sources together. See K. Chatterjee, 'Discovering India: Travel, History and Identity in late 19th century and early 20th century India', in D. Ali (ed.), *Invoking the Past: The Uses of History in South Asia* (Delhi, Oxford University Press, 1999), pp. 192–227; and H. Bury, 'Novel spaces, Transitional moments: Negotiating Texts and Territory in 19th century Hindi travel accounts', in I. Kerr (ed.), *27 Down: New Departures in Indian Railway Studies*, (Hyderabad, Orient BlackSwan, 2007), pp. 1–38. Relevant here will be to note that translations from Bengali and Hindi sources, unless otherwise stated are mine.
64 These include: the East Indian Railway Company, the Eastern Bengal Railway, the Calcutta and South-Eastern Railway Company, the Bengal and North-Western railway the Oudh and Rohilkhand Railway and the Sindh, Punjab and Delhi Railway.

1 On time?
Railway time and travel-discipline in colonial India

The opening scene of '*Mahapurush*', directed by Satyajit Ray, is set on a railway platform.[1] Here, the god-man *birinchi baba* is receiving homage from a motley crowd of devotees who have gathered at the railway station to bid adieu to him. Interestingly, the scheduled departure time of the train is clearly overdue as is evident from the anxious glances of the guard and the engine drivers. But despite their anxiety, the railway staff wait for the 'signal' (pun intended) from the god-man. Eventually, the train departs, but only after receiving a nod from *birinchi baba*. The awaiting guard too, receives his share of religious merit in the form of a dried petal thrown at him by the god-man from the already moving carriage.

The scene is thought provoking on many levels. Evidently, it is a scathing criticism of the hold of holy men on mass psyche, especially when it is eventually revealed that the man in question was a charlatan. But for our purposes, the scene is instructive because of the ways in which it challenges the notion of what I call 'travel-discipline', arguably imposed by railway operations in colonial India.[2] Additionally, the scene questions the nature and degree of time discipline imposed and adhered to by railways in colonial India.[3] If trains failed or struggled to adhere to the timetables, then by implication, time discipline, arguably the most significant aspect of the railway-induced travel-discipline, also faltered. Evidently, as the scene reveals, there was a gap between the realities of everyday railway operations and the claims of the colonial state. Trains ran late – for a variety of reasons, including the whims and wishes of a 'native' god-man. Incidentally, the ability of *birinchi baba* to manipulate the train schedule is also suggestive of the opportunities 'native' railway users have to influence or direct railway travel-discipline. The scene therefore, offers a convenient entry point to ask critical questions about railway-induced travel and time-discipline in colonial India and its implications on Indian society, the main subject of the chapter.

Keeping time: railway timetables and travel-discipline

> Punctuality, so wanting in our native friends, will be taught more effectively by the rail than by the schoolmaster, the train waits for no one, as many a native has already found to his cost.[4]

Railway timetables has been widely acknowledged as an instrument of imposing modern time discipline.[5] Additionally, debates about the imposition of time discipline have also underlined the ways in which the nineteenth-century discourse on the subject insinuates a more fundamental difference between colonising Europe and colonised non-Europe than is apparent. Broadly speaking, for post-Enlightenment European imperialists and intellectuals the absence of modern time sense among inhabitants of non-Europe was veritable proof that the latter inhabited a different time, more primitive and inferior than their own.[6] India too, was not immune from such perceptions of inferiority and difference. If anything, the adherence to a cyclical, religious notion of time by a vast majority of the Indian population exacerbated colonial administrators' belief in India's inferiority on the civilisational scale.[7] Furthermore, the existence of religious or seasonal notions of time by which Indian lives were regulated, were often conveniently ignored to a bid to claim that Indians lived in a sort of timeless existence.

But the logic of colonial control and the rhetoric of imperial beneficence also demanded a simultaneous underscoring of difference while claiming to bestow civilisational progress on the colonised by imposing a modern sense of time and punctuality.[8] As such, efforts were made to identify the best ways to impart 'value of time' to 'natives'. Railways, or more specifically, railway timetables offered a possible solution. Colonial administrators and railway promoters enthusiastically asserted that railway timetables were to be an effective tutor of punctuality, even more than either plantation or factory managers' whips and whistles. It is certainly surprising that railway timetables were invested with such transformative possibilities as anyone related with the railway enterprise in the mid-nineteenth century India did not expect 'natives' to take to railways in any significant manner.[9] Perhaps, as noted in the introduction, this belief in the power of steam was a reflection of the acceptance of the wider nineteenth-century credo of the transformative ability of technologies. Or it may well have been the gap that usually separates colonial rhetoric from reality. Whatever may be the source of such convictions; there is little doubt that the 'imperious whistle of trains' was expected to teach Indians punctuality, as it has done to 'common folks' in England.[10] Railway timetables, in other words, were to discipline Indians by instilling a sense of time and punctuality.

Interestingly, this image of railways as an efficient tool of imposing modern time discipline through an inflexible travel discipline continues to be largely accepted by post-colonial scholars. This however, does not imply a concurrence with the assumptions that underpinned the discourse about imposition of time discipline in colonial India. Quite the contrary, works of Sumit Sarkar and, more recently, that of Ritika Prasad have successfully challenged the seeming beneficence of the colonial rhetoric of imposing time-discipline in India.[11] Of these, Prasad's contribution has also underscored heterogeneous Indian responses to the imposition of 'colonial time'.[12] These analyses are certainly valuable. At the same time however, underlying assumption continues to conform to the colonial claim that 'railway time' forced travellers to submit to 'colonial time'. Simply put, our current understanding of imposition of time-discipline in colonial

India rests on the assumption that railway operations played a key role in the process both by standardising time in India and introducing an inflexible time-discipline through railway timetables.[13] Railway timetables therefore, are argued to be the tools that imposed a rigid travel-discipline hitherto absent in India; thus, in turn forcing Indian railway passengers to submit to time-discipline.[14] At a related level, this inflexibility of railway timetables has been interpreted as one of the ways in which the colonial state disciplined colonised subjects by coercing them (including controlling their physical movements) into railway travel/time-discipline without any possibilities of the latter to either direct or influence the same.[15]

These suggestions, though not entirely inaccurate, however overlook two significant and related points: (i) the standardisation of 'railway time' in colonial India was neither quick nor linear;[16] and (ii) the inflexibility of the railway timetables was more theoretical than real. More importantly, these interpretations do not take into account the practical challenges and exigencies that guided everyday railway operations in colonial India. Going back once again to the cinematic example used in the beginning of the chapter, if the efficacy of railway timetables was contingent rather than assumed, then by implication, the imposition of railway travel/time-discipline too was compromised – a possibility that also questions the latter's ability to discipline and control the colonised. Given this, the chapter focuses on railway timetables to explore the nature and scale of imposition of colonial travel/time-discipline. Wherever possible, the analysis is accompanied by Indian passengers' responses to railway time-discipline. This inclusion of Indian responses, especially the dynamic interaction between the demands of Indian railway passengers and the responses of the railway administrations have permitted me to demonstrate the role of 'native' agency in shaping the process as well as the outcomes of the imposition of railway travel/time-discipline in colonial India.

Railway timetabling: a delayed standardisation

At the most practical level, the role of timetables is to coordinate train schedules in order to maximise capital output and minimise clash, both commercial and literal. As such, railway timetables in colonial India, as in other parts of the world, were a product of the necessities associated with safe operation of train movements. Colonial India entered the railway age with a guaranteed system and with private railway companies overlooking railway operations in different parts of India.[17] Consequently, all railway companies had separate timetables and railway travellers had to follow the specific timetables of the lines by which they wished to travel.[18] The significance of the system was underlined in a contemporary Bengali tract published in 1855, which advised travellers on the importance of accurate consultation of the timetables belonging to different railway companies.[19] For a while this arrangement worked well because the railway lines covered short distances and the train service was minimal. But as the railway network expanded and the number of trains increased, coordination among the railway companies became imperative.[20] The need to regulate the movement of trains became necessary to avoid commercial squabbles and to ensure that the trains of the various companies passed through the important stations and junctions at least once during convenient hours of the day.[21] Improved timetables were also needed to attract passenger traffic. Indian passengers preferred a timetable that would obviate the need to travel or wait for the trains in the dark.[22]

But effective organisation of timetables required more than coordinating with existing train schedules. It could be done only when the local times of different regions of India could be regulated.[23] To resolve this, the companies sought intervention from the Government of India. Among local times in colonial India, 'Bombay time', and 'Calcutta time', were the two most important time zones. The Government of India opined that the difference of 63 minutes between these two times was too great for the same 'railway time' being adopted for all of India.[24] It was decided that 'Calcutta time' should be observed from the East Indian Railway network to the North-Western Provinces, as far as the limits of the local Bengal management extended; and the 'Allahabad time' should be carried on up to Delhi and down the line towards Calcutta as far as the engine drivers, guards and points-men were subordinate to the local superintendent of the North-Western Provinces.[25] It was thought best to change the time on a system of the railways whenever the working staff changed, so that the railway drivers and guards on each section would have a constant standard of time by which to regulate the performance of their duties; while the public would not suffer any inconvenience so long as the difference between the railway time and the true local time did not exceed the ordinary errors of clocks.[26] By 1860–1861, arrangements were completed for signalling the correct time daily to all the stations on the line from Howrah by means of the electric telegraph; and all the station clocks were regulated by 'Calcutta time', signalled at noon every day.

Despite Government intervention and improvements in the signalling system, the railway timetables remained beleaguered by the co-existence of multiple time zones and were a serious source of passenger grievance and inconvenience.[27] Eventually it was only by the late nineteenth century that a slow transition was made towards standardisation of railway time across India. By the late 1880s the use of 'Madras time' became the norm, with the Bradshaws publishing timetables according to 'Madras time'.[28] It was only from 1 July 1905 that Indian Standard Time was adopted across India and it was decided that 'henceforth the railway operations will also be regulated by this time instead of the Madras time'.[29] This standard time was exactly 5½ hours in advance of Greenwich and 9 minutes in advance of Madras time. Clearly, the transition to standardised time was slow. It took approximately half a century (1905) after the commencement of railway operations in colonial India (1853) to run trains along standardised time. The pace of the event therefore puts a question mark on the possibility of any sudden and radical imposition of 'railway time discipline' on existing travel practices. Furthermore, despite the standardisation, some railway lines continued to adhere to local time.[30] Consequently, even in the early decades of the twentieth century

Bradshaws continued to publish railway timetables with reference to both local and standardised time.[31] Last but not least, in reality, this delayed standardisation forced Indian railway travellers to familiarise themselves with several local times. This possibly had the effect of either confusing them or adding more temporal notions or both. At any rate, this could not have imposed the assumed rigid time-discipline.

A slow transition to standardised 'railway time' however was not peculiar to India. Neither is it related to India being a colony. And as such this aspect should not be privileged over other narratives. Transition to railway time was experienced similarly in different parts of the world. For instance, it took Bristol a decade (1842–1852) to shift to Greenwich Mean Time or 'railway time'. Bristolians insisted on using local time despite the trains coming from London following railway time. To resolve the issue, the corn exchange clock showed both local and railway time until 1852, when the Bristolians finally accepted the chance.[32] Similarly, in Japan, Tokyo solar time was eventually adopted in 1887 as the 'railway time' eight years after it became the standard clock time (1879).[33] India's transition took longer because of its size, number of local times and the chronic differences of opinion between different levels of colonial administration – a hallmark of the colonial state. This gradual transition also questions the probabilities of the impact of the temporal changes induced by railway operations. If imposition of railway time was long-drawn, uneven and contested, as evidently it was; then its impact was more variegated and less sharp than hitherto suggested.[34]

Railway timetables: adjustments and negotiations

At another level too, the theoretical ability of railway timetables to introduce radical departures and impose standardisation was regularly qualified. Railway timetables were frequently altered, mainly to attract more passengers by offering convenient schedules. In 1865, the Director-General of the Post Office of India complained about the serious public inconvenience caused by detaining the mail trains between Calcutta and Delhi.[35] Consequently, the population of the districts of Kanpur, Fatehgarh, Etawah and Agra were almost entirely deprived of railroad due to the untimely hours at which the single train passed through these districts. It also entailed that all passengers from Calcutta had to wait at Allahabad for three to six hours 'in the hottest part of the day'.[36] To alter the situation so as to attract more passengers the Director General of the Post Office suggested altering the timetable. The Board of the Eastern Indian Railway Company accepted the advice.

One of the implications of railway time is surely that it was objective rather than diurnal or seasonal in its rhythms. From the point of view of passengers, however, this was clearly not yet the case. On that basis, inconvenient railway timetables continued to draw official attention. For instance, in 1868, the agent of the East Indian Railway Company argued that the prevalent system of two 'mixed' trains, one leaving Howrah in the morning, and the other in the evening, were not suitable for the districts of Patna, Munger and Shahabad.[37] These districts were populous and attracted considerable trade. But the timings of the trains were so that it passed through these districts after dark, failing to attract significant passenger traffic. Further, these were the only trains through which the local third-class passengers travelled and the inconvenient timing discouraged a sizeable section of them from using railways altogether. These trains also offered 'similar indifferent timing' to some districts of the North-Western Provinces. But there the damage to the company's finances was less because in the North-Western Provinces third-class passengers had the advantage of availing the mail train service, denied to them in the lower districts of Bengal. Upon investigation, 'native' passengers informed the agent of the East Indian Railway Company that they avoided taking the trains because they felt insecure while waiting any length of time in the dark. The agent noted:

> If we hope to develop the third class traffic, we should be prepared to increase facilities to induce people to travel, and must make the convenience of the people our first concern.[38]

The agent was keen to alter the train timings and the Board of the East Indian Railway Company approved of the changes to suit passengers' needs.[39]

The correspondence of the railway companies is replete with similar cases where the agents of the companies or the government altered existing time tables to attract passenger traffic. But timetables were also altered in response to demands made directly by passengers. Such demands were mostly a product of the expansion of railway network, which lead to more complications in train scheduling. Passengers, mostly local or regional, wanted more convenient schedules and often resented changes in existing timetables. In this context, the following excerpt from a lengthy petition to the Consulting Engineer to the Government of Bengal from the inhabitants of the suburbs of Calcutta is worth noting:

> We, the inhabitants of Bally, Ootturparah and other thickly populated villages in the Howrah and Hugli districts, have been subjected to a great deal of inconvenience and annoyance from March last, on account of the alterations introduced by Mr. Batchelor, Traffic Manager of the Eastern Indian Railway Company, in the time table of the Up and Down passenger trains since the 21st of that month. From the first opening of the railway line up to the date of recent alterations, we had all along an afternoon Down train touching at the Bally station between the hours of 5 and 8.00 P.M. and a morning Up train between 8.00, and 10.00 A.M. These trains had enabled us to open commercial depots and business offices, and engage in professional employments in the villages, towns and civil stations up the line, as we could then go up the morning train, transact business for the whole day and return in the evening. We need therefore hardly describe the inconvenience, trouble and expense to which we have been subjected since March last, when the Traffic Manager discontinued both these trains from our station. We have not

been informed what new circumstance necessitated the above measure on the part of the traffic manager and justified him in depriving us, who were the early supporters of the railway company, of the benefits of an indulgence which we have enjoyed for more than 12 years. We presume, however, that on account of the extension of the railway line in the Upper provinces, the railway time- table has been modified so as to detain the trains as little as possible as the stations in lower Bengal.[40]

The petitioners requested the removal of the grievance and restoration of the older timetable. In response, the Consulting Engineer investigated the grievance, found it to be true and ordered the traffic manager to restore the earlier train schedule. He confirmed the suspicion expressed by the petitioners that the expansion of the railway network in north India affected the timetable arrangements in Bengal. The Consulting Engineer reminded the traffic manager not to lose sight of *local interests*, and to facilitate the service that might be given to the populous districts in the region.[41]

Evidently, Indian passengers were aware that adjusting timetables to attract passenger traffic was important in the railway companies' commercial calculations. Consequently, they often added the need for an improved train service and increased frequency of trains in their demands for convenient timetables. A newspaper report complained that since 1 April 1894, the number of trains running daily between Brindaban and Mathura were reduced to four. The report added that these trains were also very badly timed, one leaving Brindaban early in the morning at 5.45 a.m. and the other late in the afternoon at 5.35 p.m. The trains from Mathura too, were ill-timed, one starting from Mathura at 11.30 a.m., and the other at 6.45 p.m. As a result, pilgrims arriving at Mathura at 6.15 a.m., and 4.00 p.m. had to wait till 11.30 a.m., and 6.45 p.m. respectively, if they wanted to proceed to Brindaban by rail. The paper asked 'who would be so foolish as to travel in mid-day during the hot weather?'[42] The reduced train service, and inconvenient timing was soon apparent in the railway receipts on the Mathura-Brindaban branch line. The revenue at the Brindaban station decreased from 80 rupees to about 10 a day while at the Mathura city station from 5 rupees to 10 or 12 *annas* a day. An investigation into the causes of the fall in receipts showed that people preferred *ekkas* to ill-timed trains. To redress the issue, the government ordered at least six trains to be run between Brindaban and Mathura every day, timed to suit public convenience.[43]

Demands to restore earlier timetables and train services were fairly common. For instance, a newspaper editorial complained about the lack of train service on the Eastern Bengal State Railway at convenient hours for the people at Krishnagunge and other neighbouring places and for those who worked in the Calcutta offices.[44] The report claimed an absence of any early morning train service to Calcutta on Monday compelled people to leave their homes on Sunday in order to attend office the next day. The report demanded a restoration of the stopping of the Darjeeling Mail at Krishnagunge station to offer relief to the daily commuters. In a similar demand, an alternation in the timetable was requested to suit the needs of cultivators and dealers in vegetables who brought daily supplies to the Calcutta *bazars*. The prevalent schedule necessitated a long wait at the Sealdah station until the *bazars* of Calcutta opened, and these people wanted to alter the train timing (at its point of origin) so as to reach Calcutta at daybreak. Both the demands were fulfilled by the Eastern Indian State Railways.[45] Interestingly, Indian passengers were also critical of an absence of any rules on the subject of alterations of the timetables and resented frequent changes without sufficient notice. Quick changes, it was argued, adversely affected travel plans, and often encouraged them to choose alternate modes of transport.[46] A newspaper report complained about the 'great inconvenience' caused to people due to the frequent alternations in timetables by the Oudh and Rohilkhand Railway Company.[47] In a similar complaint, another report noted that the timetable of the Oudh and Rohilkhand Railway Company was altered once in October and again in December of the same year (1894) and claimed that such frequent alterations without adequate publicity was a source of much inconvenience.[48] The traffic superintendent of the Awadh and Rohilkhand Company brought to the notice of the Railway Conference the inconvenience caused to the public and by sudden changes in timings of passenger trains. The traffic superintendent noted:

> If sufficient notice is not given, railways that may have to form connections with the one making changes either have to prepare a hurried and inconvenient time-table or probably make no change or miss a connection at the junction. Time-tables are not available to the public before the change is introduced and often also the different guides which are printed in various parts of India have not sufficient time to publish the change and continue to show the old timings and thus mislead the public.[49]

As a solution, he recommended issuing prior notices announcing impending changes in the timetables as even a slight change on any of the longer main lines lead to necessary alterations on any line with many junctions. The suggestion was accepted and implemented.

Evidently, railway timetables' ability to impose time-discipline was compromised both from within and without. Frequent alternations of timetables certainly affected their ability to impose standardisation. More importantly, as the foregoing evidence suggests, for the colonial state, the claims to impose time-discipline on Indians was more a rhetorical and theoretical objective than a pursued reality. At a practical level, what mattered were revenue returns. Not surprisingly, this required flexibility – both in responding to the changing needs of the railway lines and expressed passenger demands. This flexibility certainly questions our present assumptions about the rigidity of railway travel-discipline. Moreover, flexibility is also evident in the demands made by Indian railway passengers. While on one hand regularity was demanded and appreciated, on the other, there was not much aversion to change. Critically, such evidence also hints at the ability of Indian railway passengers to direct or influence some changes at the level of daily railway operations. Interestingly, Indian passengers, albeit some sections of it, were aware of their significance to railway finances and likewise demanded what suited their convenience.

A speedier transit to travel-discipline?

Railway timetables' ability to impose standardisation, even within a local or regional time scale was also restricted by train speed. Interestingly, in the existing historiography of colonial Indian railways a discussion about train speed and timetables is near absent. This is perhaps due to the widespread assumption that railway speeded travel, which it certainly did. But in reality, how swift was railway transport? Different kinds of trains in colonial India, as in other parts of the world, ran at different speeds.[50] Furthermore, trains that ran at a slower speed, followed more inconvenient timing than the faster ones. In India, on average, a 'mixed'[51] train ran at a speed of 16–18 kilometres per hour, while the mail or the express trains ran at a speed of 20–25 kilometres per hour.[52] In the initial decades of railway operations in India (until 1871) the bulk of Indian passengers, though not all, travelled in these slow, 'mixed' trains because the faster ones did not have third or fourth-class carriages. Officials argued that 'natives' did not mind the slower speed because they were indifferent to the number of hours spent in the trains as long as they reached their destinations for a low cost. In 1868, in a report submitted to the Board of Directors of the East Indian Railway Company, A.M. Rendel, the consulting engineer of the Company argued:

> Third class passengers, who are chiefly natives, should not be run in the same trains with the first and the second class, who are chiefly Europeans; and the trains for the former should make longer stoppages at the stations and need not run so fast as at present.[53]

A year later the East Indian Railway Company's agent in Calcutta recommended slower speed and longer halts at daybreak for trains carrying mostly Indian passengers. The following excerpt from the report is worth quoting:

> We [the railway company] have not as yet timed or arranged the running of our third-class mixed trains for the convenience or comfort of those for whose convenience they are run. There are two great wants for native travellers which we have omitted to supply and in the absence of which, not only do the natives at present travel in the greatest discomfort, but also to the great risk of their bodily health. First, the stoppage of the train every morning at day-dawn, for one whole hour to provide for the calls of nature, to which every native is accustomed at this time of day. Attached to this condition is also the necessity for native privies at the stations (noted in the margin) and for the construction of a well besides each building [. . .] It is quite clear that, in both these respects, we have altogether failed to provide the convenience absolutely indispensable for native travellers and I propose at once to re-cast the running of the slow mixed passenger trains to meet their requirements.[54]

These recommendations were accepted by the Board of the East Indian Railway Company. Even the Lieutenant Governors of Bengal and the North-Western Provinces thought the experiment was 'well worth trying', as the expenses incurred were small.[55]

But Indian passengers resented slow speed and long halts, partly because they contributed to inconvenient timetables. Accounting for decline in passenger traffic in slower trains, the agent of the East Indian Railway Company noted that from 1871, when third-class passengers were allowed to travel by all trains, the fast mail trains became crowded with third-class passengers, so much so that occasionally at roadside stations passengers have been left behind for lack of space.[56] He thought probably the third-class passengers would not have been so eager to travel by the fast mail had it not been for the number and duration of stops made by the slow trains at certain stations, made expressly for the convenience of 'native' travellers. Similar views were also expressed years later, by G. Huddleston, the Chief Superintendent of the Eastern Indian Railway Company. Commenting on the demands for speedier trains by Indian passengers, particularly those travelling in slow passenger ones, Huddleston noted:

> The native of India likes to travel as fast as he could travel and at the present time there is no better proof of this than the preference given to the recently introduced third class trains over the slow passenger trains.[57]

Such observations were not off the mark. Evidence suggests that for Indians, the advantage of choosing to travel by rail primarily lay in its speed.[58] A newspaper report captured the 'native' response to the slow speed of the trains in the following words:

> While in 1865–1866 the Grand Trunk Road was almost deserted and bullock trains were no longer used, they have now again come into fashion and no few passengers content themselves with travelling on foot and all this for no other reason than because they have to suffer serious losses and inconvenience in journeying by rail.[59]

Another newspaper report expressed regret at the impending speed reduction for trains on the Oudh and Rohilkhand railways to 15 miles per hour. The paper speculated that such a reduction in speed will involve serious financial loss to the company and cause inconvenience to the public.[60] The speculation was proved right when within four months the company was forced to restore the former speed of its passenger trains. The Lieutenant Governor of the North-Western Provinces approved of this restoration 'in accordance with the public opinion' and hoped that the inconvenience it had caused to the travelling public and the loss of trade would be compensated.[61]

The railway companies were slow to respond to the demand for increasing the speed and reducing the duration of stops. This slow response was possibly a combination of two factors. First, the patronising attitude of 'knowing native needs' – a characteristic feature of colonial administrations. Second, taking a leaf from 'home', where members of the lower classes did not enjoy access to fast trains until well into the twentieth century[62] and therefore did not experience railway speed as a standardised travel experience. The railway administration in India steadfastly opposed increasing train speed until the late nineteenth century. Eventually, the speed of the passenger and 'mixed' trains was increased in the late nineteenth and the early twentieth century.[63] For a long time therefore, the influence of railways in speeding up travel had been experienced more in potential than reality, which once again questions the rigid and radical nature of the imposition of railway travel-discipline. People certainly travelled at a greater speed, but for many, particularly those travelling in slower trains, this experience was not consistent. More importantly, their inability to travel in faster trains was more for pecuniary reasons than racial reasons. That speed was related to the class of people who primarily boarded these trains is also evident from the above quoted example from the Bengali travelogue quoted above, where the author travelling in a faster train 'observed the plight' of lower-class passengers.[64] Similarly, a passing comment from the author of another Bengali travelogue confirms that slower trains were primarily meant for 'coolies'.[65] Interestingly, the author noted that slower trains also had lower ticket prices, as a matter of deliberate policy. Such evidence also suggests that social status and rank played a role in influencing railway experiences in more complex ways than currently assumed.

Imparting time-discipline? Railway timetables and punctuality

> A native's estimate of the value of time, or his inability yet to believe in a daily regularity of a train service [. . .] and when it arrives, the crushing and screaming betray surprise and unreadiness after all.[66]

Punctually running trains were one of the most acclaimed tools of the colonial state to induce time-discipline in Indians, a trait that the latter allegedly lacked. As noted before, both railway promoters and colonial administrators argued that the regularity of railway operations would 'teach' Indians the value of time. Regular train service was expected to impart another important 'lesson', viz, that the time/travel-discipline was inflexible and was not influenced by external logic or needs. For instance, Juland Danvers, the Director of the Indian State Railway Companies once claimed that Indians, especially those who belonged to higher classes, were 'taught a lesson' by railway operations. This lesson, Danvers noted, was imparted when a 'petty Raja' rebuked a station master for permitting the train to leave before his arrival; but realised that even he had to succumb to the 'imperative call' of the railway bell.[67] Evidently, such statements and numerous similar comments, including the one quoted above, assumed that trains ran on time in colonial India. But what if the trains were not as punctual as Danvers made them out to be? Clearly, this is a possibility to which neither Danvers or his ilk nor post-colonial scholars have given much thought. The silence of the former on the subject is explicable. Admitting trains failed to keep time would have amounted to challenging the foundational beliefs of colonialism. It is, however, rather surprising that post-colonial scholars have hitherto not even considered the possibility of unpunctual trains nor their implication on claims of imparting lessons in time-discipline to Indians.

Unpunctuality affected all sorts of trains, though some more than others. In one particular instance, the train service on the East Indian Railway Company's network was so consistently unpunctual that even the Viceroy on a visit to Punjab was unable to receive his post, on at least three occasions, even a week after his arrival from Calcutta.[68] This is evidently an extreme case. But even so, it is fair to assume that the unpunctuality of trains must have been a wider malaise. Evidence certainly bears out this claim. The same report that noted the non-arrival of the Viceroy's post, also complained about the 'extreme inconvenience' caused by the irregularity of the East Indian Railway Company's trains arriving at Ghaziabad (near Delhi), often detaining both passengers and freight for as long as 12 hours at the station. More importantly, the report acknowledged that the Governor-General-in-Council was aware that the unpunctuality of the East Indian Railway Company trains had reached a proportion that occasioned 'strongest remonstrance on the part of the government in behalf of the public'.[69] The report also noted that since the East Indian Railway Company's network was the main line of railway leading to north India, therefore, it was 'impossible' for the Government of India to ignore the 'habitual unpunctuality' of trains in the public's interest. Evidently, the irregularity of trains must have been a characteristic feature of railway operations in order to have garnered the attention of government agencies in a way the above instances suggest.

Interestingly, unpunctuality is a common theme in official correspondence. Evidence suggests that all trains managed by railway agencies ran irregularly, although the East Indian Railway Company line received more than its fair share of complaints, partly because of the regions it linked (Calcutta to Delhi) and partly because of the distance it covered. For instance, in 1867, while explaining 'serious deficit' of the passenger traffic between Burdwan and Calcutta, Cecil Stephenson, the Deputy Agent of the East Indian Railway Company blamed it 'in a great measure to the unpunctuality or inconvenient timing of the through trains'.[70] Two years later, a half-yearly inspection report of the East Indian Railway Company showed that mail trains ran unpunctually especially in the month February 1869.[71] Barely months later, the Chairman of the Board of Agency of the East Indian Railway Company admitted that between 18 March and 1 April seven mail trains missed the connection with the Ambala train at Ghaziabad.[72] Despite such complaints unpunctual trains continued to plague the operation of the East Indian Railway Company trains. In the same year (1869), a report in *The Englishman* bitterly complained about the unpunctuality of trains, claiming that 'an excuse was always ready for unpunctuality'. In fact, the report listed the 'excuses' offered by the East Indian Railway Company to explain irregularity of the trains.[73]

Indian passengers too, complained about unpunctual trains. In a petition submitted by the British Indian Association, North-Western Province, the petitioner (Sir Syed Ahmad Khan) noted that one of the reasons behind the long wait endured by passengers at stations was the irregularity of the trains.[74] Moreover he claimed that trains ran late rather frequently, at times by six hours or more and the upper provinces were more affected by this than Bengal. A newspaper report in 1881 published a long article about the mismanagement of the Punjab Northern State Railway. Among other complaints, the reporter noted that 'trains seldom arrive at any station at the fixed time. Delays of two or three hours frequently occur; sometimes the delay even amounts to 12 to 15 hours'.[75] A similar report in 1888 complained about 'gross mismanagement' on the Eastern Bengal Railway line and noted unpunctuality of trains as one of the causes.[76] On occasion, authors of contemporary travelogues also complained about the unpunctuality of trains and the difficulties caused by being held up in a station because of missing the connecting train for the onward journey. For instance, travelling with his family, the Bengali poet and playwright Manomohan Basu was forced to halt for an hour at Mughalserai junction for the next available connecting train to Benaras.[77] Basu complained bitterly because the missed connection delayed his planned arrival in Benaras on an important festival day. He noted how unpunctual trains left throngs of pilgrims stranded in different railway stations along the East Indian Railway network, and they too were clamouring for connecting train services. Similarly, Surendranath Ray, the author of a Bengali travelogue claimed that his connecting train from Allahabad to Etawa was late by a few hours.[78] Such grievances from the authors of the travelogues however, are rare because they mostly travelled in upper-class carriages in faster trains, which were less liable to unpunctuality. Additionally, as the foregoing evidence suggests, unpunctuality was such a characteristic feature of railway travel experience that it did not merit separate mention unless it affected the subjective experiences of travel, for instance, the possibility of having a dip in the Ganges on a holy day.

Unpunctuality of trains however, remained a persistent cause of passenger grievance well into the twentieth century. An inquiry for the renewal of contract for the Tirhut State Railways in 1904 revealed, among other things, 'dissatisfaction in Bihar on account of the unpunctuality of trains'.[79] More importantly, the report noted that the accompanying enclosures, which included letters from the collectors of Muzaffarpur, Champaran and Darbhanga were capable of 'sufficiently convincing' the Government of Bengal of the seriousness of the problem. The letters from these district officials certainly reveal the scale of the issue. The letter from the district magistrate of Muzaffarpur for instance, complained about the unpunctuality of trains running between Motihari and Bettiah, a distance of 30 miles. He further noted that such delays lead to further inconvenience to passengers as they 'frequently missed' the connection with trains running on the East Indian Railway network.[80] On a similar note, the manager of the Bettiah Raj complained about the 'chronic unpunctuality' of the trains managed by the Bengal and North-Western Railway Company.[81] In a different context, a newspaper report in 1907 hoped that the Railway Board and the Bengal Chamber of Commerce would take steps to stop 'the scandalous irregularity in the timings of local trains on the East Indian Railway network'.[82] The report urged the railway authorities to make an effort to follow timetables, and noted that the trains running behind schedule were a source of hardship especially for working men.

These criticisms certainly highlight a recurring pattern: unpunctuality of trains, on all lines, local and regional; irregularities in adhering to timetables, causing further delays, primarily by holding up passengers and freight traffic;[83] and last but not least, missing links with connecting trains, generally muddling already complicated train schedules, leading to inconveniences. But more significantly, they also question the efficacy and validity of the putative main tool of the colonial state to impose time-discipline in colonial India. At a related level, such evidence challenges the colonial stereotype of Indians being indifferent to notions of time. Interestingly, the word unpunctuality alone implies a sense of time, albeit transgressed. It is not without significance that the complaints bring out the variety of ways in which unpunctuality of trains affected Indian passengers. It affected their daily lives: office schedules and travel plans including pilgrimages. Given such practical inconveniences caused, it is hardly surprising that Indian railway passengers demanded a punctual train service. It can be argued therefore that this lack of satisfaction also challenges our theoretical notion about 'colonial time' and its impact on Indians. Colonial rule certainly introduced a different understanding of time, and the locals had to adapt to these new notions.

But such adjustments evidently did not preclude the possibility of discarding pre-existing temporal sensibilities. For instance, office/factory time, which was also a product of colonial rule, was balanced with pre-colonial notions of time such as religious time and agrarian time. More importantly, the limited evidence analysed here hints that Indian passengers wanted to be part of the 'colonial time' if only because of the practical benefits accruing from it. Notwithstanding the assertions of the colonial state and post-colonial scholars alike, these colonised subjects therefore, were sufficiently clear-headed to demand what fulfilled their needs. As such, their behaviour certainly demands more critical attention than imagining degrees of coercion involved in bringing them within the ambit of 'colonial time'. Here it is instructive to note that our current analyses of 'colonial time' is primarily based on the claims made by different colonial agencies, essentially conveying condescending superiority. But the responses of contemporary Indian railway passengers suggest otherwise.

Based on these responses, including the everyday realities of railway operations noted above, here I suggest that Indian passengers clearly did not see themselves as 'primitive' or 'standing outside the colonial time'. Evidently, 'railway time' was one of the temporal indices available to them. After all, complaints by office clerks or pilgrims about unpunctuality of trains and its impact on their plans reveal both a sense of time and flexibility to adjust and coordinate with different perceptions of time. As such, the responses of Indian passengers to 'railway time' question the colonial stereotype as much as post-colonial analyses. If anything, Indian passengers were practical; and responded to changes that affected their lives, accepting or rejecting on the basis of their needs. Last but not least, they also flexibly balanced different temporal needs, delineating the one that was more effective in fulfilling their requirements. It is no coincidence that pilgrims complained about unpunctual trains. Failure of 'railway time', they knew, would eventually affect their 'religious time', and was thus resented.

Contrary to our current understanding therefore, the chosen tool of inducing time-discipline in India, i.e., punctual railway operation, faltered rather regularly. Consequently, its ability to impart time-discipline was compromised. This therefore, qualifies the colonial rhetoric. But it also provides occasion to reappraise our understanding of the role of railway timetables to impart a timely 'lesson' to Indians. One way to do it is to underline the ways in which the rhetoric of the colonial state did not match everyday realties of railway operations. Interestingly, for many colonial officials, including railway administrators, despite a regular dose of grand claims and quotations, the reality of everyday railway operation was much different. In fact, one is struck by the frank admission of the inability to run trains punctually. For instance, responding to the criticism of the Government of India regarding unpunctuality of East Indian Railway Company's trains, Edward Palmer, the Chairman of the Board of the Agency of the Company remarked that given the length of the line at 1,000 miles, it 'scarcely called for strongest remonstrance on the part of the government and cannot fairly be stigmatised as systematic irregularity'.[84] Similarly, another government official claimed that it was 'unreasonable' on the part of the Government to expect that a line of the length of the East Indian Railway network to function in a way that was similar to double lines of 'moderate length' in Europe.[85] Such responses are not surprising. Evidently, railway officials were more prudent about the realities of railway operations in colonial India. They took into account the challenges, including one of distance and logistics. Given this, one can claim that in the quotation used at the beginning of this section, the 'surprise', which 'natives' allegedly displayed at the regularity of train service was perhaps true. Though not for the reason expounded; but on discovering that on occasions trains did keep time!

Conclusion

This chapter intended to investigate the impact of time-discipline, possibly the most significant component of railway travel-discipline on colonial India. The foregoing discussion suggests that the influence of railway time-discipline was more modest than our current understanding permits. This assumption certainly does not deny changes. Time was standardised in colonial India, with 'railway time' eventually becoming the Indian Standard Time and railway passengers had to respect the change to catch trains. As such, possibly a way better way of analysing the impact of railway travel/time-discipline will be to look at the nature and the degree of influence exerted.

Standardised 'railway time', as we saw, was a product of a long process, reaching its culminating point after five decades. Such slow transition reduces the possibility of radical departures. Of course, even in the absence of a standardised 'railway time', passengers had to adapt to their local times, which also regulated railway operations. Furthermore, these local times were not likely to be aligned with religious or agrarian time. But such adaptations perhaps required less effort than we assume, if only on the basis of the number of passengers who took to railways as soon as the operations commenced.[86] Additionally, it can be argued that the radical departure attributed to 'railway time' was less sharp because it was neither the earliest nor the only instrument through which an attempt was made to introduce a linear time-discipline in colonial India. Office/factory times and school time too, played important roles in inducing different registers of time-discipline. Of these, the office time was imposed much earlier than the railway time. And as complaints about unpunctual trains from office goers indicate, office time played a significant role in shaping responses to the railway time. Evidently, railway time-discipline had a differential impact on people travelling for different purposes. For instance, as the petitions illustrate, the impact of railway timetables on the daily commuters travelling to nearby cities for employment was sharper than say on pilgrims whose travel plans were also guided by the 'religious time'. Given this, perhaps it will be useful to think in terms of different, multiple valences of time having a wider impact on colonial Indian society.

Everyday realities of railway operations too, shaped the degree and the nature of the impact of railway time-discipline. Practical constraints included passenger demands for convenient timetables; slow trains, which in turn contributed to inconvenient timetables; and last but not least the unpunctuality of trains. But the need for profit too, exerted an important influence. Indeed, as discussions about convenient timetables or speedier trains indicate, it was pecuniary considerations that made railway travel/time-discipline both flexible and pervious to external factors such as government interventions and demands made by Indian railway passengers. This significance of commercial calculations (as opposed to morally charged rhetoric) also had the impact of fracturing the uniformity as well as the ability of railway travel/time-discipline to initiate changes. Simply put, if railway travel-discipline was not inflexible and varied under circumstances, then it must have had a differential impact in changeable contexts. For instance, the impact of railway time-discipline on those passengers who travelled in slower trains with long in-built halts would have been different than on those whose demands for better timetabling or speedier trains were accepted. Evidently, diverse social groups experienced railways differently; and by implication therefore, they took different 'lessons' home. At the same time however, it is instructive here to note that the varying lessons imparted by travel/time-discipline were also more influenced by notions of social rank or status than currently assumed. After all, it is not without significance that the slow speed of mixed trains, which affected the poorest passengers most, was not changed until the early decades of the twentieth century.[87]

But to return to the more specific point of the nature and degree of impact of railway travel/time-discipline on India and Indians; it may be argued that the realities (need for profit) and exigencies of the daily operation of railways in colonial India (passenger demands) moderated the abilities of this celebrated tool of colonial control to initiate radical changes. The actual impact that railway timetables had on lives was complex, with a more social than notional impact on the perception and management of time. The experiences in relation to train journeys certainly mattered more than the mere existence of standardised clocks. Evidently, Indian passengers' attitudes to railway travel-discipline continued to be influenced by different temporal sensibilities. This possibly played a singular role in qualifying the putative impact of railway time-discipline. This gradual, uneven and ambivalent impact of railway time-discipline therefore, can perhaps be better explained if we think in terms of Indians' familiarity with time regulation going beyond colonial rule, including their knowledge and use of different kinds of time (religious, agrarian), rather than the sudden imposition of a new temporal sensibility to which they had to succumb.

Notes

1 *Mahapurush* or *The Holy Man* is a 1965 film directed by Satyajit Ray. See www.youtube.com/watch?v=0maLQpjpW2k accessed on 11 March 2016. The movie is based on a short story, *Birinchibaba* by Rajshekhar Basu. See *Parashuram Galpa Samagra* (Calcutta, M. Mallick, 3rd edition, 2007).
2 Here travel-discipline implies an adherence to the new mechanics of travel that is, timetables and tickets, which were either introduced or modified by railway operations in colonial India.
3 The story is set in the early decades of the twentieth century.
4 *Rajmahal, its railway and historical association*, anonymous tract in 'Tracts', Volume 323, IOR.
5 D. Landes, *Revolution in Time: Clocks and the Making of the Modern World* (Cambridge, Massachusetts, Harvard University Press, 1983).
6 This belief provided a justification for colonial control under the pretext of bringing modernity and sense of time (historical modern) to primitive groups.
7 R. Thapar, *Time as a Metaphor of History* (Delhi, Oxford University Press, 1996), Chapter 1.
8 Though punctuality and sense of time were vaunted as civilisational progress, in reality, their value was in the ability to transform 'lazy natives' into efficient foot-soldiers (i.e., clerks, plantation labour or factory workers) of colonial capitalism. Such logic, however, was not confined to colonies. The under-class of industrial Europe was also exposed to a similar diatribe. E.P. Thompson, 'Time, Work-Discipline, and Industrial Capitalism', *Past and Present*, 38, 1967, pp. 59–97.
9 Lord Dalhousie's minute on the 'Railway Development in India', April 1853; in 'Correspondence regarding railway communication in India', Microfilm reel no. 60, National Archive of India.
10 B. Fraser and S. Spalding (eds) *Trains, Culture and Mobility: Riding the Rails* (UK, Lexington Books, 2012), Introduction. Such comparisons between 'common folks' in England and colonised Indians are an interesting reminder of complex imbrication of class and race in the ideology of colonial governance.
11 S. Sarkar, 'Colonial times: clocks and Kali-Yuga', in S. Sarkar, *Beyond Nationalist Frames: Postmodernism, Hindu Fundamentalism, History* (New Delhi, Permanent Black, 2002); R. Prasad, 'Time-Sense: Railways and Temporality in Colonial India', *Modern Asian Studies*, 47, 4, 2013, pp. 1252–1282.

12 R. Prasad, *Tracks of Change: Railways and Everyday Life in Colonial India* (UK, Cambridge University Press, 2016), p. 137.
13 Even scholars with a nuanced understanding of the workings of the Indian railways assume that travel- and time-discipline were imposed; see I. Kerr, *Engines of Change: The Railroad that made India* (London, Praeger, 2007), p. 91.
14 Prasad, 'Time-Sense'.
15 M. Goswami, *Producing Nation: From Colonial Economy to National Space* (Chicago, University of Chicago Press, 2004), Chapter 3; L. Bear, *Lines of the Nation: Indian Railway Workers, Bureaucracy and the Intimate Historical Self* (New York, Columbia University Press, 2007), part I, Chapter 2.
16 Only recently Ritika Prasad's analysis acknowledged this slow transition, arguing for a long, contentious and rich history of transition to 'railway-time' in colonial India. Prasad, 'Tracks of Change', Chapter 4.
17 Railway management in India passed through several stages, from private companies to government control to a system of mixed ownership and control. Initially, private guaranteed companies owned and managed the railway lines without any government control save a guarantee of 5 per cent on their investment. See I. Kerr, *Building the Railways of the Raj* (Delhi: Oxford University Press, 1995), pp. 18–19.
18 Given the importance of commercial calculations in railway operations in colonial India the earliest railway timetables were often published as newspaper advertisements serving a dual role of notice and publicity for specific lines. For instance, the first timetable of the East Indian Railway Company was published in *The Friend of India* (1854), declaring the opening of the line between Howrah terminus to Raniganj. It also contained the fare structure. L/PWD/2/76, 1860, IOR.
19 A.K. Dutta, *Bashpiya Upadesh* (Calcutta, Tattwabodhini Press, 1855).
20 Report on the administration of the North-Western Provinces for the year 1863–1864, V/1O/20, IOR.
21 Letters of the East Indian Railway Company, L/PWD/2/78, 1868, IOR.
22 Ibid.
23 Initially train services in different regions followed different local times. For instance, the trains operated by the Great Indian Peninsular Railway mainly followed Bombay time, while trains in Bengal and Bihar followed Calcutta time.
24 Report on the administration of the North-Western Provinces for the year 1863–1864, V/1O/20, IOR.
25 Ibid. The Oudh and Rohilkhand Railway Company followed the 'Allahabad time'.
26 Ibid.
27 Correspondence between the Agent and the Board of Directors of the Eastern Indian Railway Company, in L/PWD/2/82, IOR.
28 'Madras time' was in between 'Calcutta' and 'Bombay' time and was 32 minutes behind the former. The 1885 edition of the Newman's Railway Bradshaw shows 'Madras time' for the railway movement across India.
29 'Railway Time', Note from Secretary, Railway Board to Secretary to the Government of Bengal, Public Works Department, dated April 1905, in Proceedings of the Railway Department, Government of Bengal, P/7027, 1905, IOR.
30 Ibid. For a while some sections of the Great Indian Peninsular Railway Company followed 'Jabalpore time'.
31 Bradshaw's *Handbook to the Bengal Presidency and Western provinces of India* (London, W.J. Adams, 1907), IOR.
32 The plaque under the corn exchange clock refers to this fascinating history. Notes taken during a private visit to Bristol, 2012.
33 T.R. Grunow, 'Trains, Modernity and State Formation in Meiji Japan' in B. Fraser and S. Spalding (eds) *Trains, Culture and Mobility: Riding the rails* (Lanham, Maryland, Lexington Books, 2012), p. 243.

34 Prasad, 'Time-Sense'.
35 Proceedings of the Right Honourable Governor-General of India in Council, letter dated 3 June 1865 from H.B. Riddell, DG Post Office of India to E.C. Bayley, Secretary to the Government of India, Home Department, in Proceedings of the Railway Department, Government of Bengal, P/163/35, 1865, IOR.
36 Ibid.
37 Home Correspondence, 'B' Series, Copies of letters sent, 1849–1879, L/PWD/2/73, IOR.
38 Ibid.
39 Ibid.
40 'Train accommodation for the inhabitants of Bally', letter dated 3 January 1866 from Baboo Joykissen Mookerjee and others, to Captain F.S. Taylor, Consulting Engineer to the Government of Bengal, Railway Department, in Proceedings of the Railway Department, Government of Bengal, P/433/38, 'A' Proceedings, 1866, IOR.
41 Ibid. Emphasis mine.
42 Earlier, eight trains ran daily between the pilgrim towns of Brindaban and Mathura. *Hindustan*, 28 May 1894, in 'Selections from the Native Newspaper Reports, North-Western provinces', L/R/5/71, 1894, IOR.
43 Report on the administration of North-Western provinces, V/10/157, 1893–1894, IOR. *Anna* is a unit of currency; 16 annas made one rupee.
44 *Bangabasi*, 7 January 1888, in Selections from Native Newspaper Reports, Bengal, L/R/5/14, 1888, IOR.
45 *Bangabasi*, 21 December 1889, in 'Selections from Native Newspaper Reports, Bengal', L/R/5/15, 1889, IOR.
46 Proceedings of the Railway Conference, section on timetables, 1893, V/25/720/29, IOR.
47 *Azad*, 14 December 1886, in 'Selections from Native Newspaper Reports', North-Western Province, L/R/5/63, 1886, IOR.
48 *Karnamah*, 10 December 1894, in 'Selections from Native Newspaper Reports', North-Western provinces, L/R/5/71, 1894, IOR.
49 Proceedings of the Railway Conference, 1893, V/25/720/29, IOR.
50 J. Simmons and G. Biddle (eds) *The Oxford Companion to British Railway History: From 1603 to 1990s* (Oxford, Oxford University Press, 1997).
51 Mixed trains had both freight and lower-class carriages.
52 Home Correspondence, 'B' Series, 'Copies of letters sent', 1849–1879, L/PWD/2/73, IOR.
53 A.M. Rendel, 'Report to the Eastern Indian Railway Company on the cost and maintenance of the line', dated 1 January 1868, in Letters to and from Eastern Indian Railway Company, L/PWD/2/84, 1868, IOR.
54 Proceedings of the Railway Department, Government of Bengal, P/433/46, 1869, IOR. The stations noted in the margin were: Burdwan, Sahebganj, Jamalpur, Dinapore, Buxar, Mirzapore, Allahabad, Cawnpore, Etawah, Aligarh and Ghaziabad.
55 Ibid.
56 Appendix to the Public Works Department proceedings, January 1872 [Eastern Indian Railway], in Proceedings of the Railway Department, Government of India, P/580, IOR.
57 G. Huddleston, *History of the East Indian Railway* (Calcutta, Thacker, Spink and Company, 1906), Chapter 1.
58 *Nur-ul-Absar*, 15 August 1872, in Selections from Native Newspaper Reports, North-Western Provinces L/R/5/49, 1872, IOR.
59 *Koh-i-Nur*, 14 March 1871, in Selections from Native Newspaper Reports, North-Western Provinces, L/R/5/48, 1871, IOR.

60 The speed was to be reduced from the next month i.e., July 1884. *Oudh Akhbar*, 26 June 1884, in Selections from Native Newspaper Reports, North-Western Provinces, L/R/5/61, 1884, IOR.
61 *Oudh Akhbar*, 1 November 1884, in Selections from Native Newspaper Reports, North-Western provinces, L/R/5/61, 1884, IOR.
62 C. Divall and H. Shin, 'Cultures of Speed and Conservative Modernity: Representations of Speed in Britain's railway marketing', in B. Fraser and S. Spalding (eds) *Trains, Culture and Mobility: Riding the rails* (UK, Lexington Books, 2012), p. 9.
63 The speed of the trains was increased partly also due to doubling of tracks and better rolling-stock.
64 S. Shastri, *Dakshinapath Bhraman* (Calcutta, B. Banerjee and Company, 1911), p. 130.
65 S.K. Ganguly, *Uttar Bharat Bhraman O Samudra Darshan* (Calcutta, Tara Press, 1913), p. 8.
66 'Indian Railways', *Cornhill Magazine*, July 1869, IOR.
67 J. Danvers, *Indian Railways: Their past history, present condition and future prospects* (London, Effingham Wilson, 1877).
68 'Unpunctual running of trains on Eastern Indian Railway and delay in completing through booking arrangements with Delhi railway', Telegram dated 4 April 1869, from Colonel Strachey, Officiating Secretary to the Government of India, to the Officiating Joint Secretary to the Government of Bengal, PWD, in Proceedings of the Railway Department, Government of Bengal, P/433/46, 1869, IOR.
69 Ibid.
70 Note by Cecil Stephenson, Deputy Agent, Eastern Indian Railway Company, dated 26 April 1867, in Proceedings of the Railway Department, Government of Bengal, P/433/41, 1867, IOR.
71 Letter Number 24, dated 13 May 1869, from E. Palmer, Chairman, Board of Agency, Eastern Indian Railway, to the officiating Consulting Engineer to the Government of Bengal, Railway Department, in Proceedings of the Railway Department, Government of Bengal, P/433/46, 1869, IOR.
72 Ibid.
73 Extract from Englishman, enclosed as an evidence in the letter from Major E.C.S. Williams, Under Secretary to the Government of India, Public Works Department, to the Officiating Joint Secretary, Government of Bengal, Public Works Department, Railway Branch, dated 8 May 1869, in Proceedings of the Railway Department, Government of Bengal, P/433/46, 1869, IOR.
74 'The Humble Petition of the British Indian Association', dated 16 October 1866 from Syud Ahmed, Secretary and others, British Indian Association, North-Western Provinces to His Excellency the Viceroy and Governor-General of India in Council, in Miscellany Railway Letters, L/PWD/2/190 (1865–1867), IOR.
75 *Panjabi Akhbar*, 15 January 1881, in Native Newspaper Reports, North-Western Provinces, L/R/5/58/1881, IOR.
76 *Bangabasi*, 4 February 1888, in Indian Newspaper Reports, Bengal, L/R/5/14/1888, IOR.
77 S. Das (ed.), *Manomohan Basu-r aprokashito diary* (Unpublished diary of Manomohan Basu), (Calcutta, SahityaLok, 1989). Diary entry for 26 January 1887. Authors of other travelogues too, noted instances of trains running late. Surendranath Ray noted how his train from Allahabad to Etawa ran late. See S.N. Ray, *Uttar-Bharat Bhraman* (Calcutta, Pashupati Press, 1907), p. 66.
78 S.N. Ray, *Uttar Paschim Bhraman* (Calcutta, Pashupati Press, 1907), p. 66.
79 Letter number 12, dated 14 March 1904 from E.F. Growse, Officiating Additional Commissioner to the Patna Division, to the Chief Engineer and Secretary to the Government of Bengal, Railway Department in the Proceedings of the Railway Department, Government of Bengal, P/6787, 1904, IOR.

80 Ibid. Letter number 14, dated 5 March 1904 from E.V. Levinge, District Magistrate Muzaffarpur, to the Commissioner of the Patna Division.
81 Letter dated 4 March 1904 from J.R. Lowis, Manager, Bettiah Raj under the Court of Wards, to the collector of Champaran, in the Proceedings of the Railway Department, Government of Bengal, P/6787, 1904, IOR.
82 *Bengalee*, 3 February 1907, in Selections of the Native Newspaper Reports, Bengal, L/R/5/33, 1907, IOR.
83 Unpunctuality was not restricted to passenger trains alone. Goods trains too, were frequently delayed and were a cause of concern for falling railway revenues. A discussion of this interesting topic, however, is beyond our scope. For an interesting instance see Eastern Indian Railway Company's inspection report of the lower division [Bengal] for the second quarter of 1866, in Miscellany Railway letters, L/PWD/2/190 (1865–1867), IOR.
84 Letter Number 24, dated 13 May 1869, from E. Palmer, Chairman, Board of Agency, Eastern Indian Railway, to the officiating Consulting Engineer to the Government of Bengal, Railway Department, in Proceedings of the Railway Department, Government of Bengal, P/433/46, 1869, IOR.
Idem, letter dated 2 June 1869 from Major J. Hovendon, Officiating Joint Secretary to the Government of Bengal, Public Works Department, Railway Branch to the Secretary to the Government of India, Public Works Department, IOR.
85 Ibid., letter dated 2 June 1869 from Major J. Hovendon, Officiating Joint Secretary to the Government of Bengal, Public Works Department, Railway Branch to the Secretary to the Government of India, Public Works Department, IOR.
86 G. Huddleston, *History of the East Indian Railway* (Calcutta, Thacker, Spink and Company, 1906), Chapter 1.
87 Though third-class passengers were allowed to use speedier mail trains from 1871, fourth-class passengers were denied this benefit.

2 A ticket to control?
Limits of railway travel-discipline in colonial India

In Bharatendu Harishchandra's famous play *rel-ka-vikat-khel* a village bumpkin is accosted by a junior railway employee in an unspecified railway station, when he is trying to buy tickets on the behalf of the former.[1] In reality however, this seemingly kind offer was made in order to cheat and procure a bribe from the traveller. The intention to swindle the unsuspecting passenger is evident as the railway employee mutters to himself, lamenting his luck about the absence of a suitable 'prey' since that morning. His demeanour however, changed when he identified the prospective victim. Interestingly, this choice was made after careful consideration, which included: the potential victim's evident ignorance about the rules and regulations associated with ticket booking; his wealth as displayed by the amount money he was carrying on his person; his travel group consisting of two young children and a wife; and last but not least the youth and nubile charms of his wife, offering a subtle hint of the railway employee's sexual desire.

The traveller, unaware of the intentions of the railway employee, accepts the offer of help, setting in motion a series of events in which he is forced to bribe railway employees at several stages. Eventually, the traveller is successful in getting tickets for their onward journey to Gaya and is shoved inside a railway carriage with his family. The play illustrates well the harassments and predicaments that were usually experienced by an average railway passenger in procuring tickets. As this story amply demonstrates, the travel-discipline imposed by ticketing practices was also compromised and subverted at several levels including, but not limited to, bribery and cheating. Moreover, contrary to current historiographical assumptions, travel-discipline must have been flexible since it responded to an individual's ability to demand, accept, offer or resent bribes. In other words, despite the presence of ticketing rules, which implies rigidity as a theoretical possibility, the reality was rather different. At a related level, as the story underlines, Indians, both passengers and railway employees, influenced this travel-discipline. As a literary bridgehead therefore, this story unravels our current understanding of the implications of railway-induced travel-discipline, especially ticketing rules, on colonial Indian society, the theme of this chapter.

Tickets and railway travel-discipline

Tickets were perhaps the most unique feature of the travel practices associated with the introduction of railways in colonial India. More than railway timetables, the rules associated with tickets were unfamiliar and elaborate. The idea that one had to pay to travel was not new. But rules of railway travel imposed certain rigidities. For instance, tickets could be bought only with cash and at a price fixed beforehand. Tickets also had a physical life, by which I mean that they had to be bought prior to travelling and from specific sites – the ticket booking counters. Subsequently, tickets required safe keeping, if lost, the passenger had to either pay a fine or face imprisonment. Also, upon reaching the final destinations, tickets or a part of them had to be physically presented as a sign of proof of payment for the journey, an act which finally allowed passengers to exit the railway precincts. In short, ticketing regulations represented a significant departure from existing travel practices and Indian railway passengers had to comprehend these changes to use a new system of transport successfully.[2]

Curiously however, hitherto, ticketing regulations have not received serious scholarly attention. In the post-colonial historiography of Indian railways there is little or no understanding of this crucial aspect of railway travel besides a general awareness that Indian passengers were ill treated at the ticket booking counters or harassed by the railway employees. These experiences of Indian passengers are explained as either a struggle to adhere to a new, colonial travel-discipline, or as an evidence of maltreatment in the hands of European and Eurasian railway employees, thereby underlining the racial dimension of these encounters.[3] Such assumptions, though not entirely inaccurate, miss vital details. For instance, most lower level railway employees, such as ticket booking clerks, were Indians.[4] The harassment faced by Indian railway passengers therefore, needed a better explanation than just the racial one.

This vagueness of the current state of knowledge has also contributed to the conclusions drawn about the wider, social implications of travel-discipline engendered by ticketing regulations. Broadly speaking, there is a scholarly consensus that ticketing regulations 'disciplined' Indian railway passengers, forcing them to become more manageable colonial subjects, amenable to control and regulations.[5] Interestingly, this assessment mirrors the claims made by colonial officials and railway promoters. Like timetables, ticketing rules, thought colonial administrators, will teach 'lessons' to Indians and in the process, will discipline unruly 'natives' into becoming obedient, disciplined subjects.[6] That the colonial administrators had such a strong if somewhat simplistic faith in the abilities of railway travel-discipline is not surprising. After all, railways were expected to perform moral and social miracles in colonial India. But the conclusions reached by post-colonial scholars are puzzling if only because there is an absence of empirical details as to how (i.e., the processes) ticketing regulations as a tool of imperial control disciplined Indians. Additionally, these analyses miss a vital point, that is, the gap between the colonial state's putative desire to control Indian passengers and the realities of everyday railway operations. At a related level, these studies also overlook the presence of Indian railway employees who, as Bharatendu's play demonstrates, participated in the imposition of railway travel-discipline and influenced its nature and scale.

Ticketing regulations: background and evolution

Though unexpected, the enthusiasm for railway travel among Indians was remarkably instantaneous.[7] Consequently, railway companies had to respond to this growing need primarily by arranging for tickets to be sent from England to India. For instance, by 1856, barely a year after trains rolled in eastern India, the East Indian Railway Company had regularised the system of procuring tickets.[8] Similarly, the Eastern Bengal Railway Company had acquired ticket printing machines even before the network commenced operation in 1862.[9] Initially, as in England in the early days of railway travel,[10] in India too, the ticket booking clerks at respective stations had to write the details of fare, distance travelled and the destination on the tickets.[11] Unlike in England, in India however, the practice was not universal. The Eastern Bengal Railway Company for instance, issued machine-printed tickets right from when the line first opened. But whether handwritten or printed, ticketing arrangements were affected by financial irregularities practised by ticket booking clerks.

The method was rather simple. The clerks charged the fare for the destination to which passengers intended to travel, while printing or writing a shorter distance on the tickets. Needless to say, the clerks pocketed the difference, leaving the passengers to deal with the consequences and the railway companies with the loss. Official records, travelogues and reports in Indian language newspapers indicate that such irregularities were widespread. Thus, ticketing regulations and railway travel-discipline was compromised at a daily level, more of which in subsequent sections. But relevant here would be to note that the railway companies had to think of measures to control irregularities and fraud, which had a direct bearing on the revenue. For the East Indian Railway Company, remedial measures included both a transition from handwritten to machine printed tickets, with journey details and fares printed in both English and in the local language of the region in which the stations were located.[12] Additionally, to save passengers from being duped, the company decided to display in conspicuous positions a large timetable sheet in English and native languages to enable Indian passengers to ascertain the sum they had to pay for travel.[13] Eventually other railway companies followed suit, especially as Section 17 of the Indian Railway Act of 1879 mandated that details, including the amount of fare paid, should be printed on the tickets in the 'principal vernacular language of the district' where they were issued.[14] But with most passengers being illiterate, this measure did not prove very effective.

A workable solution was found in issuing differently coloured tickets to easily distinguish between different varieties. Differentiating tickets by colour was expected to help passengers to identify at least the class for which they bought the tickets, without being overcharged by the booking clerks. For instance, in the East Indian Railway network the first-class tickets were white, the second class were blue, red and pink, and the third-class tickets were green and yellow.[15] These measures were modelled on existing practices in England. Instructive here would be to note that in England too, the transition to printed Edmondson tickets was largely in response to the dishonesty of ticket booking clerks and its impact on revenue. Furthermore, as in India, in England too, differently coloured tickets and different patterns were printed on the reverse side of the tickets issued for passengers travelling in different classes largely to offset the problems faced by illiterate passengers as well as railway clerks.[16] In India, such measures were partially successful in allaying passenger confusion, but did not prove effective in either controlling the irregularities practised by ticket booking clerks or the harassment of passengers, more of which later.

Regardless of challenges, ticketing arrangements evolved rapidly. Alongside the supply of tickets, booking windows were constructed, at first only in larger stations to sell tickets. Separate counters were also built to sell tickets to passengers travelling in different classes. Initially the ticket windows were opened only at specific time to sell tickets, usually shortly before the departure of trains. In 1859 the Government of the North-Western Provinces agreed to a recommendation proposed by the Consulting Engineer to open the booking offices at all terminal and principal stations 45 minutes before the departure of the train.[17] Since the duration for which ticket windows were opened was short, passengers were alerted by bells ringing, the sound of which was expected to rise above the din of a railway station. Measures regarding collection and examination of tickets at the point of exit were also formalised. Ticket collectors were appointed to inspect and keep parts of tickets from exiting passengers. The Oudh and Rohilkhand Railway Company even appointed women to collect tickets at the separate carriages reserved for women.[18] Some companies also introduced platform tickets at some bigger stations to control the number of persons at any given time, largely to have a manageable amount of people at the exits.[19]

But despite such measures the ticket collection system did not work well. At one level, this was due to lack of standardisation of railway rules, which permitted different railway companies to introduce the measures that they thought to be best suited to their particular area. With the number of ticket collectors being a matter of financial outlay, the number of people appointed was not sufficient to effectively manage passenger rush at the exit points.[20] Eventually, at the turn of the century, the East Indian Railway introduced the system of Travelling Ticket Inspectors (TTE), who checked the railway tickets of passengers in transit. The formalisation of ticketing rules was also paralleled by a growth of elaborate railway-specific byelaws, which provided a legal framework for buying, selling and inspection of tickets. For instance, an abstract of the railway byelaws from as early as 1860 offered the following rules:[21]

1. No passenger will be allowed to take his seat in or upon any carriage used on the railway, without having paid his fare.
2. Passengers must show their tickets to the guards when required and deliver them up to the persons authorised to receive them, before leaving the station.

3   Passengers not producing or delivering up their tickets will be required to pay the fare from the place whence the train originally started.

The Indian Railway Bill of 1868 further elaborated these regulations by noting penalties and fines to be imposed upon those passengers who failed to produce their tickets. The Bill also laid down rules for penalising those passengers who either failed to buy a ticket prior to the journey or travelled in a higher-class carriage than the one for which they had paid. Any passengers found guilty of committing these offences had to pay a fine not exceeding 50 rupees.[22]

Such regulations certainly characterise a shift from previous travel practices. Railway passengers had to familiarise themselves with the new ticketing rules. For instance, a Bengali tract published in 1855 advised the readers to reach their departure station to buy tickets at least 15 minutes prior to the departure of the train.[23] Similarly, a contemporary Hindi tract suggested passengers to keep an ear open for the bells to ring to avoid missing the short window in which tickets were distributed.[24] Failure to adapt to these rules either resulted in loss of journey or loss of money. In short, unfamiliarity with the new rules could cost passengers dear. However, as the passenger statistics indicate, Indians adapted to ticketing regulations with alacrity. This was partly due to the availability of information with which prospective passengers prepared/trained in the new rules. The Bengali and the Hindi tracts quoted above certainly offered relevant information. Their publication indicates a desire among a section of Indian passengers (the literate ones) to be familiar or at least cognisant of the new rules.

But a sizeable section of Indian railway passengers were illiterate and often poor. Yet statistically speaking, such rules evidently did not impede them from using a new and relatively speedier form of transit to their advantage. This, I argue, at one level indicates that Indian passengers were no different to their European counterparts – both valued practical convenience that transformed their previous travel practices, though not without challenges. At another, more critical level, it demonstrates that since in most cases the success of railway enterprise hinged on profits, the railway administrations were not averse to adopt measures that would ensure a steady if not an increased revenue. The use of differently coloured tickets both in England and in colonial India indicates something more than a convenient metropole model being imported to the colony. It underlines the ways in which workable solutions had to be found for practical challenges (illiterate passengers and unscrupulous employees), which had implications for railway profits. Moreover, unlike England, in colonial India profits and passenger responses mattered more, primarily because passenger traffic constituted the most important share of the railway revenue.

The *Railway Gazette* of 1913 estimated that passenger earnings were as much as 1/3rd of the total earnings of Indian railways. Of this, the share of profit accrued from third-class passengers was 97 per cent. For instance, a report submitted by Colonel Conway-Gordon in 1888 shows that the total number of passengers carried during the year was 95.5 million. Of these, lower-class passengers constituted 97.33 per cent, second class, 2.24 per cent and first class only 0.43 per cent.[25] Such numbers had remained consistent since the commencement of railway operations in the mid-nineteenth century. Not surprisingly therefore, railway authorities were willing to devise measures and solutions to overcome practical problems, which otherwise would have adversely affected passenger traffic. In short, here I argue that as opposed to our current understanding of railway economy in colonial India, profits, despite the guarantee system, played a key role. Moreover, after 1879 the guarantee system was revoked for a period, which made railway revenue a matter of concern for the colonial state. In effect therefore, passenger revenue was significant. Ticketing regulations were certainly novel, even theoretically rigid. But in reality, they were amenable to the pressures and demands of passenger traffic. As noted already, profits mattered. Consequently, rigidity was often compromised to adopt measures that were likely to bear profit and nowhere was this more evident than the negotiations over ticket prices.

Disciplining through negotiation? Ticket pricing and railway travel-discipline

> It may be worthwhile to mention that, in early days of railways, the lower classes attempted the game, to which they are very partial, of bargaining, and tried to beat down the prices of their tickets at the booking office; I need to say that they soon *learnt* to discontinue this practice.[26]

The above quote from Juland Danvers is interesting. It ascribes rigidity to a process (ticket price), which was perhaps the most flexible component of ticketing regulations and travel-discipline in colonial India. It is true that ticket prices were not amenable to last minute negotiations at the booking counters. But unlike Danvers' imagination, in reality Indian passengers, particularly those who thronged the third-class carriages, did not have to try to 'beat down prices'. That was done for them by railway companies and the various government agencies keen to attract passengers at the lowest rates possible. In India ticket price was usually determined by the local governments. As early as 1862 the Secretary of State for India turned down a request by the Directors of the East Indian Railway Company to interfere in the scale of fares fixed by the East Bengal Railway Company by reminding the former about the role of local governments in the process.[27] This was hardly unexpected as local government agencies were likely to know more about traffic needs and operational conditions in their region than those in England. More importantly, the aim of the government agencies and the railway companies was to maximise profit, which was directly linked to passenger receipts. But this system could work well if it was flexible and could respond to changing needs at short notice. As such, any intervention from the Board of Directors of the railway companies or the Secretary of State in London was likely to delay the process, thereby affecting prospects of profit.

Broadly speaking, ticket price, especially for third-class passengers, was argued to be inversely proportional to revenue returns. For instance, in 1868,

A.M. Rendel, the then agent of the East Indian Railway Company suggested a reduction in the third-class passenger fares. Rendel claimed that the Company's tariff of 3 pies/mile for third-class was too high and wanted to reduce it to 2½ pies/mile. This reduction, Rendel argued, though not substantial, would have had the effect of experimenting with lower rates and their impact on revenue.[28] In the same year, F.S. Taylor, the consulting engineer in the railway department for the Government of Bengal, proposed a new passenger tariff (see table below), which he thought would be more suitable for the two railway companies operating in the region. Taylor argued that: 'the only way of securing the prosperity of a railway is by offering facilities to the development of traffic'.[29]

Evidently, this 'development' essentially meant reducing the existing tariff for the third and fourth-class passengers respectively. Railway administrators repeatedly underscored the connection between profit and lower-class passenger traffic. The following excerpt from a letter conveying the views of the Government of India on the subject is worth quoting:

> The lower classes are and must be the mainstay of the passenger traffic. They are carried at a high rate of profit, and the Governor General-in-Council desires to impress upon the agency that *here, as elsewhere*, there can be but one result if opportunities of making tolerably rapid journeys, at low fares [. . .] and if facilities for return journeys are afforded. The English railways have lately increased their profit largely by improvements in this direction, and the Governor General-in-council believes that much may be done in India with a corresponding result to the companies. Moreover, irrespective of direct profits to the companies, India has paid in guaranteed interests and other charges over 30 million sterling up to the present time towards the introduction of railways. The people of the country who have contributed this large sum have therefore a just claim on the Government to see that the railways thus created are worked in their interests.[30]

In a similar, but not so striking manner, a report by Juland Danvers' railway also made a case for cheap passenger fare and growth of traffic. He argued that to make railways 'serviceable and profitable', the lowest class of passengers should be carried at the 'lowest rate as far as possible'.[31]

Table 2.1

Class	*Eastern Indian Railway*	*Eastern Bengal Railway*	*Proposed Tariff for Eastern Bengal Railway*
1st	1½ anna/mile	1 anna/mile	12 pies/mile
2nd	9 pies/mile	6 pies/mile	6 pies/mile
3rd	3 pies/mile	4½ pies/mile	4 pies/mile
Intermediary	4½ pies/mile	N/A	N/A
4th	N/A	3 pies/mile	2 pies/mile

Interestingly, such administrative desires were often transformed into operational realities. For instance, in 1872, the East Indian railway company agreed to a proposal to reduce the third-class fare from one anna for stations below Bardhhaman. This proposal was accepted because the region was argued to be both populous and prosperous and therefore likely to yield more passenger traffic.[32] Consequently, the region between Bardhhaman and Howrah, the terminal station for the East Indian Railway Company, continued to receive attention through the following decade, largely in the form of low third-class passenger fares. An annual report of the Eastern Indian Railway Company justified this policy by claiming:

> It was of course natural that the traffic of the first 70 miles, where the people are in exceptionally prosperous circumstances, should have more attention than that of the rest of the line.[33]

Revenue return statistics demonstrate that the Company's strategies bore results. The chief auditor's half-yearly reports show that in a single year (1883) the Calcutta–Burdwan section (67 miles in length) contributed approximately 3,189,013 third-class passengers to the traffic, as compared to the rest of the line (1,442 miles), which contributed 6,328,249 third-class passengers. In other words, on the former section of the line, every mile contributed on average 130 third-class passengers up or down, each day – traffic nearly three times as large as the average third-class traffic/mile of any other railway in India. The latter, longer section of the line, yielded on average 12 third-class passengers up or down per day – a number smaller than the average third-class traffic per mile of any other guaranteed railways except the Great Peninsular Railway Company.[34]

This however, was not a singular instance. The annual Report of the Eastern Indian Railway Company noted that their main line passenger traffic continued to show a satisfactory increase almost wholly in third-class traffic. This sustained revenue return was attributed to the reduction of passenger fares for the lower classes, especially for pilgrims and holiday makers.[35] Similarly, Danvers's railway report for 1879 showed the increase in traffic return for the Oudh and Rohilkhand Railway Company with a reduction of lower-class passenger fare to 2 pies/mile.[36] Other lines too, showed comparable statistics. The Patna-Gaya railway line registered an increase of approximately 28 per cent over a single year primarily due to the reduction in the third-class passenger fare to 2½ pies/mile, along the lines of the East Indian Railway Company's tariff. Interestingly, the Patna-Gaya line's decision to follow the East Indian Railway Company's tariff came at a moment when the latter had registered a substantial increase in third-class passenger traffic as a result of reducing its third-class passenger fare from 3 pies/mile to 2½ pies/mile. G. Huddleston, the chief superintendent of the East Indian Railway Company claimed that the third-class passenger traffic 'at once responded' to this discount and the annual earning went up to nearly one million rupees.[37]

Evidently, railway authorities identified reduced fares with increased revenue returns. Consequently, they often extended the principle to introduce a special tariff for different categories of passengers. Taking a leaf from England, different fare structures were either introduced or revised to attract passengers who were thought to have different needs and thus were likely to respond to changes suitable for them. The first steps in this direction were taken by the Eastern Indian Railway Company in the form of issuing season tickets at a concession rate during the annual *Durga Puja* festival. This offer became popular, especially among Bengalis travelling to and from Calcutta during the autumnal holiday.[38] Similarly, a special long-distance return fare was introduced during certain holiday periods for large race meetings, and in summer for visits to the hills. Concession tickets were also regularly offered to attract pilgrim traffic for important religious occasions. But, with the exception of concessions offered to pilgrims, such tickets produced a small proportion of the profits accruing from passenger traffic. Railway companies therefore had to devise ways to make railway travel both attractive and accessible to a wide range of passengers. Here too, the East Indian Railway Company played a remarkable role, largely due to the length of the line, the area the network covered (Indo-Gangetic Plain), and the profits it earned. In 1865, the company decided to attract 'respectable natives who *despised* travelling with lower-class passengers in the third-class carriages'.[39]

The agent of the Company argued that railway travel was avoided by 'better classes of Indians'. Such social groups, he claimed, would be willing to pay a higher fare to have separate accommodation and would appreciate the railway company's efforts to uphold social distinctions. Consequently, the agent proposed the introduction of an intermediate class and fare. The Board of the Company approved the proposal and a special fare of 4½ pies/mile was introduced for intermediate class passengers. The measure became immediately popular with the intended audience, who also demanded similar facilities by other railway companies. Around the same time, the Eastern Bengal Railway Company also proposed a similar change for the intermediate class at a fare of 50 per cent above their third-class tariff and the measure was sanctioned by the Lieutenant Governor of Bengal.[40] On this network also, the intermediate class became popular, underlining the demand for such a facility. Lower-class passengers also had their share of special tariff structure. To this end, in 1864 the Eastern Bengal Railway Company introduced a fourth class with a tariff fixed at 1 pie/mile. Justifying the measure, the agent of the company claimed:

> The alteration seems to have given general satisfaction to the native passengers, and has had the desired effect in causing an observance of the same feeling of distinction between the higher and lower classes of natives that exists with them at all times, excepting when they travel by railway.[41]

The Eastern Indian Railway Company followed suit and in the following year (1865) introduced a new tariff structure, which was 'intended for the very poorest class, who could only afford to pay the minimum fare'.[42] The company anticipated the tariff to attract 'coolies and labourers', thus ensuring a steady revenue return. Fulfilling the company's expectations, the 'coolie class' tariff, as the fourth-class fare was often known, became popular, particularly with tea garden workers and other labourers who travelled from various parts of north India to eastern India for employment.[43]

Largely positive responses to the introduction of bespoke tariff structures influenced railway authorities' decisions to keep the ticket prices flexible. Indian passengers knew this well and often demanded favourable tariff structure through a complex web of petitioning and negotiations. In 1868 a group of passengers who regularly took the Eastern Bengal Railway Company's trains to work in Calcutta offices complained about the increase in third and fourth-class ticket prices. The following excerpt from the carefully drafted petition by Ambika Charan Mukherjee and others is instructive.

> We the undersigned third and fourth class daily passengers and other travellers by the Eastern Bengal line, sadly distressed at the rates of the lower class tickets being enhanced, beg most respectfully to draw your kind attention to the point that this unexpected revision of the traffic order as per accompanying timetables has been intended, as the matter stands, to subject us [poor passengers] only to still greater pecuniary inconvenience. Correspondences touching the matter have been carried on with the traffic superintendent, but to no effect, inasmuch the undersigned has received a verbal reply in negative, as the accompanying paper will exhibit.
>
> Indeed, the time and season in which the order referred to is being carried out into effect points at once to its being an oppressive measure; for in this season travelling by boat, the cheapest conveyance, is attended with dangers severe in their nature. *It must be remembered with gratitude that Lord Dalhousie, the father of the Indian Railways, left a minute which appeared in the newspapers that the third class fares will never be increased over 3 pies/mile in India.*[44]

In response, Captain Stanton, the officiating joint secretary to the Government of Bengal (railway branch) claimed that he was unaware of any hike in the third and fourth-class fares on the Eastern Bengal Railway network. Interestingly, his pithy reply also noted that the fares on the Eastern Bengal Railway Company's line was 'exactly similar to the intermediate and third-class fares on the Eastern Indian Railway network'.[45] Undaunted, the petitioners wrote back with more evidence substantiating their claims, which included fare bills after 2 March, the date since which the increased tariff was implemented and a comparative statement of fares charged by other railway network. In a clear display of their knowledge and understanding of the operational strategies of the railway administrations in colonial India, the petitioners argued:

> On the short suburban length, which contributes to more than 1/9th to the entire passenger traffic of the line the increase has been excessive, being in some instance almost 50 percent over what was previously charged [as evident from the comparative statement of fares]. The increase also appears

to be most arbitrarily fixed, being quite disproportioned to the distances travelled; the mileage having being disregarded as an element in the calculation, or regarded only as subordinate to some other more general principle. We are informed that this principle is not to charge fractions of an anna for any distance travelled, but we are not aware whether such a rule has ever yet been recognised on any other line of railways in India. [. . .] but we presume that no alternations in the rates and fares can be made without the previous knowledge and consent of government, and that this concession to the railway companies involves no right of departure from the recognised principle on which all fares are charged.[46]

A few weeks later, echoing the same grievance, another petition was signed by Beni Madhav Mukhopadhyay and other passengers demanded a reduction in the recent hike in the price of lower-class tickets. Not unexpectedly, here too, the petitioners' arguments underscored the significance of Indian passengers to the railway economy, reflecting a familiarity with official policies. The petitioners claimed:

Hitherto we had been paying at the rate of 1½ pice a mile for the fourth class journeys, and these rates we understand, were and are still prevalent and fixed in all the railways in India. But the Eastern Bengal Railway Company alone have, since 2nd March last, enormously increased their fares, as will be perceived from the accompanying statement. We fail to see why there should be a dissimilarity of practice in this respect between the Eastern Bengal Railway and the Eastern Indian Railway. The latter takes fractions of an anna, and so far as we are aware, finds no inconvenience in doing so. *The success of railway enterprise in India will depend on the cheapness of the fares for the poorer and the working classes from the bulk of the passengers*, but the cheapness of the rates has been in a great measure neutralised in the case of the stations of the Eastern Bengal Railway, which are close to Calcutta, by the adoption of an unnecessary, and we may say inequitable rule. We hope Lieutenant Governor will pass orders for the restoration of the old rates of fares.[47]

On this occasion, the petitioners' hope of government intervention was not unfounded. The Lieutenant Governor ordered the Eastern Bengal Railway Company to 'revert to the original scale of fares'. Additionally, the accompanying letter to the petitioners expressed the pleasure with which the Lieutenant Governor revoked the decision of the railway company, hoping for a perceptible rise in passenger traffic.[48] But passenger demands for scaling down tariffs were also rejected. In one such instance, in 1864, a group of daily commuters on the Eastern Bengal Railway Company's network petitioned to the Government of Bengal to reduce the passenger fares from 4.5 pies per mile to 3 pies per mile, as was the rate on the Eastern Indian Railway Company's line. The following excerpt from a letter signed by one Kailash Chandra Bannerjee, on behalf of other passengers including himself, is worth quoting:

> The Eastern Bengal Railway traverses through a part of the country which is comparatively poor; the majority of the people pay even third class fares not without some difficulty, but they are willing to bear increased expense, compared to what they used to incur by passage by boats, for the sake of speedy transit, and it cannot be just, we submit, to deny the passengers by this rail the convenience and comfort which are commonly enjoyed by the passengers of the same class by other railways, who also pay equal fares per mile. We accordingly request His Honour may be pleased to take the above circumstance into consideration.[49]

A month later another petition from the third-class passengers also demanded a reduction in tariff arguing:

> The course adopted by the company is arbitrary in the extreme, and is slight upon a class of people from whom the greater portion of the company's revenue is derived. [...] we are not aware of any line of railway in India which has adopted it.[50]

In response, the Lieutenant Governor of Bengal refused to intervene with the actions of the agent of the Eastern Bengal Railway Company. In an interesting argument, the communication from the Lieutenant Governor noted that since the memorialists claimed to be 'native gentlemen' of middle class and thus demanded a fare commensurate with their income, the existing tariff (4.5 pies/mile) should not be a cause for concern, as it was suitably low to allow 'any one above the condition of a day labourer' to pay.[51]

This consistent emphasis on the abilities or inabilities to afford railway tickets both from the passengers and railway authorities is instructive. It firmly links access to railway travel with income, a reality that remains largely overlooked in current historiography. There is no denying that the third-class passenger tariff was the mainstay of railway income in colonial India. But despite low ticket prices, indeed one of the lowest in the world at the time,[52] fares were not sufficiently low for a large number of Indians. Many continued to use non-railway transport such as boats, carts or even walked, especially to cover short distances. As early as 1868 the Indian Railway Bill acknowledged the problem by asking the railway companies to run at least one cheap train daily from one end to the other of each trunk, branch or junction line belonging to them, with fares fixed at 2 pies/mile.[53] The problem however, lingered on. In 1873 the Oudh and Rohilkhand and the Sindh Punjab and Delhi Railway Company instituted an enquiry to comprehend falling passenger traffic on the respective networks. For this the agents of the companies accosted 'native gentlemen and merchants', as these individuals frequently travelled by railway and were thus likely to be acquainted with the wants of those who travelled in lower-class carriages. Interestingly, the respondents claimed third-class passengers 'as a rule' did not travel for pleasure. They travelled for either duty or business. Consequently, they wanted to travel as cheaply as possible. If railway fares responded to this need, they took used the railway, otherwise they opted for other modes of transport. The following excerpt from the inquiry demonstrates the predicament faced by the railway administrations.

> If a man thinks he ought to go, he strains to collect the money for his fare, and he goes, but the fact of his going would be just the same whether the fare was some Rs 2 higher or lower, and consequently to lower the fare would be dead loss to the company. The feeling was that to the make the line pay the fares should be fixed well below all other modes of conveyance to secure the passengers, *but to reduce below that would be a wanton sacrifice of revenue, as the increase of passengers due to the reduction would be quite disproportionate to the loss.*[54]

In short, the link between lowering ticket prices and increased lower-class passenger traffic was not as directly correlated as the railway authorities imagined.

Some railway officials too, admitted that railway tariff was deemed rather high by a cross-section of Indian passengers, especially when compared with other modes of transit. Writing around the 1870s, Colonel R.E. Sedgwick, the then manager of the Punjab Northern State Railway noted that 'railways have altogether failed to attract the masses'. In his report submitted to the Government of India, Sedgwick claimed that the fare structure was designed for 'well-to-do classes' and the railway companies 'never thought of lowering their passenger fares sufficiently to enable an ordinary coolie to travel more cheaply by rail than he can travel on foot'. Additionally, mirroring the claims made by Indian respondents of the excerpt quote above, Sedgwick argued that the masses could be drawn to railway if only the costs incurred were similar to travelling on foot. Lower-class ticket prices, he suggested should not exceed 1 pie/mile and advocated a further reduction (¾th of pie/mile) for poorer districts.[55] Similar sentiments were also echoed by Horace Bell, the consulting engineer to the Government of India for State Railways. In a report on the issue of reduction of lowest class fares Bell noted:

> If a reduction is made, it must be so considerable as to induce people to travel who cannot now afford to do so and to stimulate more frequent journeys on the part of those now using our railways in this class.

Additionally, he argued that even very low fares on the Tirhut Railways failed to attract the large number of coolies going from Saran and Tirhoot across the Kosi River to the tea gardens of Assam and Darjeeling. Substantiating the argument Bell claimed that while working for the Tirhut Railways he had the opportunity to stop gangs of tea garden workers who walked on the road running parallel to the railways.

On being asked as to why they walked while the railway was available for a good part of the journey, the labourers 'inevitably' replied that railway fares were beyond their means. Bell concluded that 'even if time was of any value to these people, they could not afford to use quicker method of transit'. More importantly, Bell claimed that tea garden workers were not unique in their inability to access railway transport largely for pecuniary reasons. According to Bell, even pilgrims, a group that often significantly contributed to railway revenue, could ill-afford it. This claim was based on Bell's occasional interactions with groups of pilgrims who walked from different parts of northern India to Baidyanath, a prominent pilgrim centre in eastern India. On one such occasion, the pilgrims happened to be residents in villages near Lucknow and informed Bell that despite having either saved or borrowed money for the pilgrimage, they could not afford to buy railway tickets. The pilgrims noted that a two-way journey by rail from their village to Baidyanath (a distance of 478 miles) would have costed them 12 rupees. They claimed that if this could have been done at half the price, i.e., for 6 rupees, then they would of course use the railway. Concluding his report, Bell noted that:

> Many more illustrations to show that our lowest fare is still far too high for the class it is intended for and that it reaches only those who are fairly well off, or who are obliged from family or business reasons to travel quickly.[56]

Evidently, there was an incongruity between what the railway authorities thought to be low fares and the ticket price that attracted a wide range of passenger traffic. As the reports by Sedgwick or Horace Bell reveal, railway's relative advantages of speedy transit in less time was certainly appreciated by the labouring classes, though on many occasions they could ill-afford it. More importantly, despite suggestions to the contrary, ticket prices were never reduced to a level where railways became an attractive transit option for the lowest classes of Indian society. Yet as the foregoing evidence discussion about special measures and passenger petitions indicates, ticket prices were flexible and open to negotiation. Additionally, a cross section of Indian passengers, the petitioners for instance, participated in this process. In other words, at one level ticket prices were both flexible and pervious to outside influences. While at another, it was inflexible. Though it responded to changing needs, it did not scale down beyond a point. In other words, flexibility influencing ticket prices ceased to operate at the point when it would have had an adverse effect on revenues. This can perhaps be explained by the guiding principle of railway operations in colonial India: maximisation of profit.

As noted earlier, profit mattered, the significance of which was not lost on either the railway administrations or Indian passengers. The eagerness with which ticket fares were either revised or new tariffs introduced suggests an awareness of the role of revenue in railway operations. Similarly, it is no coincidence that the passenger petitions consistently highlighted their significance to the railway economy and demanded favourable tariff on the basis of the income generated from the paying portions of the network. This centrality of profit holds the key to understanding the complexity of ticket price regulations in colonial India. Railway authorities knew that reducing the tariff beyond a point was counter-productive from a profit point of view. The following excerpt from a note by F.S. Taylor, a railway official, arguing for a revision in the tariff structure of the railway companies operating in Bengal to make railway operation more profitable is worth quoting:

> 4 pies/mile for the third class is a sufficiently low rate, and one which the class for whom it is intended can well afford to pay [...] By the above arrangement the 2nd class would directly benefit, and the first class indirectly. Many *respectable natives and others who now complain so bitterly against railway management, and who travel third on East Indian Railway, because the 2nd class fare is three times the third, will gladly pay for the comfort and respectability when the charge is not excessive.* At the proposed 4 pie fare for the 3rd class, the double journey would amount to 8 pie, while the second class return ticket at the usual rate of deduction would also amount to 8 pie. The present third class return travellers would be likely, under such circumstances, to avail themselves of the second class for return tickets, and thus the second class carriages would fill and service become remunerative, and many of the present 2nd class travellers would find their way to the first class.[57]

Ingenuity for making the second and the first-class carriages more profitable aside, Taylor's argument is instructive for the ways in which it ties ticket price, an ability to afford higher fares and the social class of the travellers, with the prospect of increased profit.

Thus clearly, the aim was to attract people. But at a price which would be beneficial for revenue returns. Transporting huge numbers of coolies and labourers at the lowest price possible would have swelled the passenger traffic statistics, but would not have translated into perceptible profit.[58] It is not surprising that the introduction of an intermediate class tariff received a warm encouragement from various railway agencies. This new tariff guaranteed more profit per person than reducing the ticket price to 1 pie/mile as suggested by Sedgwick or Bell. Additionally, fares in India were based on mileage. Thus, the longer one travelled, the less they paid. Therefore, poorer people, travelling for long distances were not sufficiently attractive customers. At a related level, I argue that the comments by Sedgwick, Bell and the inquiry committee instituted by the railway companies are instructive if only because they underscore, possibly unwittingly, that railway operations in colonial India were always about profit. The rhetoric of social transformation added a moral legitimacy, which made the project justifiable to the colonial state. The fact that railway travel, which was argued to be an agent of social change that would transform Indians in more ways than one, was in reality denied to a large cross-section simply because their participation would not have added any tangible increase in railway revenues.

It is not without significance that labourers or poor pilgrims admitted to Horace Bell that despite an awareness of how railway travel would have saved time, they could not use it. In other words, as an additional caveat to the arguments made in the previous chapter, the desire to impart time-sense among Indians through railway travel was positively correlated to their ability to pay to learn the lesson! Consequently, there was little incentive for the railway authorities (beyond rhetoric of course) to make fares tractable for all varieties of passengers. More critically, this operational imperative made the imposition of putative regulatory travel-discipline through ticket prices difficult, if not impossible. As is evident, travel-discipline was compromised at two vital levels: (a) ticket prices being amenable to tugs and pulls from various quarters, albeit up to a point, weakened the sole bargaining power of the railway administrations, thereby affecting the nature of travel-discipline; and (b) the scale of the imposition of the travel-discipline also was affected, since many potential passengers either never travelled by railway for pecuniary reasons or did so occasionally. It is, therefore, mainly a question of numbers: to what extent and how many were affected by the travel-discipline. As already noted, those Indian passengers who could regularly access railway travel also had the power of negotiation. But those who did not, had at least the advantage of withdrawal of patronage, thus depriving railway administration of profit, however negligible. Combined together, these two factors had implications for both the nature and scale of railway travel-discipline in colonial India.

Standardised ticketing rules: a case of imagined uniformity?

Railway travel-discipline was also compromised by a lack of standardisation of ticketing rules. Up until the first decade of the twentieth century, railway administration in colonial India was characterised by the presence of multiple, contesting authorities, all spawning different rules and policies. This absence of standardised rules fractured the possibilities of imposing a consistent travel-discipline from above. At a related level, it also allowed Indian railway passengers who were aware of the lack of standardised rules, along with the significance that had for railway revenue to bargain for more favourable regulations. This section looks at the evolution of rules regarding opening times for ticket booking windows, return tickets and platform tickets to understand how the interactions between flexible ticketing regulations and negotiating tactics from different quarters shaped the imposition of railway discipline.

Initially ticket booking windows were opened for a short period of time, usually 30 minutes prior to the scheduled departure of the trains. Moreover, the number of ticket booking counters for selling tickets for lower-class passengers were few. Thus, this shortage added to the inconvenience of buying tickets within a short period. Furthermore, in the early years of operation, tickets were sold only at larger railway stations. Passengers therefore had to either travel to the nearest important station or while on transit they could get off at an intervening big station and buy tickets. The latter was not an attractive financial option largely because if passengers did not buy tickets at their stations of origin, they had to pay for the entire distance from the point of origin of the train to their destination.[59] Consequently, ticket booking counters often became chaotic sites with clamouring passengers pushing and shoving for tickets, even resorting to physical assault and violence. Contemporary accounts widely attest to the difficulties faced by lower-class passengers in procuring tickets. A Hindi proselytisation tract compared the difficulties of buying tickets to spiritual realisation.[60] A Hindi poem however, chose more prosaic terms and claimed that railway travel, especially the process of buying tickets produced *udbeg*.[61] A Bengali travelogue published in 1862 described the scenes at the ticketing booking counters at Howrah station as unalloyed chaos in which railway employees and petty criminals had a field day exploiting and cheating poor passengers.[62]

Another Bengali travelogue published a year before (1861) also noted similar scenes at Howrah station. The author of this travelogue Jagmohan Chakrabarti claimed that 'the pencil and the pen cannot do justice to the scene at the booking office'.[63] Railway officials too, acknowledged the inadequacies of ticket booking arrangements. An official report submitted to the Board of East Indian Railway Company noted the 'extreme difficulty' and 'universal discontent' felt by third-class passengers on the existing facilities for booking tickets.[64] In a similar report L.C. Abbott commented on the paucity of both ticket booking clerks and booking windows for lower-class passengers.[65] Not surprisingly, passengers complained about ticket booking arrangements or rather lack of them. In 1866 a memorandum submitted by V.J. Shankar Seth (a member of the East India Association and a prominent citizen of Bombay) complained that at some stations the stipulated time for selling tickets was very short and consequently a 'struggle' ensued for tickets when the counters open. Interestingly, Shankar Seth noted that in the clamour for tickets 'the rich and the stout are more successful in forcing their way to the front, leaving the weak and poor behind'.[66] A newspaper report argued that the time allowed for distribution of tickets to lower-class passengers left many without tickets, thus affecting their travel plans. The report described the policy as one 'determined to give discomfort to travellers'.[67] A similar report in the *Oudh Akhbar* demanded that the ticket windows be open for longer.[68] Another newspaper report described the scenes at the third-class ticket booking in the following words:

> One who has not had occasion to book himself at a third class booking office cannot realise the confusion that ensues among the passengers at the time of the distribution of tickets: the rush towards the booking office window is something fearful. Measures should be taken to remedy the evil.[69]

The problems faced by lower-class passengers at the booking counters were compounded by the ways in which railway employees manipulated the regulations with impunity, more of which in the following section. It is sufficient to note here that both official and unofficial sources are replete with complaints about how the paucity of time in which passengers had to buy tickets gave the booking clerks, pickpockets and railway police constables opportunities to 'collude' with one another and harass passengers. Needless to say, passengers travelling in upper-class carriages faced no such troubles. It is no coincidence that the travelogues offer only indirect and distant accounts of experiences at the booking counters. For instance, Kashinath Mukhopadhyay, the author of a Bengali travelogue travelling in a second-class carriage wondered whether his servant (travelling third class) would be able to buy a ticket given the chaotic conditions at the third-class ticket windows.[70] Writing decades later another author similarly ruminated over the conditions in which lower-class passengers bought their tickets while acknowledging that he did not have any first-hand experience of the tribulation faced by the latter.[71]

Ticketing regulations thus were beset with problems and those who suffered resented the system. As noted, railway authorities were aware of both the inadequacies of the system and passenger complaints. But the issue was lack of standardisation of rules. The time for which ticket windows remained open was not the same for all stations and railway networks. For instance, a Bengali pamphlet written as early as 1855 informed readers that the ticket windows at Howrah and Raniganj stations (the two terminating stations of the section of the East Indian Railway network open at the time) were opened for a longer time than the intervening smaller stations. The latter however, remained open for transaction up to 3 minutes before the departure of the trains, while the former closed 15 minutes before.[72] Such discrepancy was common. As the quote from the memorandum submitted by V.J. Shankar Seth suggests, at 'some stations' ticket booking windows remained opened longer than at others. In short, rules varied; not just between one railway network to another, but from one section of a long network to other. Not surprisingly, passengers were aware of these inconsistencies, as is evident from the demand made by Shankar Seth's memorandum to impose a standard time for all ticket booking windows to remain open. But more importantly, this awareness offered passengers the possibility of comparing different systems and demanding a change to something they would find more suitable.

Consequently, ticket-booking rules evolved through passenger demand and negotiations and the changes instituted by railway administrations, often as a response to the former. Broadly speaking, passenger demands included: longer opening hours for ticket windows and an increase in the number of ticket counters selling lower-class tickets. In 1865 the Eastern Indian Railway Company responded to these demands by agreeing to increase the number of ticket windows selling third-class tickets. The decision from the Board of the Company claimed that the additional expenditure involved in the construction of new ticket windows was approved because it was 'fully justified by the greater convenience afforded to the passengers of that class, which is the mainstay of the traffic'.[73] Other railway companies too, calculated similar connections between fulfilling passenger demands and prospects of increased revenue. Writing as early as 1859, the Consulting Engineer for the Government of North-Western Provinces argued:

> The duty of maintaining the rights of this class [third-class passengers] falls upon the Government and it will doubtless be fulfilled, *but the loss which results from the infringement falls upon the railway company and its dimensions are shown in no returns. It is notorious that respectable natives prefer any moderate amount of detention or delay to a very small proportion*

of rough usage. I would therefore beg to recommend the adoption of the following regulation that the booking officers at all terminal and principal stations shall be opened for the issue of tickets ¾ of an hour before the departure of a train.[74]

But despite consistent passenger demands and well-meaning and rather ambitious recommendations by some railway officials, regulations evolved slowly and remained inconsistent well into the first decades of the twentieth century. The clue to this was profit or the prospect of it. As the tone of the official sources indicates demands were unevenly satisfied, primarily guided by a belief in the ability of the proposed measure to generate substantial revenue return. This concern is clearly visible in the railway administrations responses to passenger demands to either keep the ticket booking windows at the stations and open them for longer or opening out-booking counters in big cities especially during holidays and festive occasions. In essence, the demand was to contract out ticket booking to private sellers such as shopkeepers and vendors in different parts of the towns, and even sell tickets even through post offices.[75] Passengers however, were not the only ones who wanted such measures. Some non-railway government agencies too, thought opening ticket-booking counters outside railway stations could ease both crowding and criminal activities such as pick-pocketing of passengers. The government of North Western Provinces for instance, recommended ticket booking arrangements outside stations to 'save the native public from crowding and pressure around the booking offices at the railway stations'.[76] Some railway companies implemented these suggestions, though not with consistency.

The Punjab Northern State Railway allowed the sale of railway tickets by private vendors on commission. But the practice was confined only to Rawalpindi Station.[77] Similarly, the Oudh and Rohilkhand Railway Company opened two out-booking offices in Benaras for the sale of tickets; but despite passenger demand it refused to expand the facility elsewhere on the network. The company officials claimed they were unable to defray additional capital expense involved as well as the prospect of loss of ticketing revenue from employee fraud.[78] Evidently, the main reason for such uneven implementation was cost outlay, especially for more extensive networks such as the Eastern Indian Railway and a scepticism for control over money. The latter was a real concern. Railway authorities had no control over the ways in which their own employees cheated passengers through various means and kept the proceeds to themselves. The decision to contract out ticketing services therefore required logistical preparation and financial risks, which the railway administrations could ill afford. It is no coincidence that eventually when it was decided (c.1900) to keep the ticket booking counters open for either the whole or at least a greater part of the day, the principal and terminating stations were the chosen sites.[79]

The concerns surrounding return tickets too, reflect a similar interaction between fluid regulations, profit imperatives and passenger demands. Broadly speaking, return tickets were not issued to lower-class passengers.[80] Railway authorities argued that since lower-class fares were very low in the first place, a provision for return tickets would reduce the tariff further, consequently having an adverse effect on profit margin. But given the lack of standardisation in ticketing regulations, there were exceptions as well. For instance, intermediate and third-class passengers travelling on the Eastern Bengal Railway Company's network were allowed to buy return tickets, though similar options were not offered to its fourth-class passengers.[81] Also, on all railway networks, servants of passengers whose employers were travelling in upper-class carriages were allowed to buy third-class return tickets.[82] Indian passengers demanded regularisation of return ticket rules. These demands were largely based on a clear understanding of the financial advantages, which accrued from the availability of return tickets. In a petition against the agent and the traffic manager of the Calcutta and South-Eastern Railway Company, a group of daily commuters claimed that the former had refused to extend the facility of return tickets to third-class passengers, which in turn caused 'great inconvenience and hardship'. Penned by one Baboo Madhav Chandra Mukherjee, the following excerpt from the petition is instructive:

> The majority of us are employed as clerks in public offices in Calcutta, whose official emoluments range from Rs 20 to 40 a month, seldom exceeding the last named sum, we feel confident that you will not deny that the restriction against which we complain is calculated to bear hard upon us. [. . .] *we were impressed with a belief that our prayer would be acceded to the not so much for our sake as for the interest of the company, which would be seriously affected, if the withholding of the third class return tickets caused, as it undoubtedly would do, a falling off in the number of passengers.*[83]

Official responses to such demands were gradual and uneven. In 1869, the Traffic Superintendent of the Calcutta and South-Eastern State Railway (the company to which the above petition was addressed) argued for an experimental introduction of return tickets for fourth-class passengers.[84] A few years later the East Indian Railway Company extended the provision of return tickets to intermediate class passengers. A letter to the agent of the railway company noted:

> You propose to give the same indulgence to intermediate class. This concession is equivalent to allowing a third class passenger to travel in an intermediate class carriage for the same fare which he now pays to travel third class and the Board desire me to convey their sanction to the arrangement.[85]

The same year, the company also allowed third-class passengers to buy return tickets; but only valid for a day. Sanctioning the arrangement, a railway official with the Government of Bengal argued:

> This concession would enable natives to use the railway on occasions when they would otherwise abstain, while it would not, he [the Lieutenant Governor of Bengal] believes, be difficult to check abuses and evasions on short local traffic.[86]

A ticket to control? 61

Around the same time the Consulting Engineer of the Eastern Bengal Railway Company also suggested an introduction of third-class return tickets on a specific section of the network, Goalundo to Calcutta, on the basis of a growth of 'native' passenger traffic.[87]

Clearly, here too, similar themes emerge: inconsistent rules, passenger demands based on an awareness of their significance to the railway economy and an uneven fulfillment of demands, primarily guided by profit prospects. But here it would be relevant to note that the degree to which lack of standardised rules affected return tickets regulations is rather unique. Different rules were applied even within the same network operated by the same company or government agency. For instance, as the preceding discussion indicates, while the intermediate class passengers on the Eastern Indian Railway had access to return tickets, the third-class passengers could only buy daily return tickets and it wasn't until the late nineteenth century that the same concession enjoyed by upper-class passengers were available to everyone.[88] Similarly, while third-class railway passengers could buy return tickets on much of the Eastern Bengal Railway Company's network from the commencement of its operations in 1862; the extension of the facility on the Goalundo–Calcutta section in 1877 also suggests deviations and inconsistencies. Similar variations can also be noted in Calcutta and the South-Eastern State Railway Company's network. The passenger petition quoted above clearly suggests that while the facility was demanded by a cross-section of passenger traffic; it was extended to a small section catering for an annual pilgrim traffic admittedly to increase revenue return.

Comparable tendencies can be detected in the evolution of platform ticket rules, though here the process was even more complicated and protracted. Initially, lower-class passengers needed prior written permission from the station authorities to allow any friends or family members to accompany them to the platform before the departure of the trains.[89] Passengers claimed that the system was faulty at many levels, including rampant corruption, which allowed some passengers who were either willing or capable of bribing the peons and the station masters to bring in their relations to the station precincts. Thus, although in theory passengers were subjected to regulations that may be construed as rigid travel-discipline, in reality it was flexible, albeit at a price. Additionally, many passengers noted that occasionally, despite paying bribes, they were not allowed to bring in their acquaintances since the final approval depended on the 'moods of railway peons'.[90] Not surprisingly therefore passengers wanted the system to be regularised. They were also willing to pay an entrance fee for their accompanying group. From the passengers' point of view the logic was clear. Some were already paying a sum (the bribe) to bring in their relations. Given this, a formalisation of platform entrance fee would at least have the advantage of not being dependent on the caprices of railway employees. As early as 1866, V.J. Shankar Seth in his memorandum sought the introduction of platform tickets, which would allow friends and relations of the passengers to see the latter off. He recommended a 'small cost, say 1/4th anna per person as a platform ticket or entrance fee'.[91] Two years later, an editor of a newspaper demanded a similar measure, suggesting platform tickets at a rate of 1 pice per person. He claimed that since this policy would offer an extra source of income for the railway companies, the latter should be willing to institute the change.[92] Such demands were consistently made throughout the following decades.

As the longevity of the passenger demands indicate, railway authorities were slow to respond to these requests. Also, here too, the responses were uneven, varying from one big station within a single network to another. One of the earliest responses from railway authorities came in the form of a suggestion made by G.L. Molesworth, the consulting engineer to the Government of India for State Railways. In 1872 Molesworth recommended the introduction of platform tickets, for an unspecified fee. If instituted, he claimed, this policy would have the advantage of 'excluding a number of useless loungers on the platform, and preventing unnecessary and confusing crowds'.[93] The first station to introduce platform tickets was Lahore. Here in the summer of 1883 it was decided that passengers had to pay one quarter of an *anna* for each person they wanted to accompany them onto the platform.[94] Later in the same year, platform tickets were also introduced at Delhi station, though at a higher price than Lahore.[95] The Eastern Bengal Railway authorities too, introduced the measure from October 1885, beginning with Sealdah station – the terminal point for the network.[96] But broadly speaking, the measure was unevenly applied. For instance, as late as 1896, passengers wanted the Oudh and Rohilkhand Railway Company to introduce platform tickets.[97] Similarly, even in 1904, passengers wanted its introduction across the Eastern Indian Railway Network.[98]

Evidently, the introduction of a platform ticket evolved through a complex and long process of passenger demands and official responses. Once again passenger demands highlight two realities: *one*, an awareness of the attraction of increased revenue return for the railway authorities, hence the couching of demands in these terms; and *two*, the pervasiveness of corruption among railway employees and its impact on passengers' perceptions of railway administration. It is no coincidence that after the introduction of platform tickets at Lahore station, a newspaper report sarcastically argued that the railway authorities should be grateful to the railway police employees for this new source of income because had it not been for the ill-treatment of passengers and bribes demanded by the former, such a system would not have been imposed.[99]

These demands and responses also highlight the lack of standardised ticketing rules. Clearly different railway administrations had different needs, target audiences and operational imperatives – factors that influenced their regulations diversely. Similarly, there was no standard response from the government agencies either. If approached, the decision was mostly guided by contingent factors rather than any definite rules on the subject. Thus, their intervention too, changed. This lack of standardised rules compromised the putative travel-discipline, especially the nature and scale of the process. For instance, the regulations guiding the opening hours for ticket booking counters and platform tickets were far from uniform. This punctuates the possibility of a uniform travel-discipline, imposed evenly from above. Moreover, passenger demands shaped these rules, often replicating their needs and choices – a process that again challenges the idea of the nature of travel-discipline as impervious to outside, particularly Indian passengers', influence. Given this, in everyday operational terms the likelihood of the imposition of this travel-discipline on Indian passengers in the ways envisaged by current scholarship is rather tenuous.

As for the scale of the travel-discipline, the issue is the differential impact on diverse groups. For instance, even by the turn of the twentieth century, platform tickets were not introduced across all railway networks. By implication, there was a possibility that many did not experience the system. But in areas where they did, the ticket price was not uniform, which once again questions the consistency of the scale of travel-discipline. In the case of ticket window opening times, it will be instructive to note that Indian passengers travelling in upper-class carriages faced none of the difficulties associated with ticketing regulations. Their numbers were certainly small. But their presence and different experiences do disrupt the imagined scale of the imposition of ticketing rules and travel-discipline. Last but not least, one has to consider the role of ubiquitous corruption, especially because regulations were not uniform, thereby offering opportunities for bribery. Thus, in reality it meant that many who could afford to pay bribes, and even those who could not and yet paid, were indeed able to subvert the system. This affected the purported scale of travel-discipline.

Cheating passengers, corrupting railway travel-discipline: contesting ticketing regulations from within

> Kim asked and paid for a ticket to Umballa. A sleepy clerk grunted and flung out a ticket to the next station, just six miles distant. Nay, said Kim, scanning it with a grin. *This may serve for farmers, but I live in the city of Lahore. It was cleverly done babu. Now give me the ticket to Umballa.* The babu scowled and dealt the proper ticket.[100]

This excerpt from Kipling's famous novel *Kim* does underline a ubiquitous problem faced by railway passengers in colonial India that is, corruption among railway employees. This, alongside Bharatendu's play used in the introduction, offers literary representations of a reality, which interestingly remains largely overlooked in current historiography. This oversight is surprising if only because the evidence of corrupt employees affecting everyday railway operations is widespread, pervading even literary sources. More critically, at a theoretical level, evidence of corruption offers empirical possibilities to interrogate our received wisdom about the nature of railway operations in colonial India, especially who participated, who gained and how did all these affect the famed tool of colonial control?

Thus, a focus on corruption can widen our historiographical horizons in hitherto unimagined ways. In this section however, I have more modest aims. Focusing on issues such as bribery, cheating and ill treatment of passengers, here I suggest that the alleged cohesiveness of railway travel-discipline was punctuated and challenged by corruption among railway employees. At a related level, corruption had an interesting dimension. Passengers who were either poor or ignorant or both, were more often cheated than their well-to-do counterparts, whether Indians or Europeans. This once again exhibits how the nature and scale of railway travel-discipline was variable and was liable to be influenced by factors such as social status or rank. Last but not least, the ability of railway employees to manipulate railway rules and policies demonstrates the role of Indians in shaping travel-discipline, on this occasion from within.

Though the focus on bribery and cheating as a way of exploring the role of corruption in influencing railway travel-discipline is self-explanatory; including the ill treatment of passengers in the analysis however, requires some exposition. At a theoretical level, ill treatment of passengers indicates a malfunctioning railway administration; one in which for a variety of reasons railway authorities did not have control over how the system operated. In current scholarship ill treatment of passengers is explained primarily as symbolic of uneven race relations, which defined railway operations in colonial India. This interpretation is certainly accurate, though it does not encapsulate the complexities of instances of passenger illtreatment. Indian passengers were ill treated mostly though not exclusively, by Indian railway employees. This is an argument based on statistics. Our present knowledge construes railway officialdom as either European or Eurasian in origin. But, as noted above, the reality of managing everyday railway operations on the cheap dictated employing Indians at several levels of railway administrations, particularly in those jobs that were low-paid and kept odd hours.[101] As such, these individuals were the most visible face of railway administration whom Indian railway passengers were likely to encounter during their travel. Consequently, the ill treatment meted out to Indian passengers mostly came from their compatriots – a reality that requires more complex explanation than either a race or colonised mind-set.

Official documents are replete with reference to the ways in which railway employees manipulated the system for their own financial benefits. Corruption, in other words, was a well-acknowledged reality for railway officials in colonial India. Furthermore, corrupt employees pervaded all railway operations, freight and passenger traffic. Ticketing too, was no exception. Railway authorities accepted the prevalence of corruption with a sagacious bearing, which displays inability to control rather than compliance. Among all ticketing related employees, the ticket booking clerks and the railway police constables who were deployed to manage the crowd around the ticket booking windows were reputed to be the most corrupt. For reasons discussed above, crowds only gathered around ticket counters that sold lower-class passenger tickets. The following discussion therefore mainly focuses on lower-class passengers, though occasional comparisons will be made to underline the ubiquity of corruption. Ticket booking clerks' proclivity to cheat passengers seems to parallel the commencement of railway operations. Published in the year in which the East Indian Railway company's network became operational, Akshay Kumar Dutta's pamphlet advised passengers not to succumb to bribing the booking clerks. He added that demanding bribe is illegal and the employees will be subjected to instant dismissal on the basis of passenger complaints. As a remedy, Dutta suggested passengers complain to Mr Hodgson, the then station manager at Howrah.[102] Despite such cautionary counsel the problem lingered on, primarily because in most cases, those who suffered were also illiterate and thereby unable to benefit from such suggestions even if published in vernacular. The durability of the problem can be gauged from the fact that a Bengali travelogue published in 1913 had a separate section dedicated to warning travellers about the usual tricks ticket booking clerks practised to cheat passengers.[103]

Broadly speaking, the modus-operandi employed by the ticket booking clerks included overcharging passengers; giving them tickets for a shorter distance than they had wanted, while charging them for the entire distance; refusing to pay the remaining balance, claiming shortage of change; and threatening and even abusing passengers by refusing to sell tickets in case the former insisted on fair treatment. The author of *Hutom Penchar Naksha*, a social satire in Bengali, described the tricks of dishonest ticket booking clerks in the following words:

> The third class booking office is swelling with people. Sitting inside their little wooden cabins the booking clerks are having a field day. One takes a whole rupee from a passenger while returning a ticket worth only four annas and a change of two annas. Any request to recover the remaining amount is promptly turned down. Another passenger pays for a ticket till Srirampur, but receives a ticket till Bali. One of the clerks is constantly blowing his nose, taking money, but neither producing tickets, nor appropriate change, disregarding the screaming passengers. All this while the jamaders and railway police constables are ill-treating passengers, making it impossible to speak to the booking clerks.[104]

Echoing similar behaviour a newspaper report claimed:

> There is a wall between the giver and the taker: in this wall is a window, into or through which the traveller puts his hand and gives the money [...] but when an excess amount is given, then there is a difficulty; and the traveller never gets back his change.[105]

Another newspaper report noted that if passengers required change for a rupee to pay for his ticket, neither the booking clerk nor the money changer gave him full charge of the rupee. Consequently, the passenger was 'obliged' to pay one or two pice as a kind of fee.[106] One newspaper correspondent complained that booking clerks cheated passengers by supplying tickets for places other than those for which fares are paid.[107] Another report requested that the railway companies employed 'men of integrity and obliging demenour', a complaint that clearly indicates lack of honesty among railway employees.[108] Yet another report claimed that ticket booking clerks on the Eastern Bengal Network became rather innovative and even levied fares from passengers who had return tickets issued on Saturdays and that were valid up to the ensuing working day.[109]

The difficulties passengers faced at the hands of the ticket booking clerks were exacerbated by the latter's collusion with other railway employees, most notably police constables and porters. Sources indicate that these employees often assaulted passengers, forcing them to pay a bribe either separately or to the booking clerks, an amount that they eventually shared. As illustrated in *rel-ka-vikat-khel*, it was a well-established practice. Radhacharan Goswami, the author of a Hindi tract underscored the collusion among corrupt railway employees by noting that those who paid any amount of bribe were whisked off by the police constables inside the ticket booking counters, thus saving them from the pushing and shoving in the queue, albeit at a price.[110] Echoing similar sentiments, the correspondent of a newspaper complained that when the tickets were distributed, the police constables took the passengers who had paid bribes to the windows by the exit, leaving other passengers to be insulted by the railway coolies.[111] Contemporary travelogues often substantiate the claims made by newspaper reports. For instance, the author of another Hindi travelogue noted that railway police constables who were employed to help passengers in procuring tickets did so only after being bribed.[112]

Such comments however, were mostly the product of distant observation as the authors of these travelogues were well educated, thus unlikely to be cheated by railway clerks. Also, as these authors travelled in upper-class carriages, it discounted the possibility of facing the clerks at the third-class ticket booking counters. But on occasions the authors of the travelogues too, had reasons to complain. Surendranath Ray, the author of a Bengali travelogue bitterly criticised the ways in which the luggage weighing clerks at Howrah station demanded bribes.[113] In another instance, Prabhat Chandra Dube described the ticket booking clerk at Sealdah station as 'ignorant, greedy (for bribe) and devoid of sensibility of how to behave with a respectable gentleman'.[114] Incidentally, in both these instances the railway employees being Bengalis, the criticism was couched in a language of how such behaviour showed a lack of regard even for *swajati*.[115]

An equally ubiquitous issue was the ill treatment of railway passengers. The extent of the problem is rather well documented in several sources. Thus, here I will mainly use some illustrative examples to underscore the ways in which my analysis differs from the current historiographical assumptions. But before that, it will be useful to define ill treatment. Here ill treatment includes assault, both physical and verbal. Given this, passengers were also ill treated by ticket booking clerks, whose assaults mainly constituted of verbal insults. More often however, passengers were subject to ill treatment at the hands of railway police constables and other lower-level employees such as porters or luggage booking clerks. As noted above, these railway employees often shared the spoils of booking clerks' ill-gotten income and thus constituted a triumvirate. Additionally, ticket inspectors also ill-treated passengers. Among these, both railway police constables and ticket inspectors were noted to be particularly amenable to ill-treating passengers. This was largely due to the legal powers vested in them, which safeguarded their actions in case of formal passenger complaints. Underscoring the role of police in ill-treating passengers, a newspaper report noted the ways in which 'poor and ignorant men were severely rough-handled by railway police constables, when purchasing tickets, on the most trifling grounds'.[116] The correspondent claimed that such behaviour was common in both the Eastern India and Eastern Bengal Railway Network.

Another report argued that railway police constables and ticket inspectors behaved harshly towards 'poor Hindoostanee' travellers and assaulted them if the former perceived any insolence in the latter's behaviour.[117] Yet another report claimed that railway police at several stations were in the habit of taking bribes from 'poor, ignorant villagers' and often ill-treated passengers.[118] Such charges were substantiated by another report that noted the 'free use of batons' made by railway police, especially on the occasion of a pilgrimage or fairs when stations became rather crowded.[119] Highlighting the collusion between different groups of railway employees, a correspondent of *Prayag Samachar* noted that station guards and ticket inspectors forcibly placed more passengers in already overcrowded compartments. If passengers resisted, they were beaten and abused.[120] In an interesting twist to the familiar theme of ill-treatment of passengers, a newspaper report noted that one ticket inspector (a Hindu) at Delhi station ill-treated Muslims if they did not bribe him.[121]

Indian passengers travelling by upper-class carriages were also occasionally liable to ill-treatment. Rabindranath Tagore recollected an instance of ill-treatment at the hands of the ticket inspector on his maiden railway journey. On this occasion, the ticket inspector was suspicious of the poet's actual age, and wanted his father to pay full fare for him. Indignant at the allegation of trying to save the difference between the full fare and the half-ticket, Debendranath Tagore paid the full fare. So incensed was the latter at the behaviour of a 'lowly half-caste Eurasian', that he even declined to receive the change offered and flung it across the platform instead.[122] In the same vein, a newspaper report complained that railway servants, especially ticket collectors, treated '*even* respectable native passengers having first and second-class tickets in the same rude way as passengers of the lower class'.[123] Another newspaper report noted that '*even the commonest coolie* has been seen to unnecessarily detain second class passengers'.[124]

Thus evidently, ill-treatment at the hands of railway employees was a common component of Indian passengers' railway travel experiences. But as the tone of the newspaper reports quoted above suggests, 'respectable' passengers, especially those travelling in upper-class carriages were much less liable, though not completely immune to ill-treatment. It is not without significance that the reports criticising ill-treatment of 'respectable gentlemen' were more consternated not by the incidence per se; but that it was directed towards more genteel folks, by the 'commonest coolie'. In other words, such responses illustrate that the ill-treatment of lower-class passengers was commonplace; while similar behaviour directed at upper-class passengers elicited surprise. More importantly perhaps, these responses also substantiate the earlier suggestion that Indian railway passengers were often ill-treated by Indian railway employees. After all, it is not without significance that reports in Indian language newspapers as well the authors of the travelogues conveyed their dismay at the instances of ill-treatment of railway passengers as a disregard for racial/national affinity.

Here therefore, it can be argued that race mattered; but so also social status, for both railway employees and passengers. Whether it was Debendranath's fury at being insulted by a 'half-caste European' or the use of the word 'commonest coolie'; such responses suggest that 'respectable' Indian railway passengers perceived ill-treatment at the hands of social inferiors not merely as an insult or even harassment; but as a social transgression beyond the former's imagination. The case of railway employees however, was more complex. Clearly, they treated 'poor and ignorant' passengers harshly because they were aware that the likelihood of reprisal was negligible, if not non-existent. But the occasional ill-treatment they meted out to the social superiors was done in the limited context of legal powers vested in them. They were aware of this limitation as well as the possibility of a formal complaint that could have jeopardised their employment. This also explains why statistically speaking, the ill-treatment of 'respectable' Indians by Indian railway employees is not comparable to what poorer passengers faced. The assaults against the former are more visible precisely because of their social status, which is reflected in official records and in their personal narratives.

Status had a bearing even in the ways in which complaints were construed against corruption and ill-treatment of passengers. As the newspaper reports used above indicate, the criticism of railway administrations was both widespread and protracted. Moreover, all railway employees, regardless of their racial background were accused of being corrupt or ill-mannered or both. One newspaper report captured the feeling succinctly by noting that as far as corruption was concerned railway employees formed a 'well-organised fraternity'. Interestingly however, the criticism of Indian and Eurasians employees mainly underscored their social background. The argument was: for reasons of economy, railway authorities employed 'dregs' of the society, who were both corrupt and had no concern for respectability. In this formulation therefore, railway employees were corrupted because they came from low social status, with little moral fabric. Though the low pay that such employees received also got occasional mention. A newspaper report for instance suggested the railway companies should increase the pay for railway *chaprasis* and police to eight rupees per month, which would attract a 'better class of men'.[125]

A couple of years later another newspaper report argued that the Eastern Indian Railway Company's employees were more likely to take bribes and trouble passengers than their counterparts in the service of both the Oudh and Rohilkhand Railway Company because the former employed 'impertinent persons of low social class'.[126] In a similar complaint another report linked low social status of employees with the ways in which they treated poorer passengers in the following words:

> Adverts to trouble and harassment to which native passengers, particularly those who could not read or write, are subjected at the hands of subordinate railway officials. *The latter are generally men of no education or social position, and the authority they possess at once inflates them with pride. The result is they insult passengers with impunity.*[127]

Reflecting comparable concerns another report argued:

> The upper subordinates and officers are bad enough, *but the menial servants are a thousand times worse, notwithstanding that they are nothing more than coolies.* They think themselves proprietors of the train and carriages, and never do anything without abuses [. . .] its [railway] subordinates can disobey its rule with impunity, and the most menial servant of this department considers himself a nawab or a raja.[128]

Given such attitudes, it is not surprising that Debendranath, an elite, underscored the 'lowly half-caste' status of the ticket collector to convey perceived social infringements.

Railway authorities were familiar with both widespread corruption and ill-treatment of passengers. In 1865 in a letter to its agent based in Calcutta, the Board of the East Indian Railway Company noted:

> With regard moreover to the issue of tickets to the third and fourth class passengers, it is impossible to be too careful to check the irregularities and extortion of venal native station masters.[129]

There was also an awareness that corruption among railway employees had a 'harmful and damaging' impact on passenger perception of railway administration and by implication on railway revenue.[130] As early as 1859, the Lieutenant Governor of the North-Western Provinces captured the sentiment in the following words:

> That portion of the native community, from which third class passengers are drawn have no notion whether they should prefer their complaints to the deputy agent or to any other person and in 99 cases out of a 100 they would rather suffer the wrong, than trouble themselves to obtain redress. *The effects however of inattention to their reasonable comforts and to their rights to be civilly treated will follow – natives of respectability will not travel by rail at all unless they are protected from such behaviour.*[131]

Some steps were certainly taken to curb the problem, including a decision to dismiss railway employees accused of ill-treatment or uncivil behaviour.[132] Occasionally actions were also taken against employees found guilty. For instance, in 1867, a railway official employed by the Eastern Indian Railway Company was dismissed for ill-treating a passenger called Baikunth Roy. In the ensuing investigation, the accused was found guilty and was suspended.[133] Such cases however, were rare.[134] This was partly due to a lack of standardised rules across railway networks; and partly the solution of dismissing railway employees was not sustainable, either financially or logistically.

In other words, despite an acknowledgement of the problem and its possible impact on passenger traffic flow, the railway authorities failed to control their employee behaviour. Though in the case of concern for growth of passenger traffic too, once again, as the above quote indicates, the concern was not on how third-class passengers suffered, but how this would have influenced the decision of 'respectable natives' to choose railway as a mode of transit. But more critically, these issues demonstrate the ways in which railway regulations and travel-discipline was punctuated and challenged from within, thereby qualifying its nature and scale in more complex ways than presently imagined.

Conclusion

This chapter interrogated the ability of ticketing regulations to impose travel-discipline on Indian railway passengers. It also explored the impact of this travel-discipline on colonial Indian society. If the foregoing evidence is anything to go by, it can be argued that railway travel-discipline was neither as rigid nor as uniformly imposed as claimed in current historiography. Additionally, since the nature and scale of this travel-discipline was qualified at the level of every-day railway operations, therefore, its putative capacity to exercise control can also be questioned. In other words, the disciplinary impetus attributed to travel-discipline was not as effective as presumed.

The foregoing discussion clearly indicates that the imposition of railway travel-discipline was compromised on several levels and by several means. In the first place, ticketing regulations were not impervious to outside influences. Indeed, passengers' demands, both real and perceived, shaped this process. Railway tariff structure in colonial India was locally determined, evidently to respond relatively quickly to changing needs. Whether it was the introduction of a special tariff for intermediate class or fourth-class passengers, the clue was not rigidity; but both the need and the willingness on the part of the railway authorities to respond to new demands. At this level therefore, it can be claimed that ticket prices, usually perceived as one of the most important and inflexible components of ticketing regulations, was responsive to pressures from within (railway authorities) and without (Indian passengers). But tariff structure, as we saw, is not the only instance; other aspects of ticketing regulations too (return and platform tickets) were flexible and responsive to passenger demands and the realities of everyday railway operations. This flexibility however, as noted, was also a product of a lack of standardised ticketing regulations, which in turn is a reflection of the complexities of railway management in colonial India – a discussion beyond the scope of this chapter. Crucially however, an absence of standardised rules questions the nature of ticketing regulations at theoretical and practical levels.

Clearly, the uniformity attributed to ticketing regulations by current histori-ography did not exist – different railway authorities, including government agencies had different rules. More importantly, rules varied even on the same network, all of which suggests flexibility and non-uniformity. This has a direct bearing on the conceptualisations of scale of railway travel-discipline. If ticket regulations and the travel-discipline it spawned was not quite uniform or rigid; then how many Indian passengers were affected by it; and to what extent?

Any statistical reply to these questions will be difficult. But on the basis of the evidence used in the preceding discussion some suggestions can certainly be made. For instance, regardless of the negotiations surrounding ticket price, railway travel still remained a costly proposition for a cross section of Indians. Many therefore did not come within the ambit of railway travel-discipline – a reality that also questions the wider influence of the latter on Indian society. More specifically, those who did choose to travel by railways, either regularly or occasionally were not subjected to similar regulations. Passengers travelling in lower-class carriages were evidently guided by different rules than their counterparts in upper-class carriages. Admittedly, the proportion of former was more, which increased the possibility of the scale of impact. But in this context, it will be relevant to note the following aspects: passenger negotiations; withdrawal of patronage; social status of passengers; an absence of standardised rules; and corruption – all of which subverted the regulations and punctuated the scale of control.

Passenger petitions as we saw, demanded specific, even narrow changes, often challenging existing regulations. These demands were fulfilled, albeit unevenly. But nonetheless, the scale of control was affected. In short, some passengers were affected by certain rules while others were not. For instance, the successful reversal of third-class passenger fares for daily commuters to Calcutta did not apply to the entire Eastern Indian Railway Company's network or to all third-class passengers. Absence of standardised rules too, had a similar impact. Platform tickets for instance, were not uniformly adopted over even single railway networks. Passengers using Delhi or Lahore stations, where platform tickets were available, were regulated by different rules than say those at Benaras. Thus numbers, which is central to any scale of measurement, varied both on where one was; and who one was. The latter aspect played a significant role in influencing scale of railway travel-discipline. Third-class passengers on the Eastern Indian Railway Company's network for instance, were not allowed to have return tickets. Though this facility was extended to servants whose employers were travelling in upper-class carriages – certainly a case of derived status. But nonetheless, such rules demonstrate that the scale of regulations and travel-discipline was less comprehensive than imagined.

Additionally, withdrawal of patronage, by which I mean choosing to travel by non-railway means, also posed a serious challenge to the scale of railway travel-discipline. As noted, the numbers who chose not to use the railways, at least not as frequently as say daily commuters, could be large. Consequently, the numbers affected by regulations varied from time to time. Last but not least, the role of bribery and corruption cannot be discounted. Those who paid bribes successfully subverted the regulations, thereby affecting its scale. If accompanied by family members, the number rose even more. Interestingly despite complaints, the endurance of corruption among railway employees suggests passenger participation, unwilling or otherwise. Either way, given the extent of corruption as suggested in the preceding discussion, its impact on the scale of railway travel-discipline was more than currently imagined.

The scope of travel-discipline was also modified by Indian participation, both as passengers and as railway employees. Here again, like the previous chapter, it can be argued that Indians shaped railway operations in colonial India in more ways than presently acknowledged. As employees, Indians challenged the imposition of the regulatory regime of railway travel by manipulating it at every level. This had practical consequences. It limited the scale and rigidity of the imposition of railway regulations by making it amenable to outside forces. Bribes and ill-treatment of passengers also punctuated travel-discipline by influencing individual experiences, which differed depending on whether one paid bribes or not. This subversion by Indian railway employees however, had no political aims. It was not a conscious, collective decision to challenge the railway regime and to undermine its financial roots. It was largely based on economic needs, since these employees were also poorly paid. Though ill-treatment of passengers was probably also based on the limited powers they enjoyed within railway precincts and thus abused it within a specific context.

Last but not least, the lack of authorial control over their activities for logistical reasons certainly gave their behaviour a conducive environment in which to thrive. The significance of the Indian participation as passengers on railway operations is self-evident. The revenue generated by passenger traffic kept the wheels of the trains running. Indian passengers were aware of this pecuniary reality. The petitioning section of Indian passengers, who were also the newspaper reading variety, surely had a clear idea of their financial significance. It is no coincidence that the petitions quoted above underscore how passengers' inability to access railway travel will affect railway revenue – the central concern for railway authorities. The veiled threat to use non-railway transport such as boats by daily commuters, also underlines this strategy. This framing of the passenger petitions and newspaper reports in terms of profit-making sections and how the success of railway economy crucially hinged on the revenue generated by specific groups of passengers, demonstrates a confidence in understanding how the railway system worked.

But those sections of Indian passengers who did not petition were also aware of the significance. Though this awareness was largely notional as many of these passengers were also illiterate and therefore could not decipher their significance from newspapers or annual railway reports. But they were not ignorant. If anything, as Horace Bell's account indicates, a large cross-section of poor passengers was aware of both the dimension of their numbers, especially in forms of 'coolie gangs' or as pilgrims and the practical advantages railway travel offered. At the same time however, they were also aware of their pecuniary status and the ways in which the former affected the advantages of railway travel. As the foregoing chapter demonstrated, speedier travel was often denied to lower-class passengers because they paid less. To add insult to the injury of forced slow travel, the lower-class passengers also suffered adversely if they resided in less prosperous regions. As noted earlier, railway companies often lowered tariffs for passengers living in more affluent districts. Consequently, for poorer passengers from impoverished regions, railway travel remained expensive. Thus, despite their substantial numbers, poorer passengers therefore travelled by rail only when the advantages outscored the disadvantages – a decision which influenced railway profit margins. But not to an extent (as argued above) that would have induced railway authorities to reduce ticket price beyond a point. A relationship symptomatic of the centrality of profits in railway operations.

At a related level, instructive here would be to note that passenger petitions or demands were rarely based on racial identity. This is indicative of Indian passengers' familiarity with the operating principle of railway operations in colonial India – revenue return. As such, passenger demands reflected what mattered. Once again, this is not to discount the role of race. But to argue that as a single analytical index race is inadequate to explain the complex realities of everyday railway operations. Expanding the arguments proffered in the previous chapter, here too, it can be suggested that social rank or status offers an additional and credible index. Social status clearly influenced railway operations in colonial India. Borrowing an Orwellian analogy, one can argue that all passengers mattered; but some more than others. Interestingly, though not surprisingly, passenger petitions consistently refer to their status both real and imagined, by words such as 'respectable' and 'middle class gentlemen'. More critically, in most cases, petitioners' resented changes in well-established policies not merely for financial reasons. Their umbrage is also at how changed rules may possibly compel them to travel with social inferiors. Clearly, practicality of railway travel was desired; but not at the cost of social respectability. Hence the success of intermediate class and demands for services to sequester themselves physically and otherwise from those who were both socially unequal and paid less.

This imbrication of financial and social status is instructive. It demonstrates that railway regulations sustained social distinctions in/of colonial India; but did not create it. Railway authorities and the colonial state played a critical role in the process, primarily for pecuniary reasons. The introduction of intermediate class tariff is a case in point. The measure was based on an admittedly perceptual need of 'respectable natives'. But as the success of the enterprise suggests, the need was rather real. Similarly, as F.S. Taylor's note on the proposed passenger tariff for the Bengal indicates, a cross-section of Indian passengers was willing to pay a trifle higher for 'respectability'. Given this, status modified the nature of travel-discipline. Whether it was ticket prices; access to return tickets; or even ill-treatment at the hands of railway employees, in most cases passengers' status determined what they got. Even corruption among Indian railway employees was criticised as a manifestation of their low social status, which made them susceptible to both greed and impertinence against social superiors. Status therefore was an acknowledged criterion for Indian passengers, railway authorities and the colonial state alike to negotiate a demand-supply relationship based on mutual awareness of profit and practicability. Consequently, it also modified the scope of railway travel-discipline by influencing the scale of regulations in accordance to social hierarchy.

Additionally, this pandering to social status offered two related advantages to a cross-section of Indian passengers who enjoyed or claimed elevated social rank.

One, it provided a platform (pun intended) for direct negotiation, which often fulfilled their acknowledged demands. *Two*, this platform in turn was used to proclaim and contest their roles in the social spaces created or modified by railway operations. Both passenger petitions and newspaper reports illustrate how privileged access to railway specific spaces such as platforms and carriages was either demanded or refused through self-proclaimed middle class or respectable status. From demanding platform tickets at a 'trifle amount' to resenting the possibility of commuting with fourth-class passengers, the idea clearly is to claim specific spaces as their own, while contesting others' rights to access. Surely, platform tickets at one *anna* must have been prohibitive for many passengers, especially those for whom even the ticket price was too high. Thus, demanding such a measure suggests a desire to appropriate platforms as a space, both in its physical and social dimensions.

This process however, had another dimension. The contestation of social space was also based on a parallel process of claiming representative roles albeit self-proclaimed, on behalf of other, lower social classes. Criticising ill-treatment of 'poor and ignorant' masses or demanding imposition of fines on corrupt ticket booking clerks provide such instances. Such representations are indicative of the ways in which middle-class, educated Indians endeavoured to wrest the authority that railway administrations and the colonial state exercised in railway specific social spaces, primarily by claiming that the former had the legitimate right to demand and dictate the regulations that governed such spaces. In other words, these instances demonstrate the attempts by a self-assuredly important, but not yet politically confident social group to contest the legitimacy of control over social spaces by other contenders.

This contestation too, it can be suggested, played an important role in qualifying railway travel-discipline. As demonstrated, many ticketing regulations were shaped through a process of claims and counter-claims. Broadly speaking, the former was framed in a language of paternalistic beneficence and thus claimed both overtly and otherwise the legitimacy to control railway specific social spaces. Not surprisingly, such attitudes were based both on an assured knowledge of political power and an equally strong belief in the moral mission of imperialism. The latter however, challenged these claims by noting the ways in which implementation faltered. It is no coincidence that petitions reminded government agencies that they were responsible for safeguarding passenger interests against hiked tariffs or ill-treatment at the hands of railway employees. The responses to these demands are instructive. As evidence demonstrates, though concessions were offered with an eye to protect or increase revenue return, the rhetoric of paternalism was not given up. This process indicates the ways in which colonial state and the railway authorities offered a counter-contestation by underlining their continued and legitimate control over railway operations, social spaces and regulations inclusive. This however, had an unintended consequence. It made regulations pervious to outside influences, thereby affecting its consistency.

As the foregoing discussion suggests, nature and scale of ticketing regulations and travel-discipline was both compromised and limited. Given this, its putative ability to influence wider social change in colonial India too, can be reassessed. Here again, change is not denied. Railway travel was popular, ticketing regulations were novel and passengers had to comprehend these regulations to access railway travel. Thus, one can certainly suggest both an awareness and adjustment to a new mode of transport and its demands. But beyond this it is difficult to conjure the wider social influence of travel-discipline in the manner currently suggested. This chapter demonstrates that an all-pervasive, uniform travel-discipline did not exist. On the contrary, it was uneven and its imposition was dependent on various contingent factors. Furthermore, it was flexible and amenable to influences both from within and without. Last but not least, the travel-discipline was challenged and punctuated by various means including passenger demands and corruption among railway employees. As such, it can be argued that its wider influence or social impact was variegated and differentiated. More specifically, its arguable that disciplining potential for colonial subjects was narrow, because if anything, ticketing regulations' lack of rigidity and uniformity produced disruptive, clamorous, clearly subversive (though for non-political reasons) and assertive subjects as opposed to more manageable or governable ones.

In other words, if travel-discipline spawned by ticketing regulations was a tool of colonial control, then its impact is evidently questionable. The clue to understanding this apparent puzzle is in the gap between the rhetoric of railway operations and the imperatives that shaped it on a daily basis, viz., generating sustainable revenue. Profit, as the chapter amply illustrated, mattered. At the level of everyday operations therefore, decisions were taken with an eye to maintain, if not increase profit. As such, the need and desire for profit often trumped grand rhetoric. As in the previous chapter, here too, if one concentrates at the highest level of colonial and railway administrations, then railways' socially transformative capacities appear more magnified than they really were. Additionally, at this level railway regulations also appear to be more effective if only because such claims sustained the narrative of colonial beneficence and progress. But evidently, the reality was both more compromised and complex, as is reflected in the impact of ticketing regulations on colonial Indian society.

Notes

1 B. Harishchandra, 'Rel-Ka-Vikat Khel', *Harishchandra Magazine*, 15 May 1874, IOR.
2 Judging by the passenger statistics, Indians clearly adapted to the new travel practices well. For coaching traffic statistics see Annual Reports to Secretary of State for India in Council on Railways in India, Parliamentary Papers, V/4 Series, IOR.
3 See I. Kerr, *Engines of Change: The railroad that made India* (Westport, Connecticut, Praeger, 2007), Chapter 4.
4 Though railway authorities in India employed a sizeable number of Europeans and Eurasians, especially the latter, financial consideration dictated employing Indians too, in large number. Thacker's Post Office Directory (from 1885 it becomes Thacker's Indian directory) offers a handy source of information for all railway administrations (companies) since 1856. Volumes consulted in this study: 1856–1892. The employment of Indians, especially at lower levels, can also be deduced from an

official note issued a decade after the inauguration of the Rajmahal line that expressed surprise at the absence of accidents as 'singular achievement when we consider the number of native servants employed'. Quoted in S. Sarkar, *Technology and Rural Change in Eastern India, 1830–1980* (New Delhi, Oxford University Press, 2014), p. 292. Also, a Bengali social satire published in 1863 noted how the stationmaster at Howrah station was prone to insult *swajati* (lit. one's own people). The use of the word *swajati* suggests an Indian (in this case Bengali) stationmaster. See K. Sinha, *Hutom Penchar Naksha o Onnanyo Samajchitra* (Calcutta [original publication 1863] Sahitya Parishad, re-print 1955), p. 54. Furthermore, authors of many Bengali travelogues noted presence of Bengali stationmasters whom they met in the course of their journeys. For instance, Prasannamayi Devi in her travelogue published in the late nineteenth century claimed that stationmasters from Bengal to westwards (including) Delhi were '*bhadralok*'; while their subordinate *babus* were not very good. P. Devi, *Aryavarta: janoiko banga mahilar bhraman vrittanta* (Calcutta, Adi Brahmosamaj, 1888), p. 111. Here again, the use of the word *bhadralok* and *babus* suggest Indian/Bengali employees. The Bengali word *bhadralok* (lit. the genteel people) is a curious mix of social, cultural and economic attributes in varying degrees and as a social groups(s) it was a product of the socio-political milieu of nineteenth- and twentieth-century Bengal. For a handy definition see P. Roy, 'Bhadralok/ Bhadramahila', in R. Dwyer, G. Dharampal-Frick, M. Kirloskar-Steinbach and J. Phalkey (eds), *Key Concepts in Modern Indian Studies* (New York, New York University Press, 2015), pp. 21–23.

5 L. Bear, *Lines of the Nation: Indian Railway Workers, Bureaucracy and the Intimate Historical Self* (New York, Columbia University Press, 2007), pp. 42–43; M. Goswami, *Producing Nation: From Colonial Economy to National Space* (Chicago, University of Chicago Press, 2004), pp. 118–119.

6 Such lessons included, among other things, an adherence to rules; punctuality, especially an awareness of the time-frame in which tickets were sold for onward journeys; and virtues of keeping the tickets safe for subsequent inspections and so on. See J. Danvers, *Indian Railways: Their past history, present condition and future prospects* (London, Effingham Wilson, 1877), IOR.

7 For a variety of reasons colonial administrators did not expect Indians to travel in trains. For passenger traffic immediately after commencement of railway operations see G. Huddleston, *History of the East Indian Railway* (Calcutta, Thacker, Spink and Company, 1906), Chapters 1–3.

8 Letter from London dated March 1856 to the Agent of the East Indian Railway Company, Calcutta, in Home Correspondence 'B', Copies of letters sent, 1849–1879, L/PWD2/52, IOR.

9 Letter from the Agent of the East Bengal Railway Company, dated July 1862, in Letters to and from East Bengal Railway Company, L/PWD/2/156, IOR.

10 Booking clerks wrote relevant details on tickets by hand until the widespread adoption of Edmondson card tickets in 1840s. J. Simmons and G. Biddle (eds) *The Oxford Companion to British Railway History* (Oxford, Oxford University Press, 2000), pp. 509–510.

11 Letters to the Agent of the East Indian Railway Company in Calcutta dated February 1860, in Letters to and from East Indian Railway Company, L/PWD/2/76, IOR.

12 Letter to the Agent of the East Indian Railway Company in Calcutta dated February 1865, in Railway Letters to and from East Indian Railway Company, L/PWD/2/81, 1865, IOR.

13 Indian Railway Bill, Part III (Rules as to use of railways) in Railway Letters to and from East Indian Railway Company, L/PWD/2/84 (1868), IOR.

14 Indian Railway Act 1879, Abstracts in Railway Proceedings Government of Bengal, P/1484, 1880, IOR.

A ticket to control? 77

15 Home Correspondence, 'B' Series, Copies of letters sent 1849–1879, L/PWD/2/52, OIOC. The East Bengal Railway Company too, followed the East Indian Railway Company's example, see Letter from Eastern Bengal Railway Company, L/PWD/2/156, IOR.
16 Simmons and Biddle, 'The Oxford Companion', pp. 510–511.
17 Note by Consulting Engineer to Government on accommodation of railway passengers, Allahabad, dated October 1859, in Railway Proceedings, North-Western Province and Oudh, P/237/26, IOR.
18 Administration of the guaranteed railways: report of the consulting engineer to the Government of Oudh and Rohilkhand Railway for the financial year 1873–1874, in V/24/3582, IOR.
19 The East Indian Railway Company introduced platform tickets in 1880s. Letter from the Chief Justice, Indore, to the Secretary of the Railway Conference, dated 5 September 1888, in Railway Proceedings, Government of Bengal, P/3632, IOR.
20 Letter from L.C. Abbott, Officiating Under Secretary to the Government of Bengal to the Secretary to the Government of India, Public Works Department, State Railways, dated 24 July 1874, in Railway Proceedings, Government of Bengal, P/265, IOR.
21 Bradshaw's handbook to Bengal Presidency and western Provinces of India, 1860, IOR.
22 Indian Railway Bill, Chapter II (Passengers, their fare and luggage) in Railway Letters to and from East Indian Railway Company, L/PWD/2/84 (1868), IOR.
23 A.K. Dutt, *Bashpiya Upadesh* (Calcutta, Tattwabodhini Press, 1855), p. 19.
24 Anonymous, *Yatri Vigyapan* (Allahabad, Allahabad Mission Press, 1876), p. 3.
25 Report by Colonel Conway-Gordon on Indian Railways for 1887–1888 in Railway Proceedings Government of Bengal, P/3632, 1890, IOR.
26 Danvers, 'Indian Railways'. Emphasis mine.
27 Home Correspondence, 'B' Series, Copies of letters sent, 1849–1879, IOR.
28 A.M. Rendel, Report on the cost of completing the main, chord and Jabalpur lines, from 1 January 1868, in Letters to and from East Indian Railway Company, L/PWD/2/84, 1868, IOR.
29 Note by Captain F.S. Taylor, Consulting Engineer to the Government of Bengal, Railway Department, on the subject of passenger fares on railways in Bengal, dated February 1868, in Railway Proceedings, Government of Bengal, P/433/43, 1868, IOR.
30 Extract from a letter dated Calcutta 4 March 1874, from the Deputy Secretary to the Government of India in the Public Works Department to the Consulting Engineer to the Government of India for Guaranteed Railways in Home Correspondence, 'B' series, copies of letters sent 1849–1879, IOR. Emphasis mine.
31 J. Danvers, Report to the Secretary of State for India in Council on Railways in India for the year 1878–1879 (London, George William Eyre and William Spottiswoode, 1879), IOR.
32 Letter dated March 1872 to the agent East India Railway Company, in Letters to and from East Indian Railway Company L/PWD/2/88, 1872, IOR.
33 Ibid.
34 Colonel Stanton's Administration Report on the railways in India for 1883–1884, in V/24/3533, IOR.
35 Progress and Annual Report of the East Indian Railway Company for the year 1873 in V/24/3584, IOR.
36 J. Danvers, Report to the Secretary of State for India in Council on Railways in India for the year 1878–1879 (London, George William Eyre and William Spottiswoode, 1879), IOR.
37 G. Huddleston, 'History'. Chapter 7.

38 Authors of several Bengali travelogues admitted using the puja concessions to travel. For instance, see K. Mukhopadhyay, *Railway Companion* (Calcutta, 1863).
39 Letters to the agent of East Indian Railway Company dated November 1865, in Letters to and from the East Indian Railway Company, L/PWD/2/81, IOR. Emphasis mine.
40 Letter from F. Prestage, Agent, Eastern Bengal Railway Company to the Consulting Engineer to the Government of Bengal, Railway Department, dated 10 June 1864 in Railway Proceedings, Government of Bengal, P/163/32, IOR.
41 Ibid.
42 Note by Captain F.S. Taylor, Consulting Engineer to the Government of Bengal, Railway Department, on the subject of passenger fares on railways in Bengal, dated February 1868, in Railway Proceedings, Government of Bengal, P/433/43, 1868, IOR.
43 Colonial projects, both infrastructural and plantations, factories etc. have been widely identified having created a labour regime and labour market in colonial India. Of these, railways played a dual role of using labour for construction and maintenance as well for transporting labour to other sites of work. See I. Kerr, *Engines of Change: The Railroads that Made India* (Westport, Connecticut, Praeger, 2007); Ravi Ahuja, *Pathways of Empire: Circulation, 'Public works' and Social Space in colonial Orissa* (Hyderabad, Orient Longman, 2009); L. Züvichü, 'Empire on their Backs: Coolies in the Eastern Borderlands of the British Raj', *International Review of Social History, Vol. 59, Special Issue* (2014), pp. 89–112.
44 Letter dated 5 March 1868 from Baboo Umbica Churn Mookerjee and others to Captain F.S. Stanton, officiating Joint Secretary to the Government of Bengal, Public Works Department, Railway Branch, in Railway Proceedings, Government of Bengal, P/433/43, 1868, IOR. Emphasis mine.
45 Ibid.
46 Ibid.
47 Letter dated 2 April 1868 from Beni Madhub Mukhopadhyay and others to Major J. Hovendon, Officiating Joint Secretary to the Government of Bengal, Public Works Department, Railway Branch, in Railway Proceedings, Government of Bengal, P/433/43, 1868, IOR. Emphasis mine.
48 Letter dated 7 April 1868 from Major J. Hovendon, Officiating Joint Secretary to the Government of Bengal, Public Works Department, Railway Branch to the agent Eastern Bengal Railway Company and to Beni Madhav Mukhopadhyay and others, in Railway Proceedings, Government of Bengal, P/433/43, 1868, IOR.
49 Letter from Baboo Koylas Chunder Bannerjee, Auditor's General's Office, Calcutta to the Joint Secretary to the Government of Bengal, Public Works Department, Railway Branch, dated 18 April 1864 in Railway Proceedings, Government of Bengal, P/163/32, 1864, IOR.
50 Petition from the third-class passengers of the Eastern Bengal Railway to the Consulting Engineer to the Government of Bengal, Railway Department, dated May 1864 in Railway Proceedings, Government of Bengal, P/163/32, 1864, IOR. Emphasis mine.
51 Letter from Captain F.S. Taylor, Joint Secretary to the Government of Bengal, Public Works Department, Railway Branch, to Baboo Koylas Chunder Bannerjee, dated 20 May 1864, in Railway Proceedings, Government of Bengal, P/163/32, IOR.
52 The Annual Reports to the Secretary of State for India in Council for Railways in India frequently compared railway rates from different parts of the world. See Parliamentary Papers, V/4 Series, IOR.
53 'Indian Railway Bill', in Railway Letters to and from East Indian Railway Company, L/PWD/2/84 (1868), IOR.

54 Letter from Colonel C. Pollard dated August 1873 to the Secretary to the Government of India, Public Works Department, in Proceedings of the Railway Department, Government of India, P/578, IOR. Emphasis mine.
55 Excerpts of report by R.E. Sedgwick in H. Bell, *Railway Policy in India* (London, Rivington, Percival and Company, 1894), Chapter 5.
56 Ibid.
57 Note by Captain F.S. Taylor, consulting engineer to the Government of Bengal, Railway Department on the subject of passenger fares on railways in Bengal, dated February 1868, in Railway Proceedings, Government of Bengal, P/433/43, IOR. Emphasis mine.
58 'Third class passenger fares', letter to the agent of the East Indian Railway Company, dated March 1872, in Letters to and from the East Indian Railway Company, L/PWD/2/88, IOR.
59 'Indian Railway Bill', Chapter 2, Section 50.
60 Anonymous, 'Yatri'.
61 R. Goswami, 'Railway Stotra', in K. Sishir (ed.) *Radhacharan Goswami ki chuni rachnayein* (Selected compositions of Radhacharan Goswami) (Allahabad, Parimal Prakashan, 1990), p. 42. *Udbeg*, lit. anxiety.
62 K. Sinha, *Hutom Penchar Naksha o Onnanyo Samajchitra* (Calcutta [original publication 1863] Sahitya Parishad, re-print 1955), p. 47.
63 J. Chuckerbutty, 'My First Railway to Rajmahal' in *Mookerjee's Magazine*, 1, 1, 1861.
64 Report by Major Hovendon dated August 1865, submitted to the Board of Directors, East Indian Railway Company, in Letters to and from East Indian Railway Company, L/PWD/2/81, 1865, IOR.
65 L.C. Abbott, officiating Under Secretary to the Government of Bengal, note on 'Native passengers travelling by rail', to the Secretary to the Government of India, Public Works Department. State Railways, dated 24 July 1874, in Railway Proceedings, Government of Bengal, P/265, 1871 (contd.), IOR.
66 Memorandum by the Honourable V.J. Sunkersett, 'On the regulation for the protection of passengers by railway', dated March 1866, in Miscellaneous Railway Letters, L/PWD/2/190, 1865–1867, IOR.
67 *Ukbar Unjumun*, 29 February 1868, in Native Newspaper Reports, North-Western Provinces, L/R/5/45, 1868, IOR.
68 *Oudh Akhbar*, 9 August 1870, in Native Newspaper Reports, North-Western Provinces, L/R/5/47, IOR.
69 *Surur-i- Qaisari*, 31 December 1885, in Native Newspaper Reports, North-Western Provinces, L/R/5/63, IOR. Emphasis mine.
70 Mukhopadhyay, 'Railway Companion', p. 2.
71 S.N. Ray, *Uttar Bharat Bhraman* (Calcutta, Pashupati Press, 1907), p. 7.
72 Dutt, 'Bashpiya Upadesh', p. 19.
73 Report by Major Hovendon appended to a letter to the agent of the East Indian Railway Company, dated October 1865, in Letters to and from East India Company L/PWD/2/81, IOR. The number of ticket booking windows was increased from three to six at larger stations.
74 Note by the Consulting Engineer to the Government on accommodation of railway passengers, dated October 1859, Allahabad, in Proceedings of the Railway Department, Government of North-Western Provinces and Oudh, P/237/26, 1859 (May–December), IOR. Emphasis mine.
75 *Oudh Akhbar*, 9 August 1870, in Native Newspaper Reports, North-Western Province, L/R/5/47, 1870; also, 'Measures for the comfort and conveniences of lower class passengers', by the Secretary British Indian Association to the Secretary Railway

80   *A ticket to control?*

Conference, Simla, 1888, in Proceedings of the Railway Department, Government of Bengal, P/3632, 1890, IOR.
76   Administration Report for Government of India (North-Western Provinces) for 1882–1883 V/10/33, IOR.
77   *Aftab-i-Punjab*, 7 August 1882, in Native Newspaper Reports, North-Western Provinces, L/R/5/59, 1882, IOR.
78   Administration Report for Oudh, 1875–1876, V/10/145, IOR.
79   At smaller stations, too, the opening hours were increased, though the counters did not remain open throughout the day. Railway Report for the Year 1900, Command Number 232, Parliamentary Papers, V/4 Series, IOR.
80   Proceedings of the Railway Conference, 1888, Resolution Number 67, in Proceedings of the Railway Conference, V/25/720/28, IOR.
81   Letter to from the Board of the Eastern Bengal Railway Company to their agent in Calcutta, dated July 1874, in Letters to and from Eastern Bengal Railway, Series 'C', L/PWD/2/160, IOR.
82   Proceedings of the Railway Conference, 1888, Resolution No. 67, V/25/720/28, IOR.
83   Letter from the inhabitants of Rajpoor, Hureenavee etc, to Consulting Engineer to the Government of Bengal, Railway Department, dated 18 August 1864, in Railway Proceedings, Government of Bengal, P/163/33, IOR. Emphasis mine.
84   Letter from W. Goodwin, Acting Traffic Superintendent, Calcutta and South-Eastern State Railway, to the Committee of Management, dated 4 June 1869, in Proceedings of the Railway Department, Government of Bengal, 1869, P/433/46, 1869, IOR.
85   Report by H. Drummond, dated 11 September 1876, Simla, in Letters to and from the East Indian Railway Company, L/PWD/2/93, 1877, IOR.
86   Ibid.
87   Letter from the Board to their agent in Calcutta, dated July 1874 in Letters to and from Eastern Bengal Railway Company, L/PWD/2/161 (1873–1874), IOR.
88   Return ticket facilities without any restrictions were extended to third-class passengers in 1889, when Sir Richard Strachey became the Chairman of the Board of Directors of the East Indian Railway Company. G. Huddleston, 'History'.
89   *Ukbar Unjumun*, 29 February 1868 in Native Newspapers Report, North-Western Provinces in L/R/5/45, IOR.
90   Ibid.
91   Shankar Seth, 'Memorandum'.
92   *Prayag Samachar*, 10 September 1883, in Native Newspapers Report, North-Western Provinces in L/R/5/60, IOR.
93   G. Molesworth, Report on the State Railways in India, August 1872, in Railway Letters and Enclosures from Bengal and India, L/PWD/3/79, IOR.
94   Akhbar-I-Am, 30 June 1883 and Akmalu-l-Akhbar, 18 September 1883, in Native Newspapers Report, North-Western Provinces in L/R/5/60, IOR.
95   'Measures for the comfort and convenience of native passengers', from the Chief Justice, Indore to the Secretary of the Railway Conference, dated 5 September 1888, in Railway Proceedings, Government of Bengal, P/3632, 1890, IOR. At Delhi station platform ticket costed one *anna* per person.
96   Dainik, 28 October, and Gramvarta Prakashika, 31 October 1885, in Indian Newspaper Reports, Bengal, L/R/5/11, IOR.
97   *Rohilkhand Gazette*, 27 June 1896, in Native Newspapers Report, North-Western Provinces in L/R/5/73, IOR.
98   *The Citizen*, 25 April 1904, in Native Newspapers Report, North-Western Provinces in L/R/5/80, IOR. It was only by 1908 that platform tickets were introduced at Kanpur station, leading passengers to demand its extension to Allahabad and other

major halts on the East Indian network. See *The Citizen*, 17 May 1908, in Native Newspapers Report, North-Western Provinces in L/R/5/83, IOR.
99 *Akhbar-I-Am*, 30 June 1883, in Native Newspapers Report, North-Western Provinces in L/R/5/60, IOR.
100 R. Kipling, *Kim* (London, Wordsworth Classic Edition, 2009), p. 52. Emphasis mine.
101 See endnote 4. Indians were widely employed as ticket booking clerks, porters, luggage booking clerks and railway police constables. Contemporary travelogues too, attest to this claim.
102 Dutta, 'Bashpiya', p. 20.
103 G.B. Dhar, *Sachitra Tirtha Yatra Vivaran* (Calcutta, The Bengal Medical Library, 1913). See the 'advertisement' in all the volumes.
104 Sinha, 'Hutom', p. 47.
105 *Ukbar Unjumun*, 29 February 1868, in Native Newspaper Reports, North-Western Provinces, L/R/5/45, IOR.
106 *Prayag Samachar*, 21 May 1888, in Native Newspaper Reports, North-Western Provinces, L/R/5/65, IOR.
107 *Urdu Akhbar*, 1 May 1873, in Native Newspaper Reports, North-Western Provinces, L/R/5/50, IOR.
108 *Oudh Akhbar*, 9 August 1870, in Native Newspaper Reports, North-Western Provinces, L/R/5/47, IOR.
109 *Sadharani*, 15 October 1882, in Native Newspaper Reports, Bengal, L/R/5/8, IOR.
110 Goswami, 'Railway Stotra', p. 50.
111 *Muraqqa-i-Tahzib*, 15 November 1881, and *Sulabha Samachar*, 23 December 1887, in Native Newspaper Reports, North-Western Provinces, L/R/5/58 and L/R/5/13, IOR.
112 D. Shastri, *Meri Purvadig Yatra* (Bankipur, Khadgavilas Press, 1885), p. 23.
113 Ray, 'Uttar Bharat', p. 7.
114 P.C. Dube, Darjeeling (Mahishadal, 1910), p. 20.
115 *Swajati*, lit. one's own *jati*. See Chapter 7 for a discussion on railway travel and its impact on notions of identity.
116 *Bharat Mihir*, 9 November 1876, in Native Newspaper Reports, Bengal, L/R/5/2, IOR.
117 Indian Mirror, 15 September 1869, in Native Newspaper Reports, North-Western Provinces, L/R/5/46, IOR.
118 *Bharat Mihir*, 7 November 1878, in Native Newspaper Reports, Bengal, L/R/5/4, IOR.
119 *Bharat Bandhu*, 1 March 1889, in Native Newspaper Reports, North-Western Provinces, L/R/5/66, IOR.
120 *Prayag Samachar*, 21 May 1888, in Native Newspaper Reports, North-Western Provinces, L/R/5/65, IOR.
121 *Mehr-I-Nimroz*, 21 August 1895, in Native Newspaper Reports, North-Western Provinces, L/R/5/72, IOR.
122 R.N. Tagore, *Prabasi*, Bhadra 1318/Shrabon 1319 (Calcutta, Bishwabharati Prakashana, August–September 1912/13).
123 *Agra Akhbar*, 30 August 1874, in Native Newspaper Reports, North-Western Provinces, L/R/5/51, IOR. Emphasis mine.
124 *Nasrat-Ul-Islam*, 6 April 1900, in Native Newspaper Reports, Bengal, L/R/5/26, 1900, IOR. Emphasis mine.
125 *Oudh Akhbar*, 9 August 1870, in Native Newspaper Reports, North-Western Provinces, L/R/5/47, IOR.
126 *Oudh Akhbar*, 29 March 1872, in Native Newspaper Reports, North-Western Provinces, L/R/5/49, IOR.

82 *A ticket to control?*

127 *Som Prakash*, 4 July 1881, in Native Newspaper Reports, Bengal, L/R/5/7, IOR. Emphasis mine.
128 *The Aligarh Institute Gazette*, 15 October 1875, in Native Newspaper Reports, North-Western provinces, L/R/5/15, IOR. Emphasis mine.
129 Letter to the agent of the East Indian Railway Company from the Board of Directors, dated February 1865, Calcutta, in letters to and from East Indian Railway Company, L/PWD/2/81, IOR.
130 Home Correspondence, 'B' Series, copies of letters sent, 1849–1879 in L/PWD/2/69, IOR.
131 Letter from the Lieutenant Governor North-Western Province to the Consulting Engineer to the Government of North-Western Province, Railway Branch, Public Works Department, in Proceedings of the Railway Department, Government of North-Western Province and Oudh, P/237/26, 1859
132 'Railway Bill', Part V (Regulation for protection of public).
133 Letters to the Agent of East Indian Railway Company dated August 1867, in Letters to and from East Indian Railway Company, L/PWD/2/83, 1867, IOR.
134 For another case of dismissal of railway employee see 'Assault on a native by the assistant station master, Tundla', report dated November 1879 in Letters to and from the East Indian Railway Company, L/PWD/2/96, IOR.

3 A shared space?

Contestation of station spaces and railway travel-discipline in colonial India

Mark Twain once described Indian railway stations as 'perennially ravishing shows'.[1] One suspects that such purple yet pithy description was primarily a product of the author's vantage in experiencing railway travel in colonial India from the comforts and confines of first-class carriages, with occasional alighting at important stations. At the same time however, given that Twain was writing in the late nineteenth century, a period by which some of the larger stations in India were certainly grand, there is also an element of truth in his description, more of which shortly. But whether built to impress or not, stations were primarily functional spaces where passengers bought tickets at ticket booking windows; boarded into or alighted from carriages; waited for their trains at the platforms or in the waiting rooms; and used the refreshment rooms, platforms and toilets for eating, resting and cleaning themselves. Consequently, stations and their precincts, particularly the larger ones, were also crowded spaces where passengers jostled with one another in an unprecedented proximity.[2]

Surely, pre-railway travelling also included experiences of sharing spaces as well as physical proximity either as a traveller in a group or as an individual. Demands of railway travel however, added either new norms or modified the existing ones. After all, the experience of waiting for daybreak to travel while resting in and around *ghats*, *dharmasalas* or *paraos* was hardly new. But the experience of waiting to resume a journey in packed, ill-lit waiting rooms and station platforms was certainly novel; and also entailed a significant degree of forced physical proximity.[3] Added to this was the fact that the passenger experiences of sharing railway spaces were mediated through railway regulations. Experiences engendered at the ticket booking counters for instance, acquired a specific meaning largely because passengers had to buy tickets within a given frame of time and from a specific space.[4] Such instances can be multiplied. But the implications are clear and thus do not warrant further elucidation. Moreover, passenger interactions among themselves and with railway rules were shaped by the presence of railway employees. Interactions, which were often, though not always, fraught with tension, inequity and even the possibility of physical assault. In other words, regardless of the appearance, the stations and their precincts were spaces where Indian railway passengers experienced an intersection of railway travel-discipline and social and physical propinquity and interactions.

Given this, it is perhaps unsurprising that in both colonial and post-colonial appraisals, the interactions between station spaces[5] and Indian passengers have been invested with the capacity for broader social transformation, especially underlining the role of such experiences in forging a common identity based on collective, national sentiments. Interesting as these suggestions are, at the same time however, it is possible that forced physical proximity experienced in station spaces and mediated through the presence of new travel norms and railway employees may have produced more complex and heterogeneous sentiments than currently presumed. This chapter therefore, explores the causal connections between experiences of railway travel filtered through station spaces and infrastructure[6] and its wider social impact.

Railway spaces and social change in colonial India: the historiographical debate

> A sacred Brahmin now sits in a third class carriage in contact with a Dome and preferring a saving in money to his caste exclusiveness, drops his prejudices.[7]

Broadly speaking, for colonial administrators of India, the caste system often became a symbolic shorthand for almost everything that ailed Indian society. Among other things, the caste system was often noted to be a significant impediment (if not the greatest) for Indians to foster wider affiliations based on national or racial sentiments. However, as noted in the introduction, railway promoters claimed that railway travel had the capacity to challenge and obliterate the influence of caste system. The formula was simple. Travelling by trains, it was argued, would weaken caste (and religious) prejudices merely by forcing people to experience close physical proximity in railway spaces such as stations or waiting rooms. These experiences in turn, were expected to engender other forms of affiliations, most notably, a feeling of common national sentiment.

Colonial railway promoters, however, were not the only ones who believed in socially transformative powers of steam. Responding to R.M. Stephenson's prospects of railway development and its consequences for Indian society, a handful of elites from Bengal underlined the ways in which experiences of sharing railway spaces were likely to have salutary effects on erosion of social conventions, particularly caste prejudices.[8] Similarly, approximately two decades later (1875) speaking before a London audience, Framjee Vicajee, a fellow of the University of Bombay argued:

> The railways will indirectly contribute to demolish the castes, associated as they are with their obsolete conception of progress, and create instead a new society, broad based upon the principle of the trades, which will shift and move with the movements of knowledge and experience.[9]

While there is little doubt that such 'native' enthusiasm for railway development can be interpreted as an 'uncritical acceptance of the prevalent British structure and points of reference'[10] by colonial elites; here however, I suggest an alternate explanation. The pronouncements of Framjee Vicajee or Ram Gopal Ghosh's belief in the power of steam to weaken caste prejudices, I argue, shows that Indian responses to technology were more complex than the current historiographical oppositional binary of 'colonial knowledge' and national ideology offers.[11] Though a detailed discussion of this theme is beyond the scope of this chapter, one can suggest that Indian enthusiasm (both elite and otherwise) for steam can be interpreted as a genuine belief in the transformative capacities of technology in general and railways in particular to ameliorate social ills.[12] It is perhaps not without significance that a belief in the ability of technology to initiate social change persistently lingered on and even played an important role in shaping policies of Nehruvian India despite Gandhi's powerful and influential rejection of technology as an answer to India's social problems.[13]

Interestingly, post-colonial scholarly appraisals of the impact of railway spaces on social change in colonial India largely correspond to the expectations of the nineteenth-century proponents of steam. There is a broad scholarly consensus that experiences of sharing railway spaces spawned among Indian railway passengers a notion of common identity, glossing over caste, religious or regional differences. But crucially, deviating from the nineteenth-century counterparts, the post-colonial scholars claim that the 'flattening of identity' was not simply an effect of travelling in trains while sharing railway spaces in enforced physical proximity. On the contrary, Indian railway passengers experienced a common bond primarily as a result of the systematic racial discrimination that characterised railway operations in colonial India.[14] At a related level, it has been argued that station spaces were also colonial spaces and as such, were informed by mechanisms of colonial power, which aimed to discipline the bodies and movements of colonised subjects through railway rules and employees.[15] Simply put, Indian railway passengers' experiences of the colonial state's disciplining apparatus as embodied in discriminatory railway regulations in station spaces have been identified as having produced a bond of common racial/national affinity among the former.

These assessments are both interesting and accurate, especially the ways in which they have suggested how racial discrimination, a fact grudgingly acknowledged by the colonial proponents of steam, in effect may have played a role in shaping railway-borne social changes. But these appraisals, including those that indicate tje presence of fissures in the putative 'national' sentiment spawned by passenger experiences of station spaces overlook some key elements. For instance, as the previous chapter demonstrated, ill-treatment and harassment of Indian railway passengers were not just products of discriminatory railway policies administered by racially prejudiced European or Eurasian railway employees. Indian railway employees also often ill-treated Indian railway passengers. The possible impact of such experiences on social relations both within and outside railway spaces is clearly absent from our present historiographical knowledge.

86 A shared space?

Similarly, the suggestion that station spaces were sites of colonial control and disciplining exercised through railway regulations envisages the latter as rigid and impervious and thus beyond being influenced by Indian railway passengers.

But as the previous chapters have shown, railway regulations, the putative tools of colonial control, were more amenable to external influences than presently assumed largely because of pecuniary consideration. Given this, how far railway authorities could financially afford to keep station spaces beyond the pale of negotiations and contestations by Indian railway passengers – the largest section of the paying traffic is questionable. At a related level, there is also the issue of logistics and the gap between the colonial railway authorities' desire to control (in this case their employees) and the everyday realities of railway operations in colonial India. Given the proportion of railway employees to that of Indian passengers and the ways in which the former often diluted railway regulations for petty financial gains (think bribe), it is both numerically and theoretically tenuous to conjure station spaces as efficient sites of colonial discipline.

This chapter therefore builds upon as well as crucially deviates from our current historiographical assumptions about station spaces and their broader impact. It does not discount the role of racial discrimination in shaping a 'national' identity through Indian passengers' experiences of station spaces. But at the same time, it suggests that station spaces were produced and reproduced through Indian passenger negotiations and their responses to the physical evolution of the former as well as the rules, which shaped and determined access to these spaces. This interaction in turn, I suggest, produced more heterogeneous sentiments that had implications for Indian society both within and beyond railway stations.

The evolution of station spaces: waiting sheds and rooms

> Station architecture is as a rule pleasing. The platform offers a *picturesque* sight both before the arrival of trains, with the crowds of natives squatting on the platforms or in the waiting rooms, and while the train is in, with the crowds of sellers of sweetmeats, native food, curios etc.[16]
>
> They [Kim and Lama] entered the fort-like railway station [Lahore] the sleepers [third-class passengers] sprang to life, and the station filled with clamour and shoutings, cries of water and sweetmeat vendors, shouts of native policemen, and shrill yells of women gathering up their baskets, their families and their husbands.[17]

The above quotes certainly conjure romantic images of Indian railway stations. Being written by Europeans these excerpts also reveal visualising through 'imperial eyes'.[18] But at a less analytical and more mundane level, these descriptions go some way to conveying the realities of the Indian railway stations, particularly the large, important ones as commodious spaces ensconced within grand architectural styles, bustling with activity. Stations, as hinted earlier, were indeed busy and crowded places. But similarities between stations in colonial India end here as not all stations were as big or had similar facilities as Lahore, Howrah or

Victoria Terminus in Bombay. In most stations, facilities for passengers developed slowly, mostly through a protracted process of passenger demand and railway administrations' need to strike a balance between capital expended and profit earned. Even in the case of principal stations, the growth in infrastructure was uneven. For instance, Juland Danvers, in a report submitted to the Government of India, commented on the inadequate facilities at Howrah and Bombay stations – the termini of the Eastern Indian Railway Company and Great Indian Peninsular Railway respectively. Danvers even noted that the station buildings were 'unworthy of those large concerns'.[19]

If one considers that this report was submitted in 1876, approximately two decades after the commencement of railway operations in India, then the slow growth of station facilities becomes apparent. Indeed, it was only by the end of the nineteenth century that many of the important stations in colonial India were transformed from being mere brick structures to imposing architectural splendours. This evolution of station architecture is best conveyed by the 'Victoria Terminus' – the termini of the Great Indian Peninsular Railway Company at Bombay. Completed in 1887 to commemorate the Golden Jubilee of Queen Victoria, it was one of the largest buildings constructed by the British in India, and continues to remain the biggest station building in Asia. The imperative behind the construction of such grandiose statements has been variously explained by strategic importance of specific stations like Lahore, Lucknow and Kanpur and hence their fortress-like appearance; to Company pride and loyalty; to an architectural expression of a confident colonial power.[20] Whatever be the motivation, this stylistic transformation of stations was the culmination of a wider process of the expansion of the station establishment, which began with the commencement of the railway operations in mid-nineteenth century India.

The most important factor that contributed to the development of station facilities was capital outlay. Initially, railway companies were sceptical about investing in station infrastructure. They did not want to expend money on an enterprise the outcome of which they were not confident about. For freight transport, minimal structures were sufficient and almost none of the railway promoters expected passenger traffic in colonial India – certainly not in any remarkable manner. But passenger response to railway operations was both immediate and enthusiastic. Though pleasantly surprised, as in the case of ticket booking, railway authorities however, were under-prepared to deal with the demands of a growing passenger traffic.[21] Consequently, in the early days of railway operations, stations were simple brick structures with the additional facility being ticket-booking windows, usually in the larger stations. In smaller stations, more informal arrangements prevailed. At this stage, platforms too were not many, with smaller stations often having one platform for both arriving and departing trains.

This was mainly because the railway network was both short and patchy, with few trains running up and down the lines and thus risks of collision being minimum. But while both passenger traffic and the railway network steadily expanded, there was no proportionate expansion of station facilities. Pointing out

88 *A shared space?*

this discrepancy, a circular from the Government of India in 1864 directed the Lieutenant Governor of Bengal to invite the attention of the railway companies towards developing station accommodation facilities, particularly for 'native' passengers. The report urged the railway companies to build latrines and urinals, refreshment rooms and *serais* at all stations according to their magnitude, and in 'a manner suitable to the habits of the natives of the country'.[22]

Interestingly, local district officials, not the railway companies, were delegated with the responsibility of carrying out these tasks. At a related level, the tone of the circular is instructive. It is a mix of reprimand for railway companies and paternal interest in the welfare of Indian passengers. The following excerpt illustrates the point:

> Considering the position of the third class passengers, who form nine-tenths of the travellers by rail in India and the complete absence of that powerful check on the management which in England is exercised by the public itself, the *Governor-General in Council considers it to be the duty of the Government* to cause its inspecting officers to supply this want and to press on the railway officers reasonable recommendations for the correction of any defects which may come to light. The Government of India has every confidence that the management of railways in all parts of India will be conducted in a manner that will give satisfaction to the public and fulfil the requirements of the trust placed in the hands of the railway companies; *but if occasion should require, the Government must firmly insist on the removal of all just causes of complaint and in that behalf, must exercise the powers given to it under the railway contracts if necessary.*[23]

In response, the Board of the Eastern Indian Railway Company, the biggest network operating in eastern and north India claimed that they were 'fully aware' of the lacunae in station facilities. But the company justified the lack of facilities by claiming that their energy (both financial and otherwise) was diverted in completing and opening the line through Delhi. The Board of the Company however, reassured the government agencies that after the opening of the line to Delhi, they were willing to direct capital requirement to improve station infrastructure.[24] Realisation of such promises however, was slow and piecemeal with the most basic station facilities improving approximately around a decade after the commencement of railway operations in the region.

Not unexpectedly therefore, both Indian and European passengers complained. A representation sent by European passengers underlined a general lack of bathing facilities, urinals and latrines at the stations along the East Indian Railway Company's network.[25] Indian passenger grievances too, reflected similar concerns.[26] Although interestingly, many of the complaints by Indian passengers were sent to local government agencies. Partly in response to such complaints, in 1865, the Government of Bengal appointed a committee to make adequate provision for the 'health, comfort and decency of travellers'.[27] In its report the committee admitted that the passenger complaints were 'generally well founded'.

It suggested remedial measures, which included the building of sheds, urinals and latrines at all stations and resting places (*serais* and *dak bungalows*) at the large ones. In an argument balancing humanitarian concern with the prospect of profit, the report claimed that if properly managed, the suggested measures were likely to prove 'remunerative'. In response, the Eastern Indian Railway Company Board largely agreed to the proposals, sanctioning the building of facilities in several stations along the Company's network.[28] The earliest and most common improvement in station infrastructure was the construction of waiting facilities that is, waiting sheds and waiting rooms for passengers. This is hardly surprising as the waiting sheds required minimal expenditure and the waiting rooms, since they were more expensive to build, were mostly restricted to some principal stations, catering to the needs of passengers travelling in upper-class carriages.

Broadly speaking, larger stations were equipped with better facilities for waiting passengers than smaller ones – not a surprising outcome given the railway administrations aimed to keep costs down by usually offering services in larger stations where the number of passengers justified the expenditure.[29] But at the same time, it is difficult to generalise about a link between the size of station and the facilities offered, especially in the initial decades after the commencement of the railway operation. For instance, the 1866 inspection report of the Eastern Indian Railway Company reveals that while important stations such as Howrah, Burdwan and Bhagalpur had good waiting facilities for all classes of passengers, other large stations such as Armenian ghat and Patna had indifferent arrangements.[30] Evidently, facilities were uneven. But such inconsistencies also reveal certain patterns. A closer look at the official correspondence of the Eastern Indian Railway Company for instance, brings out an interesting regional difference. The stations in the Bengal Presidency could boast of better facilities than those in the North-Western Provinces.[31]

Similarly, records indicate that waiting sheds for third-class passengers were more wanting than similar facilities for their upper-class counterparts. In 1866, a petition addressed to the Viceroy and signed by more than 3,000 persons, including Sir Syed Ahmad Khan, the then Secretary of the British Indian Association, North-Western provinces, underlined the gap in facilities in the following words:

> The want of shelter and accommodation at the different stations for third class passengers. These passengers consist of the *poor, ignorant and helpless*. Many of them are weak and feeble, some sick and old; many women and children. These have to always to wait in crowds of hundreds, for several hours at a time, in an open and unsheltered plain. *The few rich and wealthy have waiting rooms, or the sheltered platforms to accommodate, but these masses have no shelter at all*. These masses are left exposed to all the inclemency of the wind and weather, and suffer and contract diseases, and die like brute beasts [. . .] *The remedy we propose will be, if not simple justice, an act of State charity. It is simple and inexpensive and can be carried out at once*. It is the building of suitable sheds. It will be easy to estimate the space required. Large sheds will have to be erected at the several

large stations, and for most of the rest, about nine-tenths of the whole number, very small sheds will be sufficient. A large board with a 'notice' stating the use of the sheds in the vernacular will be necessary.[32]

While such complaints seemingly confirm a regional variation in the facilities alluded to in the above; indifferent arrangements for lower-class passengers however, were more widespread.[33] In 1870, a passenger petition addressed to the Lieutenant Governor of Bengal complained about the lack of waiting sheds for third-class passengers at the Kustia station on the Eastern Bengal Railway Company's network. Here, the problem was exacerbated by the fact that the policemen forbade the passengers to enter the station until the moment the ticket windows opened, thereby forcing the latter to wait at times for more than an hour outside the station, regardless of the vagaries of the weather. Underscoring the social dimension of the discrimination, the petitioners argued that 'while gentlemen go in at once; and are not prohibited by the police'.[34] An Indian language newspaper followed up on the issue and the following excerpt from its report is worth quoting.

> The rule passed by the police superintendent of the Eastern Bengal Railway Company, prohibiting passengers from entering the Kooshtea station until the arrival of the trains by which they are to start. [. . .] *The writer hopes the railway authorities will inquire into the reason for passing a rule which, however, does not operate on Europeans and influential native gentlemen.* Should such a rule be found necessary, some proper shelter should be afforded to passengers awaiting the arrival of the trains.[35]

Upon investigation by the Lieutenant Governor's office, the report was found to be true and the agent of the Eastern Bengal Railway Company was asked to build the shelter required by the third-class passengers.[36]

In the case of waiting rooms also, third and fourth-class passengers suffered from a general lack of facilities. Moreover, existing waiting sheds for lower-class passengers usually provided an excuse to avoid any additional expense incurred by building waiting rooms. Though once again, as noted above, facilities varied. For instance, an inspection report of the Eastern Indian Railway Company noted availability of waiting rooms for third-class passengers at Burdwan, Bhagalpur and Jamalpur stations were well-kept though similar facilities were missing from Armenian Ghat, Patna, Bankipur and Buxar stations.[37] A decade later another report noted the construction of waiting rooms for third-class railway passengers at the Lakhisarai station;[38] while around the same time a proposal submitted by one Nilkamal Mitra to construct waiting rooms for third-class passengers at some larger stations on the Eastern Indian Railway Company's network such as Sahebganj, Danapur and Kanpur indicated a lack of facilities.[39] In contrast, the Oudh and Rohilkhand Railway Company was noted for offering both separate waiting sheds and in larger stations even waiting rooms for third-class passengers.[40] Regardless of the availability, waiting rooms however, also suffered from a general lack of cleanliness. Interestingly, upper-class passengers were not immune from such neglect. A report by the sanitary commission appointed by the Government of Bengal noted that generally waiting rooms were kept in a 'filthy state', a condition that undermined the utility of the facility.[41] Given that the report was submitted in 1865, it can be safely surmised that waiting rooms referred to in it were most likely for upper-class passengers than otherwise. The problem however, persisted, as both European and Indian upper-class passengers continued to complain well into the twentieth century about the lack of upkeep and the dirty state in which waiting rooms were kept.[42]

Cleanliness however, was not the only issue that plagued the waiting rooms. Theoretically, waiting rooms in India were not segregated on the basis of race. Thus, Indian passengers possessing first or second-class tickets could use these facilities as much as their European counterparts, though in reality, the station masters reserved the right to permit or object to any person's presence in the waiting rooms. As such, Indian passengers complained about access being denied to upper-class waiting rooms. Not surprisingly, such encounters have received sustained scholarly attention, with the instances of denial becoming historiographical common knowledge and therefore not warranting another detailed discussion. But relevant here would be to note that broadly speaking, scholarly interpretations of the denial of entry of Indians into upper-class waiting rooms have underlined the ways in which these experiences shaped a uniform Indian identity and how such railway experiences were symptomatic of everything wrong with the colonial regime, especially its famous tool of control, i.e. railway management. A recent interpretation has added a layer to our understanding by suggesting that wearing European clothes usually, though not always, ensured an entry into waiting rooms thereby arguing that these experiences had dual elements – racial discrimination and attempted socio-cultural homogenisation through colonial policies.[43] Such interpretations are largely accurate. But here I suggest that this debate in its current state has overlooked certain critical elements, cognisance of which is likely to go beyond the 'Indian identity formation' hypothesis.

Firstly, there is the issue of number and visibility. Here number refers to the station masters who were Indians. Even a glance at the annual numbers of Thacker's directories makes it amply clear that Indians were appointed in good numbers as station masters by most railway companies and state railways.[44] This is also confirmed by official reports and contemporary travelogues by Indian railway passengers. Given this, the frequency of denial of access to Indian passengers in waiting rooms requires attention. Second, the travelogues, both Bengali and Hindi, are silent on the issue of either restricted or denial of access to waiting rooms. This is indeed surprising, as the authors of these texts travelled in upper-class carriages; waited at stations for connecting trains and by their own admission had interactions with European station masters.[45] More importantly, these authors were certainly not shy of expressing their opinions on everything that suited their fancy including railway management. Additionally, as we will see in subsequent chapters, many of these authors were critical of railway authorities, especially of instances of discrimination against Indian passengers. This omission to mention the issue of access to waiting rooms therefore is significant; unless one believes (without any evidence) that these authors always encountered either polite Europeans (both passengers and employees) or particularly upright Indian stationmasters.

An absence of any such information is suggestive of different experiences, underlining unevenness; hence bringing in the point of analysing discriminatory behaviour through the prism of visibility.[46] Instances of refusal of entry to Indian passengers and the way in which such experiences were interpreted I argue, can perhaps be better understood as a point of political contestation, both highly visible and debated within the broader context of an increasingly aggressive and strong anti-colonial struggle in the late-nineteenth and early twentieth century India. It is perhaps no coincidence that instances of denial of entry into waiting rooms are primarily, though not exclusively, gleaned from Indian language newspapers, which at the turn of the twentieth century also exhibit an unmistakably radical anti-colonial shift in the tone and contents of the reports. More significantly, at a related level, this shift I suggest made racial discrimination and putative unity of Indians the only visible and contentious issue; while ignoring and subsuming discussions about Indian railway passengers demanding separate waiting room arrangements from other Indian groups and classes – an oft-neglected issue to which we now turn.

Indian passengers travelling in upper-class carriages demanded separate waiting rooms both from European passengers as well as from Indians deemed socially inappropriate. For instance, a newspaper report noted how an Indian passenger holding a second-class ticket was forbidden by the station master [at the behest of a European] to smoke his *hookah* in the upper-class waiting room at the Mughalserai station. Such incidents, the reporter claimed warranted the necessity of separate waiting rooms for upper-class native passengers.[47] Similarly, a report in *Mirat-ul-Hind* demanded separate arrangements for 'native gentlemen and ladies' on the Oudh and Rohilkhand Company's network, claiming it as a 'great boon to the *native nobility and gentry*'.[48] Another newspaper report complained that while anglicised natives used waiting rooms for European passengers sans qualm and lower-class Indian passengers were satisfied with the sheds provided, there were no special arrangements for *educated and well-to-do Hindus* and demanded separate facilities for the aforementioned section of passenger traffic.[49] Historiographically speaking, while Indian passengers' demands for separate waiting rooms from European passengers have received attention; the former's clamouring for separation from other Indians (socially inferior) despite acknowledgement has not yet been adequately analysed. This is not surprising as the demands of separation from Europeans seamlessly dovetails with the existing narrative of Indian railway history.[50] But the presence of the latter is problematic, perhaps also because as the language in which such demands was framed disrupts the idea that railway travel produced homogenised experiences, which expressed itself in unified nationalist and racial sentiments.

Evidently, the demands outlined above demonstrate a desire among 'respectable' Indian passengers to travel in the company of real or imagined social equals. Elite railway travellers expressing such attitudes were not confined to colonial India and can thus be ignored as social anxiety unleashed by the demands of a new mode of transport requiring physical proximity, with a potential to imply social levelling.[51] But given the colonial context of railway operations in India, these demands demonstrate an almost simultaneous attempt to forge a distinct identity underlining both racial and class differences. Once again, such desires on the part of colonised elites are not unique to this context. Though relevant here would be to note that the demands for separate waiting rooms from Europeans exhibits a careful crafting of race identity, that legitimised racial difference while rejecting inferiority, more of which in a subsequent chapter. The demands for separation from lower-class Indian passengers however, are more interesting if only because they reveal that upper-class Indian railway passengers were not as alarmed at the prospect of travelling with Europeans as that of sharing the same space with those considered as socially inferior.

Additionally, the language in which separation was demanded is strident and clearly underscored social rank and distance. Indeed, it is distance that both literally and metaphorically defines the demands by upper-class Indian railway passengers. In other words, these demands demonstrate that social rank mattered; occasionally more than race. Interestingly, at a related level such expressed preference for Europeans rather than socially incompatible compatriots, also takes us back to the question raised above numbers and visibility of Indians travelling in upper-class carriages being denied entry into waiting rooms. Plainly put, if upper-class Indian passengers faced a systematic denial of access to waiting rooms to which presumably Europeans had superior claims; then why would the former prefer using these spaces (as evidenced in the travelogues and newspaper reports), unless the idea of travelling with lower orders was somehow more repugnant than racial prejudice. This suggestion is certainly conjectural; especially in an absence of relevant statistics to prove either. But this explanation at least has the advantage of indicating that Indian railway passengers interpreted experiences of sharing station spaces in a more complex manner than hitherto suggested.

The commercial logic of station spaces: the case of toilets and lighting

Like waiting spaces, toilets at stations and lighting arrangements for platforms and waiting rooms also evolved through railway authorities' pecuniary needs; Indian passenger demands and government interventions. Of these, the provision of toilets, in a striking similarity with waiting space arrangements, received the initial impetus of expansion from government intervention.[52] Railway administrations however, were not unaware of what potential impact of ignoring such basic facilities may have had on the growth of passenger traffic. But the question once again, was of capital outlay. Toilets required more money, both at the level of construction and subsequent maintenance. Furthermore, railway companies claimed that since passenger trains (in which the majority of passengers travelled) had long halts built into their schedules to stop at the principal stations to provide passengers with toilet and refreshment breaks; therefore, building toilets in smaller stations made little financial sense. As such, initially, such facilities were built only at larger stations.[53] Even where such facilities existed official records and reports in Indian language newspapers indicate varying levels of cleanliness and water supply. In most cases the toilet arrangements at stations were inadequate to cope with the demands of the passenger traffic as lower-class carriages transporting the maximum number of passengers lacked in-built latrines. Passengers travelling in these carriages therefore, had to wait until the trains reached larger stations to use the toilets. Consequently, the pressure on such facilities outscored their utility.[54]

Not surprisingly, passengers demanded better toilet arrangements, especially at the smaller, intervening stations. The first response to such passenger demands came from the Eastern Indian Railway Company. In 1865 the Company agreed to expand toilet facilities in smaller stations including Raniganj, Nalhati, Mokama, Danapur and Arah. Approving the additional expenditure entailed in this process, the Board of the Eastern Indian Railway Company noted that the outlay was 'essential to the well-being and reputation of the line'.[55] But mere expansion of the facility was not sufficient. The issue was to keep the toilets and latrines clean. Frequent complaints were made regarding the filthy state of the toilets. Even the Lieutenant Governor of Bengal acknowledged the problem when on an inspection tour he noted that 'it is plain that the latrines are not attended to'.[56] Being directed at the Eastern Indian Railway Company, even the Board of the Company found it hard to ignore such admonitions. In response, the Board recommended periodic inspection of the line and even appointed a sanitary commission to suggest improvements. The report submitted by the Sanitary Commission largely concurred with the views of the Lieutenant Governor, and suggested employment of more cleaners to tackle the problem. Additionally, Cecil Stephenson, the then chairman of the Eastern Indian Railway Company recommended station masters should take responsibility for keeping the toilets clean and attending to this matter as part of their regular duties.[57]

Faced with pressures from above, the company officials in India argued that it was difficult to keep the toilets clean because of 'native habits'. The allegation however, was untrue. The problem was not any insanitary habits of Indian railway passengers, but a reluctance on the part of the Company to employ an adequate number of cleaners in order to reduce operational costs, a decision that affected the condition in which toilets in the stations were kept. Not unexpectedly therefore, it was commercial logic that dictated availability of toilets at stations and their cleanliness. The inspection reports of the Eastern Indian Railway Company for 1865 for instance, claimed that toilets were better kept in stations below Allahabad due to heavier traffic that offered better revenue return, than those between Allahabad and Delhi, which were 'indifferently managed' due to lack of sufficient traffic.[58] Passenger complaints, even by European passengers (the cantonment towns of North-Western provinces provided a steady European passenger traffic) substantiate such differences. In one such complaint a certain Mr Dayne sent a representation to the board of the East Indian Railway Company pointing out the inadequate arrangements for baths at the stations above Allahabad and the conditions of the urinals and the latrines. The complainant was a businessman who frequently travelled on the line between Agra and Calcutta and thus had the vantage of familiarity with the facilities or rather the lack of them.[59]

When it came to upkeep of toilets however, the issue became rather complex. Bigger stations usually had better cleaned toilets and adequate water supply as opposed to smaller ones, with the former also offering better facilities for third-class passengers. But like the waiting spaces, here too, a lack of standardisation can be detected both at the level of policy and implementation, including different facilities afforded by different railway managements. To take an example, on the Eastern Indian Railway Company's network, at bigger stations such as Howrah, Burdwan and Patna, toilets for third-class passengers were usually better attended than in the smaller ones.[60] On the contrary, the toilets for the third-class passengers at the stations managed by the Oudh and Rohilkhand Railway Company for instance, were known for their cleanliness and general upkeep. Reports in Indian language newspapers often positively compared these facilities with those offered by the Eastern Indian Railway Company and chided the latter for lack of concern for the health and well-being of their passengers.[61] Thus clearly, toilet facilities at stations also evolved unevenly, with revenue return usually directing the change.

Unlike waiting arrangements and toilets however, railway companies demonstrated a noticeably early interest in lighting the stations.[62] For instance, as early as 1862, two railway companies: the Calcutta and South Eastern and the Eastern Bengal Railway discussed the possibility of sharing technical facilities and expenses for lighting the stations along their networks with gas lights.[63] Such enthusiasm however, can perhaps be explained by the fact that both the networks were short and therefore expense on lighting was likely to be less. Additionally, one can also detect a desire to introduce a fairly recent technology both to add to the prestige of the railway companies and to attract more passengers. Most other railway networks however, were more prudent and consequently in the initial years of railway operations, the stations were lit with oil lamps. Here too, the service was uneven, with larger stations being better lit than the smaller ones. Though once again, like waiting arrangements discussed above, this general pattern was punctuated. For instance, an official report in 1866 shows that while Burdwan station was insufficiently lit, Bhagalpur station had no such fault.[64]

The complexity of the situation can perhaps be gauged by the fact that the 'Up' platform of the Mokameh station (Eastern Indian Railway Company's network) lacked lighting, while the 'Down' platform enjoyed this facility. For railway companies, despite practical advantages, lighting meant additional expense and was hence circumspectly applied. At a related level, the official logic was that all railway stations did not require lights. At small stations trains, nighttime stops were rare. In larger which carried a maximum number of passengers were scheduled to stop at these stations only during the day;[65] while the faster trains, carrying upper-class passengers stopped at night, with the latter at any rate having access to overnight living arrangements either at the waiting rooms or in nearby hotels or official bungalows. But as the traffic and the railway network expanded, train schedules become more complicated leading to a growing number of passengers spending nights at various stations. Given this, passengers demanded better lighting arrangements.[66]

One of the earliest responses in this regard came from the Eastern Indian railway network. A letter from 1876 from A.M. Rendel, the then agent of the Company described the 'positive disposition' of the Company's Board to light the principal stations of the network with coal gas. The station chosen for the initial experiment was Allahabad, with the coal coming from the Company's coal mines.[67] Howrah station too, received gas lights in the same year, which was even provided in the third-class passenger waiting rooms.[68] The experience, though successful, was abandoned a year later in favour of electric lighting, which was argued to be cheaper, even more so in India than in England and more effective since the machinery needed was simple.[69] After a couple of years of experiments by Louis Schwendler (superintendent of electric government telegraph in India) it was decided to introduce electric lighting at the platforms in Allahabad and Howrah station respectively.[70] By the early 1880s both the Eastern Indian Railway Company and the Great Peninsular Railway – the two longest and biggest railway networks in India shifted to the use of electric lights at the platforms. This shift however was both gradual and uneven with coal gas lighting continuing to be used. But by the late 1880s several big stations on both the networks had electric lighting, which not surprisingly also became an object of explicit admiration in the contemporary travelogues.[71]

Conclusion

The introduction of electric lights, especially the way in which the facility was expanded alongside other modes of lighting once again underscores the centrality of profit in railway administration in colonial India. As noted above, electric lighting was chosen for its economic efficiency. The decision to bring it to Indian railway stations was primarily guided by the fact that coal was more expensive in India than in England. Consequently, electric lighting was introduced in the bigger stations, which attracted more passengers as the investment was thought to be viable. Given this, it is no coincidence that the smaller stations continued with gas lights or oil lamps for a much longer period.[72]

Thus, here too, like waiting facilities and latrines, the growth of station infrastructure was uneven and largely propelled by profit. This clearly suggests a pattern that is familiar from our previous discussions. Profit mattered and indeed dictated the direction of railway operations in colonial India. This becomes clearer when one compares the evolution of station infrastructure in India with that in the UK and USA. Indeed, a global context illustrates well the role of profit in the speculative venture that was the railways in the nineteenth-century world. Such comparisons are also helpful because they highlight that on many occasions, though not all, profit mattered more than the socio-political context. A case in point would be the growth of stations, by which I mean their transformation from basic brick structures to a space where passengers could wait and eat and rest. As foregoing discussion indicates, in India, this process was certainly slow. But in many ways such basic provisions were common to most railway enterprises, particularly in the early stages of operations. In the UK for instance, stations had basic infrastructure, with the smaller local ones usually having indifferent facilities as late as the 1880s.[73] In the USA too, most stations could not boast of decent infrastructure and more often than not small rented shops functioned as the ticket selling offices.[74]

Similarly, whether it was provision of waiting rooms, especially for lower-class passengers or even latrines at stations, easy parallels can be drawn with both the UK and the USA, especially the former at comparable stages of railway development. For instance, in the UK, waiting rooms for third-class passengers were provided in only some city stations, while at most other stations passengers waited on the platforms, huddled together to avoid the rain.[75] Additionally, in the UK, like India, a variety of waiting arrangements co-existed. First-class passengers enjoyed separate waiting rooms, with occasionally separate arrangements for even men and women. The 'general waiting room' however, served everyone else.[76] In the case of lavatories at stations too, similarities are striking. Toilet facilities at the stations in the UK were uneven and often indifferent and this was so even when as in India, the train carriages, particularly the low-class ones lacked in-built toilets up until the end of the nineteenth century.[77]

Interestingly, though not surprisingly, railway companies both in the UK and the USA (perhaps the latter even more than the former) justified absences or slow and uneven growth of station infrastructures on the speculative nature of the railway enterprise that did not allow much investment without a commensurate promise of profit. This, of course, does not take away the colonial context of the railway operations in India. Neither does it neglect the fact that in the UK, despite the nature of the railway enterprise, a powerful legislative force was regularly exerted in the name of 'public good' to introduce better facilities for passengers. Yet as the recent research by Simon Bradley shows, this exertion, though well meaning, had a slow impact and many improvements were long in coming because the railway companies resisted these changes, which they saw as expenses without any secure promise of return. Indeed, it can be suggested that railway companies resisted improvement in station buildings unless it threatened passenger traffic growth and thus profit.[78] Colonial officials in India were certainly cognisant of this reality at 'home' and perhaps it is no coincidence that occasionally while remonstrating railway companies in India references were made to the presence of controlling mechanisms in England, nothing more was suggested or done beyond offering veiled threats to exercise vague government powers.[79]

This I argue was both a product of the familiarity with the UK system and the realisation that however less effective that was and more importantly, the awareness of the benefits of running railways in India with minimal investment for passenger convenience. At a related level, both in India and beyond, such an insistence on profit, either real or imagined I argue, critically contributed to a general lack of standardisation in railway rules and practices.[80] The foregoing discussion certainly supports this conclusion. Evidently, from waiting arrangements to latrines to lighting stations no standard practice existed. Facilities varied from one network to another or even within the same network. More importantly, as in the case of waiting arrangements and availability of toilet facilities at stations showed, even the same group of passengers, in this case the third class, had access to different facilities on different networks. Additionally, rules varied from region to region. It is not without significance that the Eastern Indian Railway Company explained a general gap in facilities between the Bengal Presidency and the North-Western Provinces, claiming that the former was the 'paying portion' of the network and thus deserved more attention than the latter. This clearly suggests a critical role of profit in directing railway facilities. Thus, in the case of station infrastructure too much uniformity in railway rules was more theoretical than real. Contingencies of everyday railway operations, dictated by profit, successfully challenged standardisation of railway rules and practices. At a related level, once again here I suggest that a concern for profit made railway practices fluid and flexible and more importantly, amenable to pressures from all sides including government intervention and passenger negotiations.

Of these, government intervention had institutional advantage. Interestingly, as we saw above, government intervention, though cautiously and limitedly applied, often played an important, at times even a critical role in initiating improvements or admonishing the railway companies for the lack of it. This is curious as the intervention was evidently articulated through a paternal rhetoric, but was also sufficiently careful not to step into what was considered to be the rightful territory of the railway companies, a behaviour largely commensurate with similar practice back in England. Interestingly, and not unlike England, in India too, the pressure exerted by the government bodies worked, though profit often determined the final outcome. Thus, though circumstantially circumscribed, government interventions worked. This I suggest had the effect of buttressing the colonial state's superior position in the context of contending authorities, which as we will shortly see, the former used with considerable panache, especially with the rising Indian political voices.

Passenger negotiations, unlike government intervention, mostly relied on numbers. This as noted earlier, is not surprising since passengers knew the link between numbers and profit and the significance of the latter. It is not without significance that passengers often used uneven facilities on different networks or regions as the rationale for demanding expansion of the same in a more equitable manner. Such awareness reveals a clear knowledge of the significance of profit in railway matters as measures deemed popular were likely to be replicated than those which were not. Not surprisingly therefore, the negotiating tactics, such as complaints to government agencies or petitions involved a tacit or even direct acknowledgement of profit as a motivating factor. One can only interpret the underlining cost factor in Sir Syed's petition demanding waiting sheds for third-class passengers as a clear instance of such awareness. Thus, while lack of standardisation of railway and practices offered a negotiating platform window for improvement, its success critically depended on the prospect of profit.[81] At the same time, though limited, passenger negotiations about station spaces also indicate that railway policies were punctuated by 'native' agency, with Indian passengers influencing the ways in which station spaces evolved.

Given this, I suggest that the nature and consequences of the broader social impact of railway travel experiences filtered through the evolution of station spaces appear much more complex than currently imagined. In the first place, the gradual and uneven growth of station facilities punctuates the notion of uniform station experiences. Facilities varied and thus passenger experiences too.[82] Simply put, if passengers' travel itinerary entailed bigger stations, their experiences were likely to be more positive than those who travelled through smaller stations, while spending only a part of their journey at larger stations, waiting for connecting trains. That such deviations in travel experience were real can be surmised from the fact that the travelogues are largely silent on the theme of station facilities or the lack of it. Once again, this is not surprising, as the authors of these travelogues lived in cities and travelled between one big station to another. More importantly, their silence also reflects that facilities including seemingly standardised rules, varied with the social status of passengers. In itself this is neither surprising, nor unexpected if only because, as noted above, colonial India was not the only place where such incongruities existed. But such divergences do challenge our present historiographical assumptions of a homogenous mass of 'Indian' railway passengers who were evenly discriminated against by uniform and unvariegated railway rules. This, as we saw above, was not true. 'Native gentlemen' had access to facilities that were not available for other not-so-respectable 'natives'.

The acknowledgement in Sir Syed's petition about existing facilities for 'rich and wealthy' passengers, is nothing but instructive. Similarly, Shankar Seth's grievance too, did not allude to lack of facilities for passengers travelling in the upper-class carriages. Such variations evidently cut in both direction, race and social rank, more so because upper-class Indian passengers, like the petitioners themselves, must have had access to the facilities since no reference was made to any preferential treatments based on the colour of skin. Surely, an absence of such a reference is critical, as the language of the petition is assertively political, and thus would not have spared any possibility of criticising policies deemed racially discriminatory. Such evidences certainly challenge the ability of race as the only analytical tool to interpret railway experience in colonial India. Of course, most Indian passengers travelled in low class carriages and thus the question of numbers is raised, underlining the issues of how many experienced differential treatments based on their superior social class. As valid as this argument is, relevant here also would be that not all Indians travelled in low class carriages. A cross-section of Indians, as personal memoirs and travelogues reveal, always travelled in upper-class carriages. In other words, there was a possibility, albeit small, that Indian railway passengers' travel experiences were filtered through social rank.

This was indeed possible as is evident from the silence of the authors of the travelogues on the absence of station facilities. More telling however, both literally and metaphorically, are their references to absence of facilities for lower-class passengers. For instance, Saratchandra Shastri, the author of a Bengali travelogue noted the lack of waiting rooms for third-class passengers at the Bhusawal junction. His description of the ways in which third-class passengers sprawled in and around the station, busying themselves with cooking food and taking care of other needs displays a picturesque scene, which, though not devoid of sympathy was distant and thus clearly indicative of different railway travel experience.[83] In other words, if travel experiences of Indian railway passengers differed, so must their interpretation of these experiences.

Here too, as in previous chapters, I am not attempting to discount race. But the experiences of this small minority significantly illustrate the often-neglected aspect of social rank in the narrative of railway operations in colonial India. Interestingly, the evidence that rank mattered is proffered by the demands of Indian railway passengers for separate waiting rooms for those considered social inferior. The implication is clear. Railway travel practices entailed physical proximity that had the possibility of being interpreted as a social levelling. This prospect was clearly not enjoyed by a section of the Indian railway passengers, who preferred physical separation as symbolic of the social. The consequences of such sensibilities on our understanding of railway travel experiences as a unifying force is self-explanatory and does not require elucidation. Of course, it can be argued that since such demands were not met, the point is rather moot.

This is certainly a valid argument, though only partially, as demands were varyingly met, mostly dictated by profit. For instance, despite demands, separate waiting rooms for different groups of Indian railway passengers meant large additional expenses, which the railway administration did not want to expend. But as we will see in the following chapters, demands for other kinds of separations were met. More importantly, this demand for physical distance I argue, articulated a desire for social control occasionally explicit but mostly implied. This again is not surprising as station spaces were also social spaces and were thus continuously produced and reproduced through social contestation. This process is clearly noticeable in the ways in which issues of access to facilities were played out between Indian passengers, railway companies and government agencies – the three contending groups in this interaction.

A case in point is the petition by Sir Syed Ahmad Khan. Evidently, the petitioners were not asking for the facilities for themselves. It was a plea on the behalf of the 'poor, ignorant masses'. The language of the petition is stridently political, claiming a representational position vis-à-vis the colonial state. In a similar instance, the memorandum by Shankar Seth appropriates the opportunity to claim better facilities on behalf of the passengers. Such posturing by colonised elites was not unique to India and more often than not it was a characteristic feature of the baseline for subsequent anti-colonial politics. In other words, the petitioning on behalf of those who were not able to is neither a new nor particularly innovative discovery. But as the demands for separate waiting rooms for lower-class Indian passengers indicate, these contestations interestingly include a clear desire to enjoy superior access to railway spaces that in turn serves a dual purpose: *one*, claiming an elitist right to represent non-elites in perpetuity; and *two*, using the same logic to deny equality to non-elites. Thus, while there was a general agreement among the aspiring political representatives of the 'hapless masses' that improved facilities to be accorded to the latter; at the same time, there was clear disavowal of equality.

An awareness of this dichotomy, I suggest, is crucial because in many ways this was a mirror image of the paternalistic concerns occasionally expressed by the government bodies – empty and largely devoid of any intent to transform. Interestingly, the language in which government intervention is framed confirms this claim. This is not to claim that government interventions had no impact. As the chapter showed, it did; though within the limits of honouring private enterprise and profit. The latter was especially important since railway management in colonial India moved in and out of government control, and thus interventions were also directed by a desire for sustainable revenue return. But more importantly, government interventions were influenced by a desire to contest a superior claim over railway spaces, over both railway companies and Indian elites. Interestingly, as noted above, on several occasions an appeal to intervene from Indian railway passengers provided the occasion to legitimise the role of the colonial state as an arbiter. This is palpable in the language of the interventions wherein the paternalistic tone of imperial beneficence is unmistakably present. Such occasions therefore offered readymade opportunities to contest rival claims made by railway companies or elite Indian railway passengers.

Admonitions to railway companies were certainly a way of disregarding the formers' claims over passenger welfare and thus claiming a dubious but nevertheless moral high ground. But the message to Indians – either as passengers or as elite petitioners was more critical. It was certainly a way of hinting at the colonial state as the protectors (*maa, baap, sarkar*) of the poor – as opposed to Indian elites. Moreover, as the nineteenth century progressed, these utterances increasingly became smug and often empty; though retaining the characteristic of criticising the growing Indian anti-colonial movement as elitist and thus out-of-touch with the realities of 'real' India. Needless to say, passenger petitions seeking government intervention often offered the welcome and even convenient beating stick.

This chapter has shown that station spaces were contested sites of political and social control. Furthermore, this contestation, as the foregoing discussion suggests, shaped the production and the reproduction of these spaces by weakening the ability of any contending group to assert their superior rights over station spaces. As such, station spaces, as argued in current historiographical assumption were not produced only through disciplinary impetus of the colonial state. On the contrary, Indian passengers participated in the process and shaped its outcome. As such, this chapter suggests that although Indian passenger experiences of station spaces created opportunities for shared feelings (national or racial); it also produced heterogeneous and not-so-unifying impulses.

Notes

1. M. Twain, *The Complete Works of Mark Twain: Following the Equator*, Volume 2, (New York, Harper and Brother, 1925), p. 76.
2. Passengers, especially those who travelled in lower-class carriages, thronged railway stations at almost all hours of day and night, an issue that often elicited comments from contemporary observers. See the previous chapters as to why lower-class passengers had to endure longer hours at stations.
3. Here the word forced imply necessities of railway travel that translated in a relatively small place being occupied by several people at the same time.
4. See Chapter 2.
5. Station spaces include: platforms; waiting rooms and sheds and toilets at the stations.
6. Here station infrastructure includes station/platform lighting.
7. E. Davidson, *The Railways of India: with an account of their rise, progress, and construction written with the aid of the records of the India Office* (London, E. & F.N. Spon, 1868), p. 3. Interestingly, in the pages of his book, Davidson claimed that he was himself witness to the scene quoted above and noted 'the horror of the high-caste baboo, when, on entering the carriage, he saw the sweeper'. Davidson notes that the high-caste *baboo* in question finally took his position in the carriage when the guard informed him that the alternative was to be left behind. The next chapter will focus on railway carriages as contested social spaces.
8. See R.M. Stephenson, 'Report upon the practicability and advantages of the introduction of railways into British India with the official correspondence with the Bengal Government and full statistical data respecting the existing trade upon the line connecting Calcutta with Mirzapore, Benaras, Allahabad and the North-West frontier', 1844, London, L/PWD/2/43, IOR. The individuals responding to Stephenson included: Moti Lal Seal, Ram Gopal Ghosh and Debendranath Tagore. Of these, Ram Gopal Ghosh's response especially underscored how railway travel will denude hold of caste prejudice among Bengalis/Indians.
9. F.R. Vicajee, *Political and Social Effects of Railways in India*: Being a paper read before the National Indian Association, London, on 25 May 1875 (London, R. Clay, Sons and Taylor, 1875), p. 36.
10. D. Chakrabarty, 'The Colonial context of Bengal Renaissance: a note on early railway-thinking in Bengal', *Indian Economic and Social History Review*, II, 1 (March 1974), pp. 92–111.
11. Similar suggestions have been made by some recent (and not-so-recent) forays into history of science and technology in colonial India. For instance, see the introduction in A. Ramnath, *The Birth of an Indian Profession: Engineers, Industry, and the State, 1900–1947* (New Delhi, Oxford University Press, 2017). Also, S. Sarkar, 'Technical Content and Colonial Context: Situating Technical Knowledge in Nineteenth Century Bengal', *Social Scientist*, 38, 1/2, 2010, pp. 37–52; P. Chakrabarti, *Western Science in Modern India: Metropolitan Methods, Colonial Practices* (Ranikhet, Permanent Black, 2004); D. Arnold, 'Europe, technology, and colonialism in the 20th century', *History and Technology: An International Journal*, 21, 1, 2006, pp. 85–106.
12. Vernacular tracts (in Bengali and Hindi) about railway technology and its positive social impact suggest a wider audience than a handful of elites. See Introduction, section II.
13. For a succinct summary of Gandhi's views on technology, see M.K. Gandhi, *Hind Swaraj* (Ahmedabad, Navjivan, 2008). Though Gandhi's views on technology became popular and influential, there was no dearth of detractors. For instance, while physicists like M.N. Saha favoured science-based industry outright, individuals such as P.C. Ray, while supporting Gandhi's programme of social and economic regeneration of rural India, continued to emphasise role of technology in the process. In the long run, as is well-known, independent India under Nehru deviated from Gandhian notions

and chose science and technology for economic growth and progress. See D. Kumar, 'Reconstructing India: Disunity in the Science and Technology for Development Discourse, 1900–1947', *Osiris*, 2nd series, 15, 2000, pp. 241–257; R. Chopra, *Technology and Nationalism in India: cultural negotiations from colonialism to cyberspace* (New York, Cumbria Press, 2008), especially the introduction and Chapters 3 and 4.

14 M. Goswami, *Producing India: From colonial economy to national space* (Chicago, University of Chicago Press, 2004), Chapter 3; L. Bear, *Lines of the Nation: Indian Railway Workers, Bureaucracy, and the Intimate Historical Self* (New York, Columbia University Press, 2007), Part I, Chapter 2; R. Prasad, *Tracks of Change: Railways and Everyday Life in Colonial India* (New Delhi, Cambridge University Press, 2015), Chapters 1 and 2.

15 Bear suggests that railway spaces and regulations such as marshalling passengers in and out of train carriages to outside the stations made surveillance easy, subjecting colonised bodies to control hitherto unexperienced. Bear, *Lines of the Nation*, pp. 42–43. Recently Smritikumar Sarkar has made a similar though not identical observation. See S. Sarkar, *Technology and Rural Change in Eastern India, 1830–1980* (New Delhi, Oxford University Press, 2014), pp. 290–292.

16 Railway Gazette: A journal of transportation, engineering, docks, harbours, contracts and railway news (Special Indian Railway Number, May 1913). Emphasis mine.

17 R. Kipling, *Kim* (London, Wordsworth Classics, 2009), p. 52.

18 Visualising the colonised 'other' has long drawn critical and sophisticated scholarly attention. See (among others) M.L. Pratt, *Imperial Eyes: Travel Writing and Transculturation* (New York, Routledge, 2008); D. Spurr, *The Rhetoric of Empire: colonial discourse in journalism, travel writing and imperial administration* (Durham and London, Duke University Press, 1993).

19 J. Danvers, 'Personal Inspection Report', published in the Report Submitted to the Secretary of State for India in Council for Railway in India, Parliamentary Paper (Command Number 1584), 1876, IOR.

20 The railway stations were meant to convey a range of meanings symbolising the colonial state's ability to control India as well as advanced technical knowledge. See T.R. Metcalfe, *An Imperial Vision: Indian Architecture and Britain's Raj* (New Delhi, Oxford University Press, 2002); V. Oldenburg, *The making of colonial Lucknow, 1856–1877* (New Jersey, Princeton University Press, 1984); and Bear, *Lines of the Nation*, pp. 36–45.

21 See A.M. Rendel's 'Report on the Progress of Eastern Indian Railway Company', 1858 in L/PWD/2/63 Home Correspondence 'B' – copies of letters sent, 1849–1879, IOR.

22 'Administration of railways in Bengal', Circular No. 13, dated 27 August 1864, from Colonel R. Strachey, Secretary to Government of India, [PWD] to the Joint Secretary, Government of Bengal, [PWD] in the proceedings of the Railway Department, Government of Bengal, P/163/33, 1864, IOR. Provision of refreshment rooms and eating arrangements for Indian passengers is discussed in Chapter 5.

23 Ibid. Emphasis mine.

24 Letter to Edward Palmer, Agent, East Indian Railway Company, dated December 1864, Calcutta, from The Secretary, Board of Directors, East Indian Railway Company, London, in Letters to and from East Indian Railway Company, L/PWD/2/80, IOR.

25 Letters to the agent of the East Indian Railway Company, dated February 1865 with the Board's observation to documents sent in December 1864, in Letters to and from East Indian Railway Company, L/PWD/2/81, IOR.

26 Ibid.

27 Memorandum on Report of the Sanitary Commissioner, dated June 1865, in Letters to and from East Indian Railway Company, L/PWD/2/81, IOR.

104   *A shared space?*

28 Ibid. The chosen stations were: Howrah, Burdwan, Raniganj, Sahebganj, Bhagalpur, Jamalpur, Mokama, Danapur, Buxar, Patna, Bankipur and Arah.
29 'Native Passengers Travelling by Rail', by L.C. Abbott, Officiating Under Secretary to the Government of Bengal to the Secretary to the Government of India Public Works Department, State Railways, dated 24 July 1874, in Proceedings of the Railway Department, Bengal P/265, IOR.
30 East Indian Railway Company's inspection report for the lower division [Bengal] for the second quarter of 1866 in Miscellany Railway Letters, L/PWD/2/190 (1865–1867), IOR.
31 Though boundaries of the Bengal Presidency changed over time and included different regions at different periods, generally Bengal proper and stations up to Patna enjoyed better facilities than those in the upper division.
32 The Humble Petition of the British Indian Association, dated 16 October 1866 from Syud Ahmed, Secretary and others, British Indian Association, North-Western Provinces to His Excellency the Viceroy and Governor-General of India in Council, in Miscellany Railway Letters, L/PWD/2/190 (1865–1867), IOR.
33 For similar absences along the Great Indian Peninsular Railway Company's network, see the memorandum by Honourable V.J. Sunkersett in Miscellany Railway Letters, L/PWD/2/190, IOR.
34 'Complaint of natives intending passengers being kept outside the Kooshtea station', dated 10 February 1870, from Ram Chunder Lahoree and others, to the Honourable Lieutenant Governor of Bengal in Railway Proceedings, Bengal, P/433/49, IOR.
35 Extract of a report on Native papers for the week ending 5 March 1870, in Railway Proceedings, Bengal, P/433/49, IOR. Emphasis mine.
36 Note from Major F.S. Taylor Joint Secretary to the Government of Bengal, Public Works Department, Railway Branch, to the Secretary to the Government of India, Foreign Department, dated 14 April 1870, in Railway Proceedings, Bengal, P/433/49, IOR.
37 Eastern Indian Railway Company: Inspection Report of the lower division of the second quarter of 1866, in Miscellany Railway Letters, L/PWD/2/190 (1865–1867), IOR.
38 Letters to the agent in Calcutta dated July 1876, in Letters to and from Eastern Indian Railway Company, L/PWD/2/92, IOR.
39 Proposal to construct waiting and refreshment rooms for natives at Burdwan, Sahebganj, Danapur and Cawnpore, in Extract from minutes of official meeting held on 27 May 1886 in Railway Proceedings, Bengal, P/433/44, IOR.
40 *Bharat Mihir*, 9 November 1876 and *Navavibhakar*, 9 October 1882, in Newspaper Reports from Bengal, L/R/5/2, and L/R/5/8, IOR. Reports in these Indian languages newspapers argued that the Eastern Indian Railway Company should emulate the Oudh and Rohilkhand railway network in providing better facilities for third-class waiting passengers and even underlined the link with profit by claiming that the former should not shy away from the expenses as it earned reasonable revenue return.
41 Memorandum on the report of the sanitary commissioner, dated June 1865, in Letters to and from Eastern Indian Railway Company, L/PWD/2/81, IOR.
42 For instance, Surendranath Ray and Dharani Kanta Lahiri Chaudhuri authors of Bengali travelogues published in the early decades of the twentieth century complained about lack of cleanliness in upper-class waiting rooms. See D. Lahiri Chaudhuri, *Bharat Bhraman* (Calcutta, Kuntolin Press, 1908), p. 223; and S.N. Ray, *Uttar-Bharat Bhraman* (Calcutta, Pashupati Press, 1907), p. 197.
43 R. Prasad, *Tracks of Change: Railways and Everyday Life in Colonial India* (Cambridge University Press, Delhi, 2015), pp. 90–96.
44 See Chapter 2, endnote 4.

45 For instance, Bengali poet and colonial administrator Navin Chandra Sen's travelogue 'Prabaser Patra' is a compilation of letters the author wrote to his wife sitting at waiting rooms of different railway stations while taking a break between legs of his journey. See N. Sen, *Prabaser Patra: Bharater Bhraman Vrittanta* (Calcutta [originally published 1875] Goshtha Vihari, 1914), see publisher's note before preface. Authors such as Atul Chandra Mitra described their positive experience with European station masters. A. Mitra, *Prabas Prasoon: katipay pauranik sthaner itihas* (Purulia, 1915), p. 12. For more on this theme see Chapter 7.
46 I am not denying exclusionary and discriminatory behaviour against Indian passengers. I am merely suggesting that passengers had different experiences, which indicates a more complex formulation than denial based on race.
47 *The Hindustani*, 6 April 1890, in Native Newspaper Reports, North-Western Provinces, L/R/5/67, IOR.
48 *Mirat-ul-Hind*, 15 December 1878, in Native Newspaper Reports, North-Western Provinces, L/R/5/55, IOR. Emphasis mine.
49 *Hindustan*, 13 October 1900, in Native Newspaper Reports, North-Western Provinces, L/R/5/77, IOR. Emphasis mine.
50 In current historiography, such demands are interpreted (quite rightly) as Indian passengers wanting to avoid Europeans in transit to preclude or reduce the possibilities of ill-treatment on grounds of race.
51 For similar if not identical concerns outside the Indian context, see S. Bradley, *The Railways: Nation, Network and People* (London, Profile Books, 2015), pp. 74–78.
52 Circular (no. 13) dated 27 August 1864 from Colonel R. Strachey, Secretary to Government of India, Public Works Department to Joint Secretary to Government of Bengal, Public Works Department, Railway Branch, in Railway Proceedings, Bengal, P/163/33, IOR.
53 For instance, the stations with toilet facilities on the East Indian Railway Company's network included, Howrah, Burdwan, Bhagalpur, Jamalpur, Patna, Bankipur, Buxar, Benaras, Allahabad, Kanpur, Agra and Delhi. See Minutes of a special meeting held at the Agent's office, East Indian Railway Company, on Wednesday 25 January 1865 in Proceedings of the Railway Department, Government of Bengal, P/163/35, IOR.
54 *Akhbar-i-Alam*, 23 March 1871, in Native Newspaper Reports, North-Western Provinces L/R/5/48; also, *Sulabha Samachar*, 3 November 1877, in Indian Newspaper Reports: Bengal, L/R/5/3, IOR.
55 Memorandum on Report of the Sanitary Commissioner, in Letters from Eastern Indian Railway Company, L/PWD/2/81, 1865, IOR.
56 Letter to the Agent of the East Indian Railway Company, dated August 1869, in Letters to and from the East Indian Railway Company, L/PWD/2/85, IOR.
57 'Note on question of keeping latrines clean and changing lamps of passenger carriages at about midnight', from Cecil Stephenson, Chairman Board of Agency, East Indian Railway Company to the Traffic Manager, East Indian Rail, Jamalpur, dated 7 June 1869, in Proceedings of the Railway Department, Government of Bengal, P/433/47 (1869), IOR.
58 Excerpts from the Inspection Reports of the Eastern Indian Railway Company for the year 1864–1865 in a letter dated August 1865 to the Agent of the Eastern Indian Railway Company in Calcutta, in Letters to and from Eastern Indian Railway Company, L/PWD/2/81, IOR.
59 Letter to the agent of the Eastern Indian Railway Company in Calcutta, dated February 1865, in Letters to and from, Eastern Indian Railway Company, L/PWD/2/81, IOR.
60 Excerpt from the report of the Sanitary Commission in the Eastern Indian Railway Company's inspection report of the lower division [Bengal] for the second quarter of 1866 in Miscellany Railway Letters, L/PWD/2/190, IOR.

61 Excerpts from Indian languages newspaper reports quoted in Letters to the agent of the Eastern Indian Railway Company, dated 5 November 1875, in L/PWD/2/91, IOR.
62 This attention I suggest, reveals a practical need to tackle crimes that were rife in station precincts. See A. Mukhopadhyay, 'Lost in Transit? Railway Crimes and the Regime of Control in Colonial India', in S. Ghosh, E. Rashkow and U. Chakrabarti (eds), *Memory, Identity and the Colonial Encounter in India: Essays in Honour of Peter Robb* (New Delhi, Routledge, 2017).
63 Letter to the agent of the Company, dated 17 January 1862, in Letters to and from Railway Companies, 'C' Series, Register VIII, Calcutta and South-Eastern Railway, L/PWD/2/164, IOR.
64 Eastern Indian Railway Company's Inspection Report of the lower division of Bengal for the second quarter of 1866, in Miscellany Railway Letters, L/PWD/2/190 IOR.
65 See Chapter 1.
66 Passenger demanded better lighting of railway stations on the Awadh and Rohilkhand Railway Company's network in the first year (1873–1874) of its operations. This is not surprising as passengers by this time had varying experiences of station lighting over other networks. See Administration of the Guaranteed Railways: Report of the Consulting Engineer to the Government of India on the Oudh and Rohilkhand railway for the financial year 1873–1874, in V/24/3582, IOR.
67 Letter from the agent of the Eastern Indian Railway Company to the Board of Directors, dated May 1876 in Letters to and from Railway Companies, Eastern Indian Railway Company, L/PWD/2/92, IOR.
68 Ibid.
69 The Chairman of the Eastern Indian Railway Company visited the ironworks at Stockton to inspect the working of the lighting system and found it to his satisfaction. Letter from A.M. Rendel, the agent of the Eastern Indian Railway Company to the Board of Directors, dated April 1877, in Letters to and from Railway Companies, Eastern Indian Railway Company, L/PWD/2/93, IOR.
70 'Electric lighting and Allahabad and Howrah stations' in Letter from the agent of the Eastern Indian Railway Company to the Board of Directors, dated February 1879, in Letters to and from Railway Companies, Eastern Indian Railway Company, L/PWD/2/95, IOR.
71 See P. Basu, 'Travels in north India', 1887, in *Tracts Volume, Oriental and India Office Collection*, Volume 697, IOR. Authors of other travelogues too comment on electric lighting and the pleasing effect it had on the station 'scenes'. See Ray, 'Uttar Bharat', p. 35; D.C. Ray, *Debganer Martye Agaman* (Calcutta [originally published 1880], Dey's Publication, re-print 1984), p. 55; H. Devi, *London ki Yatra* (Lahore, 1885), p. 9; and Mitra, 'Prabas Prasoon', p. 6. Between them, these authors noted electric lights at Howrah, Mokameh, Bankipur, Allahabad, Jabalpur, Katni, Tundla, Agra and Delhi stations.
72 For instance, a Bengali novel set in the early decades of the twentieth century refers to gas lights on the stations of the Eastern Bengal State Railway Network in 1912. N. Chakrabarti, *Pitripurush* (Calcutta, Ananda, 1973), p. 73.
73 D. Turner, *Victorian and Edwardian Railway Travel* (Great Britain, Shire Publications, 2013), pp. 7–8; also J. Simmons and G. Biddle, *The Oxford Companion to British Railway History* (Oxford, Oxford University Press, New York, 2000), pp. 473–474.
74 C. Wolmar, *The Great Railroad Revolution: The History of Trains in America* (USA, PublicAffairs, 2013), Chapter 3.
75 Bradley, 'The Railways', pp. 136 and 469. In USA too, this was common, perhaps even more than in the UK, see Wolmar, 'The Great Railroad', Chapter 3.
76 Bradley, 'The Railways', p. 469.
77 Bradley, 'The Railways', pp. 472, 201–202.

78 Bradley, 'The Railways'. This theme runs through most of the chapters in this excellent volume. Also see a similar point made in Turner, 'Victorian and Edwardian', p. 8.
79 See the excerpt quoted above (note 22) from a note by Richard Strachey, especially the italicised portions for the comparison with the UK and the threats of intervention.
80 Here, however, the discussion will be primarily about colonial India.
81 For instance, despite demands by Indian passengers, separate waiting rooms were never built for different groups of passengers as it would have had inflated expenses beyond control.
82 For instance, third-class passengers waiting for trains at the Awadh and Rohilkhand Company's stations had a different experience then say passengers waiting at Kanpur on the Eastern Indian Railway Company's network.
83 S. Shastri, *Dakshinapath Bhraman* (Calcutta, B. Banerjee and Company, 1911), p. 130.

4 Chariots of equality?

Travelling in railway carriages and social transformation in colonial India

Saratchandra Shastri, the author of a Bengali travelogue denied a group of passengers entry into the intermediate carriage in which he was travelling because they were Muslims and he preferred to travel alone.[1] In another instance, Manomohan Basu, the author of another Bengali travelogue, took turns with his servant to stand at the carriage door through the night to ensure that other passengers did not force their way into the carriage in which they were travelling. Basu claimed that such an action was deemed necessary because he wanted to travel in comfort, but did not relish the idea of paying more money for a reserved compartment and because their travelling coincided with an important Hindu religious occasion, crowds at the stations en route to Benaras were anticipated.[2] Evidently, these instances underscore the idea that railway passengers in colonial India faced a real possibility of travelling in overcrowded carriages, surely a prospect not welcomed by most travellers. Moreover, these instances suggest that over-crowding, especially on occasions such as important religious gatherings, was not always confined to lower-class carriages and both literally and metaphorically spilled over to the upper-class carriages.[3]

But here I suggest that there is more to these examples than meet the eye. The authors' behaviour was not merely an expression of anxiety at the possibility of travelling long distances in a crowded space and thus having limited opportunity for enjoying physical comforts such as a good night's sleep. On the contrary, these denials or even resistance to share carriage space with others, I argue, indicate that railway carriages were contested social spaces, wherein passenger interactions were clearly influenced by the idea of class, caste or religious affiliation. Also, while Saratchandra Shastri's denial of entrance to Muslim passengers can be conveniently explained and even dismissed as yet further proof of the growing antagonism between Hindus and Muslims in the late nineteenth century, and thus adds little to our existing knowledge; the response of Manomohan Basu, I argue, requires more explication than we currently possess.

At a related level, such evidence of refusal to share carriage space with others having valid tickets, alongside a steady demand for separate carriages for passengers of every possible variety in the contemporary newspapers,[4] critically challenges the idea that railway carriages were successful agents of imposing railway travel-discipline that coerced 'colonised bodies' to function in specified ways imposed from above. Evidently, as the examples used above suggest, railway passengers possessed and demonstrated more agency than presently imagined. In short, as shown in preceding chapters, here too, such instances show gaps between reality and rhetoric of railway travel-discipline.

Clearly, travel-discipline was influenced by official policies, that is, selling more tickets than the carriages could carry. But it was also influenced by Indian passengers. If the descriptions quoted above are anything to go by, then passengers, like Shastri or Basu (and possibly others), even possessed the ability to subvert railway travel-discipline. Simply put, if overcrowding was the norm, then some passengers bypassed it either by reserving a carriage and thus precluding the possibility of sharing space with others or by denying entry to others on grounds of religious or other social differences. Either way, this has the effect of challenging the demands of railway travel-discipline. Last but not least, these episodes also suggest that passenger travel experiences of railway carriages varied, with social status of the travellers often determining the former. It will not be unfair to assume that the travel experiences of Shastri and Basu, both possessing costlier intermediate class tickets and in the case of the latter, travelling with a servant in tow, differed from those whom they had successfully prevented from entering carriages. Given this, these examples provide me with a critical entry point to reappraise our historical understanding of train carriages as spaces of imposition of railway travel-discipline that in turn contributed to the creation of homogenous racial/national experiences with wider social implications.

Confined bodies, unfettered minds? Railway carriages in colonial India

> As they [Indians] go to and fro, they will see and learn much that they never thought of before. *There will also be more intercourse and friction. The power of caste will likewise be shaken.* Rather than pay for his fare, a high caste Hindoo travels in the same carriage with a fellow creature whose presence in the same room would be considered pollution.[5]

Juland Danvers, a resident of the upper echelons of the colonial Indian railway administration clearly had an optimistic notion of the ability of railway travel to propel wider social change in colonial India. As argued before, Danvers and many colonial administrators like him expected various aspects of railway travel, most notably the experience of close physical proximity in a railway carriage, to alter Indian society by breaking down the rigid barriers of caste and religious distinctions. And though Danvers did allude to friction alongside intercourse; colonial administrators claimed that the impact of railway travel on Indian society would be largely positive, with older notions of identities (caste or religious) eventually giving way to a common national identity. As in the case of station spaces, here too, our current historiographical assumptions broadly correspond with such lofty claims, though not without a vital disagreement. Unlike the colonial proponents of railways in India, post-colonial scholars claim that it was racial discrimination, especially the experiences of travelling in crowded, insanitary carriages and the ill-treatment and harassment at the hands of railway employees 'amplified the hierarchies of colonial society'; and consequently, forged a shared common bond among Indian railway passengers.[6] As a related point, Manu Goswami and Laura Bear have argued that railway carriages were spaces wherein Indian passengers experienced the disciplinary impetus of the colonial state more powerfully (as compared to say station spaces) given their physical confinement in small, often cramped carriages.[7] As such, Indian railway passengers' experiences of travelling in railway carriages produced affiliation underpinned by shared racial/national sentiments.

These analyses are certainly accurate. There can be little doubt that 'hierarchies of colonial societies materialised in the space of railway carriages'.[8] Also, railway travel-discipline, especially as expressed through locked and crowded third-class carriages, can be interpreted as the widening ambit of the presence of the colonial state in the lives of the colonised subjects. But as Ritika Prasad's recent analysis shows, Indian railway passengers' experiences of travelling in carriages were also shot through with many complications that hitherto has been largely overlooked by post-colonial scholarship.[9] Simply put, Indian passengers' experiences of railway carriages varied. Pushing this argument in a more radical direction, in this chapter I suggest that not only did Indian passengers' experiences of railway carriages vary; but their interpretations of these experiences also differed. At a related level, I argue that the presence of diverse experiences and interpretations also indicate a less pervasive and effective role of railway carriages as a disciplinary tool of colonial control. After all, if railway travel-discipline was uniformly imposed from above, then the likelihood of diverse passenger experiences was negligible if not non-existent.

But as the examples in the opening paragraphs of the chapter indicate, one cannot deny Indian passenger experiences varied. Nor can one claim that such experiences were interpreted in ways that produced only racial or national affinities. In other words, while agreeing in principle to the point made by Manu Goswami about the inability of the colonial project to 'colonize consciousness'; I argue that Indian passenger experiences of carriage spaces was more complex and display Indian agency, though evidently not always in the direction hitherto suggested. Additionally, such divergences indicate that the category of Indian railway passenger needs more nuanced explication, more of which later. Here however, it will be sufficient to note that clearly not all passengers were similarly treated either by the railway administrations or by their fellow passengers – a process that I suggest holds the key to understanding diverse interpretations of railway experiences.

This chapter therefore, moves beyond our notion of railway carriage travel experiences as 'mobile incarceration',[10] inasmuch as it offers a historiographical as well as a methodological departure. Historiographically speaking, the chapter focuses exclusively on railway carriages, expanding the purview of analysis to all kinds of carriages, a focus missing in existing scholarship. For instance, the chapter discusses in detail intermediate class carriages and experiences emerging therein, a theme that hitherto has received at best scant and at worst no scholarly attention. At a methodological level, the departure is mainly visible in the attention paid to a wide range of themes, many of which are either absent or have received passing reference in current historiography. In other words, while this chapter discusses overcrowding; provisions of *zenana* carriages and lack of lavatories in lower-class carriages; it also focuses on lighting in carriages and the debate surrounding benches or lack of them in third- or fourth-class carriages.

The decision to focus on such a diverse range of themes has been influenced by a variety of factors that include: new and hitherto unexplored archival evidence; my methodological aim to interrogate railway carriages as social spaces as opposed to merely colonised spaces; and last but not least by the amount of the attention some of these themes, such as overcrowding, continue to receive in current scholarly debate. This last point is significant also because while I broadly agree with the conclusions reached by post-colonial scholars on issues such as overcrowding or *zenana* carriages; continued concentration on the same analytical indices I think, has had the inadvertent consequence of both overlooking vital evidence that reflects contrary impulses; and analysing the role of railway carriages as spaces in which Indian railway passengers negotiated with the railway administrations. The latter, I argue is particularly critical because though fraught with inequality, this process, as I hinted above, also provides occasion to display the ways in which passenger experiences varied, thereby producing diverse interpretations. In short, this chapter suggests diverse outcomes of railway carriage experiences, while indicating that confined and 'colonised bodies' behaved in complex manner, displaying agency.

Black hole or football field: overcrowding in railway carriages

> Travelling by rail very much resembles migrating in one vast colony, or setting out together in a whole moving town or caravan.[11]
>
> When the train starts to move [I was told] one has to sit tight, gathering all strength of the body as the jolt of the movement throws off people to different directions. [. . .] But when the train started to move smoothly without any hint of possible [bodily] danger, I felt sad.[12]

Railway carriages were possibly the most novel site of railway travel practice to which passengers had to adapt. The experience of being in a closed carriage with a number of strangers while moving at an average speed of 15 miles per hour was at one level, both novel and exciting, and at another, somewhat alarming. If one adds to this the long hours or even days a train journey took in the nineteenth century, then tediousness and fatigue too, gets added to the list of feelings railway travellers had to endure. In short, as the quotes by Bholanath Chandra and Rabindranath Tagore suggest, travelling in railway carriages entailed both social and physical adjustment.[13] Certainly, pre-railway travellers too, shared somewhat similar experiences. But what made railway carriages unique was the number of people who took to trains, thus magnifying the dimensions of both physical and social adjustments. Additionally, the conditions of railway travel, particularly the fact that passengers could not alight from the train carriages anywhere (except at scheduled halts) or anytime even if they found the travelling conditions unappealing, had the potential of making the confinement more galling. Thus, travelling in railway carriages added a degree of inflexibility that was integral to the mode of transport.

Needless to say, more often than not, the degree of this inflexibility and by implication therefore, the nature of railway carriage experience varied, depending upon the class of carriage in which the passengers travelled.[14] This leeway was particularly evident in the amount of space allocated to each passenger inside the carriages. Upper-class passengers undoubtedly enjoyed more elbow room (pun intended) than those travelling in the lower-class ones. But statistically speaking, even on a global scale, the number of passengers who travelled in lower-class carriages usually outnumbered those who travelled upper class. Thus, broadly speaking, for a large section of railway passengers across the world, travelling in crowded lower-class carriages was an integral component of wider travel experience.[15] This was particularly true in the context of colonial India wherein most passengers, though certainly not all, travelled in lower-class carriages. The issue was also exacerbated by the number of passengers that trains in colonial India carried.[16] Given this, in colonial India, for passengers travelling in lower-class carriages, over-crowding was the norm rather than the exception.

Third-class carriages had been overcrowded ever since the commencement of railway operations in colonial India. Consequently, most railway passengers experienced travelling in extremely cramped spaces. The ubiquity of the experience was such that contemporary accounts, both official and non-official, record overcrowding. A satirical Bengali novel published in 1863 graphically described the travails of third-class passengers who were forced by the railway employees to enter already full carriages. In a comment that can be interpreted as an act of political subversion, the author claimed that the experiences of these third-class passengers would have had the effect of assuaging the outraged feelings of even the survivors of the Black Hole.[17] Another Bengali tract published in the same year (1863) underlined the unpleasantness that the passengers felt in overcrowded carriages in a more lurid sense. Hinting at the way in which the forced proximity invaded physical space and provided occasion for unwanted bodily contact, the author suggested that during peak time in suburban commuter trains one barely had the ability to detect 'who was touching whose arse'.[18] In the same year, an anonymous passenger letter to the editor of *The Englishman* noted that the third-class carriages were overcrowded in a 'disgraceful' manner.[19]

One can go on adding such instances, but the drift is clear and thus does not warrant further illustration. But relevant here would be to note that while in normal circumstances overcrowding was bad enough, during big or special religious festivals the situation worsened.[20] Also, the effect of overcrowding was more sharply felt in the third-class carriages because for a number of years after the commencement of the railway operations these were kept locked from the outside and were opened at bigger stations where passengers where permitted to alight for refreshment and other personal needs. Though varyingly implemented by different railway networks and in different regions and not even peculiar to colonial India, the practice however, did enhance the feeling of forced confinement.[21] Fourth-class passengers faced even worse travelling conditions than their counterparts in third-class carriages. As discussed in Chapter 2, often called 'coolie' class carriages, fourth-class compartments were mere enclosed boxes, without seats or venetian blinds, wherein passengers were forced to spend the duration of their journey in utter and complete discomfort. The degree of discomfort can be gauged by the fact that in the fourth-class carriages belonging to the Eastern Indian Railway Company, the authorised number of passengers for each carriage was 75.[22]

In one particular instance, doctor F.N. Macnamara and the superintendent of labour transport of Calcutta, bitterly complained to the Agent of the Eastern Bengal Railway Company and to the wider medical community about the 'torture' that was inflicted on 'coolies' heading for the tea gardens of Assam via Kushtia. These labourers boarded the fourth-class carriages of the Eastern Bengal Railway Company at Sealdah, the Calcutta terminus of the network, and here they were packed into the carriages in a group of 60–70 persons.[23] Also, being passengers travelling in lower-class carriages, the labourers were not allowed to get off at the intervening stations even for attending calls of nature, as a result of which after a six hour journey when they arrived at the destination, the carriages were usually in an 'abominable' state. This however, was not an isolated incident. At the administrative level, too, there was an awareness that fourth-class passengers were carried 'like cattle' and in a manner 'opposed to civilised ideas'.[24]

But overcrowding, as the introductory paragraphs alluded, also afflicted passengers travelling in upper class carriages. Though such cases were few when compared to the ubiquitous crowding of lower-class carriages and consequently the suffering of passengers was less; nonetheless, travelogues, stray official documents and even contemporary newspaper reports attest to overcrowding in upper-class carriages. Judging by the nature of the complaints, especially the reports in the Indian newspapers, it seems that intermediate class passengers faced overcrowding more than their first or second-class counterparts. Broadly speaking, overcrowding in intermediate class carriages was a product of the following factors. *One*, third-class passengers, often without a ticket for intermediate class, went in the carriages, either by force or if by chance they found it empty. *Two*, intermediate class carriages were a popular choice of travel, especially for those who considered themselves sufficiently respectable to not mix with third-class passengers but clearly could not afford a second-class ticket. The occurrence of the former is not surprising given the fact that the intermediate class carriages were most proximate (in physical as well as in the tariff sense) to the third class and thus were most likely to bear the brunt of overflowing third-class carriages. Passenger grievances in newspaper reports and acerbic comments of the authors of some of the travelogues certainly support this hypothesis.

For instance, a newspaper report in *Akhbar-i-Alam* complained about insufficient accommodation in intermediate class carriages.[25] Echoing similar sentiments, 'Professor' Priyanath Bose, the owner and manager of the Great Bengal Circus, begrudged his experience of travelling in a crowded intermediate class carriage on his way to Porbandar, during the *durga puja* season. Bose complained that his plight (he had to sleep in the hanging bed) was due to the fact that all second-class carriages, wherein he originally intended to travel were 'reserved' by groups of Bengalis heading for either Mathura-Vrindavan or Benaras.[26] Similarly, Surendranath Ray, the author of another Bengali travelogue referred to overcrowding in intermediate carriages while choosing a seat for his overnight travel to Benaras. Though, unlike Basu, Ray noted that he chose the hanging bed because once mounted, the seat afforded the safety of seclusion amid the crowd and would thus allow him the luxury of sleeping through the journey.[27] The most damning criticism of overcrowding in an upper-class carriage possibly comes from the pen of Bharatendu Harishchandra. Not the greatest fan of the railway administration even on a good day, the author was distinctly livid on a trip to Janakpur, when he experienced cramping while travelling in a second-class carriage, though primarily due to the smaller dimensions of the latter.[28] On another occasion, while travelling to Baidyanath, Bharatendu and his travelling companion, the Raja of Benaras, were forced to share a second-class carriage with 12 more people on the Eastern Indian Railway Company's network.

The searing remarks Bharatendu's pen elicited on this occasion are worth quoting if only because they clearly demonstrate that occasionally overcrowding produced sentiments that were certainly neither 'national' nor 'homogeneous' in the manner of reflecting the views of most Indian railway passengers. On the contrary, Bharatendu's comments underline the ways in which social status informed railway travel experiences in colonial India. To begin with, Bharatendu bitterly complained about the lack of wide berth and cushions. He was particularly galled by the fact that second-class passengers who paid thrice more than the third-class passengers were forced to travel in carriages without facilities commensurate with the amount of money paid. Indeed, he accused the railway company of injustice and cheating. But more importantly, he suggested that such ill-maintained carriages should either be set on fire or auctioned off in Calcutta (the seat of the Company's India headquarter) and in case the Company was unduly attached to this rolling stock, it should use them for carrying third-class passengers.[29] Evidently, Bharatendu was indignant. In this however, he was not an exception. Faced with over-crowding, authors of other travelogues also displayed a mixture of indignant surprise indicating unfamiliarity with the challenges posed by the situation.[30]

Given the expansive nature of the overcrowding of carriages, not surprisingly, passengers of all varieties frequently complained about the accommodation arrangements or rather the lack of them. Most of these passenger complaints come to us from the Indian language newspapers, which mirror passengers concern and distress very well.[31] Of these, the manhandling of pilgrim traffic came under particular ire, largely because the newspapers expressly claimed to speak on behalf of dumb, mute millions.[32] But a fair amount of passenger grievances were also directed at government officials and railway companies. For instance, in 1865, a petition from a 'frequent traveller' to the Viceroy and the Governor-General-in-council complained that the carriages, especially those in the upper provinces were filled in 'on the strict principle of tight booking'.[33] Another petition by a group of suburban daily commuters to Calcutta complained to the then Lieutenant Governor of Bengal that as a result of paucity of rolling stock, they were forced to travel in 'shadeless malgaries', thus suffering from discomfort and even the prospect of suffocation.[34] Such complaints were many and based on this evidence one can safely suggest that these clearly demonstrate the nature of the discomfort suffered by railway passengers, especially those who travelled in lower-class carriages.

In current historiography, such passenger complaints against overcrowding are construed as a symbol of railway policy informed by racial discrimination. Broadly speaking, most historians argue that despite repeated and persistent complaints against overcrowding, the issue was never resolved because the passengers who suffered were Indians and thus by implication racially inferior and consequently, their suffering did not elicit any sympathy. This interpretation is certainly correct. But here I suggest that many passenger complaints also reveal something more complex than mere criticism of a racially informed railway policy. This is evident in the language in which many passenger complaints against overcrowding was framed. An excellent starting point would be the comments made by Bharatendu Harishchandra. The poet's criticism upon experiencing less than ideal travelling circumstances is instructive for two reasons, *one*, it critically links the issue of facilities with tariff in a direct manner; and *two*, at a related level, he enunciates the idea, possibly inadvertently, that indifferent accommodation for lower-class passengers would have been a perfectly acceptable behaviour on the part of the railway company. After all, it is not without significance that he suggested the decrepit carriages be used for third-class passengers.

Once again, Bharatendu was not unique among Indian railway passengers who demanded facilities commensurate with tariff. For instance, a letter from the Chief Justice of Indore (an Indian) complained about the overcrowding in second-class carriages and especially the way in which more passengers were allowed than would be permitted on the basis of the 'fare charged'.[35] More importantly, such complaints were not confined to Indian passengers who travelled in upper-class carriages. A report in *Najmu-l-Akhbar* argued that intermediate class passengers on the Eastern Indian Railway Company's network were charged 'nearly double the third-class fare' and yet they suffered from overcrowding as well as lack of facilities commensurate with the tariff. The demand for better facilities included an increasing number of intermediate class carriages so as to avoid overcrowding and provision of cushions in these carriages. Demanding such reforms, the report averred was not unprecedented, since Oudh and Rohilkhand Railway Company already offered the aforementioned facilities for the same class of passengers.[36] In a similar vein, a report in *Prayag Samachar* noted that on the Eastern Indian Railway Company's line intermediate class passengers paid 4½ pies/mile as opposed to 2½ pies/mile by the third-class passengers. And despite this difference of '2 pies/mile', the report begrudged the lack of 'additional comforts' in the intermediate class carriages, which included a wider berth (and cushions) and more compartments to reduce overcrowding.[37]

Another report claimed that though the Eastern Indian Railway network was the 'best managed' railway line in India, its intermediate class carriages 'were no better' than the third-class carriages and consequently suffered from indifferent furnishings and overcrowding.[38] But it is a report in *Nasim-I-Agra* that exposed the connection between overcrowding with tariff in a particularly succinct manner. The report argued that the problem of overcrowded intermediate class carriages can be resolved by reducing second-class fares by an amount that would permit 'well-to-do Indian gentlemen' to travel in the latter carriages while leaving the former 'for their less fortunate countrymen'.[39] A passenger petition from daily suburban commuters to Calcutta too framed the issue of overcrowding within the context of tariff. This case is particularly instructive as these petitioners travelled in third-class carriages and thus significantly widen the ambit of Indian passengers who linked an ability to pay with services received and social respectability. In this petition a group of clerks who were employed in various public offices in Calcutta argued that in the absence of return tickets for third-class passengers, they were forced to travel back from work in overcrowded fourth-class carriages, '*with the lowest dregs of society*, on payment of 2 rupees and 6 pies in excess of what they had to pay before'.[40]

The petitioners' demand however, was refused on the ground that the second-class tariff was marginally higher than the third class and also afforded the possibility of return tickets and less crowded carriages.[41] Evidently, passengers resented overcrowding. At the same time however, many linked this with an ability to pay and by implication social rank. In other words, Bharatendu's outrage at the experience of travelling in an overcrowded carriage was more galling because he, unlike third-class passengers, had paid more and thus deserved better.

Status on move: the debate around seats in carriages

Interestingly, connections between price paid, facilities provided and ideas of social respectability is perceptibly revealed also in the debate surrounding provision of seats in the lower-class carriages – an issue intimately related to overcrowding. Broadly speaking, there was an awareness among railway officials that it was easier to fill in seatless carriages with an excessive number of passengers – a possibility that added to the prospect of profit. Additionally, it was argued that since Indians were not used to sitting on raised benches, seatless carriages were closer to their idea of comfort.[42]

The real issue, however, was expenditure, as carriages with seats cost more, and railway companies were divided on the question of offering seats in third-class carriages. Consequently, here too, as in many other cases of railway administration in colonial India, arrangements varied. For instance, the third-

Chariots of equality? 117

class carriages of the Eastern Indian Railway Company had seats, a fact hitherto egregiously ignored by historians.[43] The popularity of seats with carriages was immediately apparent and not surprisingly therefore, the Eastern Bengal Railway Company and the Oudh and Rohilkhand Railway Company – the two networks who competed with the Eastern Indian Railway network at various points, also decided to introduce seats in the third-class carriages. But despite the presence of seats, there was a general agreement among railway administrations as well as the colonial state (in this case the government of Bengal) that the third-class carriages should be '*so constructed that may be suitable for persons of the lowest class only and not for those who can afford to pay higher fares*'.[44]

Given this, in 1864 the Eastern Bengal Railway Company decided to remove the seats from their third-class carriages arguing that the provision was 'excessive in comparison with the amount charged for their [third-class passengers] conveyance', while noting that 'increased accommodation' was available for passengers on 'payment of a higher rate'.[45] Third-class passengers resented the modification and immediately petitioned demanding a reversal of the decision. Describing themselves as 'middle class' the petitioners noted:

> We, the undersigned passengers by the Eastern Bengal Railway Company's third class carriages, beg to submit for the consideration and orders of Government [. . .] with a view to redress of the great inconvenience to which we are at present subjected by the removal of seats and venetians from those carriages [. . .] *the indifference which has been shown to the simple convenience and comfort of the third class passengers has created a degree of distrust in their mind, which, we may be permitted to state, is by no means favourable to the interests of the company. The course adopted by the company is arbitrary in the extreme, and is a slight upon a class of people from whom the greater portion of the company's revenue is derived. The innovation complained of is unjustifiable also, because singular, as we are not aware of any line of railway in India which has adopted it.*[46]

The Eastern Bengal Railway Company ignored the petition by blankly refusing to rescind the decision. At this stage, the petitioners demanded an intervention from the Lieutenant Governor of Bengal. The Lieutenant Governor declined to interfere in the affairs of the Company. But the following excerpt from the response from the Lieutenant Governor's office is worth quoting in some detail:

> Now, the very low fares payable by the third class passengers are fixed to suit the humblest classes of the population, those who are accustomed to exposure to sun and rain and who habitually sit upon the ground [. . .] *the memorialists who describe themselves as belonging to the middle class of the community have no right to complain of inconvenience or hardships, if they choose to travel in carriages designed for the classes below them* [. . .] those who desire to travel comfortably can do so at an extremely moderate price [second-class fare]; *while those who prefer their money to their comfort and*

choose to travel in carriages intended for the poor must be content with suitable accommodation.[47]

Third-class passengers, however, persisted in their demands. Eventually the Eastern Bengal Railway Company decided to re-introduce seats in few third-class carriages, especially in those that transported the suburban passenger traffic to and from Calcutta, while keeping the rest with moveable seats.[48]

Clearly, seats had a practical bearing on overcrowding inasmuch as they provided a slight increase in accommodation per passenger and thus a slim reprieve against indiscriminate filling of carriages practiced by the railway companies. Not surprisingly therefore, as the above instance illustrates, passengers resented any possibility of removing seats. But this resentment I suggest also had a social dimension. The self-reference as 'middle class' by the third-class passenger/petitioners of the Eastern Bengal Railway Company and the repeated use of the word 'class' in the government of Bengal's response to their demands above indicates that the debate around removal of seats and associated discomfort was framed within a language wherein social rank or class played a central role. More importantly, the instance used above was not an isolated one.

In an official correspondence describing the development of passenger traffic, Captain F. Firebrace the then manager of the Calcutta and South-Eastern State Railway argued that contrary to what most railway authorities claimed, Indians preferred carriages with seats provided that the ticket price remained the same as that of seat-less carriages. This observation came in the wake of the tariff re-adjustments that followed the transfer of the Calcutta and South-Eastern Railway's management in the hands of the Bengal Government from the Eastern Bengal Railway Company. Firebrace claimed that the ten months during which the Government ran third and fourth-class carriages at the same tariff (3 pies/mile):

> A great rush was always made towards the carriages with seats, and these carriages were always filled before many passengers would go into the seatless carriages.

Firebrace attributed this preference to the social rank of the passengers who provided the main bulk of traffic for the line. Noting that the 'majority of native passengers are baboos and field labourers', Firebrace argued that the former needed to travel in a carriage with seats, largely to keep his clothes clean. The latter, he noted, did travel in fourth-class, seatless carriages, a space that most often attracted passengers 'of very low caste or else railway servants'.[49] Interestingly, Firebrace also claimed that one of the reasons that influenced Indian railway passengers' preference for carrriages with seats was their awareness that 'English people' regarded the latter 'to be of higher class than those without seats'. Firebrace's comments certainly provide a strong rebuttal to the colonial stereotype that Indians preferred to crouch on the floor of a railway carriage than sitting on benches. But, the connection he made between accommodation commensurate with tariff and social rank is more relevant to our discussion.

Evidently, passengers chose better accommodation if the price suited them. A practical decision indeed. However, as the image of *baboos* flocking to carriages with seats effectively conveys, the choice was both economic and social. Additionally, it is not without significance that even if there is a grain of truth in Firebrace's assertion that Indians preferring carriages with seats wanted to make a point to their European co-passengers, the logic provided was not racial but social. This evidence is critical, more so because it comes from a railway official and as such has the potential to underline a more hackneyed and even convenient line of reasoning that Indian passengers challenged the implied racial inferiority by buying tickets for relatively better-furnished carriages. But Firebrace's comments clearly do not do so. Also, it is unlikely that the word 'class' in Firebrace's comments was in reality a veiled shorthand for race. In other words, travelling in a railway carriage that provided facilities in accordance with the price of the ticket had acquired a symbolic meaning and became a critical component in issues of social identity. Thus, unsurprisingly, in the instance to alluded above, passengers belonging to 'very low-castes' or railway servants, a group more often than not associated with low social and even racial status, travelled in seatless carriages.

Given this, the discussion about seats and overcrowding in fourth-class carriages also revolved around the commensurability of the accommodation with the price of the ticket and the social background of the passengers. Fourth-class carriages lacked seats. Indeed, in official circles, it was widely acknowledged that the fourth-class carriages were intended for the 'very poorest class' and thus were provided with 'sufficient' accommodation (seating on the floor) in proportion to the price of the ticket.[50] This language is clearly reminiscent of similar arguments proffered for third-class carriages and the facilities to be provided therein. In other words, the idea was to have two distinct groups of lower-class carriages with differential facilities – an arrangement justified by the difference in the cost of tickets.[51] For instance, in 1874, a decade after the fourth-class carriages were introduced by the Eastern Bengal Railway Company, it declined a proposal from the Government of Bengal to introduce seats in these coaches on the grounds that 'there must be distinction between the third and the fourth class carriages' and arguing that 'beyond the provision of jilmils'[blinds] nothing else was required.[52]

In a rebuttal of the government of Bengal's suggestion that the seatless carriages transported passengers 'like cattle' and was 'opposed to civilised ideas', the Board of the Company claimed that they were not 'indifferent to the comforts of native passengers'. On the contrary, the correspondence noted that since 'it is to the native passenger traffic that the company are indebted for the success', scrupulous care was taken to provide *'reasonable comfort* of all classes of passengers'.[53] Additionally, in their response, the company claimed that they have not received any complaints from the 'mass of natives', the actual users of these carriages, a fact taken to imply that the lack of seats was not a cause of particular consternation among fourth-class passengers. The Company's position was further bolstered by a report from H.J. D'Cruz, one of the consulting engineers to the Government of Bengal. D'Cruz argued that seatless fourth-class carriages answered the 'native idea of comfort' as most Indians were not familiar with sitting on benches and chairs and thus found them 'useless'. D'Cruz however, did not stop at this. He strongly argued in favour of maintaining a 'marked difference between the classes of passengers and kind of accommodation' and the following lines from his correspondence are instructive:

> The tendency appears to be in the direction of assimilating the lower class accommodation with that of the higher. And thereby deprecating the value of higher class carriages. This coupled with low fares appears to be a retrogressive step.[54]

Evidently, the issue at stake was revenue, the company was concerned that once seats were introduced it would be difficult to fill in the fourth-class carriages indiscriminately – the raison d'être for introducing these carriages. At a related level, it was also concerned that third-class passengers would flock to fourth-class carriages with seats (as Firebrace claimed) thus affecting passenger receipts further. In short, the seatless carriages were favoured because it allowed for increased revenue receipts, but this need, as we saw, was conveniently couched in the language of 'native' customs and usages. Regardless of the language and logic offered, the steadfast refusal to introduce seats directly contributed to overcrowding in fourth-class carriages. Consequently, as discussed above, fourth-class carriages were routinely overcrowded in a manner that drew criticism from Indian language newspapers and even from official quarters.[55] These criticisms certainly question overcrowding, but interestingly without challenging the basis of the grievance, that is, the link between the price of the tickets and the facilities (no seats) offered – the key ground on which railway companies defended themselves. For instance, on the question of carrying 'coolies' to Kushtia alluded to above, the debate never referred to the claim by the Eastern Bengal Railway Company that the price of tickets determined the amount of accommodation (in this case quite literally) provided.

Similarly, a newspaper report complained that despite paying much higher fares for the intermediate carriages of the Eastern Indian Railway Company, they were as crowded as their fourth-class ones.[56] Obviously, here the complaint was against overcrowding in intermediate class carriages. But the wider implication of the logic is clear. Overcrowding was not bad per se, especially for those who paid low fares. More critically, such reasoning was neither singular nor merely official or colonial. For instance, while travelling on the Great Indian Peninsular Company's network, Bharatendu Harishchandra noted that 'coolies or similar low-class' people, those who paid 1 pie/*kos* travelled in seatless, fourth-class carriages, wherein they were packed like a herd of sheep.[57]

Clearly Bharatendu was not impressed by the way in which fourth-class carriages were filled. But his oblique, even vague criticism in conjunction with the word low-class and the reference to cheap fares is indicative of the way in which the debate was framed. Perhaps it is not without significance that Bharatendu's words fare echoed in the opinion expressed by a certain official of the Government of Bengal, who, on the occasion of discussing seats in low class carriages and overcrowding, underlined the link between cheap fares 'suitable for humblest of classes who habitually sit upon the ground' and the conditions in which they travelled in trains.[58] This congruence of opinion, of arguably opposing interests, on matters such as overcrowding and seatless carriages I argue was not random. On the contrary, as claimed in previous chapters, here too, it demonstrates that at the official level, as well as for a sizeable cross-section of Indian railway passengers social rank mattered. The prominence and the consistency of reference to facilities commensurate with tariff and by implication with social rank are unmistakable. As the tone and content of the grievances or petitions reveal, overcrowding and seatless carriages were not condemned *per se* – a position that tacitly acknowledged the railway companies' commercial need to maximise profit by offering cheap tickets while tempering it with a vaguely equitable and humanitarian demands. Clearly then, many Indian passengers interpreted and often criticised or opposed overcrowding and concomitant lack of facilities with a language of social respectability not race. Not unexpectedly therefore, experiences of travelling in railway carriages varied. Given this, it is perhaps no coincidence that while for many passengers in colonial India carriages felt like suffocating 'black holes'; for some others, carriages were as big and roomy as a football field, offering the prospect of a pleasant journey.[59]

Seating together separately: rank and respectability in railway carriages

> There has been a deficit in the budget, which necessitated travelling, not second-class, which is only half as dear as first-class, but by intermediate, which is very awful indeed. There are no cushions in the intermediate class, and the population are either intermediate, which is Eurasian or native, which for a long night journey is nasty or loafer which is amusing though intoxicated. [...] that is why in the hot weather intermediates are taken out of the carriages dead, and in all weathers, are most properly looked down upon.[60]

Irrespective of one's opinion on the ideology underpinning Kipling's literary oeuvre, from the above quote one thing is certain: for Kipling, travelling in intermediate class carriages represented loss of social prestige. Surely, Kipling was not the only one who felt this way, especially given the reasons espoused by him, which interestingly also echo some of the themes etched out in the previous section. Given this, I use this rather long quote from 'the man who would be king' as an entry point to explore the impact of travelling in railway carriages on notions of social rank and respectability in colonial India – the main theme of this section. Linking social prestige with the class of railway carriage in which one travelled was not unique to colonial India; if anything, it is a well-acknowledged historical fact that characterised railway operations across the globe and as such does not warrant detailed discussion. In the case of colonial India however, the question of social rank in the context of railway travelling has received fleeting attention. Historiographically speaking, as discussed above, hitherto, the focus has been on the ways in which conditions of travelling in railway carriages made internal divisions of Indian society 'less salient' while highlighting the differences between the coloniser and the colonised.[61] While broadly agreeing with these interpretations, here however, I suggest that for Indian passengers, social rank too mattered, the prospect of social levelling being either real or imagined.

Indian passengers frequently demanded separate carriages. Not surprisingly, such demands included separation from European/Eurasian co-passengers with a clearly acknowledged desire to avoid racially aggravated behaviour.[62] Significant as this is however, race is not the only component of these demands. Indeed, social rank is often an important ingredient that either hardens or softens the racial edge. For instance, Bharatendu Harishchandra, a supporter of separate upper-class carriages for Indians and Europeans claimed that the latter could be 'civilised and amusing' co-passengers if they belonged to a better social class. The context for this remark was his European co-passenger whose amicable presence Bharatendu thought was a product of the latter's social rank.[63] Prasannamayi Devi, Baradakanta Sengupta and Satyendrakumar Bose, authors of Bengali travelogues, voiced similar sentiments, noting their co-passengers' civil behaviour.[64] It was however, Sir Syed Ahmad Khan who in a petition addressed to the Viceroy, most clearly enunciated the role of social rank in the debate surrounding separate carriages. Though the petition also appealed against the 'unfailing bad treatment of native passengers of all classes and grades'; the language in which the social class of passengers, both Indians and Europeans, was linked to their comportment deserves attention.

> In a variety of ways attempts are incessantly made to degrade and insult the native second-class passenger. These attempts are chiefly made by a low class of Europeans who are either 'on the tramp', or are permitted by the railway companies, as being their servants to travel free second class. Even English gentlemen, especially when with their ladies and families, have been inconvenienced by such people. We would beg to suggest that such low Europeans, [. . .] be placed in some carriage specially set apart for them, to be called by some special name [. . .] this is only due to the respectable portion of the community, both Europeans and Natives, and specially due to the ladies [. . .] it would obviate much evil complained of.[65]

Contemporary newspaper reports too, reflect a similar bias, indicating a wider resonance of the idea. Demanding separate carriages for Indians travelling in higher class carriages, a newspaper argued that irrespective of their social background, all European passengers travelled in these carriages, thus 'native gentlemen find it inconvenient' to share the space with the former.[66] In 1887, a similar concern was raised when a report demanded separate carriages for Eurasians and Indian passengers by arguing that the former was 'often a nuisance to *respectable native gentlemen*, who find it impossible to bear them company in railway carriages'.[67] Another report demanded that railway authorities should confine 'low-born' Eurasian passengers to the carriages meant for them, without permitting them to enter upper-class carriages.[68]

Clearly, some European passengers were more desirable than others, a feeling that used the yardstick of social rank to measure suitability of social and physical proximity. But 'respectable' Indian passengers were not the only ones who demanded such maintenance of social boundaries. Indeed, official debates mirror similar concerns in the debate surrounding separate carriages for Indian and European passengers. These official correspondences are worth looking at since they freely use social status as a lynchpin justifying the arrangement. For instance, in 1868, J.C. Batchelor, the traffic manager of the Eastern Indian Railway frankly acknowledged the inability to prevent 'European loafers' who travelled in lower-class carriages from entering other third-class carriages and harassing Indian passengers. As a remedy, Batchelor suggested strict seclusion of such Europeans and East Indians (Eurasians) in a carriage exclusively provided for them and a complete ban on their ability to travel in any other carriages. To ensure strict implementation, Batchelor suggested these carriages be fitted with perpendicular bars, dividing the compartments from one another and also made the guards responsible for any dereliction of duties. The measures were eventually approved by the Board of the Company, indicating consensus for the measure as well as the reason proffered.[69] In another instance, this time reflecting demands made by 'respectable native' passengers F.S. Taylor (consulting engineer to the Government of Bengal) argued:

> By all trains there will be limited class of Europeans and natives, whose main object is economy, but who are ready and willing to pay for separation from the masses, and the question is – how best to meet this requirement. [. . .] But not only has railway company in India to meet the requirements of two distinct races, it is further necessary to protect the public from the rudeness of a small number of uneducated Europeans, to which class many of their own servants unfortunately belong; to meet this difficulty I would suggest that one of the two brake vans attached to every passenger train might be fitted up to carry a limited number of poor European passengers at reduced rate, and the lower orders of the company's servants, who would thus be under the eye of the guard and out of the way of the better disposed class of travellers.[70]

On occasion, such official credo was also expanded to validate wider behaviour. In 1869, one Mr Stewart, the enquiry officer of the Eastern Bengal Railway Company was accused of turning out an Indian passenger from the first-class carriage in which the former was travelling. Stewart interestingly denied this charge by claiming that he did not have 'the slightest objection to travel with respectable native gentlemen' and that he often did so while in the process of gathering a fair amount of 'interesting information'.[71] Given such broad accord on the subject, the Oudh and Rohilkhand railway company introduced the provision of separate railway carriages for Indian and European upper-class passengers.[72] The company justified this arrangement by claiming to fulfill a 'reasonable demand' made by 'native passengers of rank', an argument that both implicitly agreed to racial difference and thus separation; while also underlining that a specific cross-section of Indian passengers was valued more merely because of their social status. Unsurprisingly, this measure became rather popular, and middle-class Indian passengers demanded similar provisions, especially from the Eastern Indian Railway Company. The Company however, steadfastly refused to offer similar services to their upper-class passengers largely on grounds of increased expenditure; though the company did introduce the system in their intermediate class carriages.

Issues of social rank and respectability also permeate Indian passengers' demands for separate travelling arrangements from other Indians who were deemed socially inferior. The clearest articulation of the desire for separation on the basis of social rank is visible around the issues of separate carriages for Indian women passengers and for passengers belonging to low class/caste. Of these, the former has attracted sustained scholarly attention and thus requires little repetition.[73] Though relevant here would be to note that the debate about *zenana* carriages was also largely framed in a language of social respectability that unambiguously tied the need for separate or safe travelling arrangements as the prerogative of women of rank. The latter issue however, is more instructive for this chapter if only because the evidence is pervasive and the language is clearly informed by notions of social rank and respectability. For instance, a newspaper report in 1871 suggested some railway reforms that included a proposal for carriages of a special kind:

> For people of lower classes, in order to save native gentlemen, the trouble and annoyance of siting with them. The fare for a seat in these carriages should be less than that taken from passengers using other carriages.[74]

In the same year, echoing a similar feeling, the Urdu Akhbar argued:

> Men of the higher classes should not be allowed to sit in the same carriage with those of the lower ones, in order not only to avoid the disgust which the former feel in being to sit with the latter, but also to prevent their health from being injured by the bad smell emitted by the persons of the latter.[75]

A few years later, two reports in different newspapers expressed comparable grievances claiming them as 'prevalent complaints'. Moreover, these reports argued that the failure to comply with these demands was 'inconsistent with the tolerant policy pursued by the government'. The following excerpts from these reports are worth quoting:

> The seating of sweepers, *chamars* and the like class of people in the same carriage with Hindustanis of the higher order. [. . .] it is extremely offensive to the religious feelings of the people [. . .] it is high time that the abuse

should be removed, and a separate carriage set apart for sweepers etc., and other low caste persons.[76]

The editor sees no reason why separate carriages should not be assigned for Hindus, Mussulmans and the people of the lower class, such as sweepers, chamars etc.[77]

These however, are not isolated instances. Contemporary newspaper reports are replete with such demands. One report even claimed that while Muslims of rank considered seating with low class people as 'disagreeable', for Hindus of similar background, the prospect was 'intolerable'.[78] As a remedy to this problem, the report demanded creation of fourth-class carriages. Demanding separate carriages for sweepers, another report noted that railway companies disregarded the fact that Brahmins considered the touch of a lower castes as 'unholy' and thereby ran the risk of 'outraging' the latter's religious prejudices.[79] Echoing similar concerns, another report argued that railway companies could improve their profit if they provided separate accommodation for the 'lowest class of people', in the process attracting a sizeable section of 'respectable natives' who avoided railway travel for loss of religious and social status.[80] Not surprisingly, this language of exclusion was also extended to demands for separate carriages for Hindu and Muslim passengers respectively, a well-known theme that does not warrant reiteration.

Clearly cross-sections of Indian railway passengers desired separation. Such desires can certainly be interpreted as anxiety unleashed by the realities of railway travel wherein (as Danvers and others had predicted) upper-caste/class passengers were forced to share physical proximity with 'social inferiors'. Here however, I suggest that these demands also underscore a wider process to delineate both the boundaries of 'respectable middle class' as well as a contestation of the railway carriage space as legitimately belonging to certain groups and not others. This is evident in the ways in which separation from other Indian railway passengers was framed in a strident demand for either introducing more intermediate class carriages or objecting to any proposals to abolish the facility alongside asking for strictly restricting intermediate carriages for 'gentlemen' and better facilities in these carriages commensurate with the tariff imposed. For instance, in 1880 the Sindh, Punjab and Delhi railway authorities decided to abolish the intermediate class. The decision drew prompt and strong criticism as is evident from the contemporary newspaper reports. A report in the *Koh-i-Nur* 'deeply regretted' the decision by noting that the measure will cause 'great inconvenience to the native nobility and gentry'. It also demanded a rescindment of the decision.[81]

This general mood was reflected in other newspapers, which not only demanded the decision to be reversed, but also took the opportunity to ask other railway companies to increase the number of intermediate class carriages on their networks.[82] A few years later (1888) the Eastern Indian Railway Company floated a proposal to abolish the intermediate class carriage. Once again, the proposal was received with consternation. Referring to the proposal a letter to the Secretary of the Railway Conference argued that such a measure would cause 'great hardship' for the travelling public. Explicating further, the letter claimed:

> Middle class genteel people cannot, as a rule afford to travel in upper class carriages, and would on no account travel in lower class carriages with coolies, mehters and dhangurs. It is absolutely necessary that there should be on all the lines a class of carriages to suit the class of men who are of humble means, but who nevertheless keep themselves apart from the lowest class of people. The reason which induced the Eastern Indian Railway Company to have intermediate carriages on their lines are as applicable to day as when they were first introduced.[83]

Other reports too, expressed similar concern. The ones in *Sanjivani* and *Bangabasi* disapproved of the proposal of abolishing intermediate class on the grounds that 'middle class native gentlemen' travel in these carriages, and bolstered their claim by arguing that these carriages yielded a large profit as opposed to the first and second classes. The report in the latter paper added:

> The middle class people of this country, who being members of the respectable castes, will be unable to travel with third class passengers consisting mostly of low class people [. . .] and whose [respectable] means will make it difficult for them to travel in the second class, the railway authorities are therefore requested to consider the matter very carefully.[84]

Another newspaper report around the same time demanded a reversal of the proposal, while insisting on an increase in the number of intermediate carriages attached to the mail trains. The report also demanded special treatment of intermediate class passengers such as separate ticket windows and not being 'huddled' together with third-class passengers.[85]

Given the proposal to abolish the intermediate class carriages drew such ire from 'respectable natives', it is perhaps unsurprising that the plan was not implemented. Railway authorities however, also drew robust criticism for their inability to ensure that intermediate class carriages were not occupied by those who were not meant to be there, that is, the third-class passengers. The Eastern Bengal Railway authorities were often singled out for such complaints with one report claiming that third-class passengers were pushed to intermediate class carriages that inconvenienced the passengers.[86] Interestingly, quite often the complainants claimed that the third-class passengers entered intermediate class carriages because the latter were not distinctly respectable in their appearance and lacked furnishing that would physically set them apart from lower-class carriages. For instance, in criticising the introduction of return tickets for intermediate class carriages, which made the fare equal to an ordinary third-class ticket, a newspaper report claimed that 'many low people' travelled in the intermediate class, thus causing 'great inconvenience to native gentlemen' – the original beneficiaries of the system.[87] Singing the same tune, a report in the *Sulabha Samachar* noted that though the intermediate class fare on the Eastern Bengal Railway network was nearly double the third-class fare, the former were 'not distinguished' in any respect.[88]

When profit met rhetoric: railway carriages and the question of social progress

> A high caste will rather submit to the indignity of sitting cheek-by-jowl with his servant than pay the extra cost of a second-class fare; and what is more, he does not find himself the worse for it at the end of the journey.[89]

As the ongoing discussion indicates, the image conveyed in the above excerpt was not entirely true. Clearly, a cross-section of Indian railway passengers did resent the physical proximity with anyone who was not deemed equal – a feeling that underpinned persistent demands for separate carriages. But interestingly, these demands were largely unmet, except for the introduction and expansion of intermediate class carriages that partially allayed concerns of 'respectable native' passengers. This refusal to provide separate carriages for lower-class passengers I argue does not imply a loyal adherence of the colonial state to its self-proclaimed ideal of inducing railway-borne social progress in India. On the contrary, it displays an interplay between colonial rhetoric and everyday realities of railway operations in India that were primarily informed by profit – a balancing trick that also provided, possibly inadvertently, a negotiating corner to Indian railway passengers. This process is most clearly visible in the ways in which railway authorities and the colonial state responded to Indian passenger demands for improving railway carriage facilities – the focus of this section.

Hitherto historiographical consensus suggests that passenger demands were rarely, if ever, fulfilled – once again underlying the colonial context of railway operations in India. Recently however, Ritika Prasad's analysis shows a departure from this received view, with an acknowledgement that passenger demands were fulfilled, albeit varyingly. Though limited in scope,[90] Ritika's contribution is both timely and accurate. Thus here, while building upon Prasad's suggestions, I expand my scale of analysis to include all the demands that were made to improve carriage facilities and the railway travel experiences of Indian passengers. These include a mix of demands – some already discussed above and a few new ones (most notably demands for lighting and lavatories in lower-class carriages). But before proceeding, relevant here would be to note that since these demands, especially the lack of toilets, have received sustained scholarly attention, my analysis will focus on the nature of the interaction between passenger demands and administrative responses and inasmuch any discussion of passenger grievances *per se*, will be peripheral.

Lower-class carriages lacked lights as well as lavatories. Unsurprisingly therefore, as soon as the railway operations commenced, passengers resented the lack of these basic facilities especially as most railway journeys were long, and involved many stops. Passenger discomfort is clearly evident from the contemporary newspaper reports and petitions to various railway and government agencies. Interestingly, the railway administrations' response to these demands differed considerably. Broadly speaking, lights in carriages were provided much earlier than lavatories. Though here too, arrangements varied from one railway administration's network to another. In short, there was no standardised response towards providing either of these facilities. In the case of carriage lighting for instance, as early as 1865, the Eastern Indian Railway Company provided oil lamps in the third-class carriages.[91] But, underlining the lack of standardisation, this time even on the same network, this measure was introduced only in the Bengal division. Consequently, as soon as the measure was introduced, a petition to the Viceroy requested the introduction of lights in the carriages of the upper division. The following excerpt from the concluding paragraph of the petition is worth quoting:

> If light is given to every third class carriage on this this side [north-western provinces] as I believe is done in Bengal line, it would meet all the necessary requirements to make the passengers comfortable. Four annas worth of oil is quite enough for one light to burn the whole night [. . .] it will cost the company five or six rupees only to light ten or twelve third class carriages. [. . .] this is nothing, the company can well afford to lose the fare of a single passenger in order to give comfort and ease to 500 or 600 of them.[92]

Though one is unclear how much a single petition mattered; nevertheless, the following year (1866) lamps were indeed introduced in the Eastern Indian Railway network's 'upper division' carriages. The system however, was not without defects and the most frequent complaint included dimness of the lamps and their inability to burn through the night.[93]

The company responded by appointing *furrush* (lamp-cleaners) and introducing mid-light 'lamp stations' where lamps were changed.[94] Interestingly, while admitting the provision of lamps was imperfect, the company claimed that the carriages with poor lighting were borrowed from the Great Indian Peninsular Railway Company, thus indicating that the latter too, provided similar facilities in their third-class carriages. Eventually by 1870s, gas lighting in the third-class carriages was also introduced by the Eastern Indian Railway Company – a measure widely welcomed by passengers. By 1887, the Company was keen to introduce electric lights. Interestingly, this suggestion received lukewarm passenger response as stronger lights were argued to be detrimental for sleeping as well as passenger privacy, especially that of women.[95] Not all railway administrations however, followed the example of the Eastern Indian Railway Company.[96] Indeed, very few except the Awadh and Rohilkhand Railway company provided elaborate and upgraded lighting facilities in the carriages. The discrepancy of the system can be gauged by the fact that as late as 1892, the Eastern Bengal Railway Company was transitioning to the system of lighting third-class carriages with Pintsch's system.[97] Similar uneven provision also characterised the introduction of latrines in lower-class carriages. For instance, while the third-class passengers travelling on the Great Indian Peninsular Railway network had access to toilets in carriages from 1896; the Eastern Indian Railway network introduced the facility only in 1902.[98] Neither were such inconsistencies confined to lower-class carriages. Provision of lavatories in intermediate class carriages varied between networks.

In 1890 the North-Western Railway network was one of the first to offer this facility for intermediate class passengers, creating a wider demand for other railway administrations to follow suit.[99] In one case, a newspaper report claimed that on the Eastern Bengal Railway network, even the second-class carriages lacked toilets.[100]

Evidently, passenger demands were met haltingly and unevenly. However, some demands, such as overcrowding in lower-class carriages, were never resolved; while some others such as seclusion of upper-class Indian passengers from their European counterparts, or introducing more and better furnished intermediate class carriages were met. The inconsistency thus is striking, if one considers that demands to do something about overcrowding and lack of latrines in carriages were long-lasting and were more or less ignored; while apparently trivial grievances were redressed. Despite appearances, this however, is not a conundrum. Neither is this an illustration of the ailing nature of a colonial railway system that allegedly ran on rules imposed from above. On the contrary, here, as in the previous chapters, what made some demands more likely to be fulfilled than others was determined by the point where the colonial claims of steam induced progress on one hand, converged with the railway administrations' desire for profit on the other (either actual or the prospect of it) alongside passenger pressures. Overcrowding was never redressed because of two related factors. The first, as Ritika Prasad correctly notes, was chronic lack of rolling stock; and second, at a related level, an unwillingness on the part of the railway companies to invest in more carriages.

This argument appears counter-intuitive if one considers the popularity of railway travel in India. But coupled with the knowledge that the price of a lower-class ticket in India was one of the lowest in the world, the imperative for shoving an unaccountable number of passengers in a single carriage makes good business sense. This was particularly relevant to overcrowding because as noted above, railway authorities made a direct correlation between tariff and the 'amount of accommodation to which passengers were entitled'.[101] Making the connection rather bare, in a report that calculated the cost of the construction of the Eastern Indian Railway Company's network, A.M. Rendel, the then agent of Company claimed that:

> In regard to the reduction of the number of person put in one carriage [third class], I think the proper way of considering the question is the amount which each carriage, when full, ought to earn, and not the bare space into which it is possible to make a man sit.[102]

Based on this belief Rendel suggested that a third-class carriage on the company's network ought to carry 40 passengers at the rate of 3 pies/miles. Such views however, were not confined to guaranteed railway companies. After 1869, the government agencies too, supported policies that contributed to overcrowding. For instance, an official correspondence in 1874 argued that 'lower classes are carried at a high rate of profit' and as such low fares had to be maintained to attract passengers.[103] Such sentiments were also bolstered by flexible railway rules that left the number of passengers to be accommodated in each compartment of the carriages in the hands of different railway companies. Though in theory, the railway company's decision had to be approved by the Government of India, in reality, the decision was made by local railway authorities, thus creating an unchecked and unregulated system.[104] More often than not, the station masters and ticket booking clerks sold more tickets than the carriages were allowed to carry, thus flagrantly disobeying railway rules, but upholding the principle of profit outlined above.

Similar tendencies also affected the provision or rather the lack of lavatories in lower-class carriages. Providing latrine arrangements in lower-class carriages necessitated an improvement in the existing rolling stock. This entailed an increased expenditure that the railway companies were certainly not ready for. But interestingly, the official correspondence on the subject completely side-stepped the issue of profit and expenditure and instead blamed 'native habits'. Resonating the debate about providing toilets in all stations, here too, the argument was that Indians left toilets dirty. The argument was simple: providing toilets in carriages would involve additional costs as then the companies would have to employ *mehters* (cleaners) on each train. Additionally, railway authorities argued that since toilets were provided at the principal stations where slower passenger trains carrying lower-class carriages were scheduled to stop for longish halts; therefore, in-built lavatories were unnecessary. Thus, despite persistent pressure from passengers, including wide use of humanitarian arguments, since expenditure involved was not expected to contribute to existing levels of profit accrued from lower-class passenger traffic, the measure was delayed until the late nineteenth century; and was finally approved by the newly constituted Railway Board. This long-awaited improvement however, I suggest, was also influenced by the changing tone of nationalist politics in early twentieth-century India – a point when political concern became more expedient than railway profit, more of which in the concluding section.

Clearly, railway reforms stood at the intersecting point of profit and passenger demands. The latter was usually fulfilled when the former seemed to be the outcome. It is as such not surprising that fulfilment of passenger demands reveals a distinct pattern. Broadly speaking, either inexpensive demands such as cushions in intermediate class carriages and lighting lower-class carriages were met; or, smaller railway networks, which had the potential to expend less but earn more, usually invested in palpably costly reforms. For instance, the Oudh and Rohilkhand railway network – a rather small line, provided separate carriages for upper-class Indian and European passengers respectively, a measure that certainly cost less (very few upper-class carriages). On the other hand, the Eastern Indian Railway network, the longest in India, refused the same measure in upper-class carriages (express and mail trains) as it would have led to increased expenditure; but introduced it in the lower-class carriages (in passenger trains), where the number of European passengers was insignificant and thus providing separate arrangements cost next to nothing. Given this, Indian passengers too, had a clear awareness of the significance of profit to the railway authorities. For instance, in a letter demanding separate carriages the Chief Justice of Indore argued that since 'higher classes of natives' used first, second and intermediate class carriages, railway administration could provide such facilities without worrying about its impact on profit levels.[105] Another report claimed that a network like the Great Indian Peninsular Railway, 'which has a large income',[106] should not begrudge providing better lighting in their third-class carriages. As argued in the previous sections, here too, these demands reveal a commercial language – one framed in the context of passenger numbers and profit. Indeed, while referring to decrepit second-class railway carriages, Bharatendu Harishchandra argued that the railway company was unjustified in treating their *grahak* (Hindi: customers) shabbily, even though they paid a substantial amount for an upper-class ticket.[107]

Conclusion

Bharatendu's self-identification as a 'customer' I argue, was not random. On the contrary, his explicit use of the phrase alongside a wide evidence of passenger demands being framed in a language of commercial logic once again underlined the agency of Indian passengers. Surely, this was circumscribed within the needs of the railway authorities and the political agenda of the colonial state (not always identical, but often enough). But here I suggest that this profit, which inspired a narrow ground of passenger negotiation, had significant social implications as it provided Indian railway passengers with opportunities for differentiated railway carriage experiences that in turn were interpreted in clearly more heterogeneous ways than presently assumed. Needless to say, an absence of standardised railway rules also contributed to this process, if only by adding to the diversity of railway carriage experiences. It is not without significance that experiences of overcrowding in lower-class carriages – a lingering and widely resented issue, too, could vary from one network to another.[108] In short, this chapter suggests that railway carriage experiences of Indian railway passengers varied. Consequently, passengers interpreted these experiences through a diverse range of filters that included race; but also, social rank including class and caste and religion.

At a related level, this heterogeneity, I argue, demonstrates that the impact of differentiated railway carriage experiences was both practical and notional. In other words, on the one hand, if the fulfilment of a demand based on an explicit logic of superior social rank materially reinforced the role of status; on the other hand, similar demands were made because a specific group of passengers imagined their social position superior vis-à-vis anyone deemed inferior and thus demanded separate and better facilities. This process is clearly suggestive of the fact that Indian railway passengers thought of themselves and others in more complex and nuanced terms – a process that questions an easy correlation between Indian passengers versus colonial railway authorities/employees and European passengers. More critically perhaps, the presence of this process once again highlights Indian passenger agency if only by offering a sobering reminder of the limits of the colonial/railway travel-discipline to control or discipline 'colonised' bodies. Evidently, as opposed to what is currently claimed, confinement did not 'discipline' Indian passengers in becoming more suppliant colonised subjects.

For what it is worth, it did not even make them more accommodating of their fellow compatriots cum co-passengers. This however, is neither a dismissal of race as an analytical index, nor an attempt to suggest that all Indian passengers had pleasant railway travel experience. But this is to suggest that experiences of travelling in railway carriages produced impulses that went beyond 'national' (i.e., if one implies some sort of unity as the basis of nation) and were firmly based in notions of socially unbridgeable (both literally and metaphorically) 'differences'. After all, as the ongoing discussion clearly indicates, although conditions of railway travelling created a long list of socially undesirable travelling companions, the vehemence against either actual or possible sharing of space with lower-class/caste passengers is particularly striking.

Here too, as in previous chapters, this attitude towards 'social inferiors' I suggest, illustrates the significance of social rank. In the context of the carriages however, status or the lack of it was more keenly felt simply because despite clamouring for separation, a sizeable section of Indian passengers had to share close physical proximity with those who were not considered equals. Clearly, the issue at stake was social levelling, both real and imagined. Thus, railway travel conditions posed a challenge to established notions and habits of rank and respectability. Evidently, the resentment is directed against the reality that railway travel has forced some sort of social levelling, albeit uneven, and thus the desire is for old practices in new contexts. It is not without significance that a newspaper report claimed that 'railways have made the poor ease loving, for they can no longer walk long distances on foot'.[109] But this, as we saw in the second chapter, was more a perception than reality. Thus, here I claim that the issue at stake is that definitions of status came to be re-assessed according to the new measures provided by railway travel – a point excellently illustrated in the context of over-crowding and lack of seats in lower-class carriages. Additionally, these demands I argue were framed with an awareness that the railway authorities and the colonial administration understood the lexicon of social rank.

For the Britons, as to why any references to social rank resonated is not hard to comprehend.[110] As for Indian passengers, as argued in Chapter 2, the ways in which railway companies created intermediate and fourth-class carriages with a frank acknowledgement to respect 'needs of native passengers' made the latter's position self-evident. In short, the railway authorities and the colonial state acknowledged social class and even upheld the existing norms, albeit whenever it suited their agenda (think: the rejection of separate carriages for lower-class/caste passengers and provision of intermediate class carriages). This however, is not surprising if one considers the gap that separated the colonial state's socially progressive rhetoric of steam from the imperative of profit that dictated day-to-day operations of railways in India. Nevertheless, it cannot be ignored that these interactions did offer additional currency to social rank by transforming it into a legitimate basis for providing facilities in a commercial enterprise. More importantly, this process, I suggest, offered a cross-section of Indian passengers with a convenient logic (because railway authorities understood it) to contest the new social space, that is, the railway carriage.

As noted, demands for separate carriages for lower-class/caste passengers were never met. Yet these demands cannot be ignored if only because they demonstrate an unequivocal desire to wrest the social space of railway carriages from lower-class passengers. Persistent demands for keeping out 'social undesirables' are clearly suggestive of an effort, albeit unevenly achieved, to claim that the intermediate class carriages were the social space of 'respectable Indians', largely imagined as Hindus. However, as we have seen, occasionally it included upper-class Muslims. At a related level, these demands also represent an attempt to define the boundaries of 'respectable middle class' vis-à-vis the railway authorities and by extension the colonial state. After all, it is not without significance that railway authorities were routinely blamed for either not furnishing intermediate carriages well, or for shoving lower-class passengers into these spaces. Similar attempts at self-definition are clearly noticeable in the debates surrounding removal of seats in the third-class carriages of the Eastern Bengal Railway Company's network. These and other similar sentiments outline above, I suggest, are significant attempts to assert a collective self-identity that required clear delineation of social boundaries.

This demarcation however, was not just directed against Indians. Indeed, the demands for separate carriages for upper-class Indian passengers can be seen as undermining the racial hierarchy and implied inferiority by claiming a common ground i.e., higher social rank, with the rulers. And nowhere is this more clearly noticeable than in Sir Syed's petition, which conflated the needs of 'respectable' European and Indian passengers for physical and social separation from lower-classes/races as identical. Clearly, it was an act of using a social parallel to make a wider political one. If being upper class was a common ground; then this assertion of identity was also a stab at political competition largely by criticising railway policies – a process that provided the dual advantage of claiming clearer social boundaries as well as greater political presence through representative claims. This desire to represent 'meek' masses is particularly visible in the debates surrounding overcrowding and lack of toilets in lower-class carriages. The choice is not surprising given the complete refusal of the railway authorities, which left a conveniently gaping political hole.

But more significantly, though occasionally overlapping, one can identify a distinctly suggestive pattern in these criticisms: from the end of the nineteenth century into the early decades of the twentieth, the tone became increasingly political, and the language redolent with collective (racial, national) sentiments. This was a clear shift from the kind of grievances discussed earlier, which did not question the commercial logic of the arrangements; if anything, overt references to tariff implied affordability and consequently better social status. The link of this shift with the changing nature of the anti-colonial movement is self-evident, and thus does not require elucidation. But here I argue that regardless of this shift, the 'national' continued to be imagined, at least partially, through social status or lack of it. After all, it is not without significance that as late as

1904 a newspaper report recommended 'only third-class carriages for a through trains to carry *coolies* directly from the upper provinces to Assam'.[111] Given this, as a concluding note, one cannot but speculate as to what extent the diverse sentiments generated by Indian passengers' railway carriage experiences cemented the colonial state's assumption that the basis of Indian society was division not unity – a theme beyond the scope of this chapter.

Notes

1. S. Shastri, *Dakshinapath Bhraman* (Calcutta, B. Banerjee and Company, 1911), pp. 3–5. Author, however, was not the only one who denied entry to Muslim passengers waiting at Asansol station for their onward pilgrimage to Mecca. The carriage he boarded had in total seven other Bengalis who according to the author collectively decided to keep the Muslim passengers out also because of the 'stinking' food (meat broth cooked with garlic) they carried.
2. S. Das (ed.), *Manomohan Basu-r aprokashito diary* (Unpublished diary of Manomohan Basu), (Calcutta, SahityaLok, 1989). Diary entry for 26 January 1887.
3. Though for passengers travelling in upper-class carriages, such experiences could have only occurred by the end of the nineteenth century when faster mail or express trains were allowed to carry third-class carriages and thus lower-class passengers. See Chapter 1.
4. This theme is discussed in detail later in the chapter.
5. J. Danvers, *Indian Railways: Their past history, present condition and future prospects* (London, Effingham Wilson, 1877). Emphasis mine.
6. M. Goswami, *Producing India: From colonial economy to national space* (Chicago, University of Chicago Press, 2004), pp. 104 and 116; L. Bear, *Lines of the Nation: Indian railway workers, bureaucracy, and the intimate historical self* (New York, Columbia University Press, 2007), Part I, Chapter 2.
7. Bear for instance describes carriages as lock-ups. See Bear, 'Lines of the nation', p. 36. A similar analogy underpins Goswami's analysis as she chooses the title 'mobile incarceration' for the chapter on railway carriages as state spaces is. Goswami, 'Producing India', Chapter 3.
8. Bear, 'Lines of the nation', p. 46.
9. Goswami, 'Producing India'. I use the word hint as Goswami refers to how 'the conditions of travelling in third class railway carriages made internal divisions of the Indian society less salient', but does not develop the argument further. R. Prasad, *Tracks of Change: Railways and everyday life in colonial India* (New Delhi, Cambridge University Press, 2015), pp. 56–57.
10. Goswami, 'Producing India', Chapter 3.
11. B. Chunder, *Travels of a Hindoo to Various Parts of Bengal and Upper India* (London, Trubner and Company, 1865), Vol I, p. 140.
12. R. Tagore, *Jeevansmriti* (Calcutta, Bishwabharati, 1959). Translation mine.
13. In this context, social adjustment implies, among other things, physical proximity with people who were more likely to be strangers than not, while physical adjustment includes but is not limited to putting one's body and luggage in the closed, often strictly marked spots for each passenger.
14. A case in point would be the above quote by R. Tagore wherein the young poet notes a feeling of dismay for not experiencing any physical jolt when the train started to move. This was simply due to the fact that Tagore was in a first-class carriage and the cushioned berth absorbed the shocks of the movement.
15. C. Wolmar, *Blood, Iron and Gold: How the railroads transformed the world* (New York, PublicAffairs, 2010), Chapter 10.

16 There is evidence to believe that in India the volume of passengers travelling in trains was higher than continental Europe. See Goswami, 'Producing India', p. 109.
17 K. Sinha, *Hutom Penchar Naksha O Onnanyo Samajchitra* (Calcutta [original publication 1863] Sahitya Parishad, 1955), pp. 50–51.
18 Azim-al-din, *Ki Majar Kaler Gadi* (Calcutta, Sri Siddheshwar Ghosh, 1863), p. 7.
19 'Railway delinquencies': letter to the editor of the Englishman, in Proceedings of the Railway Department, Government of Bengal, P/163/30, IOR.
20 It is widely acknowledged that railway connections magnified the number of pilgrims to *tirthas*. See K. Maclean, *Pilgrimage and Power: The Kumbh Mela in Allahabad, 1765–2001* (New York, Oxford University Press, 2008); also, I. Kerr, Reworking a popular religious practice: the effects of railways on pilgrimage in nineteenth and twentieth century South Asia, in I. Kerr (ed.), *Railways in Modern India* (New Delhi, Oxford University Press, 2001), pp. 304–327.
21 S. Bradley, *The Railways: Nation, network and people* (London, Profile Books, 2015), p. 267.
22 'Overcrowding of carriages', a note by Major Hovendon, dated 14 March 1865, in Proceedings of the Railway Department, Government of Bengal, P/163/35, IOR.
23 Letter from Dr F.N. Macnamara to Dr N. Chevers, dated March 1865; also, Letter from C. Burbank, Superintendent of Labour Transport, Calcutta to the Agent, Eastern Bengal Railway Company, dated 17 April 1865, in Proceedings of the Railway Department, Government of Bengal, P/163/35, IOR.
24 Government's Consulting Engineer's proposal relative to passenger fares and accommodation, dated 14 June 1877, in Letters to and from Eastern Bengal Railway Company, L/PWD/2/163, IOR.
25 *Akhbar-i-Alam*, 5 January 1892, in Native Newspaper Report, North-Western Provinces, L/R/5/69, IOR. Newspapers are replete with similar complaints, asking for more intermediate class carriages per trains.
26 P. Bose, *Professor Bose-r Apurba Bhraman brittanta* (Calcutta, Manomohan Library, 1902), pp. 76–77. Interestingly, Priyanath Bose was the younger son of Manomohan Bose, the individual we have encountered in the opening paragraphs of this chapter. See endnote 2.
27 S.N. Ray, *Uttar Bharat Bhraman* (Calcutta, Pashupati Press, 1907), p. 11.
28 B. Harishchandra, 'Janakpur ki Yatra', in *Bharatendu Granthavali*, Volume III (Nagari Pracharani Sabha, Kashi), p. 666.
29 B. Harishchandra, 'Baidyanath ki Yatra', in Bharatendu Granthavali, Volume III (Nagari Pracharani Sabha, Kashi), pp. 649–650.
30 Priyanath Bose, for instance, complained that railway companies were unable to control both the amount of luggage passengers carried and the number of tickets the clerks sold without any regard for passengers' plight. Similarly, looking at the swarm of daily commuters thronging Howrah station in the evening, Surendranath Ray admitted that he had little knowledge how the former will commute back home (in suburbs around Calcutta) in crowded carriages. Bose, 'Professor Bose-r', p. 76; Ray, 'Uttar Paschim', p. 6.
31 See *Baranagar Samachar*, 30 December 1874; *Hindu Ranjika*, 23 July 1879; *Charu Varta*, 24 September 1888, in Indian Newspaper Reports, Bengal. Many such complaints also appeared in the Native Newspaper Reports for the North-Western Provinces.
32 For one such instance, see *Bharat Mihir*, 9 November 1876, in Indian Newspaper Reports, Bengal, L/R/5/2, IOR.

136 *Chariots of equality?*

33 Petition from a frequent traveller by rail to the Right Honourable the Viceroy and Governor-General in council, dated 31 October 1865; also, 'Measures for the comfort and convenience of lower class passengers', letter from the Secretary of the British Indian Association to the Secretary of the Railway Conference, dated 15 September 1888, in Proceedings of the Railway Department, Government of Bengal, P/163/36, and P/3632, IOR.

34 'To the Honourable Alexander Mackenzie, Lieutenant Governor of Bengal, the humble memorial from the residents of so many villages lying along from Ampta to Howrah and adjacent places, and from the passengers who travel from and to the said places by the Ampta and Howrah engine tramway, signed by Sarat Chunder Mukerjee and others, in Proceedings of the Railway Department, Government of Bengal', P/5396, IOR. Emphasis original.

35 Measures for the comfort and convenience of native passengers from the Chief Justice of Indore to the Secretary of the Railway Conference, Simla, dated 5 September 1888, in Proceedings of the Railway Department, Government of Bengal, P/3632, IOR.

36 *Najmu-l-Akhbar*, 4 March 1887, Native Newspaper Reports, North-Western Provinces, L/R/5/64, IOR.

37 *Prayag Samachar*, 10 March 1888, Native Newspaper Reports, North-Western Provinces, L/R/5/65, IOR.

38 *Police News*, 8 March, Native Newspaper Reports, North-Western Provinces, L/R/5/71, IOR.

39 Nasim-i-Agra, 3 January, Native Newspaper Reports, North-Western Provinces, L/R/5/84, IOR.

40 'Third class return tickets in Mutlah Railway' from the inhabitants of Rajpoor, Hureenavee etc., to the consulting engineer to the Government of Bengal, Railway Department, dated 18 August 1864, in Proceedings of the Railway Department, Government of Bengal, P/163/33, IOR. Emphasis mine.

41 Ibid.

42 Extract of a report by Mr H.J. D'Cruz sent to the agent of the Eastern Bengal Railway Company, in letters to and from Eastern Bengal Railway Company, L/PWD/2/163, IOR.

43 'Overcrowding of carriages', note by Major Hovendon, dated 14 March 1865, in Proceedings of the Railway Department, Government of Bengal, P/163/35, IOR. The Eastern Bengal Railway Company as well the Oudh and Rohilkhand Railway Company, followed suit and introduced seats in their third-class carriages. The question of seats in third-class carriages have received some scholarly attention but largely as an off-shoot to underline the sufferings of third-class passengers in seat-less crowded carriages, an image, as we will see, not uniformly valid.

44 Letter dated November 1863 from the Board of the Eastern Bengal Railway Company to the agent of the company, concurring to the opinion expressed by the Lieutenant Governor of Bengal on third-class carriages, in letters to and from the Eastern Bengal Railway Company, L/PWD/2/157, IOR. Emphasis mine.

45 Letter from Franklin Prestage, agent of the Eastern Bengal Railway Company to superintendent of the labour transport at Calcutta, dated 14 April 1864, in Proceedings of the Railway Department, Government of Bengal, P/163/30, IORs. The number of persons to be carried in these carriages was fixed at 75.

46 Petition from the third-class passengers of the Eastern Bengal Railway to the consulting engineer to the Government of Bengal, railway department, dated 18 April 1864, in Proceedings of the Railway Department, Government of Bengal, P/163/32, IOR.

47 Letter from Captain F.S. Taylor, Joint Secretary to the Government of Bengal to Baboo Koylas Chunder Bannerjee, dated 20 May 1864, in Proceedings of the Railway Department, Government of Bengal, P/163/32, IOR. Emphasis mine.

48 Letter from the Government Consulting Engineer's proposals relative to passenger fares and accommodation, dated 14 June 1877, in Railway Letters to and from Eastern Bengal Railway, Series 'C', L/PWD/2/163, IOR.
49 Note by Captain F. Firebrace, Manager of the Calcutta and South-Eastern State Railway, on the passenger traffic on the line, dated January 1871, in Proceedings of the Railway Conference, V/25/720/27, IOR.
50 Ibid.; also, see 'Successful introduction of a fourth class on the Eastern Bengal Railway' letter from F. Prestage, Agent Eastern Bengal Railway Company to the consulting engineer to the Government of Bengal, dated 10 June 1864, in Proceedings of the Railway Department, Government of Bengal, P/163/32, IOR.
51 'Overcrowding of carriages', note by Major Hovendon, dated 14 March 1865, in Proceedings of the Railway Department, Government of Bengal, P/163/35, IOR. Third-class carriages had seats and venetians (though without cushions) and fourth-class carriages had nothing but the carriage floor to sit on.
52 Letter from the Board of the Eastern Bengal Railway Company, dated 25 June 1874, in Letters to and from the Eastern Indian Railway Company, 'C' series, L/PWD/2/161, IOR.
53 Ibid. Emphasis mine.
54 Letter to the Eastern Bengal Railway Company's agent in Calcutta from H.J. D'Cruz, Consulting Engineer's Office, dated July 1877, in letters to and from Eastern Bengal Railway Company, L/PWD/2/163, IOR.
55 'Government Consulting Engineer's proposals relative to passenger fares and accommodation', dated 14 June 1877, in letters to and from Eastern Bengal Railway Company, L/PWD/2/163, IOR.
56 Najmu-l-Akhbar, 4 March 1887, in Native Newspaper Reports, North-Western Provinces, L/R/5/64, IOR.
57 B. Harishchandra, 'Jabalpur ki Yatra' in *Bharatendu Granthavali*, Volume III (Kashi, Nagari Pracharani Sabha), p. 640. Bharatendu interestingly used the sentence '*coolie aadi neech log*' (lit. low-class people such as coolies etc) to define the groups of people who travelled in fourth-class carriages.
58 Letter from Captain F.S. Taylor, Joint Secretary to the Government of Bengal to Baboo Koylas Chunder Bannerjee, dated 20 May 1864, in Proceedings of the Railway Department, Government of Bengal, P/163/32, IOR.
59 The reference to black hole alludes to the comment made by Bengali author Kaliprasanna Sinha about the ways in which third-class carriages are crowded. Sinha, 'Hutom', p. 50. The football field analogy comes from Surendranath Ray, the author of a bengali travelogue who praised the Eastern Indian Railway Company for offering carriages as big as 'football fields' for the passengers travelling in upper-class carriages. See Ray, 'Uttar Paschim', pp. 10–11.
60 R. Kipling, 'The Man who would be king' in R. Bond (ed.), *The Penguin Book of Indian Railway Stories* (Penguin, New Delhi, 1994).
61 Goswami, 'Producing India', Chapter 3.
62 Reports in Indian languages newspapers often underlined this concern.
63 B. Harishchandra, 'Janakpur ki Yatra', in *Bharatendu Granthavali*, Volume III (Kashi, Nagaripracarani Sabha), pp. 665–666. Though on his trip to Janakpur Bharatendu admitted to have suffered (without specifics) because he had Europeans as travel companions; but he narrated a previous travel experience earlier that year when he had an amicable and hilarious chat with a European co-passenger.
64 P. Devi, *Aryavarta: Janoiko Banga Mahilar Bhraman Kahini* (Calcutta, 1888), pp. 5–6; B. Sengupta, *Bharat Bhraman*, Volume II (Calcutta, K.C. Daw and Company, 1877), pp. 227–228; 20; S. Basu, *Bharat Bhraman* (Calcutta, 1911), p. 10. Of these, Prasannamayi Devi admitted that her purpose of narrating civil behaviour from her European co-passengers was to offer a variant on the theme. For more on this, see Chapter 7.

138 *Chariots of equality?*

65 'The Humble Petition of the British Indian Association', dated 16 October 1866 from Syud Ahmed, Secretary and others, British Indian Association, North Western Provinces to His Excellency the Viceroy and Governor-General of India in Council, in Miscellany Railway Letters, L/PWD/2/190 (1865–1867), IOR. Emphasis mine.
66 The Samaj, 24 November 1893, Newspaper Report Bengal, L/R/5/19, IOR.
67 *Dainik and Samachar Chandrika*, 10 October 1887, Native Newspaper Reports, Bengal, L/R/5/13, IOR. Emphasis mine.
68 *Samaya*, 9 December 1887, Native Newspaper Reports, Bengal, L/R/5/13, IOR.
69 Working Order No. 267: Third Class European Passengers dated 27 July 1868, in Proceedings of the Railway Department, Government of Bengal, P/433/44, IOR.
70 Memorandum of matters for discussion at the Railway Conference by Major F.S. Taylor, dated 11–14 January, Calcutta, in Proceedings of the Railway Department, Government of Bengal, P/264, IOR.
71 'Regarding a Mahomedan gentleman being refused admittance into a first-class carriage at Kooshtea', dated September 1869, in Proceedings of the Railway Department, Government of Bengal, P/433/47, IOR.
72 Report of the Consulting Engineer to the Government on the Oudh and Rohilkhand Railway for the financial year 1873–1874 in V/24/3582, IOR.
73 Bear, 'Lines of the nation', part I, Chapter 2; Prasad, 'Tracks of change'.
74 *Koh-i-Nur*, 15 July 1871, Native Newspaper Report, North-Western Provinces, L/R/5/48, IOR. Emphasis mine.
75 *Urdu Akhbar*, 16 November 1871, Native Newspaper Report, North-Western Provinces, L/R/5/48, IOR. Emphasis mine.
76 *The Hindu Prakash*, 17 July 1874, Native Newspaper Reports, North-Western Provinces, L/R/51, IOR.
77 *Khair Khwah-i-Alam*, 15 August 1874, Native Newspaper Reports, North-Western Provinces, L/R/5/51, IOR.
78 *Khair Khwah-i-Alam*, 4 December 1877, Native Newspaper Reports, North-Western Provinces, L/R/5/, IOR.
79 *Bharat Bandhu*, 28 May 1880, Native Newspaper Reports, North-Western Provinces, L/R/5/57, IOR.
80 *Aftab-i-Punjab*, 30 June 1882; also *Surur-i-Qaisari*, 31 December 1886, in Native Newspaper Reports, North-Western Provinces, L/R/5/59 and L/R/5/63, IOR.
81 *Koh-i-Nur*, 25 December 1880, Native Newspaper Report, North-Western Provinces, L/R/5/57, IOR.
82 *Oudh Akhbar* (18 March), *Shola-i-Tur* (15 March) and *Rahbar-i-Hind* (17 March), Native Newspaper Reports, North-Western provinces, L/R/5/58, IOR.
83 Letter from the Secretary of the British Indian Association to the Secretary to the Railway Conference, Simla, dated 15 September 1888 in Proceedings of the Railway Department, Government of Bengal, P/3632, IOR. Emphasis mine.
84 *Sanjivani* and *Bangabasi*, 3 November 1885, Native Newspaper, Bengal, L/R/5/11, IOR.
85 *Navavibhakar*, 11 September 1882, Newspaper Reports Bengal, L/R/5/8, IOR.
86 *Bangabasi*, 4 February, Newspaper Reports Bengal, L/R/5/14, IOR.
87 *Navavibhakar*, 27 December 1886, Newspaper Reports Bengal, L/R/5/13, IOR.
88 *Sulabha Samachar*, 2 September 1887, Newspaper Reports Bengal, L/R/5/13, IOR.
89 'Indian railways' in *Cornhill Magazine*, July 1869, IOR.
90 Prasad, 'Tracks of change'; Chapters 1 and 2. Prasad's analysis mostly focuses on why the problem of overcrowding in lower-class carriages was never resolved despite strident protests and demands. She identifies a chronic lack of rolling stock as the main culprit.

91 Note by Captain F.S. Taylor, Consulting Engineer to the Government of Bengal, Inspection Report of the EIRC for the second quarter of the year 1866, in 'Miscellany railway letters', L/PWD/2/190 [1865–67], IOR.
92 'Petition from a frequent traveller by rail' to the Honourable the Viceroy and Governor General in Council, Cawnpore, 31 October 1865, in Proceedings of the Railway Department, Government of Bengal, P/163/36, (July–December) 1865, IOR.
93 'Extract from a report in Native Paper on imperfect lighting of third class carriages on the Eastern Indian Railway' in the Proceedings of the Railway Department, Government of Bengal, P/265, 1871, IOR.
94 Letter from Cecil Stephenson, Chairman, Board of Agency, Eastern Indian Railway Company to the Traffic Manager, Eastern Indian Railway Company, Jamalpur, 7 June 1869, in Proceedings of the Railway Department, Government of Bengal, P/433/46, 1869
95 *Som Prakash*, 7 May 1887; and *Sahachar*, 9 May 1887, in Native Newspaper Reports Bengal, L/R/5/13, IOR.
96 For passenger demanding similar facilities see Hindustan, 15 July 1892, in Selections from Native Newspaper Reports, NWP, L/R/5/69, IOR.
97 Annual Railway Report for the year 1892–1893, Chapter VIII, 'Details of revenue earning and expenditure'.
98 *Prayag Samachar*, 9 April 1896, Native Newspaper Reports, NWP, L/R/5/73 and *Bangabasi*, 2 March 1902, Native Newspaper Reports, Bengal, L/R/5/28, IOR.
99 Correspondence regarding the provision of latrines to intermediate class carriages, and the inconvenience and discomfort of native female passengers, dated July 1890, in Proceedings of the Railway Department, Government of Bengal, P/3632; and *Hindustan*, 20 September 1892, Native Newspaper Reports, NWP, L/R/5/69, IOR.
100 Ananda Bazar Patrika, 24 September 1883, Native Newspaper Report, Bengal, L/R/5/10, IOR. Exception to this rule was the *Darjeeling Mail* and the local trains of the network.
101 Inspection Report by Major Hovendon, dated 14 March 1865, in Proceedings of the Railway Department, Government of Bengal, P/163/35, IOR.
102 East Indian Railway: report on the cost of completing the main, chord and Jabalpur lines from 1 January 1868, in Letters to and from Eastern Indian Railway Company, L/PWD/2/84, IOR.
103 Extract of a letter from Deputy Secretary to the Government of India, Public Works Department to the consulting engineer to the Government of India for guaranteed railways, dated 4 March 1874, in Home Correspondence, B copies of letters sent, 1849–1879, L/PWD/2/73, IOR.
104 For the Railway rule, see H. Bell, *Railway Policy in India* (London, Rivington, Percival and Company, 1894), Chapter 6. Railway companies differed widely in the rules for the maximum number of passengers in each carriage, for instance: Eastern Indian Railway authorities fixed the number of passengers to be seated at each bench of their third-class carriages at five persons.
105 Letter from the Chief Justice of Indore to Secretary of the Railway Conference, dated 5 September 1888, in Proceedings of Railway Department, Government of Bengal, P/3632, IOR.
106 *Subodh Sindhu*, 5 January 1887, Native Newspaper Report, NWP, L/R/5/64, IOR.
107 B. Harishchandra, 'Baidyanath ki Yatra', in *Bharatendu Granthavali*, Volume III (Kashi, Nagaripracarani Sabha), p. 660.
108 Judging by the Indian newspaper reports, compared to other networks in the region, the Oudh and Rohilkhand Railway network dealt with overcrowding in lower-class carriages better.

109 *Bangabasi*, 5 May 1894, Newspaper Reports, Bengal, L/R/5/20, IOR.
110 In an interesting historiographical shift historians have argued that in the colonies the 'whiteness' of colonisers was not a homogenous category; but was fractured along lines of social class and distinctions. See for instance, H. Fischer-Tiné, *Low and Licentious Europeans: Race, class and white subalternity in colonial India* (Hyderabad, Orient Blackswan, 2009); S. Mizutani, *The Meaning of White: Race, class, and the 'domiciled community' in British India 1858–1930* (New York, Oxford University Press, 2011).
111 *Sanjivani*, 29 December 1904, Newspaper Reports, Bengal, L/R/5/31, IOR.

5 To eat or not to eat?

Railway travel, commensality and social change in colonial India

In the famous Bengali author Bibhutibhushan Bandyopadhyay's novel *Adarsha Hindu Hotel*, Hajari Thakur, the main protagonist beats many financial and social odds to become the owner and eventually a contractor of a railway hotel.[1] But what makes Hajari Thakur's success particularly worth celebrating is his journey from being a low-paid hired cook in one of the numerous 'railway hotels' that dotted the precincts of the Ranaghat station[2] to being the owner of one. Thus, at first glance, Hajari Thakur's career vicissitudes reflect the classic plotline of an underdog making it to the top, and hence the enduring appeal of the novel. A closer read however, reveals that the entrepreneurial success of Hajari was largely a product of the intersection of the following two factors: *one*, inadequate, if not entirely absent official refreshment arrangements for Indian railway passengers; and *two*, largely as a response to the former, the creation of a dynamic food market by Indians catering to demands of various social groups of Indian passengers including adherence to rules of commensality.[3]

Interestingly, however, railway officials and policies are not altogether absent from this story and by implication from Hajari's success. If anything, railway policies, especially the newly established Railway Board's desire to have 'Hindu hotels' at various railway stations played a significant role in furthering Hajari's enterprise and career.[4] Additionally, more than once Hajari enjoys official attention and patronage because passengers wrote letters to railway authorities extolling his services, particularly his cooking. Indeed, recommendations by Indian railway passengers influenced the official decision to offer the contract of the first 'Hindu hotel' at the Ranaghat station to Hajari, an appointment that eventually secured him the contract to work as a supervisor of cooks at various railway hotels across the Great Indian Peninsular network. Thus, though a fictional account, the novel nevertheless brings out well the chasm between Indian passengers' needs for refreshments and the inadequacies of official responses. More importantly, the novel underlines the ways in which food arrangements were aligned along class and caste lines, a system that was also informed by imperatives of profit. Last but not least, the story illustrates Indian presence and agency both at the level of contesting (demanding better facilities) and supporting (recommending cooks) shifting boundaries of railway refreshment policies (establishment of Hindu hotels at railway stations). Given this, I use *Adarsha Hindu Hotel* as an apposite literary entry point to explore refreshment arrangements for Indian railway passengers and its wider implications on colonial Indian society.

The historiography of refreshment arrangements on colonial Indian Railways

> I love the stations of the Eastern Indian Railway Company's network dearly. Irrespective of the time of the day or the season, the food vendors shout [to sell] puris, sweetmeats, malai, warm milk, apples, guavas, pears, tea. The effect of it [on the ears] is quite pleasant.[5]

Food vendors and their shouts renting the air of the stations were certainly one of the ubiquitous experiences of railway travelling in India.[6] As such, the romantic image conjured by the above quote from a Bengali travelogue written in the early decades of the twentieth century is not entirely inaccurate. But like all romantic images, this excerpt too, conceals some not-so-appealing details. A case in point would be the specific reference to the Eastern Indian Railway network's stations. Surely, one can argue that the choice was merely a matter of personal preference and hence not worth examining. But I suggest that Chatterjee's preference was also informed by something more practical, that is, the reality that availability of food varied from one network to another. Similarly, the din created by the noises of food vendors selling their diverse offerings may have had a pleasing effect on the author; but here I argue it is also suggestive of: (*a*) refreshment arrangements being influenced by caste and religious sensibilities;[7] and (*b*) an arrangement in which Indians, both as passengers and food vendors played a critical role. Last but not least, Chatterjee's silence on refreshment rooms too, is telling. At an obvious level, it indicates that unlike food vendors, refreshment rooms were not available at every station, thus once again underscoring uneven provisions. At another, perhaps more critical level, it brings out the fact that refreshment rooms, even when available, where fraught social spaces are shaped and contested by various factors including race and food preferences informed by social backgrounds and rules of commensality.[8]

Given this, it is surprising that, except more recently,[9] refreshment arrangements for Indian passengers on colonial Indian railways has attracted little attention either from contemporary colonial observers or in post-colonial railway historiography. As for the former, railway promotional literature often implicitly assumed that imperatives of consuming food in transit would break down religious and caste prejudices of Indian passengers, reinforcing similar influences from sitting in close physical proximity in carriages or waiting rooms. Interestingly, the force of such expectations diminished as railway operations commenced in India, a response perhaps reflective of an awareness of the railway enterprise in India being a commercial venture and thus the need for arrangements that would accrue profit; as well as a sobering but clear knowledge of the practical and political challenges that could have accompanied any attempt to tamper with the existing rules of commensality in India. In other words, the growing silence of the colonial administration on the putative socially transformative impact of railway catering suggests a complex role between railway rhetoric and reality; more of which in subsequent sections. As for post-colonial railway historiography, there is little beyond the scholarly consensus about the inadequacies of refreshment arrangements for Indian passengers.[10]

Though never explicitly stated, the shortcomings of the refreshment arrangements are primarily interpreted as mirroring the ills of a colonial railway system that cared little for Indian railway passengers. For instance, Manu Goswami notes that the railway authorities ignored the inadequacies of the system with the convenient excuse of 'native caste and religious prejudices'.[11] More recently, Ritika Prasad's work has enriched our knowledge by providing a sophisticated analysis of refreshment arrangements for Indian passengers within the broader context of social issues (mainly exclusion and inclusion) raised by the everyday reality of railway travel in colonial India.[12] These assessments are certainly accurate; with Prasad's contribution coming closest to a detailed and nuanced examination of refreshment arrangements and its potential social consequences. Nevertheless, these expositions overlook some critical details. For instance, at our current state of knowledge on the subject, there is little or no awareness of the ways in which refreshment arrangements for Indian passengers evolved through the mid-nineteenth century into the twentieth. More critically, we know little about why the refreshment arrangements evolved gradually and unevenly. Neither is there enough discussion about Indian passenger responses to refreshment arrangements except the oft-repeated claim that the facilities were inadequate and consequently elicited protest and grievances. At a related level, we know little, if anything, about the interactions between the needs and demands of Indian railway passengers often expressed through dictates of the rules of commensality and railway administrations' balancing act between a desire for profit and steam-induced socially progressive rhetoric.

Clearly, these are important questions and processes; and this chapter makes an initial effort to address them, though in a rather limited manner. Inasmuch, the chapter represents a historiographical departure; especially in its focus on Indian presence and participation in the context of railway refreshment facilities. Underlining the ways in which inadequate official arrangements provided occasions for Indian entrepreneurs to provide a diverse and dynamic food market, an aspect usually ignored in current historiography, this chapter argues for visible Indian agency. At a related level, here I argue that the presence of Indians was critical as it provided dynamism and even challenged official refreshment arrangements. More importantly perhaps, the Indian participation and enterprise in the refreshment provisions illustrates how Indian railway passengers were not mere recipients of railway policies imposed from above. On the contrary, the latter's clear denunciation of the inadequate official refreshment arrangements and an ability to secure alternate sources of supply that also denuded the profit prospect of the former significantly informed the railway administrations' decision to accept Indian participation as food vendors.[13]

144 *To eat or not to eat?*

In short, this chapter is mainly about Indian passengers and their role in shaping the contours of railway refreshment policies. The analysis has the advantage of not only widening and complicating our existing assumptions about refreshment provisions in colonial Indian railways; but it also provides vital clues to understand any links between railway operations and wider social change in colonial India, a widely accepted idea, though rarely investigated.

Catering to commensality: water supply arrangements for Indian railway passengers

It will not be an exaggeration to claim that catering provisions for Indian railway passengers was primarily an awkward combination of humanitarian gesture and economic common sense. The former, though periodically visible, was largely ineffective as its application was either too late or too little. The latter, on the contrary, played a more prominent role and was essentially guided by the reality that 'native' passenger traffic was the mainstay of railway revenue in colonial India. This awareness however, was counter balanced by a clear knowledge that the food habits of Indian passengers were likely to be guided by rules of commensality. As such, the aim was not to offend the caste and religious sensibilities and consequently risking a loss of revenue. Needless to say, following both elaborate as well as variable rules of commensality posed a logistical and a financial challenge to the railway companies. As such, railway companies were divided between investing in catering provisions to attract a greater number of Indian passengers and the prerequisite for doing so ironically entailed additional capital outlay. Given this, it is possibly not surprising that even the initial attempts at providing refreshment facilities to passengers came a decade after the commencement of railway operations in India. For instance, in 1867, the Eastern Indian Railway Company decided to supply drinking water to passengers at the various stations along its expanding network, thus initiating catering arrangements for Indian passengers.[14]

From a financial point of view, supplying water made good sense; the arrangement did not entail substantial investment, and the vast size of India, the length of train journeys, and a severe and prolonged summer provided ennobling, humane justifications to bolster the former. Additionally, by 1867–1868, the East Indian Railway Company's network from Calcutta (Howrah) to Delhi was nearing completion and the need to attract more Indian passengers by offering a new and a vital source of refreshment propelled the decision to supply water. The aim was to secure more passengers; hence unsurprisingly, the Company decided to respect the existing rules of commensality and provided a rather elaborate arrangement by employing *bhistis* (water carriers) of each caste to supply 'native passengers with pure water through earthen filters'.[15] So keen was the Company to know if the arrangements had met 'prejudices of the different castes' that the Board demanded regular inspection reports from the agent to gauge passenger responses. The inspection report of 1868 noted or rather gloated with satisfaction about passengers' acceptance of the service and the facilities having received their approval.[16] If the correspondence of the Eastern Indian Railway Company and sundry other reports are anything to go by then passenger endorsement of the system played an important role in both sustaining water supply arrangements at stations and expanding it towards different directions such as the construction of wells in station precincts to keep a steady source of supply at hand.[17]

For instance, an anonymous passenger petition in 1865 complained about the lack of wells 'close to the stations' from which travellers could drink water.[18] Interestingly, excerpts from this petition found their way to the agent of the Eastern Indian Railway Company who used it to seek greater capital outlay to construct wells and piping at various stations of the network.[19] Though here too, repeating a pattern noted in previous chapters, bigger stations usually received facilities quicker than the smaller ones.[20] Eventually, other railway companies too followed the Eastern Indian Railway Company's water supply arrangement pattern and usually employed high caste Hindus and Muslims as *bhistis* to provide drinking water at the railway stations to Hindu and Muslim passengers respectively. Some companies even employed Brahmins to cater specifically to the Brahmin passengers. For instance, Saratchandra Shastri, the author of a Bengali travelogue noted how Ratlam-Godhra branch line employed Brahmin children to supply *Brahmanchya Paniya* (Brahmin water) exclusively to its Brahmin passengers.[21] However, there were some exceptions too. The Madras Railway Company for instance, did not employ *bhistis* and the water was supplied in buckets through pipes and the passengers either drank directly from the pipe or filled up their *lotas* (water vessels) from the bucket.[22] Similar arrangements were also made by the Bengal and Nagpur railway company. Though the guidebook of the company wherein this arrangement is described also made it clear that 'under no circumstances passengers were allowed to dip their lotas in the bucket', implying scrupulous care was taken to maintain caste rules.[23]

The growth of drinking water facilities was thus slow. The arrangement was also uneven with facilities varying between the size of the stations as well as the network. As alluded to above, passengers at smaller stations usually suffered more than those in larger or principal stations. For instance, an inspection report of the Eastern Indian Railway Company noted that *bhistis* were in attendance on the platforms of all stations barring those which were classified as 'fourth class'.[24] Better facilities at larger stations is also attested to by travelogues; though here too, facilities varied from one network to another. For instance, Surendranath Ray, the author of a Bengali travelogue deeply appreciated an early morning stop at the Patna station (on the Eastern Indian Railway Company's network) where not only did the *bhisti* supply him with an adequate amount of warm water, but also with sprig of a neem tree with which to clean his teeth. Albeit, this generous service came in anticipation of a suitable reward and Ray did not disappoint his 'eager' servitor.[25] As opposed to this image of generous and timely service, Bharatendu Harishchandra complained that on his way to Ayodhya (Awadh and Rohilkhand network) passengers were not only refused water; but were also threatened in abusive language by the woman who supplied it.[26] On another occasion too, Bharatendu noted a similar lack of service; though this time on the

Great Indian Peninsular Railway Company's network. The author was on his way to Itarsi from Jabalpur and he noted that the passengers' cries for water were blatantly ignored by employees at various railway stations along the way.[27]

Given such variability in water supply arrangements, it is not surprising that Indian railway passengers complained. Their grievances reveal two distinct, though at times, overlapping concerns. Of these, not surprisingly, one is about the inadequate and varying water supply arrangements.[28] But Indian passengers were equally, if not more, anxious about the maintenance of rules of commensality or its putative violation by either some of the railway administration or even by passengers and, consequently, blamed the railway authorities for being biased towards one or other religious community or social group. For instance, a report in the newspaper *Hitakari* complained that the water supply arrangements on the Eastern Bengal State Railway's network were 'intended specially and almost exclusively for Hindus'. Questioning the validity of these arrangements the report enquired:

> Do not Mahomedans travel on that line, or are Mahomedans such mean creatures as not to deserve any attention at the hands of the railway authorities.[29]

Echoing a similar concern, another report noted that on the Sindh, Punjab and Delhi Company's network 'satisfactory arrangement has not been made for supplying water to mussulman passengers'.[30] While acknowledging the presence of Hindu and Muslim water carriers at every station, the report argued that the former served only Hindu passengers; the latter Europeans as well as Muslims – an arrangement that, according to the report, did not serve Muslim passengers well.

Voicing concern over violation of rules of commensality *Oudh Akhbar* published a report, excerpts from which are worth quoting, if only because they clearly illustrate an interplay between railway policies and notions of identity.

> Sometimes Mussulman bhistis give water to both European and Mussulmans in the same cup or glass. The Hindu water carriers are also not very careful. [...] a Bengali went to a place where the Hindu carrier's bucket and brass vessel was placed, filled the vessel with water from the bucket, put it to his mouth, drank the water and again placed the vessel into the bucket. Soon after the train arrived, and the water carrier gave water to the passengers with the same bucket without cleansing them. Such things are opposed to the prejudices of Hindus and Mussulmans. The railway officers should exercise a check overt the water carriers in this matter.[31]

Using the absence of copper cups for Muslim passengers, another newspaper report argued that the Eastern Indian Railway Company favoured Hindu passengers and even demanded an intervention from the Government of India to 'force reform'.[32] Singing contrary tunes, another newspaper report complained about the dismissal of Hindu water carriers from some of the smaller stations on the Oudh and Rohilkhand Railway Company's network. In this case, the report alleged the network of favouring Muslim passengers (since Muslim water carriers were retained) and sarcastically noted that maybe the railway authorities thought that Hindus did not feel thirsty?[33]

Clearly, these reports demonstrate that for Indian railway passengers an adequate supply of water was as important as adherence to the religious and caste rules. Indeed, as the foregoing discussion suggests, more often than not, the two issues were intertwined in a pattern in which the inadequacy of supply became more apparent or a cause for concern when compared to the arrangements being provided for another social group. In other words, absence of sufficient drinking water in transit was more acutely felt if passengers belonging to other religious groups received relatively better treatment, either real or perceived. Interestingly, such passenger grievances drew official attention and were even redressed. For instance, in 1869, Edward Palmer, the then agent of the Eastern Indian Railway Company claimed to redress persistent sources of passenger complaints by introducing two reforms: one, replacing tin vessels with glass tumblers to supply water to European and Muslim passengers; and two, separating the supply of water for engine drivers thus allowing the *bhistis* to 'devote their attention entirely' to the passengers. Incidentally, Palmer argued that the second reform was aimed at making less demands on the Brahmin *bhistis*' time so they could supply water unhurriedly and thus take care to avoid any physical contact.[34]

In the same year, in response to passenger complaints, the Eastern Indian Railway Company also decided to keep two to three 'good-sized ghurras' of water in reserve, especially at larger stations, to ensure steady supply of water.[35] J. Dyer, the travelling inspector of the Company noted that this reform was instituted to ensure both a sufficient reserve of water, especially at larger stations, as well as to avoid Hindu and Muslim water carriers from using the same ghurra for supplying water to all passengers regardless of their religious differences. In another instance of conflating the two demands, in 1873, a missive from the Government of India noted:

> Considering that the line to Saharanpur has been opened several years, the railway company must have been aware of the ordinary wants of natives, especially when moving in crowds during the hot season, the defective arrangement on this occasion to supply good drinking water in sufficient quantity is not creditable to the traffic department. *I am further directed to state that such disregard of the comfort of travellers should not continue, and to request that you will distinctly report on the provision of drinking water for Mahomedans and Hindoos in all future inspection reports of the Sindh, Punjab and the Delhi Railway.*[36]

Similarly, in 1874, the agent of the Eastern Bengal State Railway network decided to employ 'one Brahmin water bearer' at all large stations largely to offset demands from high-caste passengers who did not drink the water supplied, being unsure of the caste background of the *bhistis*.[37]

Thus, railway authorities responded to passenger demands, even to those based on issues of commensality. At one level, I suggest this displays the gap between the everyday railway operations, including the need for profit and the colonial rhetoric of railway borne social progress. At another, though related level, the demands made and the responses received indicate that railway rules were more flexible and permeable to passenger demands than currently imagined. Albeit, here too, as argued in previous chapters, there were limits to the flexibility of railway rules; and consequently, passenger demands were more easily met if it did not entail huge capital expense or presented a veiled threat of withdrawal of patronage. Thus, modest reforms such as buying new *ghurras* or appointing a handful of Brahmin *bhistis*, were instituted as these certainly did not translate as big expenses; yet the benefit of ensuring passenger traffic was satisfied with the arrangements clearly scored even with the investment required. As noted previously, Indian passengers also were aware of the fact that for the railway authorities profit mattered; and thus, demanded facilities that promised putative passenger satisfaction with a potential for steady traffic in return.

These demands, however, as we have seen, were by no means a call for fair distribution of water to all passengers regardless of their caste or religious identities. If anything, it was based on what can be called a negative principle of feeling affronted if either in reality or imagination rules of commensality were violated or differential treatment of different social groups leading to uneven access to drinking water supply was suspected. Thus, interestingly enough, standardisation was both demanded and rejected; the latter mainly as a response to potential loss of social status. This, I argue, is clearly visible in the language in which grievances were framed, an articulation that often plainly privileged one social identity over another. Indeed, as the foregoing evidence indicates, there is an unambiguous use of notions of identities by Indian passengers that is hard to ignore. Deviating from current historiographical assumptions, here therefore, I argue that Indian passenger grievances played an important role in shaping both water supply arrangements as well as notions of identity. The frequent conflation of two separate concerns, i.e., inadequate drinking water supply and social issues, most notably rules of commensality suggest that Indian passengers (at least those who expressed their grievances through the newspaper columns) often filtered (pun intended) the former through the prism of identities.

This process, as we have seen, had a real impact on the ways in which water supply arrangements were organised, especially by sustaining social differentiation as opposed to levelling. This, however, is not to suggest that railway authorities did not play any role in this process of social differentiation. If anything, railway companies instituted water supply arrangements with a clear eye towards maintaining rules of commensality. Though relevant here would be to note that the nods to maintain rules of commensality was largely in response to existing rules that were appreciated by Indian passengers – a process that fuelled further demands for the same. Nevertheless, as is evident from the responses to passenger complaints, especially the acceptance of explicit demands for separate arrangements for different social groups; railway authorities certainly played an important role in adding a new layer of legitimacy to existing notions of identity. In other words, the imperatives of running a railway system with an eye towards profit certainly undermined its putative socially transformative role, if not making it entirely hollow.

Sharing food, contesting spaces: dynamics of dining in transit

Arrangements for offering food for Indian passengers were both prolonged and uneven. This was largely due to the fact that railway companies were aware that food habits of most Indian passengers were influenced by rules of commensality and thus to provide for separate arrangements to satisfy the needs of different caste and religious groups posed a serious financial challenge. Furthermore, the railway managements were cognisant of the presence of Indian food vendors, both in and around the stations – an arrangement that offered a practical and cheap solution to the issue. Adding another layer of advantage for the railway companies, these food sellers catered to the rules of commensality and as such sold a diverse range of food for different social groups of passengers. Indeed, travelogues confirm the idea that Indian food sellers were a common sight from the early days of railway operations. For instance, writing as early as 1860, Jagmohan Chakrabarty, the author of a Bengali article on the novelty of railway journeys attested to the presence of various food vendors in and around Burdwan station while on his first railway trip to Rajmahal from Calcutta.[38]

Similarly, in 1863, Kashinath Mukhopadhyay, the author of a Bengali travelogue described his experience of eating at a shop selling dry food (thus alluding to his inability to ascertain the caste status of the seller) in the precincts of the Burdwan station.[39] Evidently, Indian vendors fulfilled a crucial role in providing much needed food for passengers in transit, more of which later. Nevertheless, it did not take railway authorities long to realise providing food to 'native' passengers could be financially advantageous as well as increasing the popularity of the railways. Writing in 1864, on the eve of the opening of the Eastern Indian Railway Company's network from Calcutta to Mirzapur, the consulting engineer to the Government of North-Western provinces noted that the menus of the existing refreshment rooms catered to the taste of European and Westernised Indians while drawing a blank for the rest of the 'native' passengers who formed the bulk of traffic. This negligence was noted to be detrimental to the popularity of the railway company and consequently, the agent of the Eastern Indian Railway Company was advised to construct separate refreshment rooms for Indian passengers and even to provide sweetmeat stalls (authorised by the company) on the platforms. Interestingly, such measures were recommended also because of the presence of Indian vendors at the platform 'selling confectionary from a basket to third class native passengers in the carriages'. In other words, the aim was to offer competition to existing Indian food vendors by providing official arrangements and thus hoping to make a profit.[40]

The consulting engineer was certainly not far off the mark when he thought that despite the presence of the Indian food vendors a gap existed between the supply and passenger demands. There was indeed a demand among railway passengers for an official arrangement providing refreshment at all hours and at a reasonable price. This demand was exacerbated by the fact that the journeys, especially in slow trains, were very long and when the train stopped during the night (either for a short or long time) the passengers often faced the prospect of involuntary starvation. In fact, a petition from the British Association of North-Western Provinces and signed by Sir Syed Ahmad Khan (among others) described the lack of official provision of food as 'forced starvation for thousands'. The following lengthy excerpt from this petition is worth quoting both for the representative position it takes (on behalf of the third-class passengers, poor, helpless and ignorant) as well as the remedy proposed that demonstrates a clear awareness of what drove railway administrations to action, i.e., profit or the prospect of it.

> The want of proper nourishment, especially in long journeys, is no less the fruitful source of disease and suffering than the want of proper shelter and accommodation. Life, indeed, is often sustained during the railway journeys under great difficulty by the Hindus and Mahomedans. To speak of it in mildest term it is an enforced starvation to thousands [. . .] *but the remedy for this is as simple and inexpensive* [. . .] one large room at one of the sheds for the Hindus and one small room at the other end for Mahomedan portion of the travellers, specially devoted to supplying food of all sorts, cooked and otherwise, will be amply sufficient. *These restaurants could be placed in the hands of Mahomedans and high caste Hindu cooks, bakers and confectioners who would supply the needful. There might be even a profit to the railway company if the right of these restaurants were framed out to these cooks and confectioners. They would be erected only at the principal stations.*[41]

Such suggestions aside, railway companies were aware of the link between providing food for Indian passengers and additional profit. Indeed, as one of the inspection reports of the Eastern Railway Company noted:

> There are no stalls [company owned or contracted] for the sale of these [food] at any of the stations, but hawkers of sweetmeats, paan etc. are to be found on the platforms of almost all stations.[42]

In reality however, the solution proffered by the passenger petition quoted above or from the government's consulting engineer and Eastern Indian Railway Company's inspector was difficult to implement. The primary concern was certainly financial. As noted above, railway companies knew that attracting Indian passengers through facilities offering food would require elaborate and scrupulous arrangements for maintaining rules of commensality. This essentially translated as constructing and maintaining separate refreshment rooms, food stalls and cooks (as Sir Syed suggested) for Hindu and Muslim passengers, if not for different caste groups. Needless to say, for railway authorities the initial financial outlay needed for such elaborate arrangements often outweighed their potential advantages.

Eventually however, regardless of the misgivings, the Eastern Indian Railway Company decided to undertake some basic means of supplying food to Indian passengers. The timing of this decision by the Eastern Indian Railway Company was perhaps also influenced by a fairly lengthy harangue in the form of a circular from the Governor-General in Council against the workings of the former in Bengal. This government missive called for the provision of food and water at all stations that had refreshment rooms for the first-class passengers and these arrangements were expected 'for all classes in a manner suitable to the habits of the natives of the country'.[43] Thus, pressures, both commercial and otherwise prompted the Eastern Indian Railway Company to introduce official arrangements for supplying food to Indian passengers.[44] The preliminary arrangements were a mix of constructing refreshment rooms for Indian passengers and scheduling long halts at larger stations particularly for those travelling in slower passenger trains. However, given the costs involved, the ambit of the former measure was limited to some of the larger stations along the network.[45]

The latter system on the other hand, was more widely favoured largely because in many ways it resembled the 'refreshment stops' – an arrangement popular among railway companies in England during pre-refreshment rooms at the stations era essentially designed to avoid the expense of constructing refreshment rooms.[46] In the case of India however, railway officials argued that in-built halts for refreshment purposes would be popular among Indian passengers also because of their religious/caste need to wash and relieve themselves before eating in the morning. Such official claims were bolstered by a letter sent to the Lieutenant Governor of the North-Western Provinces by Nilkamal Mitra, a Bengali entrepreneur interested in providing food for Indian passengers at the network's larger stations.[47] While making a case for acquiring the right to build refreshment rooms for Indian passengers at the stations on the Eastern Indian Railway Company's network, Mitra argued that 'native comfort and convenience' remained unfulfilled in the ways in which slow passenger trains were run and suggested refreshment halts to improve the existing arrangements.[48] Interestingly, the Government of North-Western provinces concurred with the conclusions reached by Mitra and noted:

> There are two great wants for native travellers which we have omitted to supply, and in the absence of which, not only do the natives at present travel in the greatest discomfort, but also to great risk of their bodily health.[49]

These two 'great wants' were identified as there being a need for passenger trains to halt at daybreak for an hour to provide time for passengers to relieve themselves; and another halt between 9.00 and 12.00 in the morning, once again for an hour to enable Indian travellers to bathe and eat. The proposal to schedule two halts at refreshment stations for slow passenger trains was approved on the grounds that the 'experiment was well worth trying and as the expenses to be incurred will be small'.[50] Additionally, the Government of the North-Western Provinces approved Nilkamal Mitra's proposal to build 'rent-free, refreshment rooms' for Indian passengers – a choice that was made perhaps also because Mitra had strong recommendations from the Lieutenant Governor of the province.[51]

In eastern and northern India, these decisions largely paved the way for building separate refreshment rooms for Indian passengers. Though broadly speaking, most railway managements operating in the region followed the model already established by the Madras Railway Company and built separate refreshment rooms for Hindu and Muslims passengers; the precise arrangements however, varied among different networks. For instance, while the Oudh and Rohilkhand Railway Company established separate refreshment rooms for Hindu and Muslim passengers all along its network; the Eastern Indian Railway Company did so only at the larger stations.[52] Such differences were essentially a reflection of the costs involved in building separate refreshment rooms. Indeed, writing in 1872, G. Molesworth, Consulting Engineer to the Government of India for State Railways, frankly acknowledged the potential financial liability by noting:

> Refreshment rooms will be required on some of the longer lines of railway, though it is doubtful whether the traffic will be sufficient to induce any one to take them up as a commercial speculation. If this be the case, it may probably be necessary for Government to hold out some inducements for their establishments.[53]

At one level, Molesworth's concern about lack of traffic primarily alludes to the wider notion that after 1869 the Government agencies had concerns about the feasibility of state railways as being commercial simply because the earlier built guaranteed networks were considered to have taken the traffic rich regions. At another level, more relevant to our discussion, Molesworth's note also illustrates that it was finances that determined the availability of refreshment rooms for Indian passengers. Furthermore, the anxiety for capital outlay involved was exacerbated by the fact that there was a demand among 'native' passengers for separate arrangements for those who considered themselves as 'respectable' and did not savour (pun intended) the prospect of sharing a refreshment room with their social inferiors. The pressure from the passengers can be gauged by the fact that in the initial phase of building refreshment rooms for the former, the management of the Eastern Indian Railway Company decided to make the arrangements for 'respectable natives' without any reference to similar facilities for those who were not deemed socially worthy.[54]

Last but not least, separate refreshment rooms, even where they were built, at least in its early days, were not very popular with Indian passengers, notwithstanding the presence of Muslim and Brahmin cooks respectively. The railway companies' claim of employing Brahmin cooks was thought to be dubious and many Indian passengers were averse to accepting food cooked by someone whose caste status was unknown.[55] The presence of unofficial food vendors at the platforms and food sellers in precincts of the stations certainly contributed to the relative unpopularity of the refreshment rooms as the diverse range of food offered by the former could not be matched by the restrictive menu of the refreshment rooms. Prices too, are likely to have played a role, as with the unofficial food vendors passengers could negotiate a bargain, or even had access to an option commensurate with their ability to spend; whereas at the refreshment rooms the rates were fixed. For instance, in the hotels/shops around the railway stations along most of the networks, separate menus at differing prices and appropriately titled as 'first class' or 'second class' were available clearly with the intention to serve a wide range of budgets.[56] In short, the unofficial arrangements were flexible in the broadest sense; and attuned to meet the diverse needs of an equally diverse passenger traffic.

Given this, it is not surprising that the railway authorities looked for a cheaper solution to the issue, one that would also be acceptable to a large cross-section of Indian passengers, if not all. This conundrum engendered a process in which Indian entrepreneurs such as Nilkamal Mitra became part of the official arrangements for supplying food to Indian passengers. Though Mitra's case is more widely known because initially he was given a five-year contract by the Eastern Indian Railway Company to build refreshment rooms for Indian passengers on behalf of the latter and his enterprise became popular with the Indian passengers.[57] Mitra however, was not the only one who acquired such rights.[58] The appearance of Indian enterprise however, was not an instance of imperial largesse. Quite the contrary, for the railway authorities the system had obvious advantages. It reduced the cost as well the responsibilities of maintaining an establishment.[59] Beyond this, the railway authorities were also confident that Indians were more cognisant of the needs of the 'native passengers', and as such would provide a service that even if it goes wrong would exonerate the former from much culpability. Despite the shift to Indian management, the popularity of the refreshment room languished. This was partly due to the inflexibility alluded to above. But more importantly, the system suffered from being part of a corrupt railway financial system in which railway authorities often contracted out the right to maintain refreshment rooms to those Indians who promised better revenue-sharing arrangements or even paid a bribe.[60]

This affected the quality of the food as well as the service as the contractors were keen to recover the money by selling low quality food at a high price to passengers.[61] Consequently, besides complaining,[62] Indian passengers continued to patronise unofficial food vendors both in and outside the stations. Interestingly, this continued competition from Indian food sellers was a constant reminder to the railway authorities that profit could be made if an official arrangement could be put in place that would respond to the needs of the Indian passengers. The answer was found in providing a license to Indian food vendors enabling them to sell their wares at a fixed price determined by the railway authorities. Though some railway authorities were cautious about the plan,[63] in 1875, the Eastern Indian Railway Company formalised the arrangement by appointing licensed

Indian food vendors across its lengthy network. Profit, or at least the prospect of it, clearly played a part in this process as these official vendors sold their food at a price that was 'calculated to render them cheaper'.[64] The arrangement eventually became popular with railway authorities, because once again it subcontracted both cost and responsibility from the hands of the former, while devolving it in the hands of Indians. Additionally, for smaller networks, licensed food vendors provided an opportunity to save on the cost of building separate refreshment rooms for Indian passengers.[65]

Licensed food vendors certainly provided an additional source of food supply for Indian passengers in transit and as such were popular inasmuch as they provided more choice and competitive price. But the system of offering a license to vendors was liable to abuse and corruption. Here too, as in the case of refreshment rooms, contracts were usually given to those who offered better revenue-sharing deals to the companies. For instance, at most stations vendors had to pay a fee of 10 or 25 rupees to the railway company for permission to operate. In 1886, a newspaper report noted that the North-Western Railway Company offered the right to sell food at Lahore station for the following year to a trader who agreed to pay 2,000 rupees to the railway company instead of the earlier license holder who paid 300 rupees.[66] Similarly, another report in 1900 claimed that the Eastern Indian Railway Company 'extracted' 1,600 rupees per year from Haripada Dey, the owner of the sweetmeat shop at the Burdwan station.[67]

Unsurprisingly, Indian food vendors who obtained licenses were keen to recover the amount by overcharging customers and selling low quality, stale and unwholesome food.[68] A letter from the Chief Justice of Indore complained about the quality of food sold to Indian passengers by claiming that it was 'often badly cooked and is sometimes quite unfit to be eaten'.[69] Newspaper reports too, frequently voiced passenger grievances especially against the contract system.[70] Reports in *Naiyar-i- Azam* and *Jami-ul-Ulum* laid bare the links between license/contract fees and poor food by claiming that the contractors appointed by the Oudh and Rohilkhand Company (Messrs Chunni Lal and Muhammad Hussain) continued to sell bad food at the stations of the network leading people to suspect the integrity of Mr A. Pope, the traffic superintendent of the Company.[71] Indeed, around the turn of the century, such complaints became sufficiently rife for the government of the North-Western provinces to interfere in the process of administering contracts at stations on the Awadh and Rohilkhand railway network.[72] This intervention abolished the system of granting license to traders at stations on the Oudh and Rohilkhand Railway and empowered one Hindu and one Muslim manager to supply refreshments to Indian passengers.[73] The solution however, did not produce the desired results as these managers were accused of selling food at an even higher rate than the vendors leading one newspaper report to sarcastically comment that 'the remedy has proved worse than the disease'.[74]

At the turn of the twentieth century, railway authorities came under mounting pressures to reform the provision of food for Indian railway passengers. Much of these criticisms were voiced in the contemporary newspapers and thus have a strong political flavour decrying the unmet demands of Indian passengers as symptomatic of the inequalities of colonial system.[75] Such allegations were also bolstered by the report submitted by a committee organised in 1901 that intended to enquire about the operating and managerial conditions of railways in India. Headed by Thomas Robertson, this report suggested 'root and branch reform', and condemned the existing refreshment arrangements in words that did not please the Government of India.[76] Nevertheless, one of the suggestions advocated by Robertson was eventually adopted, a decision that finally combined the disparate railway administrations under the umbrella of the Railway Board. This new entity responded to some enduring passenger grievances such as need for *pakka* (cooked) food at the station platforms and control of the quality of food sold by vendors by the permitted opening of 'Hindu restaurants' owned and managed by Indians thus redressing the former; as well as by appointing food inspectors to ascertain the latter.[77] By 1907, even dining cars were introduced on some trains in some networks, an arrangement that eventually eroded away due to lack of accruing sufficient profit.[78]

Significant as these changes were, the Railway Board too, like the previous railway authorities, neither questioned nor introduced measures that challenged existing rules of commensality. On the contrary, the ownership and management of the railway hotels were handed out to Brahmins and Muslims.[79] Similarly, the food inspectors who were appointed were Brahmins; and the menu of the railway dining cars was calibrated to suit rules of commensality, with separate arrangements on-board for Hindus and Muslims.[80] At one level, such official responses can certainly be dismissed as a bland acceptance of 'colonial norms of commensality'[81] that the former accepted as a social prerequisite guaranteeing the financial success of railway enterprise in colonial India. This analysis enjoys an additional traction by underling the role of stereotypes in colonial governance that provided the initial impetus to introduce measures that upheld rules of commensality. Valid as these interpretations are, especially the role of stereotypes, here however, I suggest that though presumed knowledge of 'native behaviour' influenced official decisions; in reality, Indian passengers preferred facilities that respected rules of commensality. In a petition, Hindu railway passengers demanded separate railway carriages to avoid contact with Muslim passengers who ate food that contained meat, onion and garlic, the presence of which arguably threatened the ritualistic status of the high-caste Hindus.[82] Demands were also made to ban the sale of beef on railway platforms, as it 'offended' the religious sensibilities of Hindus.[83]

Such demands for 'Hindu passengers' however, did not preclude the possibility of demanding separate arrangements for different castes or resenting any arrangement that violated caste norms. For instance, a report in the Advocate underscored the issue by publishing a letter from a passenger who belonged to the 'orthodox' Bhatia community. The following excerpt from the letter is worth quoting as it amply illustrates the dual, if opposing demands of standardisation with differentiation.

The natives do not want refreshment rooms set apart for them, because they will not suit them, or, in other words, they cannot leave the prejudices of caste. But is it fair that [for] this reason they should be left to their own fate? Much might be done towards the supply of vendors selling the worst possible kind of puris and sweetmeats [. . .] In my humble opinion a permanent shop of sweetmeats and puris should be established [. . .] and the vendors should be compelled to supply good articles of food to the passengers for their money. The North-Western railway authorities have taken the lead quite recently in this direction, and excellent results, I hear have been obtained. I hope other railway companies will follow the example set by the North-Western Railway.[84]

In another instance, passengers demanded the dismissal of the Hindu vendor at the charge of the food stall at the Burdwan station because the latter's claims of being a Brahmin and thus being able to provide cooked food for all castes were contested by the former.[85] Thus, if anything, such demands demonstrate that Indian passengers preferred provisions that respected norms of commensality; demanded expansion of similar facilities; resented real or suspected cases of violation of such rules; and expected their numerical significance for railway revenue to influence official compliance. If to such sentiments one adds the list of Hindu and Muslim hotels or refreshment rooms appended in the guidebooks and some travelogues;[86] or the demands made by Sir Syed's petition about separate facilities for different religious groups; then one can safely suggest that these arrangements enjoyed wide popularity and acceptance. Wider approval can also be gauged by the fact that in the absence of official arrangements, passengers articulated notions of difference through their behaviour. For instance, Sarat-chandra Shastri, the author of a Bengali travelogue and a Brahmin, refused Muslim passengers entry into his carriage because he thought their food and body odour, reeking of garlic and meat, would make his journey unpleasant.[87]

Furthermore, though such demands and behaviour indicate that caste or religious separation was the primary concern; class too, mattered. A report in the newspaper *Hindustan* exposed the issue by claiming that while third-class passengers were 'content' with the arrangements provided and there were refreshment rooms for European passengers at every large station that was also used by 'anglicised natives'; nothing was done to meet the needs of 'educated and well-to-do Hindus'. Proffering a solution to this 'problem', the report recommended 'special refreshment rooms' for the said group, arguing that such arrangements already existed on the Awadh and Rohilkhand network.[88] Similar demands were expressed in the columns of other newspapers.[89] That social rank mattered is also reflected in the presence of first or second-class menus, suitably tailored to reflect the budget and the social status of the patrons as well as separate seating arrangements, in both official and unofficial facilities, thus underlining wider approval. Evidently, Indian passengers demanded or even desired facilities that were differentiated along social status. Interestingly however, they also demanded standardisation, even parity; though with European passengers or a handful of 'Anglicised' Indians.

In other words, here too, as in the case of water supply arrangements, dual, if opposing demands of standardisation with differentiation were made. Such discrepancies do not undermine the significance of the demands for parity, especially with European passengers. Nevertheless, the unambiguous fault lines of social status that delineate these demands does complicate our current understanding of the nature of the processes through which the arrangements for food for Indian passengers evolved and the role of the latter in shaping it.

Given this, once again, here I argue that Indian passengers played a critical role in influencing the official arrangements for providing food by demanding specific measures. Their demands and official responses demonstrate a dynamic interaction that was based on an acknowledgement of mutual strengths and weaknesses. Indian passengers were aware of their numerical strength and did not hesitate to use it to claim facilities that were considered vital or practical or both. The railway authorities conceded to this reality; illustrating that railway rules were permeable and flexible. For instance, in response to the passenger demands for dismissing the Hindu food seller at Burdwan station, the Eastern Indian Railway Company not only complied, but in addition, issued four new contracts to Brahmins to meet the passenger demands. However, here too, such concessions were circumscribed within official considerations for the profit and capital expenses involved – a process evident from the ways in which separate refreshment rooms for Hindus and Muslims were provided only at larger stations; or Indians such as Nilkamal Mitra were permitted to become part of the system. In short, though passenger demands were met haltingly and unevenly; the everyday operational realities of managing the railway network, provided occasions to each contending sides to frame negotiations in terms of identity, wider implications of which will be analysed in the next two chapters.

Conclusion

As this chapter shows, contrary to our current assumptions, railway refreshment arrangements sharpened social relations. Interestingly, as the foregoing discussion clearly indicates, demands by Indian passengers played a crucial role in this process. Passengers demanded differentiated facilities. At an obvious level, such demands question the validity of the category of 'Indian passengers', both as a colonial stereotype and post-colonial scholarly index of analysis. Additionally, this once again underlines the role of social rank and the ways in which such sentiments shaped the contours of refreshment arrangements. Evidently, Indian passengers attached significance to their religious or caste identities. This however, as we saw, did not preclude the possibility of forging wider connection based on notions of race or nationality, more of which later. But at a more critical level, the presence of the former I argue unmistakably demonstrates that Indian passengers preferred differentiation, especially based on social status, any violation of which, either real or imagined was resented. This I suggest is also clearly reflected in their enduring patronage of unofficial refreshment arrangements, particularly food. Of course, passenger decisions were also a product of inadequate official arrangements, including lack of flexibility in terms of availability or timing. But relevant here will be to note that as the evidence above illustrates, at times, passengers rejected official arrangements if they noticed or perceived an absence of lack of adherence to rules of commensality. An excellent case in point will be the petition signed by Sir Syed Ahmad that demanded separate refreshment for Hindu and Muslim passengers. Yet, as we know, such facilities, even when available, remained unpopular primarily because passengers were unsure about the credentials of the cook and had little desire to jeopardise their social rank.

Given this, it is unsurprising that the belated and inadequate official refreshment arrangements eventually attempted to replicate the prevailing unofficial model as closely as possible; also, because the latter enjoyed the additional advantage of being commercially viable. This, however, is not an attempt to dismiss the role of railway authorities in introducing measures that had put caste and religious identities and that of social rank (at any rate, implicit in acceptance of caste hierarchy) at the centre of refreshment arrangements. Neither is it to argue that the colonial stereotyping of Indians and Indian society did not play a role in this process. Nevertheless, as the explicit demands by Indian passengers for differential facilities indicate, refreshment arrangements evolved through a complex process of interaction between railway authorities and the former – a system that was informed by an awareness of mutual need. As for the railway authorities, the need was profit and more often than not, it was clearly articulated. Indian passengers knew this reality that governed everyday operations of railways and thus demanded facilities that suited their agendas.

Indeed, as Sir Syed's direct reference to profit that the railway companies could make by erecting separate food halls for Hindu and Muslim passengers or newspaper reports that clamoured for separate arrangements for Hindus based on their numerical preponderance in passenger traffic suggest, Indian passengers comprehended their significance, even if notionally. More importantly, here I suggest that this awareness of the functional realities of railway operations provided opportunities to different social groups to contest the social spaces engendered by the former. In other words, passenger demands were attempts to assert social precedence using existing notions in a new context, that is, the railway spaces. This is neither surprising nor unique to India. As argued before, railway travel produced social anxieties, primarily deriving out of prospects of social levelling. But what makes the Indian example interesting is its colonial context, that adds a political layer to the contestations, demonstrating a desire particularly on the part of educated, middle-class, Hindus to position themselves as representative of Indian masses and thus eligible to demand action on a collective (read national/racial) basis; while at the same time asserting a superior position vis-à-vis other Indian social groups.

This is amply illustrated if one compares the passenger grievances that claimed parity with European passengers, as opposed to those that were about uneven refreshment arrangements. Of course, occasionally such demands overlapped; and in such instances, the political nature of contestation of railway spaces is clearly visible as the inadequate facilities were criticised as indicative of racial or national or both indignities. But as shown above, interestingly, such claims did not impede either demands for boundaries or preference for differentiated refreshment facilities. If anything, the language in which such demands were framed is clearly indicative of a desire to contest new railway specific social spaces as well as to assert superior rights over the same. Given this, it is no coincidence that the passenger demands essentially asked questions such as to whom do the refreshment rooms belong? Or for that matter, which social group will have greater access to drinking water? Or last but not least, what kind of food platform vendors should sell? As such, it is perhaps not surprising that the selling of beef was resented. Neither is it without significance that the number of *bhistis* serving Muslim passengers created a ruckus. Thus, here I suggest that the underlining issue that drove such demands and grievances was not the inadequate arrangement *per se*; though as noted, that too mattered. But, more crucial was how refreshment arrangements could or should conform to superior rights of one social group or another.[90]

Indeed, as the appeals to railway authorities and occasionally government agencies to upheld putative norms indicate, contestation, as opposed to a conclusive decision as to whom railway spaces belonged marked the evolution of refreshment facilities. As a concluding note, such interactions and interventions between authorities, both railways and otherwise, and Indian passengers once again show that railway rules were amenable to passenger demands, if only to ensure profit. Nevertheless, this pursuit of profit certainly challenged both the intent and implementation of the colonial state's exalted rhetoric of steam borne social progress.

Notes

1 B. Bandyopadhyay, *Adarsha Hindu Hotel* (Calcutta, Mitra and Ghosh, 1940).
2 In the late nineteenth century, Ranaghat was an important junction on the Eastern Bengal Railway network and the Bengal Central Railway Company.
3 The name 'Hindu hotel' itself is suggestive of rules of commensuality being maintained while in transit.
4 This will be discussed later in the chapter.
5 F.C. Chatterjee, *Pather Katha* (Calcutta, 1911), p. 20.
6 Travelogues by Indian and European railway passengers routinely described similar 'scenes' at railway stations. Such descriptions suggest an influence of the tropes and literary sensibilities of English language guidebooks on railway passengers. For an analysis of how guidebooks influenced Indian railway passengers' experiences and interpretations of train journeys, see A. Mukhopadhyay, 'Colonised gaze? Guidebooks and journeying in colonial India', *South Asia: Journal of South Asian Studies*, 37, 4, 2014, pp. 656–669.
7 Chatterjee's list of food sold at the platforms consists of only *kachha* or uncooked food. This does not indicate an absence of cooked food, but demonstrates the variety of food choices available, a diversity that was certainly influenced by caste or religious sensibilities of Indian railway passengers.
8 This theme will be explored later in the chapter.
9 Ritika Prasad's recent work being an exception inasmuch as it offers a relatively detailed discussion of refreshment arrangements for Indian passengers. See R. Prasad,

160 *To eat or not to eat?*

    Tracks of Change: Railways and everyday life in colonial India (Cambridge University Press, New Delhi, 2015), Chapter 2.
10 I. Kerr, *Engines of Change: The railroads that made India* (Praeger, USA; 2007), pp. 98–99; M. Goswami, *Producing India: From colonial economy to national press* (University of Chicago Press, Chicago, 2004), p. 118.
11 Goswami, 'Producing India', p. 118.
12 Prasad, 'Tracks of change', p. 6.
13 As we will see later in the chapter, this included both private entrepreneurs and contracted employees of the railway companies.
14 The timing is significant as the network reached completion (from Calcutta to Delhi) in 1864/65. As such, passenger traffic increased with an uninterrupted network. See G. Huddleston, *History of the East Indian Railway* (London, Thacker and Smith, 1906).
15 'A note on supply of drinking water to passengers', dated 8 July 1867, in Letters to and from Eastern Indian Railway Company, L/PWD/2/83, IOR.
16 Quarterly Inspection Report, Eastern Indian Railway Company, dated May 1868, in Letters to and from the Eastern Indian Railway Company, L/PWD/2/84, IOR.
17 Board's letter to the agent of the Eastern Indian Railway Company, dated October 1875, in Letters to and from the Eastern Indian Railway Company, L/PWD/2/91, IOR.
18 Translation of an anonymous petition, dated 24 February 1865, in Proceedings of the railway department, Government of Bengal, P/163/35, IOR.
19 'A note on drinking water at stations', dated November 1876, in Letters to and from the Eastern Indian Railway Company, L/PWD/2/92, IOR.
20 'Well at Mughalserai', dated May 1878, in Letters to and from the Eastern Indian Railway Company, L/PWDP/2/94, IOR. In this case, a sum of 1700 rupees was sanctioned by the Eastern Indian Railway Company's Board to construct a well at the compound of the Mughalserai station.
21 S. Shastri, *Dakshinapath Bhraman* (Calcutta, B. Banerjee and Company, 1911), p. 132.
22 Ibid. Also see *Illustrated Guide to the South Indian Railway* (Madras, Higginbotham, 1900).
23 Travel in India or city, shrine or sea-beach: antiquities, health resorts and places of interest on the Bengal Nagpur Railway (Bombay, The Times Press, 1916).
24 Inspection report by Major Hovendon, dated 14 March 1865, in Proceedings of the Railway Department, Government of Bengal, P/163/35, IOR.
25 S.N. Ray, *Uttar Paschim Bhraman* (Calcutta, Pashupati Press, 1907), p. 16.
26 B. Harishchandra, *Sarayupar ki Yatra* in *Bharatendu Granthavali*, Volume III (Kashi, Nagaripracarani Sabha), pp. 653–654.
27 B. Harishchandra, 'Jabalpur ki Yatra', in *Bharatendu Granthavali*, Volume III (Kashi, Nagaripracarani Sabha), p. 650.
28 *Amrita Bazar Patrika*, 18 May 1876, Newspaper Reports, Bengal, L/R/5/2; *Charu Varta*, 24 September 1883, Newspaper Reports, Bengal, L/R/5/9; *Koh-i-Nur*, 5 August 1871, Newspaper Reports, North-Western Province, L/R/5/48, IOR.
29 *Hitakari*, 2 April 1891, Newspaper Reports, Bengal, L/R/5/17, IOR.
30 *Sadiq-ul-Akhbar*, 3 June 1880, Newspaper Reports, NWP, L/R/5/57, IOR.
31 *Oudh Akhbar*, 2 October 1880, Newspaper Reports, NWP, L/R/5/57, IOR.
32 *Najmu-i-Akhbar*, 4 March 1887, Newspaper Reports, NWP, L/R/5/64, IOR.
33 *Tahzib*, 19 December 1888, Newspaper Reports, NWP, L/R/5/65, IOR.
34 Report on the supply of drinking water to passengers on Eastern Indian Railway for the second half of 1869, by Edward Palmer, dated 29 January 1870, in Proceedings of the Railway Department, Government of Bengal, P/433/49, IOR.
35 Half Yearly Inspection report of the supply of drinking water to passengers on the Eastern Indian Railway Network, dated 1 June 1869, from J. Dyer, officiating travelling

To eat or not to eat? 161

inspector to the Chairman of the Board of the Agency, Eastern Indian Railway, in Proceedings of the Railway Department, Government of Bengal, P/433/47, IOR.

36 Letter from the Government of India, Public Works Department to the Consulting Engineer to Government of India for Guaranteed Railway System, dated 28 June 1873, in Proceedings of the Public Works Department (Railway Branch), Government of India, P/578. This Government order was in response to a particularly scathing letter from A.C.C. DeRenzy (the sanitary commissioner of Punjab) that criticised the Sindh, Punjab and Delhi Railway Company's inadequate water supply arrangements for pilgrims returning from the Haridwar fair. For DeRenzy's letter see Letter from A.C.C. DeRenzy, Sanitary Commissioner of Punjab to the Secretary to the Government of Punjab, dated 18 April 1873, in Proceedings of the Public Works Department (Railway Branch) Government of India, P/578 (Guaranteed Railways). Emphasis mine.

37 A note on native passengers travelling by rail, dated July 1874, in Proceedings of the Railway Department, Government of Bengal, P/265, IOR.

38 J. Chakrabarty, 'My first railway to Rajmehal', in *Mookerjee's Magazine*, 1, 1 February 1860 (Calcutta, 1861), IOR.

39 K. Mukhopadhyay, *Railway Companion* (Calcutta, 1863), pp. 6–7.

40 'Inspection of railway stations', a note by the consulting Engineer to the Government of North-Western Provinces, on the stations in the North-Western Provinces between Allahabad and Agra, dated 15 March 1864, in Proceedings of the Railway Department, Government of NWP and Oudh, P/217/37, 1864, IOR.

41 'The Humble Petition of the British Indian Association', dated 16 October 1866, from Syud Ahmed, Secretary and others, British Indian Association, North-Western Provinces to His Excellency the Viceroy and Governor-General of India in Council, in Miscellany Railway Letters, L/PWD/2/190 (1865–1867), IOR. Emphasis mine.

42 Inspection Report for the year 1865 by Major Hovendon, dated March 1865, in Proceedings of the Railway Department, Government of Bengal, P/163/35, IOR.

43 Administration of Railways in Bengal, Circular Number 13, dated 27 August 1864, from Colonel R. Strachey, Secretary to the Government of India, Public Works Department, to the Joint Secretary to the Government of Bengal, Public Works Department, Railway Branch in Proceedings of the Railway Department, Government of Bengal, P/163/33, IOR.

44 In this context, unlike water supply arrangements, the Eastern Indian Railway Company was not the initiator of the reform. That distinction goes to the Madras railway company that had separate eating rooms constructed for Hindu and Muslim passengers respectively.

45 These stations were Armenian ghat, Howrah, Mirzapur, Allahabad, Etawa, Aligarh and Ghaziabad, see 'Proposal to construct waiting and refreshment rooms for natives at Burdwan, Sahebganj, Danapur and Cawnpore', dated June 1868, in Proceedings of the Railway Department, Government of Bengal, P/433/44, IOR.

46 S. Bradley, *The Railways: Nation, network and people* (London, Profile Books, 2015), pp. 46 and 473.

47 Excerpts of a letter from baboo Nil Comul Mitter, dated 14 May 1869, in the Extract from Minutes of official meeting held on 27 May 1869, in Proceedings of the Railway Department, Government of Bengal, P/433/44, IOR.

48 Ibid.

49 'Proposal to construct waiting and refreshment rooms for natives at Burdwan, Sahebganj, Danapur and Cawnpore', dated June 1868, in Proceedings of the Railway Department, Government of Bengal, P/433/44, IOR.

50 Ibid.

51 Ibid.

52 *Oudh Akhbar*, 29 March 1872, in Newspaper Reports, North-Western provinces, L/R/5/49; 'Proposal to construct waiting and refreshment rooms for natives at Burdwan,

162   To eat or not to eat?

   Sahebganj, Danapur and Cawnpore', dated June 1868 in Proceedings of the Railway Department, Government of Bengal, P/433/44, IOR.
53 Report on State Railways in India by Guilford Molesworth, Consulting Engineer to the Government of India for State Railways in Proceedings of the Railway Branch, Public Works Department, Government of India, P/586, IOR.
54 'A note by Major Hovendon', Officiating Consulting Engineer Bengal, dated August 1869, in Railway Letters and enclosures from Bengal and India, L/PWD/3/70, also see 'A note on refreshment rooms for natives' dated February 1877, in Correspondence of the Eastern Indian Railway Company, L/PWD/2/93, IOR.
55 See D.C. Ray, *Debganer Martye Agaman* (Calcutta [originally published 1880], Dey's Publication, re-print 1984), pp. 20–21; *Education Gazette*, 13 June 1890, in Newspaper Reports Bengal, L/R/5/16, IOR.
56 For instance, the novel *Adarsha Hindu Hotel* refers not only to different classes of menu at differing prices; but also, how the quality of the ingredients varied in the two menus.
57 'A note by Major Hovendon', Officiating Consulting Engineer Bengal, dated August 1869, in Railway Letters and enclosures from Bengal and India, L/PWD/3/70, IOR.
58 The travelogues and guidebooks in Indian languages (both Bengali and Hindi) attest to refreshment rooms maintained by Indians. See S. Prasad, *Bharat Bhraman* (Benaras, Hariprakash Yantralaya, 1902–1903); *Ochterlony hoite Qutub parjyanto: orthat purvabharat rail path sanlagna katipay pradhanato sthaner drashtabya padartha shokoler patha pradarshika* (Calcutta, Umesh Chandra Nag, 1892); A. Rasheed, *The Travellers' Companion, Containing a Brief Description of Places of Pilgrimage and Important Towns in India* (Calcutta, Indian Railway Board, 1910).
59 'Proposal to construct waiting and refreshment rooms for natives at Burdwan, Sahebganj, Danapur and Cawnpore', dated June 1868 in Proceedings of the Railway Department, Government of Bengal, P/433/44. Cost was reduced since the land was rent-free, being given out from 'railway land' that in the first place the railway companies had acquired free of cost from the Government. For a detailed and useful discussion of how railway companies acquired land see S. Sarkar, *Technology and Rural Change in Eastern India, 1830–1980* (Delhi, Oxford University Press, 2014), especially Chapter 1.
60 Corruption in railway administration, though palpably present (as preceding chapters showed) has hitherto not received adequate scholarly attention.
61 Here again comparisons can be drawn with existing conditions in England. Bradley, 'The railways', p. 473.
62 Indian language newspapers often published passenger grievances regarding quality of food being disproportionate to its cost.
63 The weariness of the railway authorities in India can be partly attributed to similar feelings that guided the introduction of licenced food vendors at railway stations in England. See Bradley, 'The railways', p. 47.
64 'Refreshment at stations', letter to the agent of the Eastern Indian Railway Company, dated October 1875 in correspondence of the Eastern Indian Railway Company, L/PWD/2/91, IOR.
65 Travel in India or city, shrine or sea-beach: antiquities, health resorts and places of interest on the Bengal Nagpur Railway network (Bombay, The Times Press, 1916). Chapter 18.
66 *Khair Khwah–i-Kashmir*, 22 December 1866, in Native Newspaper Reports, NWP, L/R/5/63; also, Samay, 7 September 1894, in Native Newspaper Reports, Bengal, L/R/5/21, IOR.
67 *Burdwan Sanjivani*, 13 November 1900, in Newspaper Reports, Bengal, L/R/5/26, IOR.

To eat or not to eat? 163

68 *Koh-i-Nur*, 15 July 1871, in Native Newspaper Reports, NWP, L/R/5/48, IOR.
69 'Measures for the comfort and convenience of native passengers' from the Chief Justice of Indore to the Secretary of the Railway Conference, dated 5 September 1888, in Proceedings of the Railway Department, Government of Bengal, P/3632, IOR.
70 *Samay*, 7 September 1890, in Newspaper Reports, Bengal, L/R/5/16. The report claimed 'native' sweetmeat sellers at stations had to pay about 1000 rupees each per annum. Also, see *Hitavadi*, 15 April 1898, Newspaper Reports, Bengal, L/R/5/24, IOR.
71 *Naiyar-i-Azam*, 21 May 1900 and *Jami-ul-Ulum*, 12 May 1900, in Newspaper Reports, North-Western Provinces, L/R/5/77, IOR.
72 *The Rohilkhand Gazette*, 24 February 1900, in Newspaper Reports, North-Western Provinces, L/R/5/77, IOR.
73 'Minutes of the meeting resolving Messrs Chunni Lal and Muhammad Husain given the responsibility of supplying refreshment to native passengers', dated 24 November 1899, in Proceedings of the Railway Department, Government of India, P/1386, IOR.
74 *Jami-ul-Ulum*, 14 April 1900 in Newspaper Reports, North-Western Province, L/R/5/77, IOR.
75 Clearly, the timing of such reports was influenced by the changing nature of the anti-colonial movement and thus is not surprising.
76 Kerr, 'Engines of Change', Chapter 4.
77 In many ways, this was an expansion of an earlier system introduced by Lord Curzon in 1902 that however, remained restricted to the Great Peninsular Railway network. See Railway Circular Number 13, in Proceedings of the Railway Conference, 1902, Simla, 25/720/32; and *Darus Saltanat*, 10 June 1910, Newspaper Reports, Bengal, L/R/5/37, IOR.
78 For a recent and good coverage of the ways in which facilities for providing food to Indian passengers developed especially after the creation of the Railway Board see Prasad, 'Tracks of Change', pp. 79–81.
79 A case in point would be the main protagonist of the novel used in the introduction.
80 *Hindi Hindustan*, 29 April 1904, in Newspaper Reports, North-Western Provinces, L/R/5/80, IOR.
81 Prasad, 'Tracks of change', p. 81.
82 *Bharat Jiwan*, 5 December 1898, in Newspaper Reports, NWP, L/R/5/75, IOR.
83 *Dabdaba-i-Qaisari*, 5 July 1890, in Newspaper Reports, NWP, L/R/5/67, IOR.
84 *The Advocate*, 13 April 1902, in Newspaper Reports North-Western Provinces, L/R/5/79. Emphasis mine.
85 *Education Gazette*, 13 June 1890, in Newspaper Reports, Bengal, L/R/5/16, IOR.
86 For such lists see S. Prasad, Bharat Bhraman (Benaras, Hariprakash Yantralaya, 1902–1903); Ochterlony hoite Qutub parjyanto: orthat purvabharat rail path sanlagna katipay pradhanato sthaner drashtabya padartha shokoler patha pradarshika (Calcutta, Umesh Chandra Nag, 1892); A. Rasheed, *The Travellers' Companion, Containing a Brief Description of Places of Pilgrimage and Important Towns in India* (Calcutta, Indian Railway Board, 1910).
87 Shastri, 'Dakshinapath', p. 5.
88 *The Hindustan*, 13 October 1900, in Newspaper Reports, North-Western Province, L/R/5/77, IOR.
89 See *Burdwan Sanjivani*, 13 November 1900; *The Bengalee*, 7 September 1909, in Newspaper Reports, Bengal, L/R/5/26 and L/R/5/36, IOR.
90 A process that inevitably contested if not entirely ignored claims of those who lacked strident voices, both political or social, a discussion beyond the scope of this chapter.

6 A nation on the move?
Railway travel and conceptualisations of space in colonial India

A still popular song from a rather old Hindi movie *Jagriti* portrays a school teacher travelling with a group of students exhorting them to feel reverential awe and pride in their nation, especially in its historical past.[1] The mode of transport that made this geo-historical perambulation possible was a train, clearly underlining the links between railway travel and conceptualising 'national' space, the main theme of this chapter.[2] But interestingly, despite this telling admission of the role of a modern technology of transport in envisioning 'national' past (as the use of the word Hindustan, alongside a clear delineation of 'national' boundaries as bound by the Himalayas on the north and the sea on the south suggests), when it came to filling in the details of this space, the regions that received attention are Rajputana, Maharashtra, Punjab (more specifically Jallianwala Bagh) and Bengal. Upon listening however, what becomes clear is that this truncated territorial conceptualisation is justified on the basis of the aforementioned regions' long and glorious history of resisting invaders and by implication, imposition of foreign rule. In other words, 'India' as envisaged in this ditty was a historical space evidently defined in equal measure by its aggression against two foreign groups: the Muslims and the British.

Additionally, if somewhat unsurprisingly, this imagined territory is imbued with quasi-religious, quasi-historical significance where description of a land washed by the sacred waters of the Ganges and Yamuna conflates with a narration of stories of valour of Rana Pratap, Padmini, Shivaji, the victims of Jallianwala Bagh massacre and Subhash Chandra Bose. While it can be argued that this particular spatial imagery can either be the poet's personal thought and thus not worth exploring as a historical clue; or the sentiments reflect the mood of the hour, i.e., a song composed in the aftermath of independence and partition. Here however, I argue that this poetic vision was neither singular, nor a mere creation of the escalating communal politics in the decades leading up to 1947. On the contrary, I suggest that the song is clearly suggestive of the role of differentiation as the basis of imagining India – a process that I claim was a product of a much longer and evidently extant tradition of conceptualising India in more heterogeneous ways than presently acknowledged. It is perhaps not without significance that the use of the word Hindustan, presumably to denote the entire length and breadth of India, in reality connotes a specific territorial vision of India that challenges both the notion and the nature of a homogenous 'national space'. More critically, this heady conflation of religion, mythology, history and geography demonstrates that the 'colonised and incarcerated bodies' of Indian railway passengers possessed agency inasmuch as in conceptualising territories in more complex ways than currently imagined. In short, in this chapter I use the famous song by Kavi Pradeep as an apposite cinematic allusion to critically reappraise our notions of the impact of railway travel on imagining spaces, particularly as a nation.

Travelling as imagining? Railway travel and conceptualisation of space in colonial India

Railways may do for India what dynasties have never done – what the genius of Akbar the magnificent could not effect by government nor the cruelty of Tipu Sahib by violence – they may make India a nation.[3]

The benefits the railway has conferred are incalculable [. . .] [it] has brought distant, barbarous places within the reach of civilization.[4]

Railways have afforded unprecedented opportunity to travel from one corner of India to another [affording] a possibility for *desh bhraman*.[5]

The author of the first excerpt is Sir Edwin Arnold, who among other things was the earliest biographer of Lord Dalhousie, the 'architect' of Indian railways. As such, unsurprisingly, Arnold had a very sanguine and possibly genuine belief in the ability of the railways to forge India as a nation. Interestingly, such belief was underpinned by an equally if not greater confidence in the knowledge that India has never been a nation before; and therefore, the British rule in general, and railways in particular, were about to perform an historically unprecedented accomplishment. Needless to say, Arnold's views were not unique. If anything, Lord Dalhousie, the principal subject of Arnold's intellectual output, felt similarly, although his famous minutes focused more on the commercial and military prospects of railways than on the probable consequences on the political imaginings of Indians in some unspecified future.[6] Thus, broadly speaking, as discussed in the introduction, even a quick glance at the railway promotional literature confirms that transforming India into a nation was an important component of railway building, at least in ideological terms.

But, evidently, as the other two excerpts quoted alongside Arnold's suggest, Indians too, or certainly a cross-section of them, believed in the transformative role of steam, anticipating diverse outcomes, some corresponding with colonial claims of civilising influence of the iron-horse; while others added new, even unanticipated dimensions.[7] Such conflation of ideas between the coloniser and the colonised is not surprising if one bears in mind that assertions underlining the use of the railway network in either creating or strengthening existing feelings of belonging to a nation, imagined as a spatial whole were the *zeitgeist* of the nineteenth-century world.[8] In other words, sentiments expressing a belief in the ability of steam to foment a national bond by bringing different regions closer were neither merely 'colonial', by which I mean coming from the colonial authorities and by implication therefore somehow tainted with the desires of the imperial project; nor were they 'derivative', if only because, despite converging with the 'colonial', Indians adopted the ideas with discernment.[9] However, despite expressing varying levels of affinity with the imperial opinion on the benefits of steam, there was a broad consensus that travelling in trains helped imagine nation primarily though not exclusively by engendering spatial proximity. Indeed, it may be argued that until Gandhi's complete rebuttal of the positive influences of steam, railway's role in making India a nation was not challenged in any serious manner.[10]

In post-colonial historiography also, a broad consensus continues to exist, underscoring the railway network's role in making India a nation in both practical and notional terms. Scholars continue to agree that the railway's impact on imagining and even 'creating' India was a positive outcome of an otherwise deleterious colonial enterprise.[11] The persistence of this historiographical assumption however, is rather surprising given the existence of sophisticated and multi-dimensional analysis of space in colonial India.[12] Interestingly, a wide, non-railway scholarship too, contributes to this debate, though indirectly.[13] One of the main contentions of this vast and critical literature is that by the end of the nineteenth century, India increasingly came to be imagined/identified as a unified nation, though clearly delineated in Hindu and gendered terms – a conclusion that also accepts the political role of railways in this historical process as *a priori*. These assessments about the sectarian ways in which India came to imagined is valid and incidentally also matches with the inferences drawn in the railway literature alluded to above. Thus, inasmuch, this chapter builds on and contributes to this railway and non-railway scholarship.

But at the same time, the chapter also diverges from both the historiographical consensuses in critical ways. Based on an exhaustive and analytical reading of travelogues, here I suggest that railways' role in spatial imagining of nation was more complex than currently assumed. More specifically, I argue that railway travel added a strong regional narrative to this seemingly national story, illustrating how the latter was both fractured and contested at various levels. At a related level, therefore, this chapter indicates Indian agency, especially in the ways in which the subjective experience of railway travel was interpreted, including but not limited to contesting spaces – a claim that evidently challenges, albeit obliquely, the limits of the colonial knowledge production's role as 'masks of conquest'.[14] In short therefore, historiographically speaking, this chapter adds a new layer of understanding to our existing knowledge about the role of railways in imagining space in colonial India, an awareness of which is not just historically significant but also offers a vital clue to understanding the wider, social implications of railways in colonial India.[15]

Aryavarta as Bharatvarsha: conceptualising nation, contesting boundaries

Railways made travelling popular.[16] Despite less-than-ideal conditions of travelling in trains, especially in the lower-class carriages, there is no denying that an increasing number of people travelled because railways offered a relatively faster and cheaper mode of transit. Given this, trains often became a practical choice, if not for optimum comfort or pecuniary considerations. Unsurprisingly therefore, the introduction of railways also played a crucial role in transforming attitudes towards travel in colonial India, a discussion of which is beyond the scope of this chapter.[17] However, suffice here will be to note that among other things, availability of railway connections engendered a new category of travel, *desh bhraman* (lit. travelling around the country), that simply put, was likely to spawn a common bond of togetherness among Indians riding the rails by visiting different parts of India and meeting compatriots both in and out of transit. Not surprisingly therefore, *desh bhraman* also came to be regarded as a practice that was beneficial in both social and political senses, particularly the latter, and as such, highly recommended in the context of late nineteenth-century colonial India.[18] Thus clearly, *desh bhraman* was not a product of railway operations in any direct sense. Nonetheless, it was the presence and expansion of the railway network that made *desh bhraman* practically achievable.

This connection between the railway network and *desh bhraman* therefore, was not lost on the authors of the travelogues. If anything, authors of many travelogues claimed that their journeys were a dual product of availability of trains and a desire to travel for a purpose aka *desh bhraman* that was at once more compelling and morally superior than any other form of travel, occasionally including pilgrimage.[19] Many of these authors even exhorted their potential readers to take advantage of the unprecedented opportunity of *desh bhraman* made possible by the railway network. In other words, most of these travelogues make a strong case between railways and *desh bhraman*, an argument so deceptively simple and direct that the crucial component of this prescription, i.e. what exactly did *desh* mean, is often lost.[20] In other words, when *desh bhraman* was prescribed and promoted in the pages of these travelogues how was *desh* territorially conceptualised? This I argue, is a question worth asking if only because *desh* was the pre-requisite of *desh bhraman*;[21] and thus, an analysis of what *desh* denoted permits an investigation of the wider question of the creation of a national space and the role of railways in it.

If taken literally, the word *desh bhraman* in most of these travelogues is misleading. While the authors claimed these texts as products of their *desh bhraman*, most often these were accounts of travel to north India (the Indo-Gangetic plain), though few included parts of central and western India.[22] The discrepancy is also evident in the titles of the travelogues, especially the ones that were ambitiously titled as *Bharat Bhraman* (lit. travelling around India/Bharat). Irrespective of such titles as well as an accompanying claim of a desire for *desh bhraman* propelling the travels, more often than not the geographical ambit was confined to parts of north India, Rajasthan and Maharashtra. For instance, while Baradakanta Sengupta, the author of a Bengali travelogue titled his travel narrative as 'Bharat Bhraman', in reality, the first volume is an account of a train journey between Calcutta and Delhi and the second covers parts of Rajasthan, Maharashtra and Central India.[23] Similarly, Nabin Chandra Sen, the famous Bengali poet was also a deputy magistrate in the colonial administration and had no misgivings in describing his travels to parts of north India and Rajasthan as 'Bharater bhraman vrittanta' (lit. tales of travelling around Bharat).[24] Echoing comparable territorial conceptualisations, Satyendrakumar Basu's travelogue 'Bharat bhraman' too, is an account of railway journeys to Bombay, Saurashtra and Gujarat.[25] One can continue to add such instances; but the drift of this incongruity is evident.

Judging by the actual travel destinations, as opposed to the titles of the travelogue or even claims of *desh bhraman*, there is a clear discrepancy between *desh* as envisaged by these authors and the actual geographical contours of India. At one level, one can certainly argue that this preference for some parts of north, western and central India was a product of railway routing that made some parts more accessible than others. This was clearly the case for the Indo-Gangetic plain, especially places such as Benaras, Agra or Delhi. The Great Indian Peninsular railway network too, helped in connecting parts of western and central India effectively with north India thus easing movement. Significant as this practical concern may have been, relevant here will be to note that reaching Rajasthan, particularly places such as Chittor – a fixed destination in the itinerary of most if not all authors of the travelogues, was not easy. This was partly because the railway network developed slowly in Rajasthan and wherein available, travelling included changing networks and gauges that added to the inconveniences. As such, the presence of railways and the relatively easy travel it promised certainly offers a necessary but not sufficient explanation to understand the truncated nature of purported *desh bhraman* by the authors of these travelogues. Given this, here I suggest this territorial inconsistency underlines a deliberate[26] choice made by the authors of the travelogues largely to conceptualise India as a space narrowly defined in terms of religious and caste identities.

The desire to imagine India in spatially constricted terms is perhaps best exemplified by authors who avowedly confined their *desh bhraman* to different parts of north India, identifying the region as *Aryavarta* (lit. land of the Aryans). Prasannamayi Devi, the author of a Bengali travelogue pushed this connection to its logical extent by titling her travelogue as *Aryavarta*, and declaring the region as 'infused with history'.[27] Though admittedly this use of the word *Aryavarta* as a title is singular; the sentiments expressed however, were more widespread. Priyanath Bose, the owner and manager of the Great Bengal Circus alluded to north India as *Aryavarta*, a land strewn with 'past accomplishments of *arya jati*, or fantastic achievements of Hindus'.[28] Surendranath Ray, a well-known journalist, explicitly acknowledged that his desire for *desh bhraman* aka travelling around north and north-western India was influenced by the desire to witness '*arya-gaurav*', albeit the historical vestiges of it.[29] Broadly speaking, many other authors too, shared similar sentiments by claiming that their choice of *Aryavarta* was determined by the region's historical significance and connections, and a desire to catch a glimpse of the glorious past of *Aryans* or Hindus, often using the words interchangeably, without making any attempts at nuanced explication between the two.[30]

As such, travelling in *Aryavarta* meant venerating peregrination of those sites of historical actions that presumably determined India's past and consequently shaped her present. Though the list of such 'historical sites' varies from one travelogue to another, thus indicating more diversity than claimed; most itineraries included places such as Delhi, Benaras, Mathura and Vrindavan, and parts of Rajasthan, usually Chittor. At an apparent level this identification of north India as *Aryavarta* and associating a glorious Hindu past to the region seems to be the mirror image of the history lessons taught in schools, thus confirming the putative hegemonic sway of the colonial curriculum on the colonised.[31] But a careful reading of the travelogues reveals a more complex image. Interestingly, many of these authors acknowledged that their attraction for travelling across *Aryavarta* was not purely historical. If anything, history or historical knowledge substantiated already well-established mythical and religious value of Aryavarta as *punyabhumi*,[32] an association that allowed coalescing of categories of travel through an emotive classification of travelling in *Aryavarta* as pilgrimage, thus adding a layer of religious legitimacy to *desh bhraman*. For instance, Prasannamayi Devi forcefully claimed that *Aryavarta* was *punyabhumi* and thus the region was more than a conglomeration of historical sites and decisive battles. Furthermore, making a strong case against describing *Aryavarta*'s 'glorious history as fantastic' and thus by implication suggesting myth as a legitimate source of construction of historical past, she argued that:

> The mountain ranges of the Himalayas and the Vindhyas were silent witness to this [Aryan/Hindu] history and the Ganges, the Yamuna and the Sarayu continue to lament its [India's] fate. The ruins of Ayodhya, Hastinapur and Indraprastha bore past memories of this scared land.[33]

Such views were widely shared by authors of other travelogues.[34] Indeed, Surendranath Ray contested the ability of historical knowledge to convey historical truth in its entirety by quoting noted historian Romesh Chandra Dutta in the following words:

> A visit to northern India is an education which our schools do not impart; it tells a history which our text-books do not record.[35]

After such strident undermining of the credibility or even the privilege of historical knowledge production in explaining past in an authentic manner; the authors of these travelogues liberally drew upon *Ramayana*, *Mahabharata* and the wider corpus of Hindu religious texts to supplement information about *Aryavarta* and its glorious past, often at tandem with modern history books.[36] For instance, in a unique display of latitude concerning historical sources, Saratchandra Sastri, the author of a Bengali travelogue 'Dakshinapath Bhraman' used *Ramayana* and *Mahabharata* alongside books by colonial administrators and district gazetteers.[37] Once again, being a teacher of Sanskrit in a school, Shastri's example though possibly extreme, was by no means singular. Other authors too, deployed a similar tactic of combining sources that shows an interesting disregard for historical authenticity. Some travelogues even have a list of sources that the authors used to supplement their narratives. Not surprisingly, such lists display an eclectic array of sources such as *Vishnu purana* or *Jagannath Mahatmya* jostling alongside Hunter's *Imperial Gazetteers* or Francis Buchanan's travel narrative through southern India.[38] Given these authors' backgrounds, especially the educational training most of them received, it is indeed striking that they were unequivocal in support of religious and mythological sources and even local legends and hearsay. In a remarkable posture that certainly questions the limits of colonial education's ability to hegemonically influence the minds of the colonised, some of these authors claimed that if their mythical or religious interpretations of events that defined *Aryavarta*'s past were at variance with modern knowledge then the former was equally valid.[39]

Evidently, these authors had a very elastic view of historical evidence and sources. This, I suggest, was neither a casual oversight; nor any lack of understanding of how modern historical knowledge is constructed.[40] If anything, this flexible attitude towards historical methodology I argue, simultaneously mounted an elitist challenge to colonial claims while robustly asserting superior rights of high-caste Hindus to *desh* through a selective appropriation of historical and geographical contours of India. Accomplishing the former, was not particularly difficult once the validity of historical evidence as the only source of constructing past was questioned. If all sources about past is equally valid, then the historical is as good as mythic or religious. Given this, the latter is no longer an invalid source to bolster accounts of a glorious past, either real or imagined. At a related level, this widening ambit of valid 'historical' evidence permitted these authors to conceptualise territory in a more fluid manner than circumscribed by a narrow range of sources that perforce also imposed a fixed geographical notion of nation and national space. In other words, using mythology and religious accounts, these authors were free to imagine the contours of *desh* in ways that suited their broader social and political agenda.

The critical role played by this eclectic mixing of sources in conceptualising India as a Hindu space both due to the latter's enduring physical presence in the land and shaping the historical fortunes of it through arguably glorious accomplishments is especially visible in the ways in which authors of these travelogues used a changeable definition of the word *Hindustan*. Historically speaking, the word *Hindustan* and the territorial conceptualisations it evoked was a product of a long process of evolution. Initially, *Hindustan* was rather flexibly imagined, primarily by the Muslim chroniclers who used the word to describe the conquered land across the Indus that eventually meant a territory inhabited by Indians, mostly Hindus. For instance, Abul Fazl's gazetteer of the Mughal Empire and its *subahs* make it plain that *Hindustan* was a concept both wider and older than the Mughal Empire, though it excluded peninsular India.[41] Subsequently, in late Mughal and early Company rule era this notion of *Hindustan* was also invested with substantial 'emotional meaning',[42] a process through which a word that was once just a geographical expression also came to be endowed with political and cultural meanings. But subsequently as a consequence of the expansion and consolidation of the East India Company rule the notion of *Hindustan* increasingly came to convey a rather restricted geographical area situated between Punjab and Bengal. This shift is perhaps best reflected in the maps, geography books and the early gazetteers of the late eighteenth and the early nineteenth century. As such, the authors of the travelogues were cognisant of this shift in conceptualising *Hindustan*. Yet despite this, the authors used both older and the relatively recent definition of *Hindustan*. Occasionally, in a confusing melange, some authors used both conceptualisations of *Hindustan* in the same text without any apparent differentiation.[43] In short, many of these authors conceptualised *Hindustan* with an apparent disregard for the niceties of a few centuries of evolution of the spatial meanings associated with it.

As argued above, this glossing over variable meanings of *Hindustan* was not inadvertent. On the contrary, this vagueness provided occasions to include or exclude areas with specific histories within the spatial limits of *Hindustan*, a region that alongside *Aryavarta* was considered as an integral component of the imagined *desh*. This association of *Hindustan* as *desh* was not problematic since many authors argued that what in ancient times was known as *Aryavarta* in later period came to be known as *Hindustan*. Hinting at a territorial conflation that granted *Hindustan* the pedigree of *Aryavarta*, Surendranath Ray argued that the two regions were one and the same. Such acknowledgements however, were circumscribed within the argument that boundaries of Hindustan have been historically flexible, thus showing a clear knowledge of the complex historical process that shaped the boundaries of the region. Given this, most authors felt free to argue that for them *Hindustan* was wider than *Aryavarta*, an acknowledgement that allowed inclusion of Maharashtra and Rajasthan, two regions with a long history of 'anti-Muslim struggle', within the ambit of the former. Conceptualised thus, *Hindustan* became a territory that was invested with a special historical role of offering consistent and bold opposition to 'Muslim invasion and aggression' as opposed to *Aryavarta*, a region that supposedly 'cowered to the Muslim might'.[44]

In other words, this shift in *desh bhraman* from the narrower historical theatre of *Aryavarta* to wider *Hindustan* symbolised a broader movement (read decline) in India's historical fortune from 'glorious Aryan/Hindu rule to being subjected to Muslim tyranny'. As such, travelling around *Hindustan*, particularly those parts associated with the lives and legends of Rana Pratap or Shivaji came to be widely considered as worthy of being included in *desh bhraman*. It is not without significance that Nabinchandra Sen or Baradakanta Sengupta described Chittor as '*maha-tirtha*'.[45] That the idea had wider resonance is evident from the fact that Chittor not only appeared in most if not all itineraries; but many authors also described their visit to the fort as *darshan*.[46] Baradakanta Sengupta admittedly could not sleep the night before visiting Chittor, comparing the excitement with a visit to a venerable pilgrimage site. He was thrilled to imagine himself within the precincts of the fort 'which challenged the might of the Mughal Empire'.[47] Similarly, though Surendranath Ray described Chittor as a 'forever desirable' destination; he was also saddened by the derelict structure of the fort. For him, it was symbolic of the loss of independence suffered by the people of Rajasthan who had a history of fighting for freedom against Muslim domination. Ray argued that the fall of Chittor signified 'India's loss of freedom and glory'.[48]

Similar hyperbole, though possibly genuinely felt was associated with visiting parts of Maharashtra. Many authors claimed that travelling through the land of the Marathas they felt proud of the formidable challenge Shivaji and his descendants offered to the 'tyrannical Mughal emperors'. Patriotism and a pride in being Hindu, these authors claimed were some traits that made Marathas an ethnic group (*jati*) worth emulating. In an interesting twist of logic reminiscent of the Hindi song used in the opening paragraphs of this chapter, both Rajasthan and Maharashtra and occasionally parts of central India were considered worthy of *desh bhraman* also because these regions continued to have indigenous ruling dynasties as opposed to direct rule by the British crown. In other words, these territories were conceptualised as spaces with a long history of successfully evading 'foreign aggression', both Muslim and British. In an endeavour that privileged some regions with a visit during *desh bhraman* over others arguably on the basis of the former's role in the history of *desh*, some authors such as Prasannamayi Devi, Nabinchandra Sen and Surendranath Ray admittedly chose destinations that were related to the *Aryan*/Hindu past. Priyanath Bose even chided fellow Bengalis for visiting only the 'artificial creations'[49] of the Muslim rulers and consequently gloating about having 'seen desh'. He lamented the lack of interest in the beautiful structures made by the Hindus and the consequent lack of pride in the achievements of 'our ancestors and arya glory'. To rectify such mistakes, he even offered an alternate list of places that were to remind visitors of 'Hindu achievements'.[50]

Other authors with more inclusive destination choices did not offer a different vision of India's past either. Nabinchandra Sen thought Lucknow appeared as 'an abyss of despair for Muslims', though admittedly he could visit the city without being affected. The fall of Lucknow [after 1857]; the banishment of its ruler [Wajid Ali Shah] to Calcutta, and his subsequent loss of sovereignty, he argued, did not indicate any political loss because, India and Indians [Hindus] had lost their independence much earlier. For him, it was at Indraprastha [Delhi] where 'India' lost her freedom. While visiting Delhi, he wrote:

> Here Prithviraj fell at the hands of his adversaries; India's destiny was ruined forever and Prithviraj's fall signalled India's loss of independence.[51]

Echoing similar feelings, while Surendranath Ray noted that the minarets of mosques in Benaras reminded him of the 'brutalities of Muslim emperors in Hindu pilgrim sites';[52] Durgacharan Ray claimed that the Qutb Minar was a

Hindu achievement that was 'cunningly appropriated by Muslims'.[53] At one level, such interpretations, as Sunil Kumar has argued, was a product of reading 'authoritative' texts, which were produced from the mid-nineteenth century onwards by Indians influenced by the positivistic historiographical methodologies of the West.[54] Given this, it is not surprising that the authors of these travelogues interpreted the monument in sectarian terms. At the same time however, it is perhaps not without significance that authors such as Prasannamayi Devi or Baradakanta Sen admitted that despite an awareness of Qutb being a creation of Muslim rulers, they 'preferred' the version in which the monument is claimed to be originally a Hindu creation that was subsequently appropriated by the Delhi Sultans.[55] Thus, the influence of Western historiographical knowledge notwithstanding, these authors displayed agency in interpreting their travel experiences; more of which later. However, suffice here will be to note that there appears to be a pattern between territorial conceptualisations of India and a specific view of her past that is hard to overlook. *Desh* as it was imagined in the pages of these travelogues was essentially an assortment of sites deriving identity and legitimacy from resisting the Muslim 'aggression' or rule; and *desh bhraman* therefore consisted of travelling to these specific sites in order to encounter an exclusively Hindu past.

This conceptualisation of *desh* clearly denied Muslims any claims to a shared national space by rejecting their role in the common historical past of the nation except as 'oppressors' and 'foreigners'. It is perhaps not without significance that despite visiting places such as Lucknow or Delhi, many of these authors argued that their destination choice was not influenced by a desire to catch a glimpse of the ruins of a Muslim past to rekindle a feeling of national glory. On the contrary, the authors claimed that their travel to these sites was propelled by a longing to extricate a glorious Hindu past that was 'forcefully erased' by generations of Muslim ruling dynasties. Significantly, these attempts to 'reclaim' the religio-mythical glory of such 'fallen Hindu sites' included an alternate territorial conceptualisation in which pre-Muslim names of places were used to restore a broken connection between Hindu past and present. For instance, Delhi became *Indraprasth*a – the capital of *Yudhishthira*; Lucknow: *Lakshmanavati* – a city built by Lakshman, the brother of Ram; and Agra: *Agravan*, literally the land before Vrindavan and thus part of the sacred territory of *Braj*. It is instructive that authors such as Prasannamayi Devi or Nabinchandra Sen argued that Agra's association with the Mughals led to an erasure of its importance as *Agravan*. These authors claimed that the identity of Agra as a part of *Braj* and thus sacred to Hindus had been long forgotten and should be renewed and celebrated.[56]

Similarly, some authors noted that a visit to Lucknow, particularly the vision of the 'Islamic monuments' were merely reminders of the 'excesses of the Muslim rule', while the real significance of the place was its association with Lakshman and its proximity to Ayodhya, the city of Ram.[57] Delhi's identity as Indraprastha was repeatedly underlined by several authors, most claiming that the 'pious' city became a 'den of debauchery and sensual pleasure' under the Muslim rulers. Additionally, many authors even celebrated Delhi's connection with Prithviraj, arguing that with the debacle of the latter, a long period of 'Hindu ruin and decline' ensued. An author of a Bengali travelogue even claimed that the lack of the material remains of Indraprastha does not signify an absence of historical evidence of Yudhishthira's capital; on the contrary, it showed that Muslims have used the physical remains of the site to build mosques and monuments.[58] Interestingly, these attempts at creating a pre-Muslim spatial identity of some places also included an effort to wrest a pre-colonial identity. In a remarkable instance of invention of spatial identity, Darjeeling became *Durjaya-Ling* – an ancient and venerable site associated with the Hindu god *Shiva*; while Simla, the summer capital of the *Raj* was imagined as '*Shyamala-Khestra*' – the land of Hindu Goddess *Kali*.

Thus, as the foregoing evidence clearly indicates, the authors of these travelogues conceptualised *desh* in rather narrow terms that by implication denied Muslims any claims to the national space. Muslims however, were not the only groups who were excluded from this imagine *desh*. Lower castes too, suffered a similar fate, though I argue that in the latter case, this refusal is not as apparently visible as in the case of Muslims. This was possibly due to the fact that a direct denial of historical and geographical scope to the lower castes had serious potential to crack the myth of Hindu whole and as such was not attempted. Nevertheless, it cannot be denied that repeated emphasis on the identifying *desh* as *Aryavarta* had a spatial dimension of excluding peninsular India that by implication peddled a wider idea – the putative and dubious claim of superior status (both racial and otherwise) for high-caste Hindus. In essence, the idea regurgitated what Thomas Trautmann calls the 'indigenous Aryan' position[59] – a view of India's historical past that suggested a linear link between high-caste Hindus as direct descendants of *Aryans* and their historical accomplishments that included driving out the indigenous inhabitants of pre-Aryan India from *Aryavarta* and a subsequent establishment of a 'superior' Hindu civilisation in the region. A detailed analysis of the highly sophisticated, if somewhat confusing lineaments of the scholarly debates of the 'Indo-European controversy' is beyond the scope of this chapter. But evidence gleaned from this scholarship certainly indicates that the notions of high-caste Hindus as *Aryans* of yore; *Aryavarta* as the posited homeland of the said group and their role in establishing the foundations of 'Hindu/Indian civilization'[60] enjoyed widespread currency and legitimacy in nineteenth-century India.[61]

Given this, it is perhaps not surprising that the authors of the travelogues were familiar with the concept and used it to conceptualise *desh* in ways that established superior claims of high-caste Hindus. In short, here I suggest that conceptualising *desh* as either *Aryavarta* or *Hindustan* was an unambiguous assertion of contestation of national space by elite, high-caste Hindus. More importantly, this contestation I argue, was directed as much against the colonial government and its wider claims of political legitimacy based on putative racial superiority as it was aimed at outrivalling Muslim or low caste claims to the 'national' space, especially in the narrow political and social ground provided by the colonial context. Nowhere perhaps is this clearer than asserting an *Aryan* identity for high caste Hindus and identifying *Aryavarta* as north India, thereby undermining the racial basis of the European claims of superiority to rule over Indians;[62] or at least over a cross-section of them. The contestation to the colonial state's claims over national space is also evident from the ways in which British and Muslims were clubbed as 'foreigners'; or pre-British and pre-Muslim spatial history of places were invented and celebrated. At an apparent level, Agra was different from Simla and thus, such associations may seem far-fetched. But if one considers that all of these places were also seats of political power, albeit intermittently, and in different historical periods, then there seems to be a clear desire to contest the superior claims and the legitimacy of Muslims and the Colonial state alike to these spaces by underlining a pre-Muslim, pre-colonial spatial past. Last but not least, the significance accorded to the travels in the princely states as well as to 'Hindu' sites in Rajasthan or Maharashtra also underscore a desire to make a wider political point that some spaces within India remained 'unoccupied', and thus by implication beyond contestation by Muslims or the colonial state. Evidently, such interpretations ignored the complex historical realities of these regions.[63] But once again, such oversight was not a product of lapse in historical knowledge. On the contrary, they reflect a desire to contest spatial imaginings of *desh* through a selective appropriation of past that interestingly, also reveal Indian agency, more of which in the concluding section.

Limits of desh: railway travel and imagining swadesh

> Those who are inclined to appreciate natural beauties [of places] can now travel [by trains] *from their own desh to that of others with ease.*[64]
>
> With the advent of pujo vacation, on our way to Buxar [we] ride the rail to travel westwards [going out] of desh.[65]

Divided by more than half a century, what connects these excerpts from a Bengali pamphlet written by Akshay Kumar Dutta and a poem appropriately titled *dur* by Rabindranath Tagore, is an awareness of one's 'own *desh*' or *swadesh* as a territorial concept. However, neither Dutta nor Tagore were isolated voices. Similar sentiments were expressed by various authors of the Bengali travelogues published through the course of the late nineteenth and the early twentieth century. Dinanath Gangopadhyay, author of the Bengali travelogue *Vividha Darshan Kavya* poetically claimed that his desire for travelling resulted in 'envying swadesh', thus leaving it behind.[66] Nabinchandra Sen subtly underscored the difference between his chosen travel destinations and swadesh by using the word *prabas* in the title of his travelogue.[67] Though most other authors were more prosaic; nevertheless, they routinely noted how their travels either took them away from *swadesh* or their delight in coming back to 'their desh' after spending days away from it.[68] Writing in the late nineteenth century, Priyanath Bose, the peripatetic manager of the Great Bengal Circus was perhaps underlining a wider trend when he noted in his travelogue that 'these days Bengalis often boast about their *desh bhraman* after returning back to *swadesh*'.[69]

Such precise use of the word *swadesh* by the authors of the travelogues reveals a distinct territorial conceptualisation, including a clear delineation of the boundaries of the former. Anticipating Tagore in more ways than one, Kashinath Mukhopadhyay in his travelogue published in 1863 wrote that he decided to spend his annual Durga Pujo vacation by travelling 'westwards from his desh'.[70] Echoing comparable geographical orientation that influenced conceptualisation of *swadesh*, Haricharan Bandyopadhyay, a student of the Hugli Normal School wrote an account of his school trip to the 'countries in the west'.[71] Writing 40 years later than Bandyopadhyay, Surendranath Ray too, noted that his decision to travel to the 'west' in January was taken regardless of an awareness of the region being very cold during that time.[72] In another instance, Baradakanta Sengupta described Rajmahal as the 'meeting point of Bengal and Bihar', while noting that beyond Rajmahal were the 'regions of the west'.[73] In short, for these authors, *swadesh* aka Bengal was a distinctly identifiable territorial entity – not a surprising outcome given the educational training the former received. But significantly, many of these authors argued that in their minds what made *swadesh* distinguishable was not merely definite boundaries but the natural beauty of the region.

Broadly speaking, in the pages of these travelogues *swadesh* appears as a verdant, flat and fertile land, with more than a hint of its natural bounties.[74] More importantly perhaps, *swadesh* also came to be conceptualised as a space that was distinct from *desh* by virtue of possessing natural beauty, a difference that the authors of these travelogues repeatedly underline through notions of proximity and difference. In other words, *swadesh* was identifiably beautiful, so much so that while travelling out or returning to it a traveller could easily distinguish between the boundaries of *desh* and *swadesh* by merely noticing the changing natural features, dry and undulating in the former, while leafy and flat in the latter. Indeed, so strong was the association between boundaries and beauty of *swadesh* that often authors claimed that their awareness of the former was informed by the latter. For instance, Kedarnath Das described his entrance in Santhal Pargana as an 'end to the familiar, beautiful and comforting scenes of swadesh'.[75] Similarly, Baradakanta Sengupta claimed that the undulating and pebbly terrain of Teenpahar signalled his going beyond *swadesh* and the commencement of *desh bhraman*.[76] This emphasis on the spontaneity of feelings is instructive because in terms of physical features the region around Teenpahar is different from the plains of Bengal and therefore capable of evoking a sense of difference. Similarly, Haricharan Bandyopadhyay 'felt' Deoghar and its surroundings was distinct from '*our desh*' because the land was uneven and full of stones.[77]

Additionally, in a clear rebuttal of the colonial stereotype of Bengal's terrain as the source of proverbial effeminacy or laziness of Bengalis, Kedarnath Das claimed that though flatness of Bengal's terrain may have 'admittedly contributed to some negative attributes'; but it was 'undeniable' that the region's fortune and prosperity depended on it.[78] Similarly, struck by the absence of greenery upon reaching Patna, Surendranath Ray blamed the general scarcity of water in the region arguing that 'unlike *swadesh*, the villages here [Patna] are not ensconced within thick foliage' and were thus not very beautiful. Though he admittedly enjoyed 'desh bhraman through Aryavarta', yet Ray claimed that he finally 'felt at peace' after coming back to *'swadesh* – the beautiful and verdant *banga-bhumi'*.[79] Saratchandra Sastri and Baradakanta Sengupta also expressed similar sentiments upon 'coming back to leafy Bengal', a feeling that they acknowledged had had the impact of amplifying the joys of *desh bhraman.*[80] Imagined thus, *swadesh* was conceptualised as a space that was both distinct and distant from *desh*, allowing the authors of the travelogues to infuse the former with emotive, collective sentiments.

Besides Bengal, some other parts of India too came to be conceptualised as distinct territorial units or *desh* of a specific ethnic group. Authors of several travelogues identified Maharashtra and Rajasthan as *desh* of Maratha and Rajput *jati*s respectively. Saratchandra Shastri used the word 'natives of this country' to describe people of the Pune and Bombay region.[81] Similarly, Surendranath Ray and Kedarnath Das wrote about Maratha and Rajput *desh.*[82] Both Nabinchandra Sen and Baradakanta Sengupta described Rajputana as the *desh* of the Rajput *jati*.[83] As in the case of Bengal (i.e. *swadesh*) here too, natural features played an important role in conceptualising these territories as distinct regions. Many of these authors noted that for them the presence of dry and craggy terrain indicated the distinctiveness of Rajasthan and Maharashtra from *swadesh*. Some took this association even further and claimed that the rugged landscape of the Rajput and the Marathas helped to produce a sturdy group of inhabitants – a combination that was argued to have spawned an 'unsurprising record of opposing foreign aggression in historical past'.[84] Evidently, for the authors of these travelogues conceptualising *swadesh* and *desh*(s) as distinct spaces did not pose any contradictions in imagining *desh* in wider geographical terms. This was neither inconsistency nor incomplete training in colonial geography. On the contrary, such conceptualisations, I argue, indicate that a prior knowledge of 'national' space as a homogeneous whole did not preclude the possibility of conceptualising the former as a spatial entity that constituted of smaller, distinct territorial units. Additionally, I claim that this conceptualisation of 'national' space in a multiple, overlapping and even contradictory manner provided these authors with occasions to acknowledge a presence of the history of strong regional identity in different parts of India and the ways in which it was invoked to assert either superior or defiant political role by specific social groups at different moments in India's past.[85]

Thus, it can be argued that for these authors, an awareness of past, especially the discussion of long and well-established traditions of 'local patriotism'[86] combined with conceptualisations of *swadesh* and *desh*(s) as an aggregate of 'national' space offered a potent way to simultaneously contest the competing claims of the colonial state and other politically strident groups over this space. It is perhaps not without significance that the authors of these Bengali travelogues chose to conceptualise Bengal or *swadesh* as a verdant region, as opposed to drier parts of north India. These authors were well aware that for the colonial state, the climatic and geographical conditions of Bengal, particularly its flat landscape and

178 *A nation on the move?*

humidity inducing heavy rain was associated with a debilitating impact on the health and the character of its inhabitants. Simply put, in the colonial stereotype of human typology Bengalis came to be described as effeminate, lazy, corrupt and venal – qualities that disqualified them from a political leadership role, despite their incessant clamour. Thus, consciously inverting this colonial stereotype of Bengal and Bengalis by claiming that the putative negative natural features of the region were in reality an asset, the authors of these travelogues were plainly making a political point through an alternate conceptualisation of *swadesh*.

Similarly, at an apparent level an acknowledgement of the positive role of dry and undulating landscape on the bodies and minds of Rajputs and Marathas seems to be an acceptance of a widely prevalent colonial stereotype in nineteenth-century India. Significantly however, such notions were simultaneously accompanied by a claim that the glories of these spaces and their inhabitants firmly belonged to the past. In other words, by challenging an orthodoxy that guided colonial policies and thus had tangible administrative and political implications, these authors argued that despite a 'valiant history of opposing Muslim rule', the ruins of palaces, forts and cities of Rajasthan and Maharashtra were in essence reminders of spaces past their prime – a claim that certainly undermined, if not altogether denied any contemporary political role to these spaces and their inhabitants.[87] In short, these claims of superior rights over 'national' space were articulated through a clearly creative and fluid interpretation of historical realities including a selective appropriation of colonial knowledge production as well as pre-colonial notions. After all, it was no coincidence that *swadesh*, as it came to be conceptualised in these Bengali travelogues, drew upon the pre-colonial idea of 'golden Bengal'[88] that was peddled by the local poets and religious movements in Bengal at least from the seventeenth century and thus these authors were consciously reviving an idea that conveniently also doubled as an explicit political act aimed at subverting the received image of Bengal and by extension, of Bengalis.[89]

Conclusion

This chapter argues that conceptualisation of 'national' space in colonial India was not as homogenous as has been currently assumed. On the contrary, it suggests that that differentiation – both spatial and of social identities, often overlapping one another, remained a valid basis for conceptualising territories in colonial India. In other words, as opposed to a single conceptualisation of 'nation' as an approximate of the real physical boundaries; the former came to be imagined diversely – as *Aryavarta*, *Hindustan*, or as an aggregate of smaller *desh*(s) each with distinct territorial and social identity. At a related level, the chapter argues that railways played a critical role in these diverse and differentiated conceptualisations of 'national' space. Railways, as noted already, made travelling easier and cheaper, thus making *desh bhraman* a viable option accessible to an increasingly wider audience. Railway routing too, favoured some regions that had a high concentration of places of religious or historical significance.

In other words, the railway's influence in shaping spatial conceptualisations was prominent and practical as it allowed adding new, visual dimensions to pre-existing textual knowledge and received wisdom. For instance, most authors admitted that a visit to Chittor or Indraprastha [Delhi] enhanced the experience of historical knowledge already available to them. There is no denying that such preconceived notions were a product of colonial education curriculum as well as guidebooks and travelogues of European travellers and as such, had the possibility of mediating spatial experiences in particular ways. Nonetheless, as we have seen in the case of visits to Lucknow, Delhi and Kanpur, visually experiencing spaces also provided occasions to interpret the former in new ways, occasionally challenging prior and arguably more authoritative knowledge. Similarly, visits to Benaras or Ayodhya resulted in privileging the knowledge that underlined the significance of these places in Hindu cosmos while ignoring or even debunking the notions that questioned the mytho-religious significance of these spaces. Thus, in short, railway journeys, especially those construed as *desh bhraman* did not remain neutral in their impact.

Evidently, railways played an influential role in familiarising these authors with the 'national' space through actual experience. But as the foregoing evidence suggests, railways clearly had very little to do with the assumptions that came to mediate experiences of travelling in trains except perhaps exacerbating existing sectarian differences by providing a new register of social differentiation.[90] In other words, the idea of *desh* was created in the mind, only partly by railway journeys. Given this, it will perhaps not be an exaggeration to argue that as railway passengers, the authors of these travelogues interpreted their travel experiences in ways that suited their wider political agenda. It is perhaps not without significance that despite claiming *desh bhraman* as the motive behind their travels, as well as expressing a clear knowledge of an expanding pan-Indian railway network that substantiated their former claim; these authors conceptualised as well as confined their travel to a version of *desh* that did not correspond with the actual geographical contours of India. More importantly, such oversight was by no means a consequence of incomplete training in modern geography. Thus, such fluid and flexible conceptualisations of *desh* can perhaps be interpreted was an attempt of elite Hindus to assert superior rights over 'national' space – a process that simultaneously contested the claims of the colonial state as well as other social groups, most notably, Muslims and lower castes to the same.

This, as we saw, is evident in the ways in which Bengal came to be conceptualised as *swadesh* or the virtues of Rajputs and Marathas as political competitors of Bengalis in the anti-colonial politics was undermined through a deliberate conceptualisation of the former's *desh*(s) as spaces void of contemporary significance. It is instructive that whether conceptualised as *Aryavarta* or *Hindustan* or as *desh*(s) of Marathas and Rajputs, the unifying theme in these territorial imaginings was a specific view of India's past as a successive narrative of subjugation and exploitation at the hands of 'foreigners', i.e., non-Hindus. Certainly, one can argue that given the political climate of late nineteenth and early twentieth-century India, such views of India's past were a by-product of

180   *A nation on the move?*

internalising a colonial view of Indian history. Additionally, the theme of 'Muslim exploitation of Indian resources' can possibly be explained as a literary strategy deployed by the authors to criticise the colonial state without drawing its wrath. Nevertheless, it cannot be ignored that anti-Muslim sentiments were not entirely colonial construction.[91] At a related level, as the following chapter will show, the authors of the travelogues did not shy away from criticising the colonial state and its exploitative and discriminatory policies in a direct and even trenchant manner. Given this, it is difficult to sustain the idea that these authors were engaging in anti-Muslim tirade merely as a veiled reference to the colonial state. Indeed, the persistent presence of anti-Muslim references in the pages of these travelogues, including a prescription for erasing Muslim spatial past, or a denial to accord significance to Muslim monuments as valid symbols of India's historical legacy, can be interpreted as having added new and vital ways to reject giving Muslims an access to the 'national' space.

Thus, railway travel experiences and the spatial conceptualisations they spawned were neither consistent with the expectations of the railway promoters/ colonial administrators; nor do they entirely converge with the post-colonial historiographical assumptions. This incongruence, I argue, shows Indian agency, especially the ways in which knowledge, both colonial and pre-colonial was appropriated or rejected in a creative manner largely to suit broader political agenda. An excellent case in point is Surendranath Ray's decision to quote R.C. Dutt's claim of a visit to north India as a lesson in history, which was absent from standard history curricula. This comment poses a rather serious challenge to assumptions of a causal link between 'colonial knowledge' and a specific view of India's past. Similarly, the claims of identifying *Aryavarta* as north India is at an apparent level an unquestioning acceptance of Orientalist knowledge. But the insistence on recognising *Aryavarta* as the posited homeland of Indians [Hindus] seriously undermined colonial notions of racial superiority by claiming Indians as original *Aryans* and thus equal, if not superior to their colonial masters. Additionally, locating *Aryavarta* in India had the vantage of debunking the Orientalist claim that *Aryans* or Hindus came from outside India and thus by implication 'foreigners'. In other words, this spatial conceptualisation provided the foundation for subsequent claims of Hindus being indigenous to India and thus having superior rights over the land. Needless to say, this formulation also did away with the prickly bits of Indo-European controversy that suggested pre-Aryan groups were indigenous to India, thus ideologically sustaining an upper-caste hegemony over 'national' space while denying any historical primacy to lower-caste groups in colonial India and beyond.[92]

Given such flexible uses of the past, it is perhaps not surprising that glorification of Marathas and their role as 'opponents of Muslim tyranny' conveniently glossed over their raids in Bengal as *bargis*, if only because the former permitted a denial of 'national' space to Muslims – perhaps a more expedient need in the political milieu of late nineteenth, early twentieth-century India.[93] Neither is it insignificant that anticipating the song used in the introduction, the itinerary of *desh bhraman* included Hindu pilgrimage sites, often dubbed as 'places of historical significance'

– an overlap that clearly did not cause much perturbation for the authors of these travelogues. This conflation is particularly vital as I argue that it was neither a mere residue of a pre-colonial notion in which India was spatially conceptualised through an extensive and intricate network of pilgrimage;[94] nor just a reflection of how pre-colonial ideas that also came to be corroborated by the textbooks of the colonial curriculum enjoyed renewed legitimacy. At a related level, this mytho-religion informed choice of 'historical places' as destinations for *desh bhraman* was certainly not a sign of incomplete training of the colonised in modern disciplines of history and geography if only because, as we have seen, a pan-Indian notion of *desh* – either religious or modern geographical was consciously rejected in favour of a smaller spatial conceptualisation confined largely to north India for patently denying specific social groups any claims to the 'national' space. In other words, such conceptualisations suggest that the ways in which the colonised elite in India engaged with past and present through consciously widening the ambit of knowledge to assert their superior claims over the 'national' space cannot be adequately explained as either derivative, or mimicry. If anything, it shows that the colonised had the opportunity and the ability to engage with a wide range of evidence to mount an anti-colonial challenge; but also, to pursue their own socio-political agenda.

Thus, to conclude, I argue that the conceptualisations of 'national' space in colonial India were exclusive, both geographically and historically. Pushed to a logical conclusion this *desh* was a Hindu nation – a conceptualisation that notionally excluded low castes as well as Muslims. In short, modern knowledge and rapid travel added new elements to an existing corpus of conceptualisations of territory in India, suggestive of a range of ideas available to these authors, which they evidently used to interpret their specific experiences. The outcome may be argued to have been a deliberate attempt to overstep colonial knowledge and to question its legitimacy. Thus, instead of conformity; notions of negation and challenge may be useful to understand the conceptualisations of space in colonial India.

Notes

1. Movie *Jagriti* (lit. Awakening). The song in question is: 'Aao bachhon tumhe dikhaye jhanki Hindustan ki, is dharti se tilak karo yeh dharti hain balidan ki'. The evident popularity of the song even to this day can be gauged by the fact that it is now available as a *deshbhakti geet* (lit. patriotic song) in cartoon format to attract children as well as from the comments that appear below the 1954 video on YouTube (see: www.youtube.com/watch?v=aZjyPrzfwUs and www.youtube.com/watch?v=lWsGPxp4s1w accessed on 5 April 2017.
2. Unless specified, here 'national' space includes both natural and social space.
3. E. Arnold, *The Marquis of Dalhousie's Administration of British India*, Vol. II (London, Saunders, Otley and Company, 1865), pp. 241–242.
4. C.N. Banerjei, *An Account of Howrah: Past and Present* (Calcutta, 1872) in the India Office Collection Tracts, Volume on 'Railways', IOR.
5. D.K. Lahiri Chaudhuri, *Bharat Bhraman* (Calcutta, Kuntolin Press, 1908). Emphasis mine. *Desh Bhraman* (lit. travelling around the country), p. 14.

6 Minute by Lord Dalhousie to the Court of Directors, 20 April 1853, in Microfilm reel number 60, Correspondence regarding Railway Communication in India, pp. 141–168, National Archives of India, New Delhi, India.
7 Here 'unanticipated' refers to both surprise on the part of the colonial railway promoters regarding instantaneous popularity of railways among Indians and how the latter used the opportunities of relatively easier and faster travel for distinct political purposes.
8 C. Wolmar, *Blood, Iron and Gold: How the railroads transformed the world* (New York, Public Affairs, 2010).
9 For instance, though admitting benefits of steam for territorial integration the authors of the travelogues discussed here never really accepted the colonial claim that India was not a nation before the British made her into one. The discussion of this theme however, is beyond the scope of this chapter.
10 M.K. Gandhi, *Hind Swaraj* (Ahmedabad, Navjivan, 2008 edition). And even then, Gandhi's ideas, as is well known despite being influential was by no means the only opinion on the issue. See Chapter three, section II.
11 S. Bandyopadhyay, *From Plassey to Partition: A history of modern India* (Hyderabad, Orient Longman, 2004), p. 128.
12 M. Goswami, *Producing India: From colonial economy to national space* (Chicago, University of Chicago Press, 2004); H. Bury, 'Novel spaces, transitional moments: Negotiating texts and territory in 19th century Hindi travel accounts', in I. Kerr (eds), *27 Down: New Departures in Indian Railway Studies* (Hyderabad, Orient BlackSwan, 2007), pp. 1–38; K. Chatterjee, 'Discovering India: Travel, history and identity in late 19th century and early 20th century India', in D. Ali (eds), *Invoking the Past: The uses of history in South Asia* (Delhi, Oxford University Press, 1999), pp. 192–227; M. Aguiar, 'Making modernity: Inside the technological space of railways', *Cultural Critique*, 68, 2008, pp. 66–85.
13 These include literature on: history of colonial education, particularly textbooks and curriculum; history of print media and vernacular literature; history of cartography and photography in colonial India.
14 G. Viswanathan, *Masks of Conquest: Literary studies and British Rule in India* (New York, Columbia University Press, 1989); M. Edney, *Mapping an Empire: The Geographical Construction of British India, 1765–1843* (Chicago, London, University of Chicago Press, 1997); S. Ramaswamy, *The Goddess and the Nation: Mapping Mother India* (Durham, Duke University Press, 2010).
15 This chapter, however, does not add to the debate about whether India was ever a nation or not if only because I think that this question is framed in a way that it inevitably privileges European historical processes of nationhood and as such any answer to the question can only illustrate either delay or deficiency of one or other kind of non-European experience. For historical accounts claiming a pre-colonial nationalism/patriotism in India see C. A. Bayly, *Origins of Nationality in South Asia: Patriotism and ethical government in the making of modern India* (Delhi, Oxford University Press, 1998); R.K. Ray, *The Felt Community: Commonality and mentality before the emergence of Indian nationalism* (Delhi, Oxford, Oxford University Press, 2002); D. Eck, *India: A sacred geography* (New York, Harmony Books, 2012).
16 This is not to suggest that pre-railway India was immobile and had no comparable experience of imagining territory. But this to highlight the role of railways in exponentially increasing the number of travellers in colonial India.
17 Post-railways, people travelled for reasons that were already well-established; while at the same time new purposes of travel, including modifying old motives for travel in novel forms came into existence. The spatial ambit of the older and more established forms of travel such as pilgrimages or marriages or employment increased, both literally and metaphorically. New meanings and forms were added to these existing

A nation on the move? 183

practices; while entirely new categories of travel such as for health or recreation were introduced.
18 These ideas were part of a wider formulation, which aimed at instilling a sense of pride and achievement in India/Bengali past. See S. Kaviraj, *Unhappy Consciousness: Bankimchandra Chattopadhyay and the formation of nationalist discourse in India* (London, School of Oriental and African Studies, 1995); T. Guha-Thakurta, *Monuments, Objects, Histories: Art in colonial and postcolonial India* (New York, Columbia University Press, 2004), Chapter 4; K. Chatterjee, 'Discovering India'.
19 The titles of the travelogues too, offer a useful pointer in this direction, as the word *desh bhraman* or *Bharat bhraman* (lit. travelling around Bharat/India) eventually became as widely used as *tirtha yatra* (pilgrimage).
20 Depending upon the context, the meaning of the word *desh* varies and may be taken to include: land (place where one was born or feels belonging to), nation or country.
21 The word pre-requisite has been used in a strictly logical sense. One cannot possibly travel around the country if it or at least the idea of it did not exist.
22 Usually central and western India included parts of modern Maharashtra and Rajasthan.
23 B. Sengupta, *Bharat Bhraman*, 2 volumes (Calcutta, K.C. Daw and Company, 1877).
24 N. Sen, *Prabaser Patra: Bharater Bhraman Vrittanta* (Calcutta, Goshtha Bihari, 1914).
25 S. Basu, *Bharat Bhraman: Bombai, Saurashtra o Gurjara* (Calcutta, 1911).
26 Here a thoughtful action is deliberately implied and by no means connotes a unified or homogenous attempt to conceptualise India if only because, as this chapter shows, homogeneity was elusive in this quest of conceptualising nation.
27 P. Devi, *Aryavarta: janoiko banga mahilar bhraman vrittanta* (Calcutta, Adi Brahmosamaj, 1888), 'Preface'. Her travels were confined to Etawa, Agra, Mathura, Vrindavan, Indraprastha and Delhi. The word Prasannamayi Devi used was 'itihasmoy'.
28 P. Bose, *Professor Bose-r apurba bhraman vrittanta* (Calcutta, Manomohan Library, 1902), p. 70. Bose was the famous manager/owner of the Great Bengal Circus. Emphasis mine. The use of the word *jati* here is not surprising; see R. Thapar, 'Some appropriations of the theory of Aryan race relating to the beginnings of Indian history', in T. Trautmann (ed.) *The Aryan Debate* (New Delhi, Oxford University Press, 2007), pp. 106–128.
29 S.N. Ray, *Uttar-Paschim Bhraman* (Calcutta, Pashupati Press, 1907). *Arya Gaurav* (lit. arya pride), p. 6.
30 See B. Sengupta, *Bharat Bhraman*, 2 volumes (Calcutta, K.C. Daw and Company, 1877); N. Sen, *Prabaser Patra: Bharater Bhraman Vrittanta* (Calcutta, Goshtha Bihari, 1914); S. Shastri, *Dakshinapath Bhraman* (Calcutta, B. Banerjee and Company, 1911); K. Das, *Bharatvarsher Pratichi Digvihar* (Murshidabad, Jadunath Bandyopadhyay, 1872).
31 Trautmann, 'The Aryan debate', p. xxxi.
32 *Punyabhumi* (lit. a sacred or consecrated land).
33 Devi, 'Aryavarta', see the dedication of the book.
34 L.L. Pandit, 'The Aryavarta or northern India': A lecture delivered before the Madras native gentlemen in Pachchappas Hall, on 25 May 1869 (Benaras, Medical Hall Press, 1870) in 'Tracts', Volume 607, IOR; Lahiri Choudhury, 'Bharat Bhraman', p. 30; Ray. 'Uttar-Paschim', p. 6.
35 Ray, 'Uttar Paschim'. The quote is in the preface.
36 S. Sastri, *Dakshinapath Bhraman* (Calcutta, B. Banerjee and Company, 1911); Sengupta, 'Bharat Bhraman'; K.N. Das, *Bharatvarsher Pratichi Digvihar*, D. Ray, *Debganer Martye Agaman* (Calcutta [originally published 1880], Dey's Publication, re-print 1984); Ray, 'Uttar-Paschim'.
37 S. Shastri, 'Dakshinapath'.

38 Baradakanta Sengupta, Kedar Nath Das and Durgacharan Rakshit are some of the authors who acknowledged the sources used. While the former does not offer specifics except hinting at the use of eclectic sources, the latter included W.W. Hunter's volume on Orissa and Buchanan's travel diary of southern India along with *Purushottam Mahatmya* and *Purushottam Chandrika*. See Sengupta, 'Bharat Bhraman'; Volume I, preface; Das, 'Bharatvarsher', p. 9; D.C. Rakshit, *Sachitra Bharat Pradakshin* (Calcutta, Sri Gauranga Press, 1907), p. 54.
39 Sastri, 'Dakishinapath', p. 74.
40 On the contrary, the questioning of authenticity of historical sources many of which were products of the scholarly endeavours of colonial officials show that these authors had a clear understanding of relations between evidence and construction of past.
41 Ray, 'The felt community', pp. 55–56.
42 Bayly, 'Origins of nationality', p. 38.
43 See, for instance, Das, 'Bharatvarsher', pp. 24–25.
44 Such claims were widely made in one form or another in almost all the Bengali travelogues consulted in this study. Largely because of this and in the interest of brevity, in the following discussion I do not specify the author or the text unless something specifically significant is mentioned.
45 Sen, 'Prabaser Patra', pp. 69 and 74; Sengupta, 'Bharat Bhraman', pp. 35–36. *Mahatirtha* (lit. the great pilgrimage).
46 The word *darshan* literally refers to the auspicious sight of a deity or a holy person. Ray, 'Uttar-Bharat', 220; Bose, 'Professor Bose-r', pp. 61, 63 and 67.
47 Sengupta, 'Bharat Bhraman', pp. 35–36.
48 Ray, 'Uttar Bharat', pp. 223, 227–228.
49 Bose, 'Professor Bose-r', p. 74. These artificial creations included: Taj Mahal and Sikandra in Agra, Jumma Masjid and Qutb Minar in Delhi and Machhi Bhavan and Hussainabad in Lucknow.
50 Ibid. This included temples at Bhubaneswar, Srirangam, the Uday Sagar Lake and Simhachalam in Vizagapatam.
51 Sen, 'Prabaser Patra', pp. 14–15, 36–37 and 38.
52 Ray, 'Uttar-Bharat', p. 18.
53 Ray, 'Uttar-Bharat', p. 220; Ray, 'Debganer Martye', p. 53.
54 S. Kumar, *The Present in Delhi's Past* (New Delhi, Three Essays Collective, 2010), Chapter 1.
55 Devi, 'Aryavarta', p. 140; Sengupta, 'Bharat Bhraman', Volume II, p. 198.
56 Sen, 'Prabaser Patra', p. 7; Devi, 'Aryavarta', p. 31. Also see Sengupta, 'Bharat Bhraman' Volume I, p. 89; Ray, 'Uttar-Paschim', p. 79.
57 Sen, 'Prabaser Patra', pp. 14–15.
58 Ray, 'Debganer Martye', pp. 52–53.
59 Trautmann, 'The Aryan debate', pp. xxxvii–xlii.
60 This implied use of Sanskrit and the evolution of the caste system.
61 For a quick look at the present status of the debate see E. Bryant and L. Patton (eds), *The Indo-European Controversy: Evidence and inference in Indian history* (UK, USA, Canada, Routledge, 2005). See the introduction by the editors and the chapters in the historiography section. Also, as Tony Ballantyne argues, the idea of an Aryan racial group was popular to both colonial administrators and different groups of Indians merely because the idea was flexible and could be used to draw different interpretations and conclusions to suit various socio-political needs. See T. Ballantyne, *Orientalism and Race: Aryanism in British Empire* (UK, Palgrave Macmillan, 2002), pp. 54–55 and 173.
62 There is a lively debate about the homeland of Aryans. For an understanding of its wider political implications see M. Deshpande, 'Vedic Aryans, non-Vedic Aryans, and non-Aryans: Judging the linguistic evidence of the Veda', in Trautmann, *The Aryan Debate*, pp. 62–83; and Thapar, *Some appropriations*.

63 By which I mean that the 'independence' of the princely state was more a result of the colonial state's post-1857 calculations of political stability than any hard-fought battles against the presence of *Raj*.
64 A.K. Dutta, *Bashpiya Upadesh* (Tattwabodhini Press, Calcutta, 1855), p. 3. Emphasis mine.
65 R. N. Tagore, 'Dur', in *Sishu Bholanath* (Calcutta, Biswabharati, 1922).
66 D.N. Gangopadhyay, *Vividha Darshan Kavya* (Calcutta, 1877), p. 3. The original line in Bengali is: 'swadeshe koriya dwesh holem biday'.
67 Sen, 'Prabaser Patra'. Prabas meaning outside Bengal.
68 Sengupta, 'Bharat Bhraman', volume II, p. 230; Ray, 'Uttar Paschim', p. 258; Das, 'Bharatvarsher Pratichi', p. 185.
69 Bose, 'Professor Bose-r', p. 74. Emphasis mine.
70 K. Mukhopadhyay, *Railway Companion* (Calcutta, 1855). Mukhopadhyay's use of the word *paschim* (lit. west) to describe regions beyond Bengal is instructive as by the turn of the twentieth century the term became commonplace enough to be used as a shorthand for north and north-western India by Tagore and numerous others. Thus, here anticipating Tagore implies both the use of the word '*paschim*', but also how railways alongside an annual autumn vacation to celebrate *durga pujo* in Bengal came together to offer time and opportunity for travel. For a nineteenth-century account of how *durga pujo* holidays and railways combined to make travelling popular, see K.P. Sinha, *Hutom Penchar Naksha o Onnanyo Samajchitra* (Calcutta [original publication 1863] Sahitya Parishad, re-print 1955), part II, the chapter titled 'Railway'.
71 H. Bandyopadhyay, *Bhraman Vrittanta* (Hughli, Hooghly Normal Press, 1876), p. 2 and 5. Despite such grandiloquent title and claims, in reality the pamphlet is a description of a short overnight trip of 22 students of Hughli Normal School from Chinsurah to Munger.
72 Ray, 'Uttar-Bharat', p. 6.
73 Sengupta, 'Bharat Bhraman', Volume I, pp. 26–27.
74 Kedarnath Das for instance described swadesh or *banga bhumi* as an 'excellent garden'. Das, 'Bharatvarsher Pratichi', pp. 6–7.
75 Das, 'Bharatvarsher', p. 8.
76 Sengupta, 'Bharat Bhraman', Volume I, pp. 26–27.
77 Bandyopadhyay, 'Bhraman Vrittanta', p. 6.
78 Das, 'Bharatvarsher', pp. 6–7.
79 Ray, 'Uttar-Bharat', pp. 15–16, 258. Emphasis mine.
80 Shastri, 'Dakshinapath Bhraman', p. 183; Sengupta, 'Bharat Bhraman', Volume I, p. 117.
81 Shastri, 'Dakshinapath Bhraman', p. 183.
82 Sengupta, 'Uttar-Bharat' and Das, 'Bharatvarsher', p. 38.
83 Sen, 'Prabaser Patra', pp. 50 and 90; Sengupta, 'Bharat Bhraman', Volume II, pp. 32–33.
84 Shastri, 'Dakshinapath Bhraman', p. 183; Das, 'Bharatvarsher', p. 48.
85 For a discussion on Maratha and Rajput nationalism see S. Gordon, *The Marathas: 1600–1880* (Cambridge, 1993); S. Wolpert, *Tilak and Gokhale: Revolution and reform in the making of modern India* (New Delhi, Oxford University Press, paperback edition 1991); and N. Peabody, 'Tod's Rajasthan and the boundaries of Imperial rule in 19th century India', *Modern Asian Studies*, 30, 1, 1996. Also, P. Deshpande, *Creative Pasts: Historical memory and identity in Western India, 1700–1960* (New York, Columbia University Press, 2007).
86 Bayly, 'Origins', pp. 29–30, 49–50.
87 Sengupta, 'Bharat Bhraman', Volume I, p. 177; Ray, 'Uttar Paschim', p. 171. This theme is discussed with greater clarity in the following chapter.
88 R. Jones, 'Dreaming of a Golden Bengal: discontinuities of place and identity in South Asia', *Asian Studies Review*, 35, September 2011, pp. 373–395. Also, Bayly, 'Origins',

pp. 29–30. If anything, it can be argued that a long usage of the word *swadesh* and its wide diffusion regardless of the ways in which the meaning shifted in different political contexts possibly made the concept (and the territorial conceptualisation) a popular and particularly potent political tool in colonial Bengal.

89 Late nineteenth and early twentieth century literary endeavours by Bengali litterateurs too played a role in this conceptualisation of Bengal as a 'verdant paradise'. From Bankim Chandra Chatterjee to Rabindranath Tagore and beyond wrote paeans about Bengal's natural beauty though their literary output was also influenced by European literary sensibilities, especially Romanticism. This, however, does not mean that figures such as Bankim or Tagore did not challenge colonial stereotypes.

90 See previous chapters on how railway travel practices added new ways of asserting social status and contesting railway spaces.

91 P. Van der Veer, *Religious Nationalism: Hindus and Muslims in India* (Berkeley and Los Angeles: University of California Press, 1994); C. A. Bayly, 'The pre-history of "Communalism"? Religious conflict in India, 1700–1860', *Modern Asian Studies*, Vol. 19, No. 2 (1985), pp. 177–203; Ballantyne, 'Orientalism and race', p. 186; T. Trautmann, *Aryans and British India* (New Delhi, Yoda Press, 2004 edition), pp. 66–80; J. Chatterji, *Bengal Divided: Hindu communalism and partition, 1932–1947* (Cambridge, Cambridge University Press, 2002).

92 It is not surprising that attempts were made to undermine the implication of this suggestion, i.e. Brahmins being 'aggressors and foreigners' as lower-caste movements in colonial India used this to assert their historically valid superior claims over the national space. For an account of how Phule and others appropriated this narrative see R. O'Hanlon, *Caste Conflict and Ideology: Mahatma Jotirao Phule and low caste protest in nineteenth century western India* (Cambridge, Cambridge University Press, 1st paperback edition 2002), pp. 80–81; 148–151. For a general historiographical discussion on the theme see A. Parashar-Sen (eds) *Subordinate and Marginal Groups in Early India* (USA, Oxford University Press, 1st edition, 2004).

93 Though interestingly some authors did refer to Marathas' political past as disruptive, especially to Bengal. See Sen, 'Prabaser Patra', p.91; Das, 'Bharatvarsher', pp. 60–63.

94 An idea usually subscribed by historians of religion. For a recent exposition see D. Eck, *India: A Sacred Geography* (New York, Harmony Books, 2012).

7 Shared spaces, shifting identities

Railway travel and notions of identity and community in colonial India

In a Bengali travelogue published in the mid-nineteenth century, the author Deviprasanna Raychaudhuri described Telengas as 'possibly the most ignorant and stupid jati in India who nonetheless have learnt superficial civility from their association with the sahibs'.[1] The author of another Bengali travelogue published in the late nineteenth century explicitly referred to 'Biharis' as 'uncivilised'.[2] A few pages later, the epithet was repeated, presumably to convey to the readers that such associations between a region, its inhabitants and civilisational accomplishments or rather the lack of them was not accidental. Interestingly, the occasions that elicited such responses were products of either encountering non-Bengalis[3] in railway spaces or musing about the latter during or after railway journeys.[4] More significantly perhaps, as we will see later in the chapter, articulation of such sentiments was not a singular occurrence.

At one level, presence of the sentiments quoted above is not surprising. After all, as shown in previous chapters experiences of sharing common railway spaces entailed both physical proximity and confinement for a fixed duration – a process that produced heterogenous, even competing ideas of identity. At another level however, if one bears in mind that the authors of the travelogues invariably travelled in upper-class carriages and consequently avoided the conditions of travel that beset most Indian railway passengers; then their evidently uncharitable assessments of fellow passengers and compatriots require more explication than we currently possess. Clearly, as the remarks quoted above indicate, regardless of the differences in objective conditions of travel, the literary narratives of Indian passengers' railway travel experiences in colonial India did not merely produce 'nationhood, or community'[5]; at least not to the exclusion of other more divisive, and hierarchical[6] notions of identity. In other words, articulations of differentiation as a criterion of asserting as well as assessing social position by the authors of these travelogues offer me an appropriate, if somewhat provocative entry-point from which to appraise current historiographical assumptions regarding the impact of railway travel on notions of identity and community in colonial India, the main theme of this chapter.

An imagined community? Railway travels and identities

> They [Hindustanis] were delighted to meet us as if we were *swadeshis*. At this place [Nathdwara] far away from Bengal, Bengalis came to be considered as *swadeshis* by *Hindustanis*. In Kashi one [Bengalis] can never expect such kinship and friendly behaviour from Hindustanis.[7]
>
> We are inhabitants of far-off Bengal and his [co-passenger] home is in Lucknow; yet he was describing us as belonging to one nation, i.e. bharatbasi.[8]
>
> It [Rajmahal] is the meeting point of Bengal and Bihar. The locals are at the least illiterate. It will not be an exaggeration to claim that there is almost an absence of bhadralok here.[9]
>
> I was surprised to notice a lapse in the duty by a European station master. It is all the more surprising because it was being done by an employee at a big station [Lucknow] and of a railway company [the Eastern Indian Railway Company] which is otherwise known for its standards of efficiency and comfort.[10]

Railway travel experiences certainly influenced notions of identity. But if the excerpts quoted above from Bengali travelogues published in the early decades of the twentieth century are anything to go by, travelling to or visiting new places, and meeting diverse groups of people beyond what was considered to be familiar, engendered feelings that were more complex than presently acknowledged. Broadly speaking, in a historiographical position largely concurrent with colonial administrators and railway promoters, post-colonial scholars note that railway travel experiences significantly contributed to a growth of 'national' or 'nationalist' sentiment in colonial India.[11] Of these, except for Kumkum Chatterjee's article exploring explore links between 'travel, history and identity' using travelogues written by Bengali railway travellers; there is a remarkable lack of detail as to *how* the putative process of forging 'national' identity through railway travel unfolded.[12] Making a strong case for railway travel experiences in enhancing an understanding of India's past as well as present; Chatterjee argues that Bengali travelogues written during the late-nineteenth and early twentieth century reflect a project of nation building by Bengali gentry that was informed by Western-educated, middle-class, Hindu/upper caste sensibilities.

At a related level, Chatterjee suggests that this process of construction of Indian nationhood was also an attempt by Bengali nationalist bourgeoisie to wrest from the colonial state and its ideologues the right to describe India on their own terms. This contestation, Chatterjee claims, was done through a dual process: *one*, by constructing a 'nationalist' ethnographic description of other, non-Bengali Indians through the conscious use of former authors of the Bengali travelogues who rejected derogatory and hackneyed colonial stereotypes; and *two*, by defining the British and the Europeans as the 'ultimate other' thus underlining a collective, racial, 'national' identity.[13]

Chatterjee's conclusions, especially the claim that the nation as imagined in the pages of these travelogues was based on a specific and narrow view of India's past and was suffused with sensibilities of the social group that undertook this project is certainly valid. At the same time however, her analysis overlooks critical details that once examined and added, significantly fractures, even complicates, the notion 'national' sentiments as articulated by the authors of Bengali railway travel narratives. If anything, the fact that the authors of the excerpts quoted above were surprised to be identified as *bharatbasi* or that they defined *Hindustanis* as non-*swadeshis* suggest that even after half a century of railway operations, steam did not miraculously transform disparate groups of railway passengers as 'Indians'. Evidently, the quotes demonstrate that though on occasion different groups did deploy a language of 'nation' and 'national' community; the reverse too was not just possible, but prevalent. Otherwise, why the surprise in being described as '*bharatbasi*'; or for that matter the claim that such behaviour was unheard of in places such as Benaras, a site noted for combining religious (Hindu) and nationalist sentiments. Certainly, such evidence can be dismissed as either fragmentary or given the nature of the source, as personal opinion. But either way, their significance in questioning current historiographical conventions cannot be denied.

Given this, primarily drawing upon Bengali travelogues written in the late-nineteenth and early twentieth century,[14] here in this chapter I suggest that railway travel did not obviate differentiation as a valid basis of notions of identity and community in colonial India. On the contrary, heterogenous notions of identity continued to compete and eventually contested the rather newly formed 'national' identity. At a related level, I argue that this differentiation was creatively used to assert regional identities over 'national' to contest both railway-specific and other spaces, a process that had consequences for Indian society. Last but not least, critically deviating from Chatterjee's and similar analyses, I suggest that attitudes of the authors of these travelogues towards Europeans or British, either as railway employees or members of the ruling race, was not quite simplistic as the 'ultimate other'. This is neither to discount evidence of political criticism in the pages of the travelogues; nor to suggest that race did not influence the interactions between Indian and European railway passengers. But as the excerpt from a Hindi travelogue quoted above indicates, Europeans elicited nuanced sentiments including even positive appraisals. Such responses I argue, require more expositions than we presently possess.

In short, railway travel played a direct as well as indirect role in influencing notions of identity colonial India. The former is rather self-evident and thus easy to define and identify. Indeed, it will not be an exaggeration to claim that in colonial India railway travel afforded a hitherto unprecedented possibility of experiencing and expressing notions of identity through increased interaction and contact among different groups, setting in motion a process of comparison and contrast. Railway travel's indirect role however, is slightly more difficult to delineate, if only because, in the pages of the travelogues it so often coalesces with the direct one. Nonetheless, as the above excerpts illustrate, railway travel did provide vital occasions to interpret railway-specific experiences in non-railway contexts. More critically perhaps, such experiences were interpreted in ways that clearly had wider socio-political consequences.

This chapter therefore, weaves through a narrative, combining interpretations of railway travel experiences both within and without railway precincts. This methodology has the advantage of underscoring the influence and overlap of the former over the latter; while also offering ways to examine disparate events around which expressions of identity were constructed, partly as a result of the former. The chapter also builds upon existing scholarship.[15] At the same time however, it also adds new evidence and perspective to our present understanding of how Indians interpreted experiences of railway travel, thereby once again underlining a gap between imperial claims and 'native' realities – a process that also crucially demonstrates the agency of the colonised.

From loyalty to challenging the Raj: railway travel in the shaping of Bengali self-identity

> Before 1857 Bengalis were the favourite jati of the King; what a contrast with present time [1911]. Now we [Bengalis] are viewed with suspicion [on account of nationalist politics] and have our luggage checked and personal history investigated [as railway passengers][16]
>
> In those days [before 1857] there was a Hindustani proverb popular in these regions [north-western provinces] that said: "fighting is done by those who wear hats [British] while the spoils are enjoyed by the ones who wear dhoti" [Bengalis].[17]

For the authors of the travelogues, the hours of forced confinement in the carriages provided ample opportunity to engage with ideas of 'self' and 'other'. Typically, non-Bengali co-passengers provided convenient occasions to launch an elaborate comparative ethnographic analysis. More often than not, the initiating point of such comparisons was a self-definition of Bengalis, for which the authors invariably chose the colonial stereotype of the Bengali persona, a curious combination of largely unflattering attributes, though not entirely without redeeming qualities.[18] The use of colonial ethnography however, was not limited to self-definition. It was also liberally applied to define non-Bengali others. The pages of the travelogues are replete with references to 'manly marathas or Rajputs', or 'cunning Muslims'. Setting aside the historiographical analysis of this use of colonial ethnography for a discussion later; in the following paragraphs, I focus on the ways in which the authors used the latter to interpret railway travel experiences largely to construct notions of 'self' and 'other' by exploring, and asserting differences.

The authors of the travelogues largely admitted the deficiencies of Bengali character outlined in the colonial ethnography. Indeed, they used these putative shortcomings to either explain or interpret experiences accrued from railway travels. Writing in 1911 Shyamakanta Ganguly, the author of a Bengali travelogue explained his struggles to buy a ticket at the crowded ticket window at Katihar junction in terms of his being an 'effete and weak Bengali' who had to expend time and energy to make his way to the counter that was blocked by 'burly north

Indians'.[19] Ganguly's views, though rare in the sense that it described a direct experience of being physically shoved around at a railway counter allegedly due to lack of superior strength;[20] was by no means new. If anything, as a theme, physical weakness of Bengalis enjoyed a long status of being discussed in the pages of travel narratives and beyond.[21] For instance, writing as early as 1861, Jagmohan Chakrabarty, the author of an English railway travel narrative claimed that it was only in Bengal that the despicable treatment of the third-class passengers at the hands of lower-level railway employees goes without affrays. For him, this was tell-tale evidence of the physical weaknesses of Bengalis.[22] Given the centrality of physical weakness in the self-definition of Bengalis, many authors tackled various aspects of the issue in the pages of their travel narratives. Unsurprisingly, their engagement with the subject was either occasioned by meeting people of 'sturdier jatis who did not eat rice'; or travelling through drier climes than Bengal, while pondering about its positive impact on the physical well-being of the inhabitants.

Echoing the colonial stereotype, most authors linked effeminacy and physical weakness to food and climate. Kedar Nath Das argued that the fertility and the evenness of Bengal's land was as much the source of fortune as it was responsible for making Bengalis effeminate, weak and lazy.[23] Saratchandra Shastri was appreciative of the ability of the Marathas to climb mountainous terrain without fatigue, and attributed this to their food. His explanation for the physical abilities displayed by the Marathas is worth quoting:

> These people [Marathas] do not consider traversing such terrain as challenging because unlike us [Bengalis] they do not survive by eating fine rice. Their appetite is satiated only after eating a substantial amount of atta mixed with generous helping of ghee along with vegetables.[24]

This strength-inducing food, he argued, enabled Marathas to endure physical labour. Given such food habits, he was not surprised that Marathas produced 'courageous characters' such as Shivaji and Peshwa Baji Rao. Similar thoughts were also expressed by Surendranath Ray. Passing through parts of north India Ray noted:

> People of this desh [north India] do not eat food only to satiate their taste buds. For them any food is delicious which offers physical strength and energy. This is why Hindustanis are physically stronger than us [Bengalis]

At a related level, Ray claimed that excessive consumption of rice made Bengalis effeminate, as well as impotent.[25] Prasannamayi Devi too, argued that 'Hindustanis prefer health and nutrition over taste', a choice she thought explained the 'manliness' of north Indians.[26]

Interestingly, the 'manliness' attributed to some groups of non-Bengalis was mainly, though not exclusively, constructed as an anti-Muslim posture. In other words, Bengalis were noted as an 'unmanly' *jati* that collectively cowered to the

Muslim rule, without putting up a military resistance worth celebrating. Such 'historical weaknesses', the authors of these travelogues argued, made Bengalis suffer for centuries. Given this, it is hardly surprising that most of the authors recommended a visit to either Rajasthan or Maharashtra as a way of witnessing the 'manlier races in action', presumably to instil a sense of purpose among 'drift less and pleasure-loving bengali youths'.[27] Surely, this choice of travel destination, as shown in the preceding chapter, also corresponded with a specific territorial conceptualisation of *desh* and as such served a dual purpose of visiting those parts of India that were also home to people who resisted the imposition of Muslim rule with 'courage and fortitude', thus drawing a lesson in history and national pride.

Significantly, for the authors of these travelogues, the lack of physical strength among Bengalis was symptomatic of a broader weakness of character or moral being. If anything, the absence of the former was seen as visible proof of more intangible, nevertheless critically important deficiencies. Undeniably, such opinions were informed by the colonial stereotype of Bengalis. Thus unsurprisingly, the symptoms of moral deficiencies too, corresponded with the colonial claims. Of all things, authors were particularly concerned about the lack of 'spirit of enterprise' among Bengalis. For authors, this translated as a 'disproportionate fondness' of Bengali males to seek employment as lowly clerks in government or mercantile offices, without exploring the option of pursuing independent business or even other manual work such as farming or factory hands. More importantly perhaps, this predilection for 'safe', though lowly as well as humiliating work was described as symptomatic of the 'slave mentality' of Bengalis.[28]

At a related level, this alleged slavishness of Bengalis was identified as the pre-eminent cause of material degradation of Bengal, since Bengalis were arguably uninterested in improving the latter by investing in capital and enterprise. Travelling through parts of northern India, watching independent farmers working at their fields, a scene that indicated material prosperity of the region, Prasannamayi Devi pointedly, if somewhat rhetorically asked her women readers why they felt so proud of their menfolk while all they did was *chakri*.[29] Echoing similar thoughts elicited by a journey through northern India, including a visit to the railway workshop in Jamalpur, Durgacharan Ray argued that Bengalis preferred to undermine the prospect of the material prosperity of Bengal; but did not hesitate to take up *chakri*, which entailed long hours, low pay and humiliation at the hands of European or Eurasian supervisors, and even exile from *swadesh*.[30] The Bengali fondness for *chakri* therefore, was argued to be a moral drawback that by implication was difficult to repair without overhauling the disposition of Bengalis.[31]

In a striking display of using a notion of causation, so central to colonial ethnography, the authors of these travelogues claimed that the moral and the physical deficiencies of Bengali character had roots in social practices and specific historical experiences of the region. Elucidating the links, many of the authors identified child marriage, social sanctions against widow remarriage and widespread apathy or even resentment over women's education as some of the most prominent reasons that lead to both mental and physical weaknesses. Citing child marriage as a curse that plagued Bengali society, authors such as Kedar Nath Das, Deviprasanna Raychaudhuri, Prasannamayi Devi and others noted that the former practice lead to weak progeny that eventually hindered the growth and progress of Bengalis. The 'women's question' also was similarly targeted. Many authors claimed that undereducated and underage brides did not make either good wives or good mothers, a combination that was once again identified a source of Bengali weaknesses.[32] For instance, travelling through Orissa, Deviprasanna Raychaudhuri argued:

> Women's education is prevalent in Utkal [Orissa]; among some castes widow remarriage too, is accepted. Noticing such practices, I pondered long and hard. *We [Bengalis] consider people of Utkal as uncivilised; and usually censure them*; [but] on social issues, they [people of Utkal] are much superior than Bengalis.[33]

Underlining the link between the low status of women in Bengal as a cause of Bengali moral and physical weakness, most authors noted with approval that women in parts of Rajputana or Maharashtra were 'freer' in their manners and movements including the relative absence of veiling faces than their Bengali counterparts. Such uninhibited social practices were further identified as one of the reasons as to why these parts of India produced more 'manly' offspring.

Interestingly, though not surprisingly, the enduring social causes that for these authors allegedly lead to Bengal and Bengali degradation were argued to be largely a product of 'ruinous impact' of a long era of Muslim rule over Bengal. Most authors invariably claimed that the 'social ills', particularly practices such as excessive care taken to veil faces or to avoid possible contact with males outside the family was a direct consequence of the arrival of Muslims in north India and Bengal. The advent of Muslim rule was arguably the point when women of these regions were forced to accept exclusionary social practices to save their 'honour' from 'depraved Muslim males'.[34] To substantiate these claims, many authors claimed that a positive correlation could be established between the places that successfully resisted 'Muslim aggression' and thus were more morally and physically superior than an average Bengali or an inhabitant of the Indo-Gangetic plain – two regions that had allegedly suffered inordinately under Muslim rule for a very long time.[35]

Significantly, some authors claimed that since Muslim rule was no longer a political force, the time was thus ripe to throw away the 'corrupted customs and rituals accrued through the long exposure to the evils of Muslim rule'. More importantly perhaps, authors argued that overthrowing customs such as veiling of faces will not be construed as acts of cultural or even religious betrayal, since in the first place these social practices were neither Bengali nor Hindu. On the contrary, such practices were claimed to be accretions of a political past that were detrimental to the 'nation' [read Bengali/Hindu]. Thus, rejecting social practices that were clearly identified as both circumstantial and harmful was prescribed as

194 *Shared spaces, shifting identities*

a remedy that will eventually improve Bengali mind and body, leading to regaining self-respect and a concomitant ability to take a more strident role in the future of India.

Critical as it was, these attempts at defining Bengali self-identity in the pages of these travelogues however, ran parallel to a process of comparing and classifying the non-Bengali 'other'. A logical follow-up choice after all, if one bears in mind that the starting point of all comparisons requires an awareness of self, particularly a hierarchy of attributes considered as either superior or inferior. Less philosophically speaking, the authors of these travelogues created an image of 'other' by radically transforming the meanings associated with ideas of 'self', though in most cases, though not all, assumptions remained implicit. This is perhaps most clearly evident in the instances where the Bengali self was defined as 'weak' or 'effeminate'. Broadly speaking, the authors of the travelogues argued that the physical deficiencies and effeminacy of the Bengali character was compensated for by their superior intellect, Western education and 'civility', which set them apart from other Indians. In a claim reminiscent of the assumptions and sentiments expressed in the excerpts quoted in the introduction, Kedar Nath Das noted:

> While people of Bhagalpur and Rajmahal area are described as strong and manly; [in reality] these people are inferior because they are neither well-educated, nor intelligent and civilised as Bengalis.[36]

Similarly, Baradakanta Sengupta implied a difference with Bengal by noting 'lack of bhadraloks' in Rajmahal; while he described the people of the region as 'grossly uneducated'.[37] Haricharan Bandyopadhyay, a student on a school trip to Munger thought the people of Deoghar were not as civilised as people of his *desh* and cited lack of education (the Western variety) as the probable reason for the former.[38]

Similar feelings were echoed by Deviprasanna Raychaudhuri who, as noted in the introduction, described Telengas and occasionally Oriyas in frankly unflattering terms. Indeed, if anything, his claim that some social practices of Oriyas made him ponder as to why Bengalis censured and looked down upon the former as 'uncivilised' indicate the presence of popular notions that were not particularly 'nationalistic'.[39] Of all authors, Prasannamayi Devi perhaps came the closest to a bold reappraisal of Bengali self-identity, despite an admittance of weakness. In her travelogue *Aryavarta*, Devi suggested inter-marriage between Bengalis and non-Bengalis as a way of improving both Bengal and north India's specific deficiencies. But such apparently radical recommendation came with a critical caveat, as is well-illustrated in the following excerpt:

> The boys from Braj region [Mathura/Vrindavan] should be adopted [by Bengalis] at a young age to be educated and subsequently married to Bengali girls. The possibility of such unions producing healthy, and strong progeny is highly probable, [a solution] that will be helpful for both groups.[40]

Clearly, Devi acknowledged where Bengalis were lacking. But it is not without significance that her solution called for an adoption of young non-Bengali boys at a very early age for social and educational training under Bengali tutelage.

The weak and effeminate self-image of Bengalis was also radically redefined by arguing that Bengalis were a political force to reckon with; and that they played a pre-eminent role in engendering the anti-colonial politics in India. More critically, these authors claimed that despite outward appearances, when it came to awareness of political rights and demanding equal treatment from Europeans, the 'manly' *jatis* did not fare well; while 'effeminate' Bengalis successfully conveyed their grievances. Travelling around, these authors noted several instances of differential treatment of Indians by Europeans and claimed Bengalis were respected more than other Indian *jatis*. Prasannamayi Devi for instance, thought the physical strength of the north Indians was of no great use vis-à-vis Europeans. She noted that Hindustanis lived in 'mortal fear of Europeans and rarely faced them while Bengalis were better off and Europeans behaved more thoughtfully towards them'.[41] For Baradakanta Sengupta, however, it was the political awareness of Bengalis that attracted European ire. He thought the reason for better relations between Europeans and the people of Bombay lay in the submissive attitude of the latter. Though not appreciative of the ways in which the people of Bombay, especially Parsis, behaved obsequiously towards the British, Sengupta nonetheless argued: 'unlike Bengalis these people do not want to be equals and Europeans prefer this behaviour'.[42]

This self-image of bold fearlessness was further bolstered by the *swadeshi* movement at the turn of the twentieth century.[43] Shayamakanta Ganguly thought his belongings were searched by the ticket collector at Lucknow station because his identity as a Bengali was enough to rouse fear in the mind of the railway official.[44] In a similar incident Satyendrakumar Basu felt he was interrogated and his luggage rummaged through at the Victoria Terminus station in Bombay 'just because he was a Bengali'.[45] Read alongside the sentiments challenging the efficacy of the 'manly' races at facing up the colonial administration at an everyday level, the authors of the Bengali travelogues were proffering tangible evidence of their ability to engage with the colonial state in ways other *jatis* were incapable of, a clearly political point, more of which shortly. The authors of the travelogues also inverted self-image of physical weakness as a result of dietary choices by replacing it with a claim that though the latter had a deleterious influence on the former; the fine culinary culture of Bengal reflected higher civilisational attainment. For instance, Baradakanta Sengupta informed his Bengali readers 'with delight' about the availability of fresh *Ilish*, arguably the favourite fish of Bengalis, in Rajmahal. The presence of the fish in the region he noted, would 'save Bengalis them from eating local food'.[46] Similarly, Surendranath Ray argued that though the Hindustani food was 'strength inducing', it was nevertheless 'coarse and inedible'.[47] Ray claimed that people of northern India had never known the pleasure of eating Bengali epicurean delights such as *luchi* and *rosogolla*; and lamented with palpable displeasure that given the absence of fine food outside Bengal, his travelling days were marked by eating 'inferior' food.[48]

Thus, the self-image of Bengalis was ensconced within a wider definition of non-Bengali 'other', the latter being patently inferior. More importantly, the claims of Bengali superiority were based on a clear notion of the elements that constituted the former. The authors were unambiguously clear that Bengalis were more accomplished than other *jatis* because of their Western education and training; a long exposure to structures of colonial power and administration that trained them in political manoeuvres, while giving them an enviable proximity to the ruling race; and last but not least, 'civility', a vague term that allowed 'flexible applications'.[49] Of these, not surprisingly perhaps, most authors considered the first two attributes as critical to claims of Bengali superiority. Gyanendra Mohan Das, the author of the Bengali tome *Banger Bahire Bangali* perhaps came closest to conveying the sentiments when he claimed that:

> Whether it was assisting in delivering government duties, or attaining and spreading European education and medical training or establishing schools, colleges, reading groups, Bengalis played a pre-eminent role as the right hand of the British. In all aspects of administration Bengalis enjoyed a monopoly; and displayed their influence and reputation [producing] a sense of awe among inhabitants of these regions [north India]; a feeling that was not unmixed with envy.[50]

Evidently, a combination of specific attributes, though in varying degrees, enabled the authors of these travelogues to contest implications of inferiority imbued in the colonial stereotype of Bengali weakness. At the same time, it also allowed the authors to make wider claims of superiority over other non-Bengali groups in ways that were underscored by the logic of the Bengali claims being based on recognisable accomplishments either unavailable or lacking in the latter. It is perhaps not without significance that Deviprasanna Raychaudhuri argued other *jatis* of India 'must admit that Bengalis possessed the greatest talent and intelligence; and that India could never have any political and social reform without Bengalis'.[51] Durgacharan Ray too, shared similar sentiments while linking what he considered as either the inability or unwillingness of 'uncivilised Biharis' to adapt to the practices introduced by a new system of transport as suggestive of a larger issue, that is, that the Biharis were incapable of independent decision making and thus needed to be led towards greater political awareness, and 'civility', presumably by Bengalis.

Clearly, such formulations and claims challenge, if not altogether reject the implications of the colonial stereotype of Bengalis by replacing it with more radical and subversive meanings. The use of colonial ethnography and stereotype is undeniable. But how far such usages are symptomatic of an internalisation of 'colonial characterisation' is questionable.[52] As the foregoing evidence clearly suggests, the use of colonial stereotypes is not significant *per se*;[53] but how this information was skilfully and selectively appropriated to create radically distinct definitions of 'self' and 'other' – a process evident in the ways in which the authors of the Bengali travelogues used the former in the new sites, contexts and

Shared spaces, shifting identities 197

issues provided by railway travel experiences. Thus, here I suggest that the use of colonial ethnography was by no means an 'inability of middle-class, educated Indians to be completely free of the influence of the British colonial presence'.[54] On the contrary, the authors of the travelogues used this handy, and rather well-diffused body of information for dual, though related purposes. On the one hand, the authors often inversed the colonial stereotypes, occasionally even rejecting or replacing it with radically different alternatives. At another level, this engagement with the colonial ethnography provided the authors with occasions to contest social spaces in colonial India, a claim mainly, though not exclusively sustained on an access to Western education. It is no coincidence that the authors skilfully critiqued unflattering attributes of the colonial stereotype of Bengalis by interpreting it in ways that undermined implications of drawbacks; while making a simultaneous claim of superiority over other *jatis*.

The ways in which the allegations of physical and moral weaknesses of Bengalis were consciously inverted to challenge alleged superiority of 'manly' non-Bengali *jatis* is plainly apparent and as such does not require repetition.[55] Similarly, at an apparent level the emphasis on Western education and training alongside a proximity to colonial structures of power may appear as either yet another indication of subjugation to the colonial norms, or worse an admission of loyalty to the *Raj*. But combined with the claims that Western training made Bengalis superior, clearly offered the vantage of favourably competing with other *jatis*; as well as using it to take a shot at claiming the reins of politics from the British. The argument that Bengalis were more respected by Europeans largely as a consequence of the former's political awareness certainly substantiates the idea that these authors were making a wider claim of Bengalis having the requisite political training to negotiate the demands of anti-colonial politics better than more 'manly' *jatis*. In other words, the admission of superiority of other *jatis* was strictly in the past, mainly in the form of anti-Muslim resistance; but when it came to modern political tactics, Bengalis clearly had an advantage of prolonged apprenticeship and thus were more eligible for political leadership over brawny non-Bengalis. As for the latter, it is instructive that the positive components of the colonial stereotype of Bengalis, i.e., keenness in acquiring Western education was transformed as an ability to replace the colonial state by providing modern political institutions, largely as a result of Bengal being the 'British bridgehead'.[56] It is perhaps no coincidence that Prasannamayi Devi claimed that though people of north India (including children) possessed lighter skin and better health than Bengalis; their faces however showed neither intelligence or brightness. Indeed, lack of these attributes, Prasannamayi Devi argued made it difficult for her to remember such beautiful faces.[57]

Thus, building upon, as well as deviating from, current scholarship here I argue that Bengali travel narratives reveal clear instances of contestation of social space. Additionally, I suggest that this contestation had specific political objectives of claiming, if not establishing superiority of Bengalis over other Indian *jatis* as much as competing with the colonial state for political power. Starting from the stereotype of effeminacy, the Bengali 'self' came to be defined in a more strident manner. In opposition to this self-image, the 'other' was defined over a range from 'uncivilised Biharis' to 'entrepreneurial but politically meek Marathis'. Evidently, these authors were claiming a pre-eminent political and social role for Bengalis. There is little doubt that the claims of superiority advocated by the authors of the travelogues enjoyed added credence in the late-nineteenth, early twentieth-century context of a heightened consciousness about Bengali accomplishments, in itself a typical product of the colonial encounter.[58] Nevertheless, the travelogues added a crucial layer by bringing in new evidence and claims as products of travel and meeting people. At the same time however, the claims of superiority could only be sustained if Bengali industry, both in terms of capital and labour, could be as successful as other aspects of Bengali life.[59] Bengalis therefore were exhorted to overcome their limitations (which by the way were mostly due to the Muslim rule) and contest for a position that would be commensurate with their accomplishments. Read along with the claim of Bengalis being on a par with Europeans, or at any rate demanding equality, while clamouring against inequities of the colonial system, the implications are rather too self-evident to require explication.

Identities in transit: ambiguities of encountering the 'ultimate other'

Railway travel provided opportunities for observation and contact to reflect upon another variant of the 'self' and 'other' theme: comparison with Europeans and occasionally Eurasians. Historiographically speaking, hitherto, Indian railway passengers encountering their non-Indian 'other' in railway travel experiences have only been interpreted as moments of discord, symptomatic of wider racial discrimination, and asymmetrical access to political power that characterised Indo-British relations. Though rather narrow, this focus however, is not surprising because tensions arising from Indians travelling in upper-class carriages with European co-passengers, or encountering European or Eurasian railway officials have been widely acknowledged as having played a critical role in engendering 'national' sentiments, underpinned by racial unity.[60] As such, scrutinising such encounters often has the self-referential quality of illustrating how the demands of the colonial railway system forged notions of collective identity by primarily uniting disparate groups of Indians through the glue of racial discrimination and arrogance displayed by the members of the *Raj*.[61]

Valid as these analyses are, here I suggest that there was more to these encounters than our current assumptions permit. Meeting Europeans and Eurasians while travelling in trains I argue elicited a range of responses that included an ambivalent assessment of the 'other', occasionally even respect, as well as antagonism and disdain based on race. In other words, a critical reading of the travelogues indicates that the authors' interpretations of railway travel experiences were complex and nuanced; with the former being informed as much by either suffering or witnessing explicit acts of racial discrimination as by being helped by a European railway employee or friendly European co-passengers. Additionally, these interactions also reveal a complex intersection of notions of race and social status/rank that qualifies the role of railway travel experiences in spawning 'national' sentiments. This section therefore reappraises present historiographical assumptions about Indian passenger experiences of encountering their 'ultimate other'.[62]

Significantly, none of the travelogues record any unpleasant occurrences while travelling with Europeans. If anything, as discussed in Chapter 4, Europeans, especially if they belonged to 'higher classes' were considered pleasant travel companions. Bharatendu Harishchandra for instance described one occasion when he and his European co-passenger shared jokes.[63] Additionally, the authors who wrote about their experiences of travelling with Europeans admittedly did so as a corrective to the general notion of Europeans as not-so-agreeable travel companions. Prasannamayi Devi for instance, noted that she felt 'duty-bound' to describe her pleasant experience of travelling with a European couple as a corrective to the oft-repeated claims of Europeans treating Indian co-passengers with discrimination and disdain.[64] Surely, Prasannamayi Devi or Bharatendu's claims hint at the existence of other, more unpleasant encounters. Nonetheless, such disclaimers also demonstrate possibilities of heterogenous railway travel experiences.[65] More significantly perhaps, such descriptions also bring to the fore an oft-overlooked possibility of class or social rank re-configuring race relations in railway encounters. After all, these authors equated better manners in Europeans as a sign of their belonging to a higher social class in England.[66] For instance, in her travelogue *Aryavarta*, Prasannamayi Devi twice linked civil behaviour to better social background and racial purity.[67] Simplistic and even inaccurate as this formulation was; there is no denying that instances of racial discrimination also came to be interpreted through notions of social rank, thus adding nuances to the former.[68]

If meeting Europeans as co-passengers prompted occasional allusions of racial tensions; encountering the latter as railway employees had no such outcomes. Indeed, it will not be an exaggeration to claim that for these authors European employees symbolised order and willingness to address grievances; with an additional advantage of not displaying a proclivity for demanding bribe.[69] Atul Chandra Mitra for instance, noted that having spent the night at the second-class waiting room at the Nasik station, the European station master woke him up at 5.00 in the morning, enabling him to complete the onward journey.[70] Similarly, Ram Shankar Vyas, the author of an Hindi travelogue candidly claimed that whenever he approached European station masters for help, the latter readily complied. In one such instance, the author praised the European stationmaster at Benaras for agreeing to convince their European (male) co-passengers to leave the second-class carriage in which the women of the author's family were travelling. On another occasion, the European station master at Hardoi honoured a similar request from the author, this time removing two inebriated white soldiers.[71] Baboo Gopalram too, expressed similar feelings when he claimed that whenever needed, European railway employees took care of the needs of a large group in which the author was travelling.[72] Manomohan Basu, the renowned

Bengali playwright, recounted in his diary an instance of a European guard apologising for a prolonged and unexpected delay in starting a train from the Mughalserai station.[73]

Of all these instances, Surendranath Ray's lengthy description perhaps serves as the exemplifier of combining positive attributes of European railway employees in a single narrative. Ray's journey to north India had a rather unsavoury beginning. Faced with demands for bribes from luggage-booking clerks at the Howrah station, Ray's luggage booking was delayed, resulting in him in missing 'Bombay Mail'. Left with little choice he booked a ticket for 'Punjab Mail', and wanted to enter an intermediate carriage before it got crowded. But his intentions were derailed (pun intended) by a '*krishanga sahib*' (lit. dark skinned/ Eurasian) ticket inspector who refused to let him in the carriage. A prolonged altercation followed, with the author's grievance finally redressed by a '*khanti sahib*' (lit. pure white), the stationmaster at Howrah. Ray noted, with some satisfaction, that the European employee not only redressed the issue; but also offered a strongly worded admonition to the Eurasian employee.[74] These characterisations of European employees were in sharp contrast to the author's opinion of Eurasian railway employees. Broadly speaking, Eurasians were described as disregardful of the needs of passengers; nasty, and intent on taking bribes.

For instance, Ram Shankar Vyas claimed that on each occasion he sought assistance from a Eurasian employee, the latter turned out to be either greedy or lazy, usually both.[75] The author of another Hindi travelogue too, made similar claims. Like Vyas, Sinha's complaint was also a result of first-hand experience, in this case having been forced to bribe railway employees at Allahabad station to ensure his onward journey to Kanpur could proceed without delay.[76] Manoranjan Majumdar also echoed similar sentiments. Narrating an incident to which he was a witness, Majumdar graphically described the ways in which Eurasian railway employees shoved an excessive number of passengers into the third-class carriages while demanding bribes in return for seats.[77] Evidently, Eurasian railway employees lacked the positive attributes of their European counterparts. As is well acknowledged in the literature, among Indians, this dislike of Eurasians was largely due to their racially mixed identity. But here I suggest that the disdain against Eurasian railway employees and resentment against their actions also underscored the crucial role social status played in interpretation of railway encounters with 'others'. Once again, this is not to undermine the role of race. But in a colonial society race and social status are not mutually exclusive. If anything, the former determines access to wealth and accompanying privileges. It was no coincidence that Eurasians lacked superior access to employment primarily because of their mixed racial identity.[78]

In other words, in the social hierarchy of colonial India, Eurasians lacked the advantage of Indians, i.e., of purity of race. Additionally, compared to Indian elites, Eurasians were disadvantaged on account of education, wealth and even access to political power. The authors of these travelogues were aware of this reality. What is more, they rightly identified railway employment as the Eurasians' only source of socially upstart manners that incidentally was also highly perceptible in railway spaces. As such, these authors' uncharitable opinion of Eurasians, with admittedly generous appraisal of European railway employees, was not just expressions of smarting under racial discrimination. Had it been so, then European employees too, would not have been spared. On the contrary, such contrasting appraisal of European and Eurasian railway employees was an assertion of superior social status by Indian elites in railway spaces, a process in which race mattered; but social status did too.

Encountering Europeans and Eurasians, members of the *Raj* also provided occasion to reflect upon the nature of colonial rule, including though not limited to evaluations of the colonial state. Interestingly, many authors admired or even praised aspects of colonial rule. Baradakanta Sengupta thought the printing press and the contribution of missionaries of Srirampur was one of the most positive aspects. The secret of Bengal's progress, he argued, lay in Srirampur; and Bengalis should be proud of its impact in transforming the Bengali language and in popularising print and education. He even suggested the Sanskrit hymn praising the five virtuous women of Hindu mythology should be re-written in favour of Marshman and his team who had lived to improve the condition of Indians (Bengalis).[79] Similarly, Deviprasanna Raychaudhuri expressed his admiration for the canal network in Orissa, comparing it favourably with the public works built by the Hindu kings of Orissa. The canals, he thought, would bring prosperity to Orissa by combatting the scourge of famine.[80] For the likes of Kalidas Moitra, Kedar Nath Das and Nabinchandra Sen, 'Pax Britannica' was the most admired contribution of colonial rule. Nabinchandra Sen for instance, was particularly impressed by the school at Jabalpur where erstwhile *thugs* were trained in activities such as carpet weaving. He was appreciative of the products made in this school and credited the colonial administration with transforming members of a 'criminal tribe' into law-abiding members of society.[81] Kedar Nath Das described the English as 'saviours' of ordinary Indians from warring and recalcitrant Indian rulers, a list that significantly included Marathas as *bargis*. He praised the English for pacifying and subjugating those 'little lords who deluded themselves as Gods and exploited their people'.[82]

It would be easy to dismiss these thoughts as products of colonised minds, which had come to believe the propaganda of the *Raj*. But here it will be instructive to note that these authors were also critical of colonial rule and its discriminatory practices.[83] The ambiguities and complexities of assessing colonial rule became pronounced as the authors travelled beyond the boundaries of British India. As noted in the preceding chapter, the travel itineraries were more or less fixed; and a visit to *Rajputana* or western India was mandatory. Consequently, most authors travelled through the princely states dotting these regions. This triggered a comparison of the administrative systems of two distinct, though not necessarily opposing forms of governance. Saratchandra Shastri was so 'impressed' by the administration of the Baroda State that he described in detail the functioning of the departments of education, industry and law.[84] For Nabinchandra Sen it was the easy yet expedient methods of dispensing justice that made a favourable impact in the court of Jaipur. He thought that, unlike in British territories, subjects in Jaipur were not trampled by incomprehensible legal jargon and 'blood-sucking lawyers'. For Sen the legal system was also reminiscent of the ways in which the ancient Hindu states governed, a loss that the author lamented.[85]

Baradakanta Sengupta compared the 'native' administration of *Rajputana* favourably to the British one. Significantly, he used the term *deshiya*, hinting at an awareness of the differences in the forms of administration, which were imported from Europe and thus by logic foreign. The lack of strict discipline in Rajputana's administrative matters, he argued, was compensated for by empathy towards the subjects, as a result of which the latter were not miserable.[86] He was not alone in thinking that the inhabitants of the princely states were materially better off than their counterparts in British India. Saratchandra Shastri was struck by the general prosperity of the people of Baroda. Similarly, Priyanath Bose noted: 'the benevolence of native rulers allows their subjects to prosper'. This sentiment was a product of his visit to Bundelkhand that coincided with a famine in the region. He described in great detail the relief measures implemented by the ruler of *Charkhari*, a small princely state in the region. He compared them with the 'inadequate' measures adopted by the British administration in their territory, and noted the steady trickle of people who crossed over to take advantage of *Charkari*'s better-managed relief measures.[87]

Colonial state was also criticised in a more explicit and strongly worded manner. Kedar Nath Das thought discrimination was the main drawback of the colonial rule. He identified race as the operative logic behind the unequal treatment of Indians and Europeans. He argued:

> Black people are subjected to humiliation at every stage, and their concerns are never redressed. Nor does their comfort, pleasure, or needs matter to the sahibs.

Highlighting the link between the loss of political freedom for Indians and the monopoly of violence enjoyed by the colonial state, Das noted that *sahibs* had the 'right' to be arrogant because they were winners and thus were 'expected' to exude pride and superiority. But at the same time Das claimed that the welfare of people too, should remain an important concern.[88] Discrimination was also at the centre of Deviprasanna Raychaudhuri's critique of colonial rule. Travelling across Orissa he visited the abandoned salt manufactorers of Balasore and trenchantly criticised the salt law. The abandoned salt factories, he argued, were proof of the English government's misrule and exploitation. He noted that the government discriminated against Orissa's salt even though it was of higher quality than that of Liverpool; accusing the English government of nepotism he claimed:

> They [the British] will never be absolved of the crime of systematically ruining one of the most profitable businesses of India.[89]

This pithy but damning appraisal was followed by a general condemnation of colonial administrative policies wherein Raychaudhuri regretted the failure of the

Oriyas to rescind the government's discriminatory salt laws despite a consistent campaign. Similarly, disrupting the standard narrative of the history of British experience in India, Nabinchandra Sen claimed that though a visit to the 'mutiny memorial' in Kanpur made him sad; there was no denying that atrocities were committed by both sides.[90]

Significantly, these authors not only distinctly acknowledged the inadequacies of the colonial rule; they also causally linked the former with the rise of anti-colonial political sentiments in India. Baradakanta Sengupta for instance, noted that Indians had turned seditious because the British rule had failed to deliver good governance. Making a causal connection between Indians' lack of loyalty and the failure of the British government to treat them well Sengupta argued:

> If the British authorities had been *fair* to their Indian subjects then they would have been rewarded by loyalty since Indians consider fealty to their rulers as dharma.[91]

Sengupta's views concurred with that of Deviprasanna Raychaudhuri and Kedar Nath Das. For Raychaudhuri, the disenchantment Indians felt towards the *Raj* was a consequence of a consistent policy of discrimination and 'divide and rule,' and this feeling, the author claimed would eventually lead to the downfall of the British Empire.[92] Kedar Nath Das argued that an earlier generation of *sahibs* had treated 'natives' well, as a result of which they were rewarded with loyalty. Using discrimination of third-class railway passengers as a wider index of mistreatment of Indians, Das claimed that actions and the behaviour of the members of the *Raj* ultimately determined the response of their Indian subjects.[93] Regardless of the accuracy of this favourable portrayal of an earlier generation of colonial administrators; this assessment nonetheless makes a strident claim for the colonial state having failed in its duty (albeit self-proclaimed), thus, eroding goodwill and undermining stability. More importantly, the basis for this critique is just and equitable treatment – things that have been clearly denied to Indians and as such, the latter's demands for self-government were justified. This was undoubtedly a political manoeuvre and one in which the rhetoric of the colonial state's superior and just government was used to upend its own legitimacy.

As the foregoing discussion suggests, encountering non-Indian 'other' in the course of railway travels engendered complex feelings. Plainly, the sentiments were more nuanced than a 'colonised' versus 'coloniser' paradigm allows. This however, is by no means a denial of railway travel producing collective identity, with clear racial boundaries. If anything, as shown above, actions underlined by notions of racial difference, or travelling through princely states expanded the ambit of communities based on linguistic or regional affiliations into a wider identity. Simply put, these experiences engendered by railway travels contributed to re-assessment and re-configuring meanings of being 'Indian'. Clearly, the experiences of railway journeys were framed in terms of 'we' as Indians and distinct from Europeans or Eurasians, sentiments that also produced assessments of the colonial rule. At the same time however, overarching identities did not subsume other, more particularistic or parochial ones. On the contrary, as the discussion around the authors' descriptions of European and Eurasian passengers and railway employees reveal, other aspects of identity such as wealth or racial purity were often sharpened in railway encounters.

This I argue is rather an unsurprising outcome given that the new spaces engendered by railway operations provided occasion for contestations, i.e., different social groups asserting rights over the former by underlining superior claims. In other words, the contestation of railway specific social spaces was influenced by notions of identity and in turn critically contributed to the intensification of the same. This is evident in the ways in which the authors of the travelogues being middle-class elites resented supercilious manners of Eurasians employees; but praised the behaviour of the European employees, who, as hinted earlier, were by no means beyond racial prejudice. This incongruity was certainly not a display of colonised elites' obsequious manner, especially given their criticism of racial discrimination as one of the biggest deficiencies of the colonial state. The difference in attitudes towards Europeans and Eurasians, I suggest, was in essence a contestation of social space. By asserting social status, both economic and racial, the authors of the travelogues were claiming superior rights over railway spaces, while denying the same to the Eurasians. More importantly perhaps, this assertion had a double edge. The emphasis on racial purity and wealth as markers of identity provided occasion to claim equality or at least contest the superior claims of Europeans; while at the same time rejecting Eurasians as irredeemably inferior offered a peculiar, though not an untypical instance of claiming the latter as beneath both comparison and competition. In short, these encounters certainly acknowledged the racial differences of the European and the Eurasian 'other', but not without challenging the implied superiority of the former and thus engaging in a literary rebuttal of the *Raj*.

Conclusion

This chapter shows that experiences of railway travel had a crucial role in shaping the notion of identity and community in colonial India – though in more complex ways than currently acknowledged. The conditions of railway travel brought people into close physical proximity for several hours and this experience was quite unlike any other previous experiences of transport. Meeting a wider range of people created both unifying and differentiating impulses. While on one hand, identities became less localised and broader; on the other, they were also defined in a narrower manner. For instance, while the railway experiences led the authors of the Bengali travelogues to imagine themselves as Indians; these also steered them to refine their Bengali identity.[94] As hinted already, such outcomes are hardly surprising as railways offered the most potent occasions for involuntary association and proximity, which gave rise to ideas about identity, religion and class. Following Lefebvre's ideas, it can be argued that railway engendered new social spaces produced through the conflicting interests of various social groups – a process that also led to re-configuration of notions of identity. The importance of railways lay in the fact that in comparison with other sites (cities or factories), they were the most accessible to most people. By providing sites for observations in quite large numbers, the railways, it can be argued, gave their experiences and interpretations greater force and salience. In addition, as the prolonged engagement with notions of 'self' and 'other' illustrate, railway travel experiences were also understood and interpreted outside railway contexts, leading to reassessment of identities and drawing of broader conclusions with socio-political implications.

Clearly, the authors of the travelogues interpreted facets of their railway travel in more complex ways than the railway promoters, and colonial administrators imagined. This once again illustrates agency of the colonised. Whether using as well as inverting colonial stereotypes and the meanings attached with it; or praising specific aspects of the colonial administration, while rejecting or criticising others, these literary narratives illustrate contestations of social space; assertion of a strident Bengali identity; and perhaps most strikingly, a use of travel experiences outside railway contexts to characterise behaviour and attributes of specific groups of people. Additionally, as noted in the introduction, the crucial point about the heterogenous and even provocative interpretations offered by the authors of these travelogues was that these were meant to be read. Given this, it is difficult to agree with the suggestion that the opinions expressed in these texts were an attempt to 'interiorise' ideas about India's past and convey them to an Indian audience by writers who could not 'shake off the silent presence of the west'.[95] On the contrary, despite the active surveillance measures taken by the colonial state to monitor sentiments expressed in the vernacular press, it is evident that these authors were using these texts to contest the claims of the colonial administration. These writers were not 'second guessing' the response of the colonial state; they were engaging with it through the medium of languages that gave them the advantage of sharing their ideas with the widest audience possible. It is perhaps no coincidence that issues of race and discrimination; exploitation of resources; the legal system of British India; and last but not least, famine relief and lack of concern for subjects were issues that were chosen to evaluate the colonial state.

At a related level therefore, neither the admiration of the colonial administration nor use of colonial ethnography suggest a subaltern elite uncritically reflecting back colonial assumptions. If anything, it suggests selective appropriation of information, largely to suit political ends. An excellent case in point is the portrayal of Muslims and their negative influence on Indian/Bengali life as it appears in the pages of these travelogues. As hinted before, such sentiments can be interpreted as reflecting uncritical acceptance of Orientalists' (in the Saidian sense) opinions. Yet, it is nothing if not suggestive that these authors peddled only those opinions that described the influence of Muslim rule on India in deprecatory terms. At a related level, these authors also ignored the big nineteenth-century shift in Orientalist tradition that Thomas Trautmann describes as a move away from 'British Indomania' towards 'Indophobia'.[96] It is not without significance that these authors consciously discarded the turn taken by Mill and his followers and rather appropriated an earlier scholarly tradition that celebrated

Indian civilisation and ranked it favourably with Europe. In other words, what is evident in the pages of these travelogues is not a reflection of some internalised attitude but a highly selective and qualified use of colonial ethnographic descriptions. At risk of speculation, it can be argued that the idea of 'interiorising' is appealing probably because it identifies the colonial intervention as the starting point of social differentiation in India. By so doing it almost denies the precolonial past any agency to initiate social (or economic) change and consequently comes alarmingly close to the colonial claim that India was inert before the arrival of the British.

Thus, evidently, as the foregoing discussion suggests, railway travel experiences were interpreted both within railway and outside railway contexts. Though this chapter has attempted the difficult task of disentangling the specific impact of railway experiences on notions of identity and community in colonial India; it needs to be underlined that those reading these travelogues and then going on journeys were being told what they were experiencing. In other words, these texts determined, at least to an extent, what people saw and also their reaction or interpretations. Evidently, some of these ideas or interpretations were projected from other sources; but some were produced anew from the direct experiences permitted by the railway.[97] This ambiguity encapsulates the role of a new transport technology in defining the notions of identity and community and is clearly reflected in the complex ethnographic descriptions in the travelogues, which can hardly be defined as 'nationalistic', though certainly national, being made by Indians. In other words, these interesting narratives of 'self' and 'other' products of railway travel experiences enable us to ask broader questions about the assumed connection between railways and social change in colonial India, the theme of the concluding chapter.

Notes

1 D. Raychaudhuri, *Bhraman Vrittanta*, Volume I (Utkal) (Calcutta, Nabya Bharat Basumati Press, 1885), p. 23. Incidentally, Deviprasanna Raychaudhuri was also the editor and publisher of a Brahmo periodical (monthly) *Nabya Bharat* (lit. New India).
2 D. Ray, *Debganer Martye Agaman* [1885] (Calcutta, Day's, 1980 reprint edition), pp. 169, 171. The author used the word *asabhya*.
3 Since most of the travelogues examined in this chapter were written by Bengalis, the authors used the word non-Bengali to refer to anyone who did not speak Bengali as their native tongue.
4 For instance, the repeated remark of Biharis as 'uncivilised' were occasioned by two separate incidents in which Bihari railway passengers wanted to board a second-class carriage with third-class tickets and refused to part with their tickets at the end of the journey at the behest of the ticket inspector respectively. See Ray, 'Debganer'.
5 K. Chatterjee, 'Discovering India: Travel, history and identity in late nineteenth- and early twentieth century India', in D. Ali (ed.), *Invoking the Past: The uses of history in South Asia* (New Delhi, Oxford University Press, 1999), pp. 193–227.
6 Here the use of the hierarchical is strictly logical as is evident from Durgacharan Ray's (the alluded in endnote 2) use of the word 'uncivilised'. One cannot identify others as 'uncivilised' without an awareness and ranking (in mind or otherwise) of what

Shared spaces, shifting identities 207

7 D.C. Rakhsit, *Bharat Pradakshin* (Calcutta, Sri Gauranga Press, 1903), p. 23. Emphasis mine.
8 D.K. Lahiri Chaudhury, *Bharat Bhraman* (Calcutta, Kuntolin Press, 1908), p. 129. Emphasis mine. *Bharatbasi* (lit. inhabitants of Bharat). Instructive here will be to note that the passenger who was describing the author and himself as *bharatbasi* was a soldier.
9 B. Sengupta, *Bharat Bhraman*, Volume I (Calcutta, K.C. Daw and Company, 1877), p. 26.
10 B. Gopalram, *Lanka Yatra ka Vivaran* (Kashi, Khadgavilas Press, 1885), p. 39. The 'lapse in duty' that surprised the author was that his travel companion and the patron of the travelogue Maharaja Bijaychand Bahadur, the raja of Bilaspur, Simla, was travelling in a first-class carriage and the station master at Lucknow should have had dangled the 'reserved' placard outside the carriage to denote the status for the former's journey from Lucknow to Mughalserai.
11 I. Kerr, *Engines of Change: The railroads that made India* (USA, Praeger, 2007); M. Goswami, *Producing India: From colonial economy to national press* (Chicago, University of Chicago Press, 2004); L. Bear, *Lines of the Nation: Indian railway workers, bureaucracy, and the intimate historical self* (New York, Columbia University Press, 2007); R. Prasad, *Tracks of Change Railways and Everyday Life in Colonial India* (New Delhi, Cambridge University Press, 2015); and Chatterjee, 'Discovering'. Though, of these, Ritika Prasad's recent and important analysis does suggest that experiences of railway travel and railway spaces 'allowed people to simultaneously pursue ideals of a horizontal society and reinstate hierarchies of difference'. See Prasad, 'Tracks of change', p. 59. Prasad, however, does not develop this argument either at a theoretical or empirical level.
12 Emphasis mine. Here lack of detail implies an *a priori* acceptance of railway travel having engendered national identity without investigating if such causal connections are valid.
13 Chatterjee, 'Discovering', pp. 210–211. Interestingly, Chatterjee dismisses the widespread use of colonial ethnographic discourse as a valid source by authors as an 'inability' of this group to be completely free of the influence of the British colonial presence, p. 204.
14 Besides Bengali travelogues however, I also draw upon contemporary newspaper reports, English travel narratives written by Indians as well as Hindi travelogues mainly to supplant and suggest wider resonance of the ideas expressed in the Bengali texts.
15 If anything, the chapter adds to the interpretative analysis of both Chatterjee and Prasad. Chatterjee, 'Discovering'; Prasad, 'Tracks of change'.
16 S.K. Basu, *Bharat Bhraman: Bombay, Saurashtra and Gurjara* (Calcutta, 1911), p. 23.
17 G.M. Das, *Banger Bahire Bangali* (Calcutta, Kalikinkar Mitra Indian, 1915), p. 59. The proverb in Hindi went thus: 'lade topiwala, khaye dhotiwala'.
18 Broadly speaking, in colonial classification, Bengalis were identified as a 'non-martial race', and thus by implication effeminate and weak. At a related level, Bengalis were also supposed to show apathy for manual labour; while displaying a disproportionate fondness for office/desk jobs. Last but not least, intertwining putative impact of climate and food on physical and moral well-being, Bengalis were portrayed as a languid group, whose excessive consumption of rice had severe debilitating impact. But such comprehensive denunciations came with some redeeming qualities. Bengalis were noted to be intelligent and quick learners, who also showed consistent interest in Western education and training. These qualities arguably made them politically precocious, a trait though positively appraised, nonetheless also offered an unsavoury

potential for the colonial administration. For a useful discussion of the colonial stereotype of Bengalis see M. Sinha, *Colonial Masculinity: The 'manly' Englishman and the 'effeminate' Bengali in nineteenth-century India* (Manchester, Manchester University Press, 1995).

19 S.K. Ganguly, *Uttar Bharat Bhraman O Samudra Darshan* (Calcutta, Tara Press, 1913), p. 13.
20 Ibid. As noted in previous chapters, the authors of the travelogues invariably travelled in upper-class carriages and thus avoided experiences of crowding, pushing and shoving at railway spaces. In this instance too, the author admitted that though he wanted to travel in a second-class carriage, the tickets were already sold out, thus forcing him to queue for third-class tickets at the crowded third-class ticket window at the Katihar junction.
21 The theme of 'weaknesses' of Bengalis was a subject of popular concern and debate in Bengal. See I. Chowdhury, *The Frail Hero and Virile History: Gender and politics of culture in colonial India* (New Delhi, Oxford University Press, paperback edition 2001), introduction and Chapter 2.
22 J. Chuckerbutty, 'My first railway to Rajmahal' in *Mookerjee's Magazine*, 1, 1 February 1861.
23 K.N. Das, *Bharatvarsher Pratichi Dig-Vihar* (Murshidabad, Jadunath Bandyopadhyay, 1872), pp. 6–7.
24 S. Shastri, *Dakshinapath Bhraman* (Calcutta, B. Banerjee and Company, 1911), p. 193. Emphasis mine.
25 S.N. Ray, *Uttar Paschim Bhraman* (Calcutta, Pashupati Press, 1907), p. 32. Ray used the word *hina-birya* that literally means low/inferior semen; though clearly the usage had metaphorical connotation, suggesting a lack of political power.
26 P. Devi, *Aryavarta: Jonoiko Banga Mahilar Bhraman Kahini* (Calcutta, Adi Brahmosamaj, 1888), pp. 14–15.
27 Ray, 'Uttar Paschim'; see Preface; and P. Bose, *Professor Bose-r Apurba Bhraman Vrittanta* (Calcutta, Manomohan Library, 1902), p. 73.
28 The Bengali word for paid employment is *chakri*. The meaning is loaded since the word is a derivative of the word *chakar* or slave, given this, the implications are self-evident. Additionally, as in the nineteenth and twentieth century for Bengalis *chakri* primarily meant working as lowly-paid clerks in the colonial office, the word assumed a connotation of political subservience alongside socio-economic one. For a nuanced discussion of *chakri* in colonial Bengal and its impact of Bengali psyche see S. Sarkar, 'Kaliyuga, chakri and bhakti: Ramakrishna and his times', in S. Sarkar, *Writing Social History* (New Delhi, Oxford University Press, 2002). Also see D. Chakrabarty, *Colonial Clerks: A social history of deprivation and domination* (Kolkata, K.P. Bagchi & Co., 2005).
29 Devi, 'Aryavarta', pp. 21–22. Emphasis mine.
30 Ray, 'Debganer', p. 52.
31 An interesting claim if only because it disregarded the well-known realities of discriminatory colonial employment as well as investment policies and its debilitating impact, especially on a province such as Bengal that produced a significant number of university graduates.
32 This aspect of public debate in late nineteenth and twentieth-century Bengal has received sustained and significant scholarly attention. See for instance, T. Sarkar, *Hindu Wife, Hindu Nation: Community, religion, and cultural nationalism* (Bloomington, Indiana University Press, 2010); S. Sarkar and T. Sarkar (eds), *Women and Social Reform in Modern India* (Bloomington, Indiana University Press, 2008); P. Chatterjee, 'The nationalist resolution of the women's question' in K. Sangari and S. Vaid (eds), *Recasting Women: Essays in Indian colonial history* (New Delhi, Kali for Women, 1989), pp. 233–253.

33 Raychaudhuri, 'Bhraman Vrittanta', p. 83; emphasis mine. Also, Das, 'Bharatvarsher', pp. 114–115.
34 Authors such as Nabin Chandra Sen, Prasannamayi Devi, Baradakanta Sengupta and others made explicit connections between Muslim rule and subsequent 'decline' of status of women in India. For instance, see Devi, 'Aryavarta', p. 15. Bengali authors, however, were not the only ones who made such claims. Har Devi, the author of a Hindi travelogue claimed that the idea of 'purdah' (veil) was unheard of before Muslims and it was the arrival of Muslims that forced Hindu women to adopt such 'unnatural' practices. See H. Devi, London ki Yatra (Lahore, 1886), p. 13.
35 See Sengupta, 'Bharat Bhraman', Volume I, pp. 46–48; N. Sen, *Prabaser Patra: Bharater Bhraman Vrittanta* (Calcutta, Goshtha Bihari, 1914), p. 34.
36 Das, 'Bharatvarsher', pp. 26–27.
37 Sengupta, 'Bharat Bhraman', p. 26.
38 H. Bandyopadhyay, *Bhraman Vrittanta* (Hughli, Hooghly Normal Press, 1876), p. 19.
39 Raychaudhuri, 'Bhraman Vrittanta', see the quotation analogous to endnote 33. It is interesting that the author admitted to Bengalis considering inhabitants of Orissa as 'uncivilised'. In other words, such sentiments were not merely the personal opinion of these authors, but had wider resonance. Echoing similar thoughts, the author of another Bengali travelogue, Chunilal Basu, argued that instead of looking down upon inhabitants of Orissa, Bengalis should be grateful to them for preserving ancient religious, historical heritages. See C. Basu, *Puri Jaibar Pathe* (Calcutta, 1903).
40 Devi, 'Aryavarta', pp. 66–67.
41 Ibid., p. 21.
42 Sengupta, 'Bharat Bhraman', Volume II, pp. 190 and 200–201.
43 *Swadeshi* movement or the socio-political and economic agitation that rocked Bengal following Viceroy Lord Curzon's decision in 1905 to partition Bengal. For a discussion on how revolutionary terrorism, a component of Swadeshi movement in Bengal had a wider romantic appeal, see S. Sarkar, *Swadeshi Movement in Bengal, 1903–1908* (New Delhi, Peoples Publishing House, 1973), Chapter 9.
44 Ganguly, 'Uttar Bharat Bhraman', p. 35.
45 Basu, 'Bharat Bhraman', p. 27. These incidents refer to 'militant nationalism' (as opposed to Gandhian non-violence) popular and consistently present in Bengal's anti-colonial politics both during the *Swadeshi* movement and beyond. See P. Heehs, *The Bomb in Bengal: The rise of revolutionary terrorism in India, 1900–1910* (New Delhi, Oxford University Press, 2004); also, Sarkar, 'Swadeshi movement'.
46 Sengupta, 'Bharat Bhraman', Volume II, p. 26.
47 Ray, 'Uttar Paschim', p. 56. Similarly, Haricharan Bandyopadhyay, a school student, described rice in the 'west' as 'disgusting'. See Bandyopadhyay, 'Bhraman', p. 6.
48 For a discussion of how food and culinary culture played a role in defining a distinct Bengali identity in the late nineteenth and early twentieth century see U. Ray, *Culinary Culture in Colonial India: A cosmopolitan platter and the middle-class* (New Delhi, Cambridge University Press, 2015).
49 For instance, as noted above, linking dietary choices as a marker of socio-cultural attainments.
50 Das, 'Banger Bahire', p. 56. The title means 'Bengalis outside Bengal' itself hints at the wider claim that Bengalis played a prominent role beyond their native region. Interestingly, this notion of non-Bengalis envying Bengalis for their accomplishments was noted quite explicitly by some of the authors of the Bengali travelogues. For instance, travelling around Punjab, Nabinchandra Sen claimed that the locals (i.e. Punjabis) 'hated Bengalis', and avoided social contact with the latter. Similarly, Prasannamayi Devi claimed that locals in north India avoided social contact with Bengalis and considered the latter as Christians. Sen, 'Prabaser', p. 29; Devi, 'Aryavarta', p. 20.

51 Raychaudhuri, 'Vividha Darshan Kavya', p. 95.
52 Chatterjee, 'Discovering', p. 213. For similar arguments see A. Nandy, *The Intimate Enemy: Loss and recovery of self under colonialism* (New Delhi, Oxford University Press, paperback imprint 2007).
53 In my view, the use of colonial ethnography is not a particularly enticing object of analysis because unlike post-colonial scholars, the authors of these texts lacked the advantage of hindsight, and as such saw colonial ethnography as ready-to-use sources of information. Moreover, as is well known, this ethnographic data was drawn from an eclectic range of materials including both Indian (pre-colonial texts) and non-Indian (e.g. quasi-scientific theories) notions imported from Europe. Thus, the label 'colonial' ignores the presence of pre-existing notions of differentiation that, as we will see, played a critical role in the comparative analyses contained in the pages of Bengali travelogues.
54 Chatterjee, 'Discovering', p. 204.
55 I do not emphasise this point because a similar analysis is available in Indira Chowdhury's work. I. Chowdhury, 'Frail hero', Chapter 2. My point, however, is distinctly different as I suggest that rejecting the colonial stereotype was a patently political choice that included challenging the superior claims on which the rule of 'colonial difference' was based as well as declaring Bengalis as the most civilised and accomplished group of people (say, for instance, as opposed to Marathas or Rajputs) to lead India into political freedom.
56 Here I use the title of P.J. Marshall's book to underline the idea claimed by the Bengali authors that an early access to British rule, especially Western education offered a political as well as socio-cultural edge to the inhabitants of Bengal. P.J. Marshall, *Bengal: The British Bridgehead: Eastern India 1740–1828*, The New Cambridge History of India, II.2 (Cambridge, Cambridge University Press, 1987).
57 Devi, 'Aryavarta', p. 13.
58 The period saw a rather unprecedented profusion of activities aimed at attempting to establish a distinct Bengali identity. For useful account of the historical processes involved see T. Raychaudhuri, *Europe Reconsidered: Perceptions of the West in nineteenth century Bengal* (Delhi, Oxford University Press, 1988); also, S. Kaviraj, *Unhappy Consciousness: Bankimchandra Chattopadhyay and the formation of nationalist discourse in India* (London, School of Oriental and African Studies, 1995).
59 Despite a general celebration of things Bengali, as noted above, the lack of Bengali enterprise and capital was widely criticised as a serious drawback plaguing Bengali society. For a discussion of this theme see R.K. Ray, *Urban Roots of Indian Nationalism: Pressure groups and conflict of interests in Calcutta city politics, 1875–1939* (Delhi, Oxford University Press, 1979).
60 Bear, 'Lines'; Goswami, 'Producing'; and Kerr, 'Engines'.
61 Chatterjee, 'Discovering', pp. 221–223.
62 The reference here (and in the title of the sub-section) is from Kumkum Chatterjee's article wherein Europeans are described as the 'ultimate other' of Indian railway passengers. Chatterjee, 'Discovery', p. 221.
63 B. Harishchandra, 'Janakpur ki Yatra', in *Bharatendu Granthavali*, Volume III (Kashi, Nagaripracarani Sabha), pp. 665–666.
64 Devi, 'Aryavarta', pp. 5–6.
65 This claim is not without evidence. Priyanath Bose, for instance, described how his journey from Peshawar to Rawalpindi (in a second-class carriage) was pleasant with Europeans keeping him company. P. Bose, *Professor Bose-r apurba bhraman vrittanta* (Calcutta, Manomohan Library, 1902), p. 141. Similarly, Baradakanta Sengupta described how more than once he had pleasant travel companions in Europeans and Eurasians; though with the latter, he ascribed the civil behaviour to his Western attire. Sengupta, 'Bharat Bhraman', Volume II, pp. 227–228 and 230.

66 For instance, Syed Ahmed Khan's petition made clear links between low-class Europeans being a threat to the respectability of both upper-class Indians and Europeans. See 'The humble petition of the British Indian Association', dated 16 October 1866, from Syud Ahmed, Secretary and others, British Indian Association, North-Western Provinces to His Excellency the Viceroy and Governor-General of India in Council, in Miscellany Railway Letters, L/PWD/2/190 (1865–1867), IOR.
67 Devi, 'Aryavarta', pp. 11 and 113. In the first instance, Devi noted that Eurasians behaved particularly nastily with Indians because, despite their relatively lighter skin, they retained the impurity of low-blood. In the second instance, Devi praised the officer in charge of the Agra Fort in issuing 'passes' by claiming that high-ranking officers of military were almost always more well mannered than civilians of low rank.
68 As noted in Chapter 4, unsurprisingly, racial discrimination was more acutely felt if the offender happened to be a white poor, or worse, a Eurasian.
69 Interestingly, none of the authors who compared Europeans with Indian employees (mostly implicitly) in respect of demanding bribes, never even alluded to the fact that Indians were very low paid, a difference that may have forced Indians to seek ways of extra income.
70 A.C. Mitra, Prabas-Prasun: katipay pauranik sthaner itihas (Purulia, 1911), p. 56.
71 R.S. Vyas, *Paribhraman athava Srinathrajyabhishek darshan* (Bankipur, Patna, Khadgavilas Press, 1909), pp. 38–39.
72 Gopalram, 'Lanka ki Yatra', p. 58.
73 S. Das (ed.) *Manomohan Basu-r aprokashito diary* (Calcutta, Sahitya Lok, 1981).
74 Ray, 'Uttar-Paschim', pp. 7–10. Interestingly, Ray quotes the admonition in detail. Though one may rightly suspect Ray's memory, unless he was writing down what was being said; the drift of Ray's argument, however, is clear.
75 Vyas, 'Paribhraman', p. 39.
76 Sinha, *Meri Purvadig Yatra* (Bankipur, Khadgavilas Press, 1885), p. 28. The demands for a bribe came from a motely group of railway employees including Eurasians and Indians. The author noted that third-class passengers faced worse fate than him, as they were also pushed around and ill-treated, especially if they refused to offer bribes.
77 Here too, as in the previous instance, perpetrators included Indian railway employees. See M. Majumdar, *Tirthayatrir Bhraman Kahini*, Volume I (Barisal, 1914), p. 45.
78 See S. Mizutani, *The Meaning of White: Race, class, and the 'domiciled community' in British India 1858–1930* (New York, Oxford University Press, 2011), also L. Bear, *Lines of the Nation: Indian railway workers, bureaucracy, and the intimate historical self* (New York, Columbia University Press, 2007).
79 Sengupta, 'Bharat Bhraman', Volume I, p. 6.
80 Raychaudhuri, 'Vividha Darshan', p. 9.
81 Sen, 'Prabaser Patra', p. 105.
82 Das, 'Bharatvarsher Pratichi', pp. 60–63.
83 A striking example comes from Nabinchandra Sen, a deputy magistrate in the colonial administration. Travelling through north India, Sen commented in his travelogue that expansion of British rule in India was based on deceit, greed and desire. See Sen, 'Prabaser', pp. 43–44. Of course, Sen was not a unique example; both Bankimchandra Chatterjee or Surendranath Banerjee, for instance, despite being members of colonial administration were nonetheless critical of it.
84 Shastri, 'Dakshinapath Bhraman', pp. 152–154.
85 Sen, 'Prabaser', p. 54. It is nothing but suggestive that Sen associated efficient and benevolent justice system with Hindu rule.
86 Sengupta, 'Bharat Bhraman'; Volume II, pp. 89 and 93.
87 P. Bose, 'Professor Bose-r', pp. 9–10. Here it needs to be noted that being the owner/manager of the Great Bengal Circus – the first Indian circus company in colonial

India, Bose significantly enjoyed patronage of rulers of princely states who often invited the circus to visit their territories.
88 Das, 'Bharatvarsher Pratichi', pp. 56–57.
89 Raychaudhuri, 'Vividha Darshan', pp. 90–91.
90 Sen, 'Prabaser Patra', p. 9. Interestingly Sen made a similar remark when looking at Mutiny ruins in Lucknow. Here he commented that though British sacrifice has been commemorated, no mention has been made of British inhumanely killing thousands of Indians in retribution (see p. 18).
91 Sengupta, 'Bharat Bhraman'; Volume II, p. 93.
92 Raychaudhuri, 'Vividha Darshan', pp. 90–91.
93 Das, 'Bharatvarsher Pratichi', pp. 56–57.
94 Recent research indicates that railway travel experiences were by no means the only medium through which a notion of Bengali *jati* and nationhood was created. See S. Gupta, *Notions of Nationhood in Bengal: Perspectives on Samaj, c. 1867–1905* (Leiden, Boston, Brill, 2009).
95 Chatterjee, 'Discovering', p. 213.
96 T. Trautmann, *Aryans and British India* (New Delhi, Yoda Press, 2004). See Chapters 3, 4 and the epilogue.
97 For a discussion of how familiarity with destinations (either from textual or other forms of information) influence travellers' attitude towards the former see H. Zhang, D. Gursoy and H. Xu, 'The effects of associative slogans on tourists' attitudes and travel intention: the moderating effects of need for cognition and familiarity' *Journal of Travel Research*, 56, 2, 2017, pp. 206–220.

Conclusion
All aboard the train? Technology transmission and social transformation in colonial India

A recent book on the British Empire and its impact on India suggests that so-called 'imperial gifts' such as the railways were never meant to benefit colonial India and if in the end the colonial largesse did have some positive influence on the former, it was unintended.[1] Regardless of whether one agrees with such summary and unflattering appraisal of the *Raj*; the inclusion of railways as an ambivalent legacy of India's colonial encounter is suggestive. At one level, one can argue that such reference to railways, especially underlining its deleterious influences on colonial Indian economy while alluding to its incidental positive social and cultural influences is an effective buttress against the view of Britain's empire as a force of good that 'made the modern world';[2] and as such, is perhaps both overdue and welcome. At another level, this need to acknowledge diverse outcomes of the decision to introduce and operate railways in India indicates a continuing historiographical tradition that illustrates the largely positive socio-cultural impact of the railways, particularly the former's role in imagining national space and community, an undoubtedly crucial component of anti-colonial struggles. In other words, as discussed in the introduction, despite differences of opinion regarding degree of change, railways' putative socially transformative role in colonial India has never been questioned. But does this historical image of colonial Indian railways accord with reality? To put it differently, if somewhat simplistically, what was the impact of railways on colonial Indian society? At a related level, did the introduction of the well acknowledged tool of the empire justify its superior moral mission by rescuing Indians from moribund beliefs and religious and caste prejudices, which arguably impeded their economic and social progress and thus by implication their march to modernity? This book had primarily set out to find answers to these questions, though in a tentative and contingent manner.

But as any reader will know by now, there is no single or simple answer to these questions. For instance, railway time and timetables were argued to be the instruments that would introduce a sense of time among Indians. It was also expected to teach Indians punctuality. But as Chapter 1 demonstrated, the railway time was neither the earliest nor the only instrument through which a distinct, linear time-discipline was imposed on Indian society. Office and factory times also played important roles in creating time-discipline. Of these, office time was imposed much earlier than railway time and it played a significant role in shaping responses to railway time. This is evident in the ways in which office-goers petitioned the railway administration to offer more convenient train schedules and demanded the punctuality of trains. Further, the standardisation of 'railway time' was a gradual process; it was uniformly implemented only at the turn of the twentieth century (1905). This gradual development obviates the possibility of any sudden change. Also, different systems of time, for instance religious or agrarian, co-existed, before as well as after the railways. This multiplicity of time had implications for any standardised time-discipline because people travelled for different purposes.

The impact of railway timetables on the daily commuters travelling to nearby cities for employment was sharper than, say, on pilgrims whose travel plans were also guided by 'religious time'. More importantly, the ability of 'railway time' to impact on behaviour was severely compromised by the routine unpunctuality of the trains. Hitherto arguments relating the railways to time have disregarded the constraints under which trains operated. At a practical level, railway companies struggled to adhere to the timetables. Their problems were increased by efforts to provide convenient timetables to suit passenger demands. But timetables were frequently altered, which affected standardisation and travel-discipline. On the other hand, interestingly, passengers were often critical of the unpunctuality of the trains, and complained about the inconvenience caused. This suggests that railways had a social and perceptual rather than a material impact on the management of time. The latter needed punctuality. In other words, railway timetables' actual impact on lives was limited, but the expectations in relation to train journeys were certainly important. The standardised clock was not reinforced so much by railway experiences as by its notional timetables.

Similarly, railway's impact on territorial imagination of India as a homogenous 'national' space too was complex, even ambivalent; though the former undoubtedly played a significant role in spatial integration of India. The railway network made the hugeness of India graspable.[3] It offered a hitherto unimaginable possibility of moving from one part of the country to another with relative ease and speed. An important feature of imagining land was through ideas of distance and proximity. By compressing the time taken to travel from one place to another the railway annihilated the space between two locations. This annihilation however, was not real and only a product of feeling nearness as opposed to distance. It altered the relation between places when areas previously considered to be relatively far away were seen as nearby destinations. Places came to be classified on the basis of re-evaluation of their relative distance. In other words, places closer to one's own region were argued to be more familiar (at least in theory) than those farther away. But, applying such assumptions after the railways, Baradakanta Sengupta, author of a Bengali travelogue, wrote less about northern India because the region he argued was not 'very different' from Bengal.[4]

On the other hand, as is evident from the instances of defining Bengal as *swadesh* underlining specific geographical and natural differences, railway experiences did not preclude the possibility of articulating notions of differences.

It is perhaps not without significance that Durgacharan Rakshit, the author of a Bengali travelogue claimed that railway travel made the ties with *swadesh* stronger and even made it impossible for Bengalis to be Hindustani or vice versa.[5] Such sentiments question hitherto held historiographical assumptions that, by the end of the nineteenth century, 'India' came to be imagined increasingly in standardised terms. As we have seen in Chapter 6, 'national' space continued to be conceptualised in fractured ways as *Aryavarta* or *Hindustan*. Such conceptualisations imagined India as land belonging to upper-caste Hindus. More importantly perhaps, these imaginations were not just the products of 'colonial knowledge'. They were a curious mixture of new geographical sensibilities available through school and university curricula, combined with pre-colonial territorial conceptualisations, including religious and mythical sources. These conceptualisations, therefore, conformed with as well as contradicted the cartographic ideal of India created by the colonial state, thus demonstrating both the limits of the ability of technology to initiate change regardless of wider contexts, as well as of the putative hegemonic desires of the colonial state.

Besides introducing a perception and value of time and territorial integration, the railway's most significant role was said to be its ability to transform social behaviour and practices and thereby dissolve social boundaries in India. It would not be an exaggeration to argue that this was the most publicised social and moral role of the railways in India. This robust belief in the ability of steam was possibly influenced by the fact that the railway promoters and colonial officials claimed that if Indians could let go of their inhibitive social practices, then they would modernise, speedily and successfully. Further, it was hoped (and claimed) that the dissolution of social boundaries would create a common bond among Indians, forging their specific caste, religious or regional identities into a national one. In short, by putting people in an unfamiliar setting, railway travel was expected to make customs change and barriers fall. Not surprisingly, this possibility offered by railway encounters, especially railway travel, has also been celebrated by Indians, both contemporary commentators and later scholars. But, as the discussion in Chapters 3, 4 and 7 showed, the reality was more complex.

Demands of railway travel necessitated physical proximity for several hours. This provided occasion to encounter and express notions of identity and community. Moreover, railways physically transported people to different places, away from the familiar, which accentuated feelings of both similarity and difference. The sentiments generated by these experiences had social implications, as they were deployed to reach wider conclusions. As Chapter 7 showed, the definition of 'self' and 'other' had two distinct levels: local or regional, and national. For instance, the authors of the travelogues defined themselves as Bengalis as opposed to Marathas, Rajputs or Biharis. At the same time, they also saw themselves as Indians, distinctly different from Europeans, but also as Hindus not Muslims. Further, Muslims were excluded from this pan-regional hierarchy. Rather they were defined as 'outsiders', who came as invaders, and failed to assimilate. This was repeatedly highlighted by classifying them with Europeans – as foreigners. As a result, Muslim achievements were undermined, and military victories were described as a loss of independence by Hindus. More importantly, by this logic, Muslims were denied a part in the shared history and culture of India and by extension a role in the nation's future. Given this, contrary to what Marian Aguiar has argued, it is not surprising that partition riots broke the 'inviolability' of railway space, if only because it was never as impervious to social norms and influences as has been imagined.[6]

At one level, however, railways did contribute to a sense of national identity. As argued in Chapter 7, railway travel also provided occasions to define 'self' in trans-regional language largely as a response to experiences shaped by encountering Europeans either as co-travellers or as railway officials. Interestingly, such meetings were described as 'pleasant', and European railway officials were noted as 'fair', and, unlike their Eurasian or Indian counterparts, not inclined to demand bribes. It might be suggested that such representations reflect the perceptions of 'colonial elites', and therefore can be safely discounted. But these authors were aware of the political and racial dynamics of these interactions; and were certainly not eager to please Europeans or the railway administration. If anything, on several occasions, they were critical of discriminatory policies of the railway companies, as well as the colonial government. We have seen how Deviprasanna Raychaudhuri criticised the salt laws or Kedarnath Das condemned the treatment of third-class passengers in unequivocal terms. Such behaviour and sentiments now appear contradictory or even conciliatory, possibly because our understanding of these events is teleological, that is, from the perspective of where things led: nationalism and binary opposition. Authors at the time were willing to report Europeans as 'friendly' and Indians as 'corrupt', without self-consciousness about how that made them seem as 'nationalists'.[7] Given this, it can be argued that expressions of identity and normative behaviour were not articulated only as binaries, in strict opposition with another. Rather there was a complex construction of notions of identity, because, while on one hand these observations admitted the presence of 'corrupt Indian railway employees' and 'friendly European co-passengers', on the other hand they did not discount the fundamental inequality of colonial relations. At a related level, these definitions question simplistic assumptions and claims that railways contributed to the creation of a uniform, homogenous, national identity.

As the foregoing discussion suggests, the impact of railway on colonial Indian society was both complex and heterogenous. Undoubtedly, consequences of the conditions of railway travel either as first-hand experience or more distant observations engendered collective notions of identity, usually underpinned by racial or national sentiments. But as the demands for separate arrangements for food, drinking water, retiring facilities and carriages illustrate, differentiation too remained a valid basis of identity formation. In other words, as opposed to colonial railway promoters' expectations, railway experience did not weaken notions of caste and religious affiliations. This however, is not to suggest that railways spawned such sentiments. But being a popular mode of travel, railway experiences possibly gave more force and salience to diverse passenger sentiments and demands, making them more effective. In other words, railways provided new contexts and indices to assert notions of caste and religious identities. For instance, we have seen how the author of a Bengali travelogue did not allow Muslim passengers to enter the carriage in which he was travelling. Similarly, the demand made by high-caste travellers to replace the cook at the railway refreshment room in Burdwan station because he was suspected to be a non-Brahmin indicates that new contexts offered by railways were used to articulate pre-existing norms and old hierarchies.

Additionally, railway experiences were also extrapolated in non-railway contexts to justify exclusionary norms based on notions of religious or caste differences. A Hindi poet for instance, caustically remarked that while Muslim passengers had access to drinking water from both *bhistis* and *paani panreys*; Hindus died of thirst. For him, this oversight was an indication of a general and wider disregard felt by the colonial authorities towards Hindus.[8] Bharatendu Harishchandra too felt similarly when he compared the decrepit state of carriage on his way to Baidyanath with the fate and courage of Hindus.[9] In short, railway experiences and the ways in which Indian passengers interpreted the former sharpened caste and religious identities. Surely, railway policies, especially those based explicitly on notions of religious or caste differences (e.g., refreshment arrangements) also played a role in reinforcing and legitimising divisive sentiments. Furthermore, there is little denying that railway policies were guided by the colonial state's specific view of Indian society as centred and ordered around caste and religious identities. But as we have seen, in many instances, railway policies responded to either existing popular demands (separation of Hindu and Muslim refreshment rooms) or anticipated passenger demands (Brahmin cooks in refreshment rooms and platform eateries). Thus, railway authorities largely responded to demands based on notions of social differentiations; but it did not create them.

This is not an attempt to exonerate the colonial state or role of colonial stereotypes in shaping administrative decisions with wider implications.[10] But at the same time, what needs to be underlined is that the notions that underpinned railway policies were influenced by Indian passenger demands, both articulated and anticipated and thus were not merely imagined or a creation of the colonial state, but had some basis in Indian realities.[11] This is also substantiated by the fact that measures such as the introduction of separate refreshment rooms for Hindu and Muslim passengers or appointment of Brahmin food inspectors or banning the sale of beef by platform food vendors became popular and were demanded in those networks that did not offer these facilities. Last but not least, not all passenger demands based on notions caste or religious differences were fulfilled, suggesting a guiding principle that was not merely *divide et impera*; more of which shortly. Differentiation as opposed to homogenisation is also visible in the ways in which railways sharpened identity based on notions of social rank or status. As the debates about intermediate class carriages or facilities commensurate with ticket prices have shown, railways provided new indices and occasions to assert social rank.

Additionally, as Chapters 2, 3 and 4 have shown, demands from 'respectable natives' were more likely to be met than those from others, thus adding credence to the formers' superior claims. This deference to social hierarchy was as much a product of British social formation[12] as it was of the colonial stereotype that Indian society was hierarchical and therefore, the 'natural leaders' should be assuaged, as they could take care of the rest of the population. Regardless of its source of inspiration however, as the discussions about the introduction of intermediate class carriages and the subsequent rescindment of the decision to abolish the former or introduce reserved carriages for 'women of rank' have shown, there is little doubt that railway policies and authorities privileged social rank. Given this, it is hardly surprising that the debate around providing toilets in the intermediate class carriages was never about the need for the facility for reasons of health, but rather about what was demanded by the middle-class, 'respectable' patrons of these carriages as its absence was interpreted as an affront to their social rank and gentility. Thus clearly, social status of passengers mattered. This provides us with occasions to re-evaluate the role of status in informing colonial relations, more of which later. But differential treatment of passengers and uneven fulfilment of their demands shows that contrary to our current historiographical assumptions, railway policies were flexible, even pervious to external pressures and influences.

As the foregoing chapters demonstrated, whether it was the question of introducing platform tickets or return tickets for lower-class passengers or lighting railway stations and platforms, railway policies were guided by local conditions and demands. The railway companies as well as the government (at all levels) recognised the pragmatism of this arrangement and did not want to introduce measures that would rankle with the locals and affect railway revenue. This fluidity had partly to do with the peculiarities of railway management in India, which was a combination of public and private initiatives.[13] Further, until about 1905, when the Railway Board was created, railway policies were decided at several levels. As a result, the railway companies (both private and the state-owned) as well as the government formulated policies to suit their particular needs, especially to attract passengers. In other words, well into the early decades of the twentieth century, one can hardly speak of standardised railway policies to which all railways operating in India responded.

At a related, possibly more critical level, flexibility of railway policies was also informed by material conditions. Indian railways were the most expensive investment ever made by any colonial power in any colony;[14] and unsurprisingly therefore, the search for ways to improve railway profitability was never far from the minds of the Boards of Directors of the railway companies, as well as the colonial government. If one adds to this the fact that profits from freight traffic grew slowly and were highly irregular until the turn of the twentieth century,[15] then it requires little to deduce that Indian passengers were the mainstay of railway income especially because they constituted 97 per cent of the coaching traffic. As such, flexible railway policies that could respond to local demands were perhaps part of the compulsion that railway authorities had to adhere to. But, as the debate around ticket price for lower-class carriages have shown, this flexibility of railway policies was circumscribed by the need for profit. Simply put, railway policies did not respond to external influences if profit or its prospect was jeopardised. Given this, it was perhaps no coincidence that separate upper-class carriages for Indian passengers were introduced on the Awadh and Rohilkhand Railway Company's line (a small network and thus less expensive); while similar demands were declined by the Eastern Indian Railway Company's network, but nonetheless measures were taken to separate poor Europeans and Eurasians from third-class Indian passengers (on a longer line with many Indians travelling in lower-class carriages, it was cheaper to sequester a handful of poor whites).

In short, it was profit not a desire for social transformation that shaped railway policies in colonial India. Perhaps this explains why some demands based explicitly on religious or caste prejudices were fulfilled while similar ones were not. After all, it was cheaper to employ *bhistis* of different backgrounds or buy tin and glass vessels for Hindu and Muslim passengers respectively than to add new rolling stock to accommodate consistent demands for separate carriages for lower-class/caste third-class passengers. Thus, neither the acceptance of the former demands nor the refusal of the latter were dictated by superior moral mission of railways, if only because there was no such thing except a pragmatic pursuit of profit, an objective shared by private companies and colonial empires alike. Historiographically speaking, the foregoing discussion questions the assumption that railway policies were efficient tools of colonial control that imposed order on unruly colonised minds and bodies. At a related, though wider level, these findings also challenge the claim that science, including technological developments, constituted a coherent strategy of power, through which colonialism exerted its authority.[16] Railway policies, as noted above, was flexible, albeit for commercial reasons. For everyday railway operations, this translated as moving away from rhetorical rigidities that marked upper echelons of railway administrations as well as being amenable to external pressures such as passenger demands and nowhere are such shifts more clearly visible than the correspondence of the railway companies with their respective Boards of Directors and various levels of colonial Indian administration.[17]

Additionally, as Chapter 2 and 7 have shown, railway policies were also influenced by widespread practice of railway employees accepting bribes that effectively subverted the putative rigidity of the former from within. Thus, railway policies varied and by implication therefore railway passengers must have experienced and interpreted its impact unevenly. There is little doubt that the likes of the main protagonist in Bharatendu's play *rel-ka-vikat-khel* interpreted the message of steam differently than several authors of the travelogues who travelled in upper-class reserved carriages;[18] or for that matter businessman and philanthropist Sir Jamshedjee Jeejeebhoy, the first Indian to be knighted in 1842 and also one of the first directors of the Great Indian Peninsular Railways, who once booked an entire train to take his family and friends on a pleasure trip.[19] If railway policies varied and railway experiences differed largely but not exclusively on the basis of social status then clearly the monolithic category of 'Indian railway passengers' needs more nuanced explication than we currently possess.

Perhaps Sir Syed's lengthy and unmistakably patronising petition on behalf of 'ignorant masses' (quoted in preceding chapters) may offer an entry point. What more, Sir Syed was certainly not the only one who emphasised difference with lower social orders and articulated a desire for distance.

Whether it was demands for separate waiting rooms for upper-class railway passengers or resentment against the Eastern Bengal Railway Company's decision to reduce the price of third-class tickets to the point when daily commuters to Calcutta offices and self-declared 'respectable middle class' were forced to travel fourth class with the 'dregs of the society', all suggest a desire for differentiation and rejection of standardisation and the social levelling the latter implied. Given this, it was no coincidence that reports in Indian languages newspapers (Chapter 4) persistently demanded intermediate class carriages to be outwardly differentiable in ways that would announce its superior status while also demanding strict prohibition on presence of 'social undesirables' in the midst of 'respectable' railway passengers. As should be clear now, this book is not discounting the role of race and racial discrimination in informing railway policies and operations in colonial India. Neither is it denying the unequal colonial relations in which railways operated in India. But evidently, Indian passengers were not a monolithic group that suffered equally from uniformly discriminating railway policies imposed from above. On the contrary, if the remarks by Bharatendu to donate decrepit carriages for third-class passengers or collective, persistent and widespread clamour (newspaper reports suggest wider currency) for amenities in intermediate class carriages to be commensurate with ticket prices is anything to go by; then Indian railway passengers not only showed a proclivity for differentiation on the basis of social rank, but they also used it to assert superior claims.

An evidence of railway policies guided by profit and thereby flexible, alongside the presence of a differentiated passenger body aware of its numerical significance, as well as social differences and not shy of asserting either, indicates a more nuanced image of technology transfer in colonial India than what I have previously referred to as the 'Headrick-Adas' model. The story of colonial Indian railways was certainly not one of an all-powerful colonial state imposing new technology from above over listless 'natives'. If anything, as argued above, the exigencies of everyday workings of railways in colonial India necessitated negotiations with Indian passengers. Though informed by the asymmetry of colonial economic and political relations, this need nonetheless deprived the colonial state/railway administrations from being the only force to shape the nature and direction of railway technology transfer in colonial India, a process most clearly visible in the ways in which railway-specific social spaces evolved. As outlined in the introduction, the necessities of railway operations created social spaces. But as the preceding chapters have shown, contrary to current historiographical assumptions, the colonial state was not the only power that shaped the contours of these spaces. If anything, these spaces were produced and reproduced through competing claims of various social groups of which the colonial state was but one. Whether it was the railway stations or the platforms or the carriages or the waiting rooms; a large number of people congregated and interacted in these spaces, perforce, as the demands of railway travel dictated.

These spaces therefore provided new occasions either to reinforce existing social practices, behaviours, norms and hierarchies, or to transform them. For instance, the demands for the introduction of intermediate class carriages illustrate the contestation of railway space around the idea of social rank and respectability. As the debate around the issue showed, the concerns revolved around an ability to pay more that would procure better facilities and concomitant social status. In other words, travelling in upper-class carriages came to be interpreted as a mark of status and by extension of this logic, those who travelled in the third or fourth-class carriages could not claim either social status or respect. Such sentiments were also amply evident in the petition sent by the 'respectable' middle-class office-goers to the Eastern Bengal Railway Company on the question of the removal of seats from the third-class carriages, a measure that was allegedly not commensurate with their social rank. But as Chapter 3 and 4 have shown, contestation of social space was not confined to assertion of superior rights based on social rank alone. Caste and religious identities too were deployed to contest railway spaces by claiming distinct and superior rights and privileges. For instance, separate carriages were regularly demanded for upper-caste Hindus in order to avoid contact with lower-castes and Muslims. In some cases, separate arrangements were also wanted for Indians travelling in upper-class carriages. Similar propensities shaped demands for separate refreshment rooms for Hindus and Muslims, or appointment of Brahmin cooks and *bhistis* of different castes.

Perhaps the most striking evidence of various social groups exerting dominance and conflict over railway space is how middle-class Indians appropriated the right to represent the poor or those lacking social status. This contestation is worth examining as it also shows a clear desire on the part of elite Indian middle-class to contest the claims of the colonial state as the protector and benefactor of Indian masses. As the petitions against over-crowding, lack of toilets in the lower-class carriages or ill-treatment of Indian passengers by railway employees have shown, a rising middle-class in late nineteenth-century India was asserting a strident political and social position, competing with the colonial state to speak for those who presumably lacked voice. At the same time, these claims of representing 'mute masses' however, was by no means intended to provide lower classes with any claim to railway spaces. This is evident in the language of newspaper reports, which claimed separate, better travelling arrangements in the form of intermediate class carriages. It is interesting to note that 'respectable' middle-class 'native' passengers demanded physical separation. Newspaper reports are replete with appeals to the railway companies and the government demanding prohibition of lower-class people from entering (even by mistake) upper-class carriages or waiting rooms because they posed a threat of social degradation and a health hazard to their social superiors. Given this, it will perhaps not be an exaggeration to argue that contestations over railway spaces added new dynamics to notions of material or political entitlement in colonial India.

Contestations over railway spaces are also obvious in the contemporary travelogues, with the most obvious and assertive instances coming from the Bengali texts. As Chapter 7 has shown, several Bengali authors carefully constructed a claim for Bengalis as politically conscious and strident, thus superior to other social groups.[20] Moreover, such claims were underpinned by both an explicit and implicit assertion of Bengalis leading other Indians towards greater political and social accomplishments. For instance, as noted in Chapter 7, Deviprasanna Raychaudhuri claimed that Bengalis were the most appropriate candidates to lead Indians towards political independence because of their education and possession of requisite talents. Similarly, Durgacharan Ray interpreted the inability of a group of railway passengers from Bihar to comprehend and conform to railway travel practices as symbolic of a wider problem that characterised them, namely the latter's lack of Western education and civilised behaviour. This, he argued, also made them 'unfit' for greater political roles. The travelogues also reveal other comparable processes of contesting railway spaces and beyond. For instance, one is struck by the ways in which the authors of the travelogues, who were mostly upper-caste Hindus, denied Muslims and lower-caste Hindus any claims to the railway spaces. As noted already, the demands for separate arrangements for travelling, food and water highlight this process. On one level, by refusing to share communal facilities, upper-caste Hindus were exerting their power over Muslims and the lower castes. At another, this was an attempt to appropriate and manipulate the new social spaces and travel practices to their advantage.

More importantly, this denial extended beyond railway spaces. We have seen how the territorial conceptualisation of *Aryavarta* meant a specific view of India's past, present and future, where Muslims and low-caste Hindus had no or little space. These contestations and claims, as Vasudha Dalmia has argued, possibly allowed for the articulation of an indigenous cultural and political identity designed in opposition to a repressive colonial power. But, as she rightly suggested, while the process was emancipatory for upper-caste Hindus, it was repressive for lower-caste Hindus and Muslims and excluded them with a potent imagining of their difference.[21] At one level however, the contestation over railway space offered an opportunity to express a collective identity as Indians as opposed to Europeans. As noted already, the railway travel experiences both in terms of symbolism and meeting Europeans or Eurasians was not necessarily unpleasant. But this did not rule out the possibility of conflicting social interests, especially because railway spaces were the product of technology transfer in a colonial context. Furthermore, it is not difficult to see why railway spaces were the appropriate sites to feel and express collective, though not necessarily homogenous, sentiments. Railways were the physical symbol of superior technical knowledge possessed by Europeans and the way in which it was operated and managed certainly provided sufficient occasions for Indians to feel discriminated against. In other words, the production and re-production of railway space was marked by a process of conflict between Europeans and Indians, primarily over issues of exerting power and control. Though this process was uneven, as the Europeans possessed institutional power and enjoyed a monopoly of violence; nonetheless, their putative superiority was also contested by critiquing discriminatory policies and exploitation of Indian resources. In short, the impact of the introduction of railways on Indian society was mediated by different competing groups and interests in contestation over railway spaces and beyond. This contestation was in itself a product of the wider socio-political context of introduction of railways in India that ironically also muted any potentially socially transformative capacities of steam.

On the basis of the foregoing discussion, one can safely argue that railway's role as a tool of colonial hegemony was limited. Indians, sometimes as a collective, at other times as diverse social groups and interests evidently contested the social and cultural hegemony that the railway promoters wanted to impose. This complex interaction, though admittedly railway-specific, however, also allows us to re-assess wider and related issues such as (*a*) agency of the colonised; and (*b*) relations between the coloniser and the colonised. As for the former, seen through the prism of railway operations, the agency of the colonised comes across as both complex and substantial. As argued in Chapter 7, the use of colonial stereotypes did not necessarily translate as accepting it. On the contrary, the skilful and selective appropriation of 'colonial knowledge' in the pages of the Bengali travelogues suggests 'colonised elites' responded in a more nuanced manner than hitherto imagined. It is perhaps not without significance that historical and spatial contours of the imagined *desh* was defined as *Aryavarta* thus denying Muslims and lower-castes any claims to it while claiming an equivalent if not superior racial status than the British. Similarly, superior attributes of Rajputs and Marathas were simultaneously accepted and rejected to assert clearly political ambitions. In short, the travelogues display an agency of the colonised in the ways in which the authors contested and inverted 'colonial knowledge'. More importantly perhaps, these texts show that not unlike their colonial masters, the colonised too were capable of using knowledge, regardless of its veracity for ideological ends.

Passenger negotiations over specificities of railway policies too, reveal agency of colonised, though at a more mundane level than articulated by the authors of the travelogues. This was largely because 'native' passengers negotiated within an asymmetrical power relation that did not permit elaborate literary engagements with the colonial state. Nevertheless, as passenger negotiations through petitions, newspaper reports or occasional withdrawal of patronage (either threatened or actual) illustrate, 'natives' contested and even rejected implications of inferiority. It is nothing but instructive that very often Indian passengers framed their demands not on the basis of race, but on economic grounds. Surely, this shows that passengers were aware of their numerical significance and did not hesitate to assert it. But it also underlines an equally clear knowledge of the role of race and the inferiority it implied; and thus, an attempt to subvert or overcome the latter by using the objective logic of commercial reasoning, a choice that for reasons of profit was also appealing for the railway authorities.

This railway-narrative also complicates our understanding of the relations between the coloniser and the colonised. Indian passengers' negotiations over various demands and the evolution of railway policies suggest that though fundamentally unequal, the relations between 'natives' and railway authorities were shaped by notions of social rank. More critical perhaps, was the awareness for both the ruler and ruled that social rank mattered. Perhaps not a particularly difficult conclusion to reach given that the language in which passenger demands and railway authorities' responses were framed was often underpinned by notions of status and respectability. After all, though seemingly from two opposing perspectives, what connected Sir Syed's outrage at the prospect of sharing carriage with 'low-bred' Europeans with that of the Eastern Indian Railway Company and the Government of India's decisions to sequester poor Europeans in a separate third-class carriage was an awareness of social rank as a marker of differentiation and the desire to uphold it. Similar propensities also guided both Prasannamayi Devi and a railway official's assertion that 'well-bred' Europeans and 'respectable natives' turned out to be better co-passengers. Evidently, social status, both as a notion and a reality informed coloniser-colonised encounters in a railway context; thus offering us an additional analytical index to understand the impact of technology transfer on colonial Indian society. At the same time however, it also opens up possibilities for future research by underlining what David Cannadine described as 'the interconnections between social visions of the metropolis and periphery'.[22]

Thus, historiographically speaking, the hegemonic powers of railway technology, arguably the pre-eminent 'tool of empire', were after all not as effectual in colonial India as currently assumed. This outcome however, should not be surprising if one does not forget or ignore the material foundations of colonial rule, which, as is widely known, also influenced the introduction of railways in India. Simply put, at the heart of colonial enterprise in India (or anywhere else for that matter) was profit for the benefit of the metropolitan economy. As such, even the desire for control of the colonial society was circumscribed by the need for profit as the railway promotional literature amply illustrates. In other words, both political and socio-cultural control was a means to an end. But as the foregoing discussion about railways in colonial India demonstrates, often the need for profit undermined the ability control if only because the former required pragmatic flexibility, including conceding to 'natives' as well as collaboration with them. As such, this study of railways in colonial India offers an additional perspective to reflect upon the nature of the colonial state. The subject already boasts of a critical and sophisticated literature.[23] The aim here therefore, is to add to this narrative by looking away from the imperial rhetoric to everyday workings of colonial Indian railway.

As is clear by now, once the rhetoric of technology transfer and social change is sifted through the sieve of complex realities that governed daily railway operations in colonial India; the ability of the colonial state to impose order or homogeneity appears much less effective. What is more, the evolution of railway policies and negotiations with Indian passengers suggest that social change, often assumed to be the central objective of colonial governance, was after all not the guiding principle. If anything, here I argue that at its best railway/colonial administration in India was ambivalent about social transformation; at worst, the latter was inconsequential as long as the prized investment of railways managed to make a reasonable profit while also justifying the moral mission of colonialism.

The story of railways and its impact on colonial Indian society shows that the context of the transmission of technology is as important as the actual process, because it determines the ways in which technology would be diffused. Seen from this angle, the railways did not deliver the expectations of colonial railway promoters, not at least without inconsistencies and ambiguities. This book therefore claims a limited and nuanced role for railways in inducing social change in colonial India. It does not deny that changes occurred; but questions their range, nature, direction and implications. More importantly, it demonstrates the participation of Indians in creating and directing this change, implying in turn that the outcome influenced Indian society in more ways than has been thought. In short, railways had unintended consequences for India, assuming that other results were intended!

Notes

1 S. Tharoor, *Inglorious Empire: What the British did to India* (London, Hurst, 2016). Also, www.theguardian.com/world/2017/mar/08/india-britain-empire-railways-myths-gifts accessed on 8 March 2017.
2 N. Fergusson, *Empire: How Britain made the modern world* (UK, USA, Penguin Books, 2004).
3 Paul Theroux, 'Foreward', in M. Satow and R. Desmond (eds), *Railways of the Raj* (New York, New York University Press, 1980), pp. 6–7.
4 B. Sengupta, 'Preface', in *Bharat Bhraman*, Volume II, (Calcutta, K.C. Daw and Company, 1877).
5 D.C. Rakshit, *Sachitra Bharat Pradakshin* (Calcutta, Sri Gauranga Press, 1907), p. 54.
6 M. Aguiar, 'Making modernity: Inside the technological space of the railways', *Cultural Critique*, 68, 2008, pp. 66–85.
7 For a somewhat similar argument see C.A. Bayly, *Origins of Nationality in South Asia: Patriotism and ethical government in the making of modern India* (Delhi, Oxford University Press, 1998), pp. 76–79. Also see C.A. Bayly, *Recovering Liberties: Indian thought in the age of liberalism and Empire* (Cambridge, Cambridge University Press, 2011), Chapters 5 and 6.
8 R. Goswami, 'Railway do-act', in K. Sishir (ed.), *Radhacharan Goswami ki chuni rachnayein* (Allahabad, Parimal Prakashan, 1990), p. 50.
9 B. Harishchandra, 'Baidyanath ki Yatra', in *Bharatendu Granthavali*, Volume III (Kashi, Nagaripracarani Sabha), p. 656. Bharatendu claimed 'gadi bhi aisi tuti-futi, jaisi Hinduoin ki kismet or himmat'.
10 B. Cohn, *Colonialism and its Forms of Knowledge: The British in India* (New Jersey, University of Princeton Press, 1996). For a more recent analysis see U. Kalpagam, *Rule by Numbers: Governmentality in colonial India* (UK, Lexington Books, 2014).
11 As both older and more recent scholarship has shown, caste, religious identity and notions of social rank go beyond an easy colonial, pre-colonial divide. Certainly, colonial rule sharpened and added new nuances but to create them would be to grant a power to the colonial state it never enjoyed. See P. Van der Veer, *Religious Nationalism: Hindus and Muslims in India* (Berkeley and Los Angeles, University of California Press, 1994); C.A. Bayly, 'The pre-history of 'communalism'? Religious conflict in India, 1700–1860', *Modern Asian Studies*, 19, 2 (1985), pp. 177–203; J. Sharma, *Hindutva: Exploring the idea of Hindu nationalism* (New Delhi, Penguin

Books, 2004); C. Jaffrelot, *The Hindu Nationalist Movement in India* (New York, Columbia University Press, 1998); S. Guha, *Beyond Caste: Identity and power in South Asia, past and present* (Leiden, Boston, Brill, 2013).

12 D. Cannadine, *Ornamentalism: How the British saw their empire* (London, The Penguin Press, 2001); F. Cooper and A. L. Stoler (eds), *Tensions of Empire: Colonial cultures in a bourgeois world* (Los Angeles, University of California Press, 1997).

13 See I. Kerr, *Engines of change: the railroads that made India* (Westport, Connecticut, Praeger, 2007), Chapter 4.

14 D. Thorner, *Investment in Empire: British railway and steam shipping enterprise in India, 1825–1849* (Philadelphia, University of Pennsylvania Press, 1950).

15 C. Dewey, *Steamboats on the Indus: The limits of western technological superiority in South Asia* (New Delhi, Oxford University Press, 2014); R. Varady, 'Rail and Road Transport in Nineteenth Century Awadh: competition in a North Indian province', (Unpublished PhD Dissertation, University of Arizona, 1981).

16 G. Prakash, *Another Reason: Science and the imagination of modern India* (New Jersey, Princeton, 1999).

17 For a discussion on the use of this hitherto unused archival source see the introduction.

18 Several authors such as Lalit Mohan Moitra, Ram Shankar Vyas, Prabhat Chandra Dube and Baboo Gopalram all travelled in exclusive reserved carriages and their travel narratives can be seen as a view of colonial Indian railways from above. As noted in preceding chapters, those authors who did not travel in reserved carriages invariably travelled in upper-class ones. A particularly striking instance is that of Priyanath Bose, the manager of the Great Bengal Circus. Though the circus was promoted as a nationalist enterprise, Bose (or Professor Bose as he was known) either travelled with his troupe in reserved second-class carriages or when reservations for one reason or another did not work out, they travelled in normal second-class carriages. Bose's travelogue-cum-memoir provides many instances of such travels. See P. Bose, *Professor Bose-r Apurba Bhraman Vrittanta* (Calcutta, Manomohan Library, 1902).

19 D. Kanwar, *Palace on Wheels: A royal train journey* (New Delhi, Prakash Books India, 2008), p. 28.

20 Recent research indicates that in colonial India, Bengalis were not the only ethnic group that expressed similar notions. See M. Sengupta, *Becoming Assamese: Colonialism and new subjectivities in northeast India* (New Delhi, Routledge India, 2016); P. Deshpande, *Creative Pasts: Historical memory and identity in western India, 1700–1960* (New York, Columbia University Press, 2007).

21 V. Dalmia, *Nationalization of Hindu Traditions: Bharatendu Harishchandra and nineteenth century Benaras* (Delhi, Oxford University Press, 1996).

22 Cannadine, *Ornamentalism*, 'Preface', p. xx.

23 D. Peers and N. Gooptu (eds), *India and the British Empire*, Oxford History of the British Empire Companion Series (Oxford, Oxford University Press, 2012); N. Dirks, *The Scandal of Empire: India and the creation of Imperial Britain* (USA, Harvard University Press, 2008); J. Wilson, *The chaos of empire: The British Raj and the conquest of India* (New York, PublicAffairs, 2016).

Bibliography

Primary sources

Archival records: unpublished

Proceedings of the Judicial Department, Government of Bengal.
Proceedings of the Judicial Department, Government of North-Western Provinces.
Proceedings of the Judicial Department, Government of India.
Proceedings of the Railway Department, Public Works Department, Government of Bengal.
Proceedings of the Railway Department, Public Works Department, Government of North-Western Provinces.
Proceedings of the Railway Department, Public Works Department, Government of India.
Railway letters and enclosures from Bengal and India.
Railway letters and correspondences of the East Indian Railway Company.
Railway letters and correspondences of the East Bengal State Railway.
Railway letters and correspondences of the Calcutta and South-Eastern Railway Company.
Railway letters and correspondences Miscellaneous.
Railway letters and correspondences of the Bengal and North-Western Railway Company.
Railway letters and correspondences of the Oudh and Rohilkhand Railway Company.
Railway letters and correspondences of the Sindh, Punjab and Delhi Railway.
Native Newspaper Reports, Bengal.
Native Newspaper Reports, North-Western Provinces.

Archival records: published

Annual Administrative Reports, Government of India.
Annual Administrative Reports, Government of Bengal.
Annual Administrative Reports, Government of North-Western Provinces.
Annual Police Reports, Railway Police Department.
Annual Reports to Secretary of State for India in Council on Railways in India.
Annual Reports of the Railway Borne Trade, Government of North-Western Provinces.
Annual Report to the Secretary of State for India on progress of Railways.
Census North-Western Province, Allahabad, 1872.
Census North-Western Province and Awadh, Allahabad, 1881.
Railway Gazette: A journal of transportation, engineering, docks, harbours, contracts and railway news.
Report on Inter-provincial crime, United Provinces, Bengal and Assam, Calcutta, 1899.

Report on river crime and river police reorganisation scheme, Calcutta, 1907.
Report of the railway police committee, Simla, 1921.
Thacker's Indian Directory.

Contemporary works

Andrews, W.P. *Indian railways and their probable results, with maps and appendix containing statistics of internal and external commerce of India, by an old Indian Postmaster* (London, T.C. Newby, 3rd edition, 1848).

Arnold, E. *The Marquis of Dalhousie's Administration of British India*, 2 volumes (London, Saunders, Otley and Company, 1865).

Banerjei, C.N. *An Account of Howrah: Past and present*, India Office Records Tracts, Volume 323 (Calcutta, 1872).

Bell, H. *Railway Policy in India* (London, Rivington, Percival and Company, 1894).

Beveridge, H. 'Notes of a holiday trip to Maldah and Bihar', *Calcutta Review*, 1891.

Chakrabarty, J. 'My first railways to Rajmehal', *Mookerjee's Magazine*, 1, 1860 (Calcutta, 1861).

Chapman, J. *The cotton and commerce of India considered in relation to the interest of Great Britain with remarks on railway communication in Bombay Presidency* (London, 1851).

Clunes, J. *Itinerary and Directory for Western India, being a collection of routes through the provinces subject to the Presidency of Bombay and the principal roads in the neighbouring states* (Calcutta, 1826).

Daniell, T. and William, D. *Early Views of India* (London, Thames and Hudson, 1890).

Danvers, J. *Indian Railways: Their past history, present condition and future prospects* (London, Effingham Wilson, 1877).

——. *Report to the Secretary of State for India in Council on Railways in India for the year 1878–79* (London, George William Eyre and William Spottisowoode, 1879).

Davidson, E. *The Railways of India: with an account of their rise, progress, and construction written with the aid of the records of the India Office* (London, E. & F.N. Spon, 1868).

Harischandra, B. *Bharatendu Granthavali*, 3 volumes (Kashi, Nagaripracarani Sabha, 1870).

Heber, R. *Narrative of a journey through the upper provinces of India from Calcutta to Bombay, 1824–1825* (London, John Murray, 1828).

Huddleston, G. *History of the East Indian Railway* (Calcutta, Thacker, Spink and Company, 1906).

Hunter, W.W. *A Statistical Account of Bengal*, 20 volumes (London, Trubner, 1875–1877).

Kipling, R. *Kim* (London, Wordsworth Books, 2009).

MacGeorge, G.W. *Ways and Works in India: Being an account of the public works in that country from the earliest times to the present day* (London, Archibald Constable and Company, 1894).

Montgomery, R. *Statistical Report of District of Cawnpore* (Calcutta, 1849).

Nevill, H.R. *Cawnpore: A Gazetteer, being volume XIX of the district gazetteers of United Provinces of Agra and Awadh* (Allahabad, 1909).

Pandit, L.L. 'The Aryavarta or northern India', a lecture delivered before the Madras Native Gentlemen on 25 May 1869 (Benaras, Medical Hall Press, 1870).

Roberts, J.S. *Routes in the Bengal Presidency* (Calcutta, 1865).

Vicajee, F.R, 'Political and social effects of railways in India', being a paper read before the National Indian Association, London on 25 May 1875 (London, R. Clay, Sons and Taylor, 1875).

Guidebooks and travelguides

Bradshaw's Handbook to the Bengal Presidency, and Western Provinces of India (London, W.J. Adams, 1864).
Illustrated Guide to the Madras Railway (Madras, Higginbotham, 1898).
Keene's Handbooks for Visitors: Allahabad, Cawnpore, Lucknow (Calcutta, Thacker, Spink, 1896).
Murray's Handbook of the Bengal Presidency (London, J. Murray, 1898).
Ochterlony hoite Qutub parjyanto: orthat purvabharat rail path sanlagna katipay pradhanato sthaner drashtabya padartha shokoler patha pradarshika (Calcutta, Umesh Chandra Nag, 1892).
The Prince's Guide Book: The Times of India Handbook of Hindustan (London, Eyre and Spottiswoode, 1875).
The Tourist's Guide: W. Newman and Company's East Indian Railway Handbook, a guide historical, descriptive, and suggestive (London, Newman and Company, 1870).
Travel in India or City, Shrine or Sea-beach: Antiquities, health-resorts and places of interest on the Bengal Nagpur Railway (Bombay, The Times Press, 1916).

Travelogues (Bengali)

Azim-al-din, *Ki Majar Kaler Gadi* (Burdwan, 1863).
Bandyopadhyay, H. *Bhraman Vrittanta* (Hooghly, Hooghly Normal Press, 1876).
Basu, B. *Tirtha Darshan*, 5 volumes (Calcutta, Sri Kali Prasanna Basu, 1891).
Basu, C. *Puri Jaibar Pathe* (Calcutta, 1903).
Basu, S. *Bharat Bhraman: Bombai, Saurashtra o Gurjara* (Calcutta, 1911).
Bose, P. *Professor Bose-r apurva Bhraman Vrittanta* (Calcutta, Manomohan Library, 1902).
Chatterjee, F.C. *Pather Katha* (Calcutta, 1911).
Das, K.N. *Bharatvarsher Pratichi Digvihar* (Murshidabad, Jadunath Bandyopadhyay, 1872).
Devi, P. *Aryavarta: Janoiko Banga Mahilar Bhraman Kahini* (Calcutta, Adi Brahmosamaj, 1888).
Dhar, G.B. *Sachitra Tirtha Yatra Vivaran*, 5 volumes (Calcutta, The Bengal Medical Library, 1913).
Dube, P.C. *Darjeeling* (Mahishadal, 1910).
Dutt, A.K. *Bashpiya Upadesh* (Calcutta, Tattwabodhini Press, 1855).
Gangopadhyay, D. *Vividha Darshan Kavya* (Calcutta, 1877).
Gangopadhyay, R. *Bharat Bhraman o Tirtha Darshan* (Calcutta, 1913).
Ganguly, S. *Uttar Bharat Bhraman o Samudra Darshan* (Calcutta, Tara Press, 1913).
Lahiri Choudhury, D.K. *Bharat Bhraman* (Calcutta, Kuntolin Press, 1908).
Majumdar, M. *Tirtha Yatrir Bhraman Kahini* (Barisal, 1910).
Mitra, A. *Prabas Prasoon: Kotipoy pauranik sthaner itihas* (Purulia, 1911).
Moitra, K. *Bashpiya Kal O Bharatiya Railway* (Srirampore, Srerampore Press, 1855).
Moitra, L. *Tirtha Yatra Vivaran* (Rajshahi, 1909).
Mukhopadhyay, K. *Railway Companion* (Calcutta, 1863).

Ray, D.C. *Debganer Martye Agaman* (Calcutta, originally published 1880, Dey's, reprint 1984).
Ray, S. *Uttar Paschim Bhraman* (Calcutta, Pashupati Press, 1907).
Raychaudhuri, D. *Bhraman Vrittanta: Utkal* (Calcutta, Nabya bharat Press, 1885).
Rakshit, D. *Bharat Pradakshin* (Calcutta, Sri Gauranga Press, 1903).
Sen, J. *Prabas Chitra* (Calcutta, 1899).
Sen, N. *Prabaser Patra Bharater Bhraman Vrittanta* (Calcutta, Goshtha Bihari Publications, 2nd edition 1914).
Sengupta, B. *Bharat Bhraman*, 2 volumes (Calcutta, K.C. Daw and Company, 1877).
Shastri, S. *Dakshinapath Bhraman* (Calcutta, B. Banerjee and Company, 2nd edition 1911).
Som, N. *Varanasi* (Calcutta, 1911).

Travelogues (Hindi)

Anon. *Yatri Vigyapan* (Allahabad, Mission Press, 1876).
Anon. *Rel ki ticket* (Agra, 1870).
Das, G. *Lanka Yatra Vivaran* (Kashi, 1910).
Devi, H., *London ki Yatra* (Lahore, 1885).
Prasad, S. *Bharat Bhraman*, 5 volumes, (Banaras, Hariprasad Yantralaya, 1902/03).
Ratneshwar, P. *Patramalika* (Agra, Agra School Book Society, 1841).
Shastri, D. *Meri Purvadig Yatra* (Bankipore, Khadgavilas Press, 1885).
Uddin, A.A. *Badri Yatra* (Lucknow, Munshi Ganga Prasad Varma Press, 1893).
Vyas, R. *Paribhraman* (Bankipore, Khadgavilas Press, 1909).

Travelogues (English)

Basu, P.C. *Travels in North India*, India Office Records Tracts, Volume 696 (London, 1887).
Chunder, B. *Travels of a Hindoo to Various Parts of Bengal and Upper India*, 2 volumes (London, Trubner and Company, 1865).

Travelogues (Marathi)

Versaikar, V.G. *Maajha Pravas: 1857 cha bandachi hakikat*, translated into English by Mrinal Pande (New Delhi, Harper Perennial, 2011).

Unpublished dissertations

Appleby, L. 'Social change and railways in north India, c.1845–1914', University of Sydney, 1990.
Bear, L. 'Travelling Modernity: capitalism, community and nation', University of Michigan, 1998.
Bury, H. 'Geographies, histories, boundaries: the formation of regional cultural idiom in colonial north India', School of Oriental and African Studies, 2006.
Derbyshire, I. 'Opening up the interior: the impact of railways in the north Indian economy and society, 1860–1914', University of Cambridge, 1985.

Robert, V. 'Rail and road transport in nineteenth century Awadh: competition in a north Indian province, University of Arizona', 1981.

Sinha, Nitin, 'Communication and patterns of circulation: trade, travel and knowledge in colonial Bihar, 1760–1870', School of Oriental and African Studies, 2007.

Internet sources

Mahapurush: The Holy Man: www.youtube.com/watch?v=0maLQpjpW2k11th accessed on 10 March 2016.

The DD Files: Shyam Benegal's 'Yatra' packed all of India in a train: https://thereel.scroll.in/800696/the-dd-files-shyam-benegals-yatra-packed-all-of-india-in-a-train accessed on 14 December 2016.

Aao Bachhon Tumhe Dikhaye: www.youtube.com/watch?v=lWsGPxp4s1w and www.youtube.com/watch?v=lWsGPxp4s1w accessed on 5 April 2017.

'But what about the railways . . . ?' – The myth of Britain's gifts to India: www.theguardian.com/world/2017/mar/08/india-britain-empire-railways-myths-gifts accessed on 8 March 2017.

Secondary works

Abbeele, G. *Travel as Metaphor: From Montaigne to Rousseau* (Minneapolis, University of Minnesota Press, 1992).

Abu 'al-Fazl ibn Mubarak. *A'in-i- Akbari*, translated into English by H. Blochmann (Volume I) and H.S. Jarrett (Volumes II and III) (Calcutta, Asiatic Society of Bengal, 1873–1894).

Adas, M. *Machines as the Measure of Men* (Ithaca, Cornell University Press, 1990).

Aguiar, M. 'Making modernity: Inside the technological space of railways', *Cultural Critique*, 68, 2008, pp. 66–85.

——. *Tracking Modernity: India's railway and the culture of mobility* (Minneapolis, London, University of Minnesota Press, 2011).

Ahuja, R. *Pathways of Empire*: *Circulation, 'public works' and social space in colonial Orissa* (Hyderabad, Orient Longman, 2009).

——. 'Opening up the country'? Patterns of circulation and politics of communication in early colonial Orissa', *Studies in History*, 20, 1, n.s. (2004), pp. 73–130.

Ali, D. (ed.) *Invoking the Past: The uses of history in South Asia* (New Delhi, Oxford University Press, 1999).

Amin, S. *Event, Metaphor and Memory: Chauri Chaura 1922–1992* (Delhi, Oxford University Press, 1995).

——. *Conquest and Community: The afterlife of Warrior Saint Ghazi Miyan* (Chicago, University of Chicago Press, 2016).

Anderson, B. *Imagined Communities: Reflections on the origin and spread of nationalism* (London, Verso, 2006).

Arnold, D. *Colonizing the Body: State medicine and epidemic disease in nineteenth century India* (Berkeley, University of California Press, 1993).

——. *Science, Technology and Medicine in Colonial India*, The New Cambridge History of India, III.5 (Cambridge, Cambridge University Press, 2000).

——. 'Europe, technology, and colonialism in the 20th century', *History and Technology: An International Journal*, 21, 1, 2006, pp. 85–106.

——. *Everyday Technology: Machines and the making of India's modernity* (Chicago, London, University of Chicago Press, 2015).

Baker, D.E.U. *Colonialism in an Indian Hinterland: The central provinces, 1820–1920* (Delhi, Oxford University Press, 1993).

Ballantyne, T. *Orientalism and Race: Aryanism in British Empire* (Basingstoke, UK, Palgrave Macmillan, 2002).

Banarasidas, P. *Ardhakathanak: A half story*, translated into English by R. Chowdhury (New Delhi, Penguin Books India, 2007).

Bandyopadhyay, B. *Adarsha Hindu Hotel* (Calcutta, Mitra and Ghosh, 1940).

Bandyopadhyay, S. *From Plassey to Partition: A history of modern India* (Hyderabad, Orient Longman, 2004).

Banerjee, P. *Politics of Time: 'Primitives' and history writing in a colonial society* (New Delhi, Oxford University Press, 2006).

Basu, R. *Mahabharat* (Calcutta, Samsad, 1975).

——. *Parashuram Galpa Samagra* (Kolkata, M. Mallick, 2007).

Batey, M. 'The picturesque: An overview', *Garden History*, 22, 2, Special Issue, Winter 1994.

Bayly, C.A. *Rulers, Townsmen and Bazaars: North Indian society in the age of British expansion, 1770–1870* (New Delhi, New York, Oxford University Press, 1992).

——. *Empire and Information: Intelligence gathering and social communication in India, 1780–1870* (Cambridge, New York, Cambridge University Press, 1997).

——. *Origins of Nationality in South Asia: Patriotism and ethical government in the making of modern India* (Delhi, Oxford University Press, 1998).

——. *Recovering Liberties: Indian thought in the age of Liberalism and Empire* (Cambridge, Cambridge University Press, 2011).

——. 'The pre-history of "communalism"? Religious conflict in India, 1700–1860', *Modern Asian Studies*, 19, 2, 1985, pp. 177–203.

Bear, L. *Lines of the Nation: Indian railway workers, bureaucracy, and the intimate historical self* (New York, Columbia University Press, 2007).

Behdad, A. *Belated Travellers: Orientalism in the age of colonial dissolution* (Cork, Cork University Press, 1994).

Bhabha, H.J. *The Location of Culture* (UK and USA, Routledge, 1994).

Bharati, A. 'Pilgrimage in Indian tradition', *History of Religions*, 3, 1, 1963, pp. 135–167.

Blumhardt, J. F. (ed.) *The Catalogue of Bengali Printed Books in the Library of the British Museum* (IOR, 1886).

——. *The catalogues of the Hindi, Punjabi, Sindhi and Pushtu printed books in the library of the British Museum* (IOR, 1893).

Bond, R. (ed.) *The Penguin Book of Indian Railway Stories* (New Delhi, Penguin, 1994).

Bonea, A. *The News of Empire; Telegraphy, Journalism, and the Politics of the Reporting in Colonial India c.1830–1900* (New Delhi, Oxford University Press, 2016).

Borocz, J. 'Travel capitalism: The structure of Europe and the advent of tourist', *Comparative Studies in History and Society*, 34, 4, 1992, pp. 708–741.

Bradley, S. *The Railways: Nation, network and people* (UK, Profile Books, 2015).

Bryant, E. and Patton, L. (eds) *The Indo-European Controversy: Evidence and inference in Indian History* (UK, USA, Canada, Routledge, 2005).

Cannadine, D. *Ornamentalism: How the British saw their empire* (London, The Penguin Press, 2001).

Cavour, C. *Des chemins de fer en Italie* (Paris, Plon Fréres, 1846).

Chakrabarti, P. *Western Science in Modern India: Metropolitan methods, colonial practices* (Ranikhet, Permanent Black, 2004).

Chakrabarty, D. 'The colonial context of Bengal Renaissance: A note on early railway-thinking in Bengal', *Indian Economic and Social History Review*, 2, 1, 1974, pp. 92–111.

Chakrabarty, D. *Colonial Clerks: A social history of deprivation and domination* (Kolkata, K.P. Bagchi & Co., 2005).

Chatterjee, K. *Merchants, politics, and society in early modern India: Bihar, 1733–1820* (Leiden, Boston, Brill, 1996).

Chatterjee, P. *The nation and its fragments: Colonial and postcolonial histories* (Princeton, NJ, Princeton University Press, 1993).

——. *Nationalist thought and the colonial world: A derivative discourse* (London, Zed Books, 1986).

Chatterji, J. *Bengal Divided: Hindu Communalism and Partition, 1932–1947* (Cambridge, Cambridge University Press, 2002).

Chattopadhyay, R. and Ghosh, S. (eds) *Goenda aar Goenda* (Calcutta, Ananda, 1994).

Chopra, R. *Technology and Nationalism in India; cultural negotiations from colonialism to cyberspace* (New York, Cumbria Press, 2008).

Chowdhury, I. *The Frail Hero and Virile History: Gender and politics of culture in colonial Bengal* (New Delhi, Oxford University Press, 2001).

Cohn, B. *An Anthropologist Among Historians and Other Essays* (New Delhi, Oxford University Press, 1990).

——. *Colonialism and Its Forms of Knowledge: The British in India* (New Jersey, University of Princeton Press, 1996).

Cooper, F. and A.L. Stoler (eds) *Tensions of Empire: Colonial cultures in a bourgeois world* (Los Angeles, University of California Press, 1997).

Cooper, M. *Brazilian Railway Culture* (UK, Cambridge Scholars, 2011).

Dalmia, V. *Nationalization of Hindu Tradition: Bharatendu Harishchandra and nineteenth century Banaras* (Delhi, Oxford, Oxford University Press, 1997).

Das, G.M. *Banger Bahire Bangali* (Calcutta, Kalikinkar Mitra Indian House, 1915).

Das, P. *Colonialism, Development, and the Environment: Railways and deforestation in British India, 1860–1884* (New York, Palgrave Macmillan, 2015).

Das, S. *Manomohan Basu-r aprokashito diary* (Calcutta, Ananda, 1981).

Davis, R.H. (ed.) *Picturing the Nation: Iconographies of Modern India* (Hyderabad, Orient Longman, 2007).

Debroy, B., Chadha, S. and Krishnamurthi, V. (eds) *Indian Railways: The weaving of a national tapestry* (New Delhi, Penguin Random House India, 2017).

Deloche, J. *Transport and Communication in India Prior to Steam Locomotion*, 2 volumes (Delhi, New York, Oxford University Press, 1993–94).

Derbyshire, I. 'Economic change and the railways in North India, 1860–1914', *Modern Asian Studies*, 21, 3, 1987, pp. 521–545.

Deshpande, P. *Creative Pasts: Historical memory and identity in western India, 1700–1960* (New York, Columbia University Press, 2007).

Dewey, C. *Steamboats on the Indus: The limits of western technological superiority in South Asia* (New Delhi, Oxford University Press, 2014).

Dewey, C. and Hopkins, A.G. (eds) *The Imperial Impact: Studies in the economic history of Africa and India* (London, Athlone Press for the Institute of Commonwealth Studies, 1978).

Dirks, N. *Castes of Mind: Colonialism and the making of modern India* (Princeton, NJ, Princeton University Press, 2001).

———. *The Scandal of Empire: India and the creation of Imperial Britain* (USA, Harvard University Press, 2008).
Dwyer, R., Dharampal-Frick, G., Kirloskar-Steinbach, M. and Phalkey, J. (eds) *Key Concepts in Modern Indian Studies* (New York, New York University Press, 2015).
Eck, D. *India: A sacred geography* (New York, Harmony Books, 2012).
Edney, M. *Mapping an Empire: The geographical construction of British India, 1765–1843* (Chicago, London, University of Chicago Press, 1997).
Ericsson, S. 'Importing locomotives in Meiji Japan: International business and technology transfer in the railroad industry', *Osiris*, 13, 1, 1998, pp. 129–153.
Fabian, J. *Time and the Other: How anthropology makes its objects* (New York, Columbia University Press, 1983).
Fergusson, N. *Empire: How Britain made the modern world* (UK, USA, Penguin Books, 2004).
Fischer-Tiné, H. and Mann, M. (eds) *Colonialism as Civilizing Mission: Cultural ideology in British India* (London, Anthem Press, 2004).
———. *Low and Licentious Europeans: Race, class and white subalternity in colonial India* (Hyderabad, Orient Blackswan, 2009).
Fitzgerald, P. *The Story of Bradshaw's Guide* (London, Field and Tuer, 1890).
Foster, W. *The English Factories in India, 1624–1629: A calendar of documents in the India Office etc.* (Oxford, Clarendon Press, 1909).
Fraser, B. and Spalding, S. (eds) *Trains, Culture and Mobility: Riding the rails* (UK, Lexington Books, 2012).
Freeman, M. *Railways and the Victorian Imagination* (New Haven, London, Yale University Press, 1999).
Gandhi, M.K. *An Autobiography: The story of my experiments with truth* (Boston, Beacon Press, 1962).
———. *Hind Swaraj or Indian Home Rule* (Ahmedabad, Navjivan, 1984).
Ghosh, S., Rashkow, E. and U. Chakrabarti (eds) *Memory, Identity and the Colonial Encounter in India: Essays in honour of Peter Robb* (New Delhi, Routledge India, 2017).
Giddens, A. *The Consequences of Modernity* (Stanford, Stanford University Press, 1989).
Gordon, S. *The Marathas, 1600–1818* (Cambridge, Cambridge University Press, 1993).
Goswami, M. *Producing India: From colonial economy to national space* (Chicago, University of Chicago Press, 2004).
———. 'From Swadeshi to Swaraj: Nation, Economy, Territory in Colonial South Asia, 1870–1907', *Comparative Studies in Society and History*, 40, 4, October 1998, pp. 609–636.
Gramsci, A. (ed.) *Prison Notebooks* (New York, Columbia University Press, 1992).
Grewal, I. *Home and Harem: Nation, gender, empire and the cultures of travel* (London, Leicester University Press, 1996).
Guha, R. *Elementary Aspects of Peasant Insurgency in Colonial India with a Foreword by James Scott* (Durham and London, Duke University Press, 1999).
Guha, R. and Spivak, G. (eds) *Selected Subaltern Studies* (USA, Oxford University Press, 1988).
Guha, S. *Beyond Caste: Identity and power in South Asia, past and present* (Leiden, Boston, Brill, 2013).
Guha-Thakurta, T. *Monuments, Objects, Histories: Art in colonial and post-colonial India* (New York, Columbia University Press, 2004).

Gupta, S. *Notions of Nationhood in Bengal: Perspectives on Samaj, c. 1867–1905* (Leiden, Boston, Brill, 2009).

——. 'Rel-Ka-Vikat Khel', *Harishchandra Magazine*, 15 May 1874.

Harvey, D. *The Condition of Postmodernity: An enquiry into the origins of cultural change* (Oxford, Wiley-Blackwell, 1990).

Headrick, D. *The Tools of Empire: Technology and European imperialism in the nineteenth century* (New York, Oxford, Oxford University Press, 1981).

——. *Power Over Peoples: Technology, environments, and Western Imperialism, 1400 to the present* (Princeton, Oxford, Princeton University Press, 2010).

Heehs, P. *The Bomb in Bengal: The rise of revolutionary terrorism in India, 1900–1910* (New Delhi, Oxford University Press, 2004).

Hoy, Van, T. *A Social History of Mexico's Railroads: Peons, prisoners, and priests* (USA, Rowman and Littlefield, 2008).

Huddleston, G. *History of the East Indian Railway* (London, Thacker and Smith, 1906).

Hutton-Taylor, G. *Illustrated Guide to India and Indian Hotels* (Calcutta, Thacker Spink, 1892).

Iqbal, I. *The Bengal Delta: Ecology, state and social change, 1840–1943* (UK, Palgrave Macmillan, 2010).

Jaffrelot, C. *The Hindu Nationalist Movement in India* (New York, Columbia University Press, 1998).

Jones, K.W. *Arya Dharma: Hindu consciousness in 19th century Punjab* (Berkeley and Los Angeles, University of California Press, 1976).

Jones, R. 'Dreaming of a golden Bengal: Discontinuities of place and identity in South Asia', *Asian Studies Review*, 35, 2011, pp. 373–395.

Kalpagam, U. *Rule by Numbers: Governmentality in colonial India* (UK, Lexington Books, 2014).

Kanwar, D. *Palace on Wheels: A royal train journey* (New Delhi, Prakash Books India Pvt Ltd, 2008).

Kaviraj, S. *Unhappy Consciousness: Bankimchandra Chattopadhyay and the formation of nationalist discourse in India* (London, School of Oriental and African Studies, 1995).

Kerr, I. *Building the Railways of the Raj, 1850–1900* (Delhi, Oxford University Press, 1995).

——. *Railways in Modern India* (New Delhi, New York, Oxford University Press, 2001).

——. *27 Down: New departures in Indian railway studies* (Hyderabad, Orient Longman, 2007).

——. *Engines of Change: The railroads that made India* (Westport, Connecticut, Praeger, 2007).

——. 'Representation and representations of the railways of colonial and post-colonial South Asia', *Modern Asian Studies*, 37, 2, 2003, pp. 287–326.

Kerr, I. and Hurd, J. (eds) *India's Railway History: A research handbook* (Leiden, Boston, Brill, 2012).

Kling, B. *Blue Mutiny: The indigo disturbances in Bengal, 1859–1862* (Philadelphia, University of Pennsylvania Press, 1966).

Kolff, D. *Naukar, Rajput and Sepoy: The ethnohistory of military labour market in Hindustan, 1450–1850* (Cambridge, Cambridge University Press, 1990).

Kosher, R. 'What ought to be seen: Tourists' guidebooks and national identity in modern Germany and Europe', *Journal of Contemporary History*, 3, 33, 1998, pp. 320–340.

Kumar, S. 'Reconstructing India: Disunity in the science and technology for development discourse, 1900–1947', *Osiris*, 15, 2000, pp. 241–257.

Kumar, S. *The Present in Delhi's Pasts* (New Delhi, Three Essays Press, 2010).

Lahiri Chaudhuri, D.K. *Telegraphic Imperialism: Crisis and panic in the Indian Empire, c.1830–1920* (UK, Palgrave Macmillan, 2010).

Landes, D., *Revolution in Time: Clocks and the making of the modern world* (Cambridge, Massachusetts, Harvard University Press, 1983).

Lefebvre, H. *The Production of Space*, translated into English by Donald Nicholson-Smith (Oxford, Blackwell, 1991).

——. *Rhythmanalysis: Space, time and everyday life* (London, New York, Continuum, 2004).

Maclean, K. *Pilgrimage and Power: The Kumbh Mela in Allahabad, 1765–1954* (Oxford, Oxford University Press, 2004).

Makdisi, U. 'Ottoman orientalism', *The American Historical Review*, 107, 3, 2002.

Markovits, C., Jacques P. and Subrahmanyam, S. (eds) *Society and Circulation: Mobile people and itinerant cultures in South Asia, 1750–1950* (Ranikhet, Permanent Black, 2003).

Marshall, P.J. *Bengal: The British Bridgehead: Eastern India 1740–1828*, The New Cambridge History of India, II.2 (Cambridge, Cambridge University Press, 1987).

Menon, D. 'Religion and colonial modernity: Rethinking belief and identity', *Economic and Political Weekly*, 37, 17, 2002.

Metcalf, T. *An Imperial Vision: Indian architecture and Britain's Raj* (London, Faber, 1989).

——. *Ideologies of the Raj* (Cambridge, Cambridge University Press, 1995).

Mizutani, S. *The Meaning of White: Race, class, and the 'domiciled community' in British India 1858–1930* (New York, Oxford University Press, 2011).

Mukherjee, M. (ed.) *Early novels in India* (New Delhi, Sahitya Akademi, 2002).

Mukhopadhyay, A. 'Colonised Gaze? Guidebooks and journeying in colonial India', *South Asia: Journal of South Asian Studies*, 37, 4, 2014, pp. 656–669.

Mukhopadhyay, B. 'Writing home, writing travel: The poetics and politics of dwelling in Bengali modernity', *Comparative Study of Society and History*, 44, 2002, pp. 293–318.

Naidu, P. *The History of Railway Thieves with Illustrations and Hints on Detection* (Madras, Higginbotham, 1915).

Nandy, A. *The Intimate Enemy: Loss and recovery of self under colonialism* (Delhi, Oxford University Press, 1988).

O'Hanlon, R. *Caste Conflict and Ideology: Mahatma Jotirao Phule and low caste protest in nineteenth century Western India* (Cambridge, Cambridge University Press, 2002)

Oldenburg, V. *The Making of Colonial Lucknow: 1856–1877* (New Jersey, Princeton University Press, 1994).

Orsini, F. *Print and Pleasure: Popular literature and entertaining fictions in colonial north India* (Ranikhet, Permanent Black, 2009).

Parasher-Sen, A. (ed.) *Subordinate and Marginal Groups in Early India* (Delhi, Oxford, Oxford University Press, 2004).

Parks, F. *Wanderings of a Pilgrim in Search of Picturesque* (Karachi, Oxford University Press, 1975).

Parsons, N. *Worth the Detour: A history of the guidebook* (London, The History Press, 2008).

Peabody, N. 'Tod's Rajasthan and the boundaries of Imperial rule in 19th century India', *Modern Asian Studies*, 30, 1, 1996, pp. 185–220.

Bibliography

Peers, D. and Gooptu, N. (eds) *India and the British Empire, Oxford History of the British Empire Companion Series* (Oxford, Oxford University Press, 2012).

Pinney, C. *Photos of the Gods: The printed image and political struggle in India* (UK, Reaktion Books, 2004).

Pouchepadass, J. *Land, Power and Market: A Bihar district under colonial rule, 1860–1947* (London, Sage, 2000).

———. *Champaran and Gandhi: Planters, peasants and Gandhian politics* (New Delhi, Oxford University Press, 1999).

Prakash, G. *Another Reason: Science and the imagination of modern India* (New Jersey, Princeton University Press, 1999).

Prasad, R. 'Time sense: Railways and temporality in colonial India', *Modern Asian Studies*, 47, 4, 2012, pp. 1252–1282.

———. *Tracks of Change: Railways and everyday life in colonial India* (New Delhi, Cambridge University Press, 2015).

Pratt, M.L. *Imperial Eyes: Travel writing and transculturation* (London, New York, Routledge, 2008).

Raj, K. *Relocating Modern Science: Circulation and the construction of knowledge in South Asia and Europe, 1650–1900* (New York, Palgrave Macmillan, 2007).

Ramaswamy, S. *The Goddess and the Nation: Mapping Mother India* (Durham, Duke University Press, 2010).

Ramnath, A. *The Birth of an Indian Profession: Engineers, industry, and the state, 1900–1947* (New Delhi, Oxford University Press, 2017).

Rasheed, A. *The Travellers' Companion: Containing a brief description of places of pilgrimages and important towns in India* (Calcutta, Railway Board, 1910).

Ray, R.K. *Urban Roots of Indian Nationalism: Pressure groups and conflict of interests in Calcutta city politics, 1875–1939* (Delhi, Oxford University Press, 1979).

———. *The Felt Community: Commonality and mentality before the emergence of Indian nationalism* (New Delhi, Oxford, Oxford University Press, 2002).

———. *Exploring Emotional History: Gender, mentality and literature in the Indian awakening* (New Delhi, Oxford University Press, paperback edition, 2003).

Ray, U. *Culinary Culture in Colonial India: A cosmopolitan platter and the middle-class* (New Delhi, Cambridge University Press, 2015).

Raychaudhuri, T. *Europe Reconsidered: Perceptions of the West in nineteenth century Bengal* (New Delhi and Oxford, Oxford University Press, 2002).

Robb, P. *Sentiment and Self: Richard Blechynden's Calcutta diaries, 1791–1822* (Oxford, Oxford University Press, 2011).

———. (ed.) *Rural India: Land, power and society under British rule* (London, Curzon Press, 1983).

Roy, T. *Traditional Industry in Economy of Colonial India* (Cambridge, Cambridge University Press, 1999).

Sahu, B.P. 'Brahmanical ideology, regional identities and the construction of early India', *Social Scientist*, 29, 7/8, 2001, pp. 3–18.

Said, E. *Orientalism* (London, Penguin Books, 2003).

Sangari, K. and Vaid, S. (eds) *Recasting Women: Essays in Indian colonial history* (New Delhi, Kali for Women, 1989).

Sanyal, N. *Development of Indian Railways* (Calcutta, University of Calcutta, 1930).

Sarkar, S. *Technology and Rural Change in Eastern India, 1830–1980* (New Delhi, Oxford University Press, 2014).

Sarkar, S. *Swadeshi Movement in Bengal, 1903–1908* (New Delhi, Peoples Publishing House, 1973).
——. *Beyond Nationalist Frames: Postmodernism, Hindu fundamentalism, history* (Bloomington, Indiana University Press, 2002).
——. *Writing Social History* (Delhi, Oxford, Oxford University Press, 2002).
——. 'Technical content and colonial context: Situating technical knowledge in nineteenth century Bengal', *Social Scientist*, 38, 1/2, 2010, pp. 37–52.
Sarkar, S. and Sarkar, T. (eds) *Women and Social Reform in Modern India* (Bloomington, Indiana University Press, 2008).
Sarkar, T. *Hindu Wife, Hindu Nation: Community, religion, and cultural nationalism* (Bloomington, Indiana University Press, 2010).
Satow, M. and Desmond, R. (eds) *Railways of the Raj* (New York, New York University Press, 1980).
Schivelbusch, W. *The Railway Journey: The industrialization of time and space in the 19th century* (Berkeley, University of California Press, 1986).
Sen, S. *Bangla Sahityer Itihas* (Calcutta, Eastern, 1978).
Sen, S. *Empire of Free Trade: The East India Company and the making of the colonial marketplace* (Philadelphia, University of Pennsylvania Press, 1998).
Sengupta, M. *Becoming Assamese: Colonialism and new subjectivities in northeast India* (New Delhi, Routledge India, 2016).
Settar, S. (ed.) *Railway Construction in India: Select documents*, 3 volumes (New Delhi, Indian Council of Historical Research, 1999).
Sharma, J. *Hindutva: Exploring the idea of Hindu nationalism* (New Delhi, Penguin Books, 2004).
Simmons, J. *The Railways in England and Wales, 1830–1914: The system and its working* (Leicester, Leicester University Press, 1978).
Simmons, J. and Biddle, G. (eds) *The Oxford Companion to British Railway History: From 1603 to 1990s* (Oxford, Oxford University Press, 1999).
Singha, R. *A Despotism of Law: Crime and justice in early colonial India* (Delhi, Oxford University Press, 1998).
Sinha, K. *Hutom Penchar Naksha o onnanyo Samajchitra* (Calcutta, Sahitya Parishad, re-print, 1955).
Sinha, M. *Colonial Masculinity: The 'manly Englishman' and 'effeminate Bengali' in the late nineteenth century* (Manchester, Manchester University Press, 1995).
Sinha, N. *Communication and Colonialism in eastern India: Bihar, 1760s–1880s* (London, Anthem Press, 2012).
Sishir, K. (ed.) *Radhacharan Goswami ki chuni rachnayein* (Allahabad, Parimal Prakashan, 1990).
Sleeman, W.H. *Rambles and Recollections of an Indian Official* (Karachi, Oxford University Press, 1973).
Smith, G.R. *The History of Bradshaw: A centenary review of the origin and growth of the most famous guide in the world* (London, 1939).
Spurr, D. *The Rhetoric of Empire: Colonial discourse in journalism, travel writing and imperial administration* (Durham and London, Duke University Press, 1993).
Srinivasan, R., Tiwari, M. and Silas, S. (eds) *Our Indian Railway: Themes in India's railway history* (New Delhi, Foundation Books, 2007).
Tagore, R. *Jeevan Smriti* (Calcutta, Bishwa Bharati, 1980).
——. *Sishu Bholanath* (Calcutta, Biswabharati, 1922).
Thapar, R. *Time as a Metaphor of History* (Delhi, Oxford University Press, 1996).

Tharoor, S. *Inglorious Empire: What the British did to India* (London, Hurst, 2016).

Thompson, E.P. *The Making of the English Working Class* (London, Penguin, 1980).

——. 'Time, work-discipline, and industrial capitalism', *Past and Present*, 38, 1967, pp. 59–97.

Thorner, D. *Investment in Empire: British railway and steam shipping enterprise in India* (Philadelphia, University of Pennsylvania Press, 1950).

Trautmann, T.R. *Aryans and British India* (Berkeley, London, University of California Press, 1997).

——. (ed.) *The Aryan Debate* (New Delhi, Oxford University Press, paperback edition 2007).

Turner, D. *Victorian and Edwardian Railway Travel* (UK, Shire, 2013).

Twain, M. *The Complete Works of Mark Twain: Following the equator*, Volume 2, (New York, Harper and Brother, 1925).

Varady, R.G. 'North Indian Banjaras: Their evolution as transporters', *South Asia: Journal of South Asian Studies*, 2, 1–2, 1979, pp. 1–18.

Veer, van der P. *Religious Nationalism: Hindus and Muslims in India* (New Delhi, Oxford University Press, 1998).

Viswanathan, G. *Masks of Conquest: Literary studies and British rule in India* (New York, Columbia University Press, 1989).

Wilson, J. *The Chaos of Empire: The British Raj and the conquest of India* (New York, PublicAffairs, 2016).

Wolmar, C. *Blood, Iron and Gold: How the railroads transformed the world* (New York, PublicAffairs, 2010).

——. *The Great Railroad Revolution: The history of trains in America* (USA, PublicAffairs, 2013).

Wolpert, S. *Tilak and Gokhale: Revolution and reform in the making of modern India* (New Delhi, Oxford University Press, 1991).

Yang, A. *Bazaar India: Markets, society and the colonial state in Gangetic Bihar* (Berkeley, University of California Press, 1998).

——. (ed.) *Crime and Criminality in British India* (Arizona, University of Arizona Press, 1985).

Zhang, H., Gursoy, S. and Xu, H. 'The effects of associative slogans on tourists' attitudes and travel intention: The moderating effects of need for cognition and familiarity', *Journal of Travel Research*, 56, 2, 2017, pp. 206–220.

Züvichü, L. 'Empire on their backs: Coolies in the Eastern Borderlands of the British Raj', *International Review of Social History*, 59, 2014, pp. 89–112.

Index

Aryavarta 167–171, 174–15, 177–178, 180, 194, 199, 215, 222–223
agency of: colonised 4, 223, 205; Indian/'native' 4, 12, 22, 166

Bell, H. 53–55
Bengali *see* travelogues
Bharatvarsha 167
bhisti 144–145, 147, 159, 217, 219, 221
black hole 111–112, 121

carriages 108–111, 121, 127: fourth-class 49, 119–120; gas lighting 128; intermediate class 49, 111, 113, 121, 125–126, 128, 132
Cavour, C. 1–2
commensality *see* rules

Dalhousie, J.A. 2, 165
Danvers, J 30, 46–48, 87, 109, 125
desh 167–168, 170, 172–177, 179, 181, 192, 223
desh bhraman 167–168, 170–172, 178–181
dharamsalas 9–10

Eurasian 68, 122–123, 198, 200, 203–204: passengers 123, 204
European: employees 199–201, 204; passengers 88, 92, 94, 122–123, 130–131, 156–158

fourth class *see* carriages

Gandhi, M.K, 85, 166
Ghosh, R.M, 2, 85

Harishchandra, B. 41, 43, 63, 114–116, 120, 122, 131, 199, 217, 219

Headrick–Adas model 4, 220
hegemony 8, 223
Hindi *see* travelogues
Hindustan 165, 170–171, 174, 178, 215
Huddleston, G. 29, 48

imagined community 3, 188

jati 66, 168, 172, 177, 187, 191, 195–197

Kerr, I.J. 2–3, 8
Khan, S.A. 89, 99–100, 133, 150, 156, 158, 220, 224

lavatories 127–130
Lefebvre, H. 9, 204

MacGeorge, G.W. 1–2

overcrowding 111–115, 119–120, 129, 131

platform ticket 44, 56, 61–63, 70–71, 74, 218
production of space 9–11, 222
punctuality 30, 214: unpunctuality 31–34, 214

railways: social change 1–2, 55, 84, 127, 206, 213, 224–225; economic and military needs 1; moral and social role 1; time 1, 23–24, 33–35, 214; timetables; 20, 22, 35–36, 42
railway tariff 48–50, 53, 70
Raj 174, 190, 197–198, 201, 203–204, 213
refreshment: arrangements 141–143, 156, 159; rooms 142, 150–152, 154
Rendel, A.M. 28, 47, 96, 129

return tickets 55–56, 59–61, 65, 71, 73, 116, 126, 218
rules: commensality 141–44, 146, 148–50, 158

standardisation: railway time 22–23; ticketing rules 44, 56, 60, 62, 71
Stephenson, R.M. 2, 31, 84
sources: official 6–7; unofficial 6–7, 11
space 9–11: conceptualisation 12, 164–165, 180–181, 192, 215; contestation; 9–11, 74, 83, 101, 149, 158–159, 166, 204, 222; national 165, 174, 177–178, 180–181, 214–215; railway 9–12, 83, 158–159, 165, 187, 222; social 9–11, 111, 132–133, 220; station 83–85
swadesh 175–179, 192, 214–215

Tagore, D.N. 2, 67–69
Tagore, R.N. 67, 111, 175

technology: transfer 4, 220, 224; transmission 213
ticket booking clerks 43, 57, 64–66, 130
ticket inspectors 44
ticketing regulations 41–43, 45–46, 56, 58, 60, 62–63, 70, 74–75
time discipline 11, 20–23, 27, 30–31, 34–36, 213–214
timetables *see* railways
tool of empire 1, 5, 224
travel discipline 12, 20, 22, 28, 30, 34–36, 41–42, 46, 56, 62–64, 70–72, 74–75, 83, 131, 108–110
travelogues 2, 7, 8: Bengali 2, 6–8, 11, 30, 57, 65, 122, 142, 187–88, 190, 215–17; Hindi 2, 7–8, 11, 189, 199–200
Twain, M. 83

waiting: rooms 86, 90–93, 97, 100, 142; sheds 86, 89

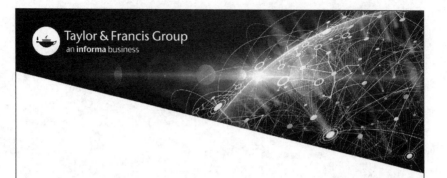